Sulla
Politics and Reception

Sulla

Politics and Reception

Edited by
Alexandra Eckert and Alexander Thein

DE GRUYTER

ISBN 978-3-11-076333-1
e-ISBN (PDF) 978-3-11-062470-0
e-ISBN (EPUB) 978-3-11-062482-3

Library of Congress Control Number: 2019946287

Bibliographic information published by the Deutsche Nationalbibliothek
The Deutsche Nationalbibliothek lists this publication in the Deutsche Nationalbibliografie;
detailed bibliographic data are available in the Internet at http://dnb.dnb.de.

© 2021 Walter de Gruyter GmbH, Berlin/Boston
This volume is text- and page-identical with the hardback published in 2019.
Typesetting: Integra Software Services Pvt. Ltd.
Printing and binding: CPI books GmbH, Leck

Coin on front cover: reverse of RRC 367/4 (ANS 1967.153.195)
showing Sulla in *quadriga* crowned by flying Victory.
Minted by L. Manlius, dated to 82 B.C.
Courtesy of the American Numismatic Society

www.degruyter.com

Acknowledgements

This book originated in a panel at the Ninth Celtic Conference in Classics held at University College Dublin from the 22nd to 25th June 2016 which focused on the politics, public image, and reception of the dictator Lucius Cornelius Sulla Felix (138–78 B.C.). It was a large conference with more than 300 delegates, and thus it was the perfect venue for a gathering of scholars working on Sulla to exchange ideas and initiate collaboration in the company of colleagues participating in other panels on related topics. The conference as a whole was organised by Alexander Thein, Alan Ross, Anton Powell, and Douglas Cairns, with financial support from the UCD College of Arts and Humanities, the Classical Association of Ireland, and Fáilte Ireland, the Irish Tourist Board.

This volume would not have been possible without the help and support of many people. Special thanks go to Stephen O'Brien, a recent UCD colleague, for proofreading and indexing, and to University College Dublin for a Seed Funding grant to cover the costs of the original conference panel. The editorial work on the volume was facilitated by two appointments for Alexandra Eckert as a Visiting Research Fellow in the UCD School of Classics, and by a discretionary research fund provided by UCD to Alexander Thein as Head of School.

Oldenburg and Dublin, February 2019
Alexandra Eckert & Alexander Thein

Contents

Acknowledgements —— V

Contributors —— IX

Alexandra Eckert and Alexander Thein
Introduction —— 1

Part I: Politics

Catherine Steel
1 Sulla the Orator —— 19

Sophia Zoumbaki
2 Sulla's Relations with the Poleis of Central and Southern Greece in a Period of Transitions —— 33

Cristina Rosillo-López
3 Can a Dictator reform an Electoral System? A Reassessment of Sulla's Power over Institutions —— 55

Alexander Thein
4 Dolabella's Naval Command —— 71

Arthur Keaveney
5 *Paludes et Silvae*: The Ruin of the Veteran —— 89

Part II: Reception

Federico Santangelo
6 Sulla in the *Bellum* Jugurthinum —— 107

J. Alison Rosenblitt
7 Sulla's Long Shadow: Sallust in Tacitus and Tacitus in Sallust —— 125

Inger N. I. Kuin
8 Sulla and the Philosophers: The Cultural History of the Sack of Athens —— 143

Alexandra Eckert
9   Reconsidering the Sulla Myth —— 159

Abbreviations —— 173

Bibliography —— 175

Index of Ancient Authors —— 197

Index of Ancient Persons and Deities —— 199

Index of Ancient Places —— 203

General Index —— 205

Contributors

Alexandra Eckert
Assistant Professor in Ancient History at Carl von Ossietzky Universität Oldenburg

Arthur Keaveney
Reader Emeritus in Ancient History at the University of Kent

Inger N. I. Kuin
Assistant Professor of Classics Academic General Faculty, University of Virginia

J. Alison Rosenblitt
Senior Lecturer in Classics at Regent's Park College, University of Oxford

Cristina Rosillo-López
Associate Professor in Ancient History at the Universidad Pablo de Olavide, Seville

Federico Santangelo
Professor of Ancient History at Newcastle University

Catherine Steel
Professor of Classics at the University of Glasgow

Alexander Thein
Lecturer in Classics at University College Dublin

Sophia Zoumbaki
Director of Research at the National Hellenic Research Foundation, Athens

Alexandra Eckert and Alexander Thein
Introduction

Lucius Cornelius Sulla (138–78 B.C.) is a pivotal figure in Roman history. His career played a key role in the fall of the Republic, not least by his decision to march on Rome with his army. In doing so, he introduced civil war into Roman politics and demonstrated the potential of the 'client army'.[1] Sulla also had a lasting impact on the *poleis* of mainland Greece and Asia Minor.

Born into an obscure patrician family, he served as quaestor to the Elder Marius in the war against Jugurtha in Africa and played a key role in the negotiations which secured the capture of the king and ended the war, in 105. From 104 to 101, he served under Marius in the wars on Italy's northern frontiers against the Teutons and Cimbri, and in the 90s, following an urban praetorship, was appointed governor of Cilicia on Rome's eastern frontier, before returning to Rome and cementing his military reputation in the Social War of 90–89. At some point the relationship with Marius broke down, and in 88, when Sulla was consul, the conflict escalated into rioting in the Forum, the son of Sulla's fellow consul was killed, and Sulla was forced to take refuge with his legions in Campania. Having lost this political battle he raised the stakes and took a decision with lasting consequences: he appealed to his soldiers and became the first Roman to march an army on the city of Rome. In its aftermath twelve men, including Marius, were outlawed as 'enemies of the state' (*hostes*).[2]

Sulla's prize was the command in the war against King Mithridates VI of Pontus (c. 120–63 B.C.), who had overrun the Roman province of Asia and extended his power to Athens and mainland Greece. Sulla defeated the king's forces in two major battles, at Chaeronea and Orchomenus in Boeotia, sacked Athens and the Piraeus after a difficult siege, and restored Roman control of the East, having imposed terms on Mithridates at the Peace of Dardanus in 85.[3] In 83, Sulla returned to Italy, and the result was a civil war which affected large parts of the peninsula and ended only after 18 months of conflict, at the battle of the Colline Gate, fought just outside Rome's city walls, on the 1st November 82. As victor, Sulla acted with unprecedented violence towards the defeated faction, but he was also celebrated as the champion of conservative political interests, and after his appointment to the dictatorship, an emergency office with almost unlimited powers last used in the war with Hannibal,

---
1 Carcopino (1931) 205–211; *contra*, e.g. Hurlet (1993) 165–167. Client army: e.g. Badian (1970) 15; Gabba (1976) 26–28. Cf. Syme (1939) 17, for the idea that 'Sulla could not abolish his own example'.
2 Sulla's early career: Badian (1970); Cagniart (1986); Letzner (2000); Keaveney (2005a) ²[1982]; Fündling (2010). Sulla and Marius: Santangelo (2016b). Sulla's march on Rome: Keaveney (1983a); Dahlheim (1993); Santangelo (2018).
3 Sulla in the Greek East: Santangelo (2007); Assenmaker (2014); Eckert (2016a); Zoumbaki (2018).

he implemented a comprehensive programme of judicial and administrative reforms which transformed the system of government and created a new Sullan Republic.[4]

Sulla's dictatorship was not limited to the standard six months, but he was not a would-be monarch, and after a short period he resigned his near-absolute powers and abdicated, retiring to the life of a private citizen after a second consulship in the year 80. Some writers of the Imperial period looked back at Sulla's abdication with admiration, for it seemed to show that, in spite of his cruelty, he had not sought power to become a tyrant.[5] In his own view, expressed in his memoirs, Sulla was a charismatic man of destiny blessed by the gods who triumphed over his enemies to become saviour of the Roman state. As civil war victor he received a series of honours which included a golden equestrian statue on the speaker's platform in the Forum and an official new surname, Felix, which celebrated his *felicitas*, the divine favour or good fortune that gave him success. But he was also a divisive figure, and soldiers were called in to prevent violent protests at his funeral in 78. In his own final message to posterity, the epitaph on his tomb, Sulla stated that no friend had ever surpassed him in kindness and no enemy in doing harm.[6]

Sulla had a lasting and negative impact on the 1st century B.C. His constitutional reforms of the Roman Republic sparked ongoing debates on whether his laws should be preserved, altered, or rescinded, and there was also a reaction against the widespread redistribution of land confiscated from Sulla's enemies to his partisans and his veteran soldiers. More generally, there was a slow economic recovery from the impact of war in Italy and the Greek East, and two of Sulla's would-be imitators, Lepidus and Catiline, exploited unrest in the Italian countryside when they took up arms against the Roman state in 78 and 63. The last decades of the Republic were likewise defined by Sulla's long shadow, an *exemplum* that was both rejected and copied, be it in Caesar's civil war policy of clemency, the renewal of the proscriptions under the second triumvirate, or Augustus' sole rule and the foundation of the Principate.

---

[4] Sulla's reforms: Laffi (1967); Badian (1970); Hantos (1988); Flower (2010). Sulla's dictatorship: Carcopino (1931); Hinard (1988); Hurlet (1993); Vervaet (2004); Hinard (2007); (2008) 43–60; Sandberg (2018).
[5] Quint. *Inst.* 5.10.71; Sen. *Dial.* 6.12.6. Sulla's abdication: Badian (1962), Badian (1970); Worthington (1992); Kunkel/Wittmann (1995) 711; Hinard (1999); Thein (2002); Keaveney (2005b); Eckert (2016a); Syme (2016); Vervaet (2018).
[6] App. *B Civ.* 1.97; Plut. *Sull.* 38. Sulla's memoirs: Calabi (1950); Pascucci (1975); Valgiglio (1975); Scardigli (1979) 89–91; Ramage (1991); Lewis (1991); Behr (1993); Mackay (2000a); Sumi (2002); Thein (2002); Russo (2002); Sonnabend (2002); Scholz (2003); Riggsby (2007); Smith (2009); Thein (2009); Wiseman (2009); Tatum (2011); Cornell (2013); Scholz/Walter (2013).

Marching on Rome
Sulla can be characterised as someone who ruthlessly transgressed social and political norms in the pursuit of his own ambitions. In 88, he was faced with political humiliation with the transfer of the Mithridatic command to Marius, at the time a mere *privatus*, and in response he escalated political violence to the level of civil war and marched his army on Rome.[7] As he entered the city through the Esquiline Gate he violated religious norms by crossing Rome's sacred boundary, the *pomerium*, under arms, and when the residents of the Esquiline pelted his army with stones and tiles from the roofs of their houses he issued the order for his troops to set fire to their houses. Plutarch states that Sulla acted in anger, giving no thought to the fact that fire was an indiscriminate weapon 'which made no distinction between the guilty and the innocent'.[8] Rome was treated as if it were a foreign city subjected to a military assault, and Appian rightly states that 'Sulla entered the city in appearance and in fact an enemy'.[9] The aftermath of Sulla's march on Rome was also unprecedented. Twelve men including Marius and his son were condemned without trial and declared public enemies (*hostes*) by a vote of the Senate or people: their property was confiscated, and they were defined as outlaws who could be killed with impunity, even by their own slaves.[10] Marius adopted the life of a fugitive, pursued by soldiers, but he was able to escape, and the sources are sympathetic to his trials and tribulations, describing, for example, how he was captured hiding naked in the marshes of Minturnae.[11] It was, however, Marius who precipitated the crisis of 88, and Cicero, in the civil war between Pompey and Caesar, felt that Sulla's march on Rome was just if not right.[12]

Sulla in the Greek East
Sulla left Italy for Greece in 87, and in his absence there was a resumption of civil strife: a conflict between the consuls led to a full-scale civil war in which the victors were Cinna and Marius. In its aftermath there was a violent purge, and Sulla was

---

7 Sulla's 'first' is noted by App. *B Civ.* 1.60, 1.63. Cf. Lange/Vervaet (2019).
8 Plut. *Sull.* 9.6–7.
9 App. *B Civ.* 1.58.
10 App. *B Civ.* 1.60; Plut. *Sull.* 10.1–2. On the role of slaves: Thein (2015).
11 Plut. *Mar.* 35.5–40.7, esp. 37.4–38.2.
12 Cic. *Att.* 9.10.2: *at Sulla, at Marius, at Cinna recte. immo iure fortasse; sed quid eorum victoria crudelius, quid funestius?* ('Sulla, Marius, and Cinna all acted properly, or perhaps one should rather say, legally, but what was more cruel than their victory, what more destructive?') This passage, written in March 49 B.C., also refers to the civil war of 87 (with Marius and Cinna marching on Rome).

declared a *hostis*, or enemy of the state.[13] The evidence for Sulla's actions in the war with Mithridates is good, and there are detailed accounts of the major battles at Chaeroneia and Orchomenus, the sieges of Athens and the Piraeus, the diplomacy which resulted in the Peace of Dardanus, and the post-war settlement of Asia. Appian devotes 36 chapters of his *Mithridatica* to the Sullan phase of the war (87–85 B.C.) and in Plutarch's *Life of Sulla* the war is given 15 chapters, nearly half the total length of the biography.[14] Ultimately, a key source was Sulla's own memoirs, and from the fragments that survive it would appear that for Sulla the most important theme in this work was the narrative of his achievements in the war with Mithridates. The ritual end to the war was the triumph, celebrated back in Rome in January 81, and it was this event – not the dictatorship – which formed the climax of the memoirs.[15]

Sulla had a positive narrative to tell about his victories on the battlefield, and in the negotiations with Mithridates he claimed a total of 160,000 enemy casualties.[16] But the terms imposed on Mithridates were lenient, and there was a suspicion that his main concern was not to punish the Pontic king but to hasten his return to Rome to deal with his own private enemies. Plutarch tells us, in fact, that Sulla's own soldiers objected to the fact that Mithridates had been allowed to sail home, with his booty, unpunished for the massacre of allegedly 150,000 Romans in the Asian Vespers of 88 B.C.[17] The conflict with Mithridates was a foreign war fought in the context of civil strife in Rome, and this had an effect on how the war was conducted. A second Roman army under a Marian commander was operating in the Hellespont, and Sulla was worried that this army might make the decisive move to secure a total victory over Mithridates.[18] A further problem faced by Sulla was the lack of financial support from the treasury in Rome, and it was in response to this that he plundered the famous panhellenic sanctuaries of Delphi, Olympia and Epidaurus to raise the money to pay his army.[19] Greek authors criticised Sulla's seizure of the temple-offerings for centuries to come, linking it to the plunder of Delphi by the Phocians in the 4th century B.C.[20] Sulla did repay the debt by granting Delphi, Olympia and Epidaurus half the territory of Thebes.[21] In this way a Greek city was made to pay, and Pausanias made the bitter remark that Sulla was 'honouring the Gods with other people's incense'.[22]

---

[13] Diod. Sic. 38/39.4.1; Livy, *Per.* 80; Vell. Pat. 2.22.1.
[14] App. *Mith.* 30–66; Plut. *Sull.* 11–26.
[15] See Thein (2009).
[16] Diod. Sic. 38/39.8; App. *Mith.* 58.
[17] Plut. *Sull.* 24.4. Alternatively, the death toll was 80,000: Val. Max. 9.2.ext.3.
[18] App. *Mith.* 51–53, 59–60 (C. Flavius Fimbria).
[19] Diod. Sic. 38/39.7.1; Plut. *Sull.* 12.5–14; Paus. 9.33.6, 10.21.6.
[20] Diod. Sic. 38/39.7.1; Plut. *Sull.* 12.6–9; Paus. 9.7.5–6; cf. 10.2–3.
[21] Diod. Sic. 38/39.7.1; Plut. *Sull.* 19. 6; App. *Mith.* 54; Paus. 9.7.5–6.
[22] Paus. 9.30.1.

Ultimately it was the Greek civilian population which paid the price of the war between Rome and Mithridates. The siege of Athens, a long-term Roman ally and centre of Greek learning, ended after months of famine with a violent sack which resulted in extreme loss of life for the civilian population, the destruction of the Erechtheion, one of the most famous Athenian sanctuaries, and the theft of many works of art.[23] Other cities in central Greece also suffered: Orchomenus was plundered after the battle there, while the nearby Boeotian towns of Anthedon, Halae, and Larymna were razed to the ground.[24] For Pausanias, Sulla's cruel treatment of Athens and the Boeotian cities was unworthy of a Roman.[25] In Asia Minor the Greek cities which had collaborated with Mithridates were forced to pay an indemity of 20,000 talents. It was a massive sum, almost double what was demanded by Sulla from the Pontic king himself in the Peace of Dardanus, and it left them crippled with debt for the next decade.[26] Privileges were granted to those cities in mainland Greece, the Aegean islands, and Asia Minor which had remained loyal to Rome, for example Thespiae, the island of Cos, and Stratoniceia, but only a few such cases are known.[27]

Civil War Violence

Sulla returned to Italy with his legions in 83, and on his arrival he found support from a diverse group of men who felt excluded from power after Rome came under the control of Cinna and his faction after the civil war of 87. The most important was the aristocratic Q. Metellus Pius, who joined Sulla with an army of his own and gave credence to Sulla's claim that he was the champion of conservative interests.[28] The war lasted 18 months and resulted in extreme loss of life. Large armies were recruited by both sides in small-town Italy, and Appian tells us that 'from 10,000 to 20,000 were killed in a single battle more than once'.[29] In the final battle of the

---

[23] On the sack of Athens: Plut. *Sull.* 14.3–4, 6; App. *Mith.* 38; Paus. 1.20.7, 9.33.6. Cf. Rotroff (1997); Hoff (1997); Mango (2010); Rathmann (2010); Assenmaker (2013a); Zychowicz (2013); Thein (2014); Eckert (2016a). On Sulla's theft of works of art: Plin. *HN* 36.5; Lucian, *Zeux.* 3. Cf. Inger Kuin's contribution in this volume.
[24] On the other Boeotian cities: Plut. *Sull.* 26.3–4; Paus. 9.7.5.
[25] Paus. 1.20.6–7, 9.33.6.
[26] Memn. 25.2; Plut. *Sull.* 24.4, 25.2; App. *Mith.* 63.
[27] Epigraphic evidence for Sulla privileging Greek cities and islands: *RDGE* 23 (Oropus); *IThesp* 397 (Thespiae); *RDGE* 20 (Thasos); *RDGE* 70 (Chios); *RDGE* 49 (Cos); *RDGE* 18 (Stratoniceia); *RDGE* 17 (Tabae); *RDGE* 19 (Cormus). Appian (*Mith.* 61) includes Chios, Rhodes, Ilium, Magnesia, and Lycia among the islands, cities, and regions privileged by Sulla.
[28] Cass. Dio fr. 106; cf. Livy, *Per.* 85; Vell. Pat. 2.25.2; App. *B Civ.* 1.80–81. On Sulla's faction: Badian (1962); Keaveney (1984); Paterson (1985).
[29] App. *B Civ.* 1.82.

war, at the Colline Gate, it is said that a total of 50,000 were killed on both sides, but in the previous battles of the war the outcome was one-sided, with the Marian armies suffering disproportionately heavy casualties and high rates of desertion or defection to the Sullan side.[30] Sulla's soldiers became used to the slaughter of a rout, and after the battle of Sacriportus it is known that prisoners were executed en masse.[31] The civilian population also suffered: there was a massacre when Sullan forces captured Naples, other Italian cities were plundered for booty, and in Rome there was famine.[32] At Praeneste, the end of the Sullan siege was marked by a massacre which violated the terms of surrender and claimed either 5,000 or 12,000 lives.[33]

The worst atrocities took place in Rome after Sulla's decisive victory at the battle of the Colline Gate, in the night of the 1st November 82 B.C. Several thousand prisoners, not all of them enemy soldiers captured on the battlefield, were killed en masse in the Villa Publica on the 3rd November, their screams interrupting Sulla's speech at a Senate meeting in the nearby temple of Bellona.[34] This massacre served as the green light for a wave of indiscriminate violence in the city of Rome in which men were killed for political reasons, but also to satisfy private enmities and greed.[35] One source puts the death toll at three times the number of those killed in the Villa Publica massacre.[36] Sulla came under pressure in the Senate to put an end to the anarchy, and his response was to publish the first proscription lists.[37] It was a system of violence in which the mass condemnation of Sulla's enemies, without trial or judicial process, was effected by the mere publication of death lists posted in the Forum. The property of the proscribed was confiscated and sold at public auction, and the death sentence was enforced by the proclamation of penalties and rewards for assisting or killing the proscribed.[38] The first three lists had 520 names, but the lists remained open to the addition of new names, and the total number of victims was estimated at around 2,000 by

---

30 App. *B Civ.* 1.93, cf. 1.84, 1.90–92. Alternatively, the death toll at the Colline Gate was 80,000: Oros. 5.20.9.
31 App. *B Civ.* 1.87.
32 App. *B Civ.* 1.88, 1.89. Booty: Thein (2016).
33 Val. Max. 9.2.1; Plut. *Sull.* 32.1.
34 Strabo 5.4.11; Val. Max. 9.2.1; Sen. *Clem.* 1.12.2; Plut. *Sull.* 30.2–3; Cass. Dio fr. 109.5. Some of the victims had been promised safety. It was a war crime to execute those who voluntarily surrendered. Discussion: Hölkeskamp (2004) 105–136.
35 Plut. *Sull.* 31.1; Flor. 2.9.25; Cass. Dio fr. 109.9–11; Oros. 5.21.1; August. *De civ. D.* 3.28. Discussion: Thein (2017).
36 Oros. 5.21.1 (9,000 and 3,000).
37 Intervention: Plut. *Sull.* 31.1–3; Flor. 2.9.25; Oros. 5.21.2–3; August. *De civ. D.* 3.28.
38 Definition of proscription: Thein (2018). Cf. Hinard (1985a); (1985b); Linke (2005) 127–130; Heftner (2006a); (2006b) 200–206; Thein (2013); Eckert (2014); Thein (2015); Eckert (2016a); (2016b).

Appian and other sources, and at 4,700 by Valerius Maximus.[39] Condemnation was reserved not just for the scale of the slaughter, but also for the fraudulent proscription of men targeted for their wealth.[40] The greatest injustice, however, was felt to be the punitive measures imposed on the sons of the proscribed, who were prohibited from standing for public office and reduced to second-class citizens.[41]

Sulla's civil war victory was defined by mass executions, in the Villa Publica and at Praeneste, and also by violent anarchy in the streets of Rome which continued after the publication of the proscription lists and may have been replicated in other towns in Italy.[42] The violence was not, however, without logic: Sulla's aim was not only to punish his enemies but also to reward his followers, and thus he was willing to turn a blind eye to abuses such as the fraudulent proscription of men of wealth. On one occasion, we are told, he even referred to the confiscated properties of the proscribed as his own booty.[43]

By the end of the Republic it had become a truism that greed was a driving force of civil war.[44]

Dictatorship and Reform

Sulla was in control of the Roman state after his victory at the Colline Gate, but it was only after the deaths of the consuls of 82, Cn. Papirius Carbo and Marius the Younger, that he formalised his position: L. Valerius Flaccus became *interrex* and proposed a law, passed by the People, to ratify all of Sulla's past acts, the proscriptions included, and to appoint him dictator 'to reform the Republic and enact laws' (*rei publicae constituendae et legibus scribundis*). As dictator, Sulla was granted near absolute powers and given the prerogative to hold office for longer than the customary six month limit if he deemed it necessary.[45]

As dictator, Sulla enacted a programme of laws which bolstered his regime and transformed the *res publica*. There were punitive measures, notably the *lex Cornelia*

---

39 First three lists: Plut. *Sull.* 31.3; cf. Oros. 5.21.4. Total more than 40 senators and 1,600 knights: App. *B Civ.* 1.95; figure of 2,000: Flor. 2.9.25; August. *De civ. D.* 3.28; total of 4,700: Val. Max. 9.2.1.
40 Sall. *Hist.* 1.55.17 (Maurenbrecher) = 1.48.17 (McGushin) = 1.49.17 (Ramsey); Sall. *Cat.* 51.33–34; Val. Max. 9.2.1; Plin. *HN* 33.145; Plut. *Sull.* 31.5–6.
41 Sall. *Hist.* 1.55.6 (Maurenbrecher) = 1.48.6 (McGushin) = 1.49.6 (Ramsey); Vell. Pat. 2.28.4; Plut. *Sull.* 31.4. On the restoration of the sons of the proscribed to their full rights, see Eckert in this volume.
42 Livy, *Per.* 88; Plut. *Sull.* 31.5; App. *B.C.* 1.96. Larinum: Cic. *Clu.* 25.
43 Cic. *Verr.* 2.3.81–2; *Leg. agr.* 2.56; *Off.* 2.27; Plut. *Comp. Lys. Sull.* 3.3. Discussion: Eckert (2016b); Van der Blom (2017); and Catherine Steel in this volume.
44 Cic. *Off.* 2.29; with Eckert in this volume.
45 Cic. *Leg. agr.* 3.5–6; Plut. *Sull.* 33.1; App. *B Civ.* 1.98–99. On Sulla's powers as dictator: Eckert (forthcoming: b).

de proscriptione, which regulated the mechanics of the proscriptions, and also laws which established Sullan veteran settlements on land confiscated from Italian municipalities.[46] Other laws reformed the workings of politics, justice, and provincial government. The Senate was doubled, from 300 to 600, the new members appointed by Sulla or elected by the tribes from the equestrian order.[47] In order to maintain senatorial numbers at this level, it was prescribed that quaestors, now increased from twelve to twenty, would be automatically enrolled in the Senate after their year in office without having to wait for the next *lectio Senatus*.[48] The expanded Senate provided a reservoir of jurors for the reformed system of six permanent criminal courts, each under the control of a praetor, the number of which was increased from six to eight. The terms of reference for each of the courts were revised, and jury service was restricted to senators to the exclusion of knights.[49] Consular elections were moved from November to July, and there was a new *lex annalis* to regulate the *cursus honorum*, with fixed minimum ages for each office, and a two-year interval between curule offices.[50] Provinces were assigned to praetors and consuls after their year of office, and the result was that the consulship became an urban magistracy, with consuls taking a more proactive role in legislation.[51] Restrictions were placed on the power of tribunes of the plebs to initiate legislation, and to make the office unattractive to ambitious populists, a law was enacted to prohibit tribunes from holding any higher political office.[52] A further measure was the abolition of the grain dole.[53]

Sulla's aim was to create a stable system of government for the future, and in doing so he adopted a conservative position and privileged the Senate at the expense of the people and knights in the legislative process and the judicial system. But he also diluted the prestige of the established aristocracy, and opened up its ranks to new men: the Senate was doubled in size, the number of praetors and quaestors was increased, and there was also a significant expansion of the four major priestly colleges, the ultimate bastion of elite privilege (although the new priests were now chosen by co-option, not election by the people).[54] Civil war and

---

46 Proscription law: Cic. *Rosc. Am.* 125–126. Veteran policy: Livy, *Per.* 89; App. *B Civ.* 1.96, 1.100, 1.104; cf. Santangelo (2007); Krawczuk (2008); Thein (2010); Santangelo (2016a).
47 App. *B Civ.* 1.100; *contra*: Sall. *Cat.* 37.6; Dion. Hal. *Ant. Rom.* 5.77.5, where Sulla's new senators are dismissed as common soldiers.
48 Tac. *Ann.* 11.22. Cf. Steel (2014a); (2014b); (2018).
49 Vell. Pat. 2.32.3, 2.89.3. Cf. Laffi (1967) 184–185; Hantos (1988) 154–161; Brennan (2000) 390–391.
50 Astin (1958) 33–34, 45–46; Laffi (1967) 182–183; Hantos (1988) 33–45; Brennan (2000) 391–392.
51 Laffi (1967) 184; Hantos (1988) 107–109.
52 Cic. *Leg.* 3.22–26; Caes. *B Civ.* 1.5.1, 1.7.3; Livy, *Per.* 89; App. *B Civ.* 1.100, 2.29; Dion. Hal. *Ant. Rom.* 5.77.5. Cf. Hantos (1988) 74–79 and 130–147; Kunkel/Wittmann (1995) 654–659.
53 Gruen (1974) 385; Seager (1994) 203; Thein (2002) 177.
54 The colleges of pontiffs and augurs both increased from nine to fifteen, the *epulones* from three to seven, and the *decemviri sacris faciundis* became *quindecimviri*. See Laffi (1967) 183; Hantos (1988) 125–129; cf. Cic. *Fam.* 8.4.1; Livy, *Per.* 89; *De vir. ill.* 75.11; Cass. Dio 37.37.1.

proscription had claimed more than 100,000 lives, according to Appian, among them 15 consulars, 90 senators, and 2,600 knights.[55] The elite had been decimated, creating vacancies to be filled by new men. But this was not enough for Sulla: he expanded the elite to maximise the patronage he could offer his faction.

Sullan Politics

As dictator, Sulla was granted almost unlimited powers, with no specified end-date, but he did step down from office, eventually retiring to his country villa near Cumae. Appian felt that Sulla's powers as dictator were monarchical, and that he abdicated from a position of unimpaired political strength: he was in good health and physically fit, he had loyal veteran soldiers throughout Italy to whom he had given money and land, in the city of Rome he had the support of the 10,000 Cornelii (ex-slaves of the proscribed to whom he had given citizenship), along with members of his faction who remained committed to partisan politics and 'rested upon Sulla's safety their hopes of impunity for what they had done in co-operation with him'.[56] Sulla's regime certainly faced no serious external threats at the time of his retirement: only one town, Volaterrae, remained under siege in Italy, and otherwise the only area of Marian resistance was under Sertorius in Spain.[57] But there were limits on Sulla's power, notably in his veteran settlement policy: land was confiscated from the Italian municipalities, but not all of it was distributed, and two decades after Sulla's death there were places such as Volaterrae where the land remained in the hands of the dispossessed, while elsewhere it had been appropriated by the leading Sullani.[58] Sometimes there are structural explanations for failure, but it is also important to consider the extent to which Sulla faced opposition, even from his own faction.[59] Appian gives the example of Q. Lucretius Ofella, who was killed in the Forum by a Sullan centurion after he stood for the consulship, in contravention of the rules, and ignored a direct request from Sulla to give up his candidacy. Appian uses this episode to highlight the coercive violence of Sulla's dictatorship, stating that 'afterwards he ruled as he pleased'.[60] But Plutarch is more open to Sulla's fallibility, and he recounts an episode of passive resistance in which a herald at one of the proscription auctions allowed the bidding to

---

55 App. *B Civ.* 1.103.
56 App. *B Civ.* 1.104, cf. 1.100.
57 Volaterrae: Cic. *Rosc. Am.* 20 and 105; Strabo 5.2.6. Sertorius: e.g. App. *B Civ.* 1.108.
58 Cic. *Att.* 1.19.4; *Fam.* 13.4, 13.5; cf. Thein (2010) 67–68.
59 In this volume, see Keaveney, Rosillo-López, and Thein.
60 App. *B Civ.* 1.101. Cf. Thein (2006) esp. 240–242.

continue after Sulla had indicated that a property should be sold to one of his adherents below the market price. The response attributed to Sulla is that of a petulant tyrant unable even to control the workings of cronyism and corruption: 'It is a dreadful wrong, citizens and friends, and an act of tyranny, if I cannot dispose of my own booty as I wish'.[61]

Sulla had unprecedented powers as dictator, but this did not necessarily translate into absolute power. In the civil war he had created a winning coalition, but his faction was heterogenous, and the hour of victory brought the potential for internal conflict, as Sulla's adherents began to look to their individual interests. But the tendency has been to assume that politics – defined as the activities of people trying to obtain an advantage within a group[62] – was absent in the period of Sulla's sole rule, and one of the problems in challenging this view is that the limited source material is dominated by Appian and his view that Sulla was an absolute monarch. There is potential for rethinking politics under Sulla, and for moving beyond the lawgiving aspects of the dictatorship. In doing so, it is worth reflecting on what we mean by 'politics', a key term highlighted in the title of this book. For the political scientists Hague, Harrop, and McCormick it is the 'process by which people negotiate and compete in the process of making and executing shared or collective decisions'.[63] This process of competitive decision-making can be perceived as 'struggle for power and resources between people and groups'.[64] Political power struggles encompass activities such as lobbying, negotiating compromises, achieving decisions, or claiming legitimacy. Policies are the decisions reached in the process of politics within a group. Policies bind and commit the members of the group.[65] In terms of questions, this lets us focus not just on Sulla's political aims, but also on his methods, his success or failure, and the input 'from below' from other groups or individuals. The papers in this volume examine patronage, persuasion, and Sulla's relationship with the Sullani, while also revising how we look at his policies at home and in the Greek East.

---

[61] Plut. *Comp. Lys. Sull.* 3.3.
[62] Cf. *Politics* in *Cambridge Academic Content Dictionary*, Cambridge (2008).
[63] Hague et al. (2016) [1982] 6.
[64] Hague et al. (2016) [1982] 7.
[65] Hague et al. (2016) [1982] 6. A different political science approach is to distinguish not only between 'politics' as the competitive process of decision-making and 'policies' as the results of that decision-making, but also to take 'polity', i.e. the overall structure of the political system (constitution, laws, norms) into consideration. When following this approach, 'the political' (in German: 'Politik') is used as a generic term for political activities in conjunction with the subcategories 'politics' (process), 'policies' (results/content) and 'polity' (structure). Cf. Holtmann (2000) ^{3}[1991] 550 (polity), 484 (politics) and 483 (policy). Cf. also 'Politik' in Rohe (1994) and Andersen/Woyke (2013).

Reception: Ancient and Modern

A second perspective employed by the papers in this volume on Sulla is 'reception'. Following Hardwick and Stray, 'reception' can be understood as 'the way in which Greek and Roman material has been transmitted, translated, excerpted, interpreted, rewritten, re-imaged and represented'.[66] Contributions in this volume specifically focus on Sulla in antiquity as well as his reception in modern scholarship.[67] The process of establishing a methodological framework in reception studies is ongoing, but it is agreed that the ideas presented by the literary scholar Hans Robert Jauß in his inaugural lecture in 1967 play a fundamental role.[68] In this lecture, on the definition and purpose of literary history, he coined the term Rezeptionsästhetik ('poetics of reception'). Highlighting the importance of readers in the communication process underlying the reception of literary sources, he argued that each reader – ancient or modern – interprets transmitted texts anew, and that different historical contexts on the part of the reader may change reception. There is an overlap between reception theory, more specifically reception history, and the field of intertextuality which is the study of both structural and contentwise interrelationships between texts.[69]

One aspect of Sulla's reception in ancient authors was his claim for *felicitas*. Sulla highlighted the divine blessing or *felicitas* that gave him success in life, above all on the battlefield, and as civil war victor he was granted the official honour of a new *cognomen*, Felix, to become Sulla the Fortunate.[70] But Sulla was also the author of the proscriptions, and writers of the Imperial period challenged Sulla's right to be called Felix on this account.[71]

---

66 Hardwick/Stray (2008) 1. In her introduction to *Die Rezeption der antiken Literatur*, published as *DNP Supplement* vol. VII, Christine Walde abstains from providing a definition of 'reception'. See Walde (2010) i–xiii, at x. For reception studies, cf. Hardwick (2003); Brockliss et al. (2012); Hardwick/Harrison (2013); Richardson (2019).
67 The modern scholarly reception of historical persons and events is sometimes called the 'history of modern scholarship'. Cf. Martindale (2006) 1.
68 The German title of Jauß's inaugural lecture was 'Was heißt und zu welchem Ende studiert man Literaturgeschichte?' For the text of the lecture, see Jauß (1970). Jauß's involvement in the Nazi regime became a matter of public debate around two decades after his death in 1997. See Westermeier (2016).
69 Cf. Jauß (1970) and Martindale (2006) 4. See also Nünning (2008) ⁴[1998] 340–341 (entry: Jauß, Hans Robert), 619–21 (entry: Rezeptionsästhetik) and 623–625 (entry: Rezeptionsgschichte).
70 App. *B Civ.* 1.97. On Sulla's *felicitas*: Balsdon (1951); Thein (2009).
71 E.g. Plin. *HN.* 22.12; Val. Max. 9.2.1; cf. Eckert (2016a) 43–85; (2018b). Seneca felt that *felicitas* was inconsistent with the coercive violence of Sulla's dictatorship: 'Is Lucius Sulla fortunate because an armed bodyguard clears the way for him when he comes down to the Forum?' (Sen. *Dial.* 1.3.8.). For the medical writer Q. Serenus, Sulla was *infelix* because he suffered from *phthiriasis*, an infestation of tiny parasites resembling lice (*Liber Medicinalis* 62–63.). On Sulla and *phthiriasis*, see Keaveney/Madden (1982); Bahmer/Eckert (2014); Eckert (2016a) 70–75 and (forthcoming: a). Pausanias thought of this disease as divine punishment for Sulla's impiety during the war in

Yet, Sulla was not just a negative *exemplum*, for his civil war victory ended a half-decade in which Rome was under the control of Cinna and his allies, a period in which, for Cicero, 'the Republic was without law and altogether without dignity' (*sine iure fuit et sine ulla dignitate res publica*).[72] Elsewhere, he praises Sulla's politics but condemns the excessive powers of the dictatorship: 'without doubt he exercised royal power, yet he had restored the Republic' (*tum sine dubio habuit regalem potestatem, quamquam rem publicam reciperarat*).[73]

Other writers focused on the antithesis between Sulla's civil war aims and the violence of its aftermath. In Sallust's view, Sulla was the most fortunate of all men before his civil war victory: 'As for what he did afterwards, I do not know if one should feel more shame or disgust in talking about it'.[74] Velleius concluded that Sulla was an example of a man in possession of two very different personalities, while Cassius Dio, with reference to the extreme violence that followed the victory at the Colline Gate, argued that Sulla 'left his former self, as it were, on the field of battle outside the walls'.[75]

In modern scholarship, Sulla's legislative and constitutional reforms have received most attention. For some, Sulla's reforms provide the basis for favourable judgements on his life and career. Mommsen felt that neither Sulla nor his reforms had been properly appreciated by posterity, and that he was to be admired as one of the most excellent, perhaps even a unique character in history.[76] Such exuberant judgements are no longer to be found, yet there is still a tendency to distinguish between the positive aims of the reforms and the violence of the proscriptions.[77] Some scholars, however, do reject the idea that any evaluation of Sulla's actions can rest on a good/bad distinction between his reforms and extreme violence.[78] More generally, scholars have focused on the logic and long-term legacy of the reforms, and the standard view is that Sulla's programme was a conservative attempt

---

Greece: either the violation of asylum, when the Athenian 'tyrant' Aristion was dragged from Athena's sanctuary on the Acropolis to be executed, or the theft of an ancient ivory statue of Athena from Alalcomenae in Boeotia (Paus. 1.20.7, 9.33.6.). Cf. Kuin in this volume.

72 Cic. *Brut.* 227, written in 46 B.C.
73 Cic. *Har. resp.* 55, written in 57–56 B.C.
74 Sall. *Iug.* 95.4; cf. *Cat.* 11.4. 2.25.3.
75 Vell. Pat. 2.25.3; Cass. Dio fr. 109.1–3. Cf. Cic. *Off.* 2.27; Livy, *Per.* 88; Val. Max. 9.2.1.
76 Mommsen (2010) ⁹[1903/1904] 2.367: 'Die Nachwelt hat weder Sulla selbst, noch sein Reorganisationwerk richtig zu würdigen verstanden… In der Tat ist Sulla eine von den wunderbarsten, man darf vielleicht sagen, eine einzige Erscheinung in der Geschichte'.
77 Cf. Laffi (1967); Hantos (1988). For Keaveney (2005) ²[1982] Sulla was 'the last Republican'. Likewise: Hinard (1985a) 277. For the good/bad dichotomy, see Dowling (2000); Miaczewska (2013); Thein (2014). For Sulla's reception see in particular: Zecchini (1993); Christ (2002); Zecchini (2002); Piepenbrink (2013); Walter (2018); Rosenblitt (2019); Seemann (2019).
78 Hölkeskamp (2000) 218; Linke (2005) 136–138. Cf. Piepenbrink (2013) 963, noting Dion. Hal. *Ant. Rom.* 5.77.5, which discusses Sulla's reforms in the broader context of Sulla's acts of violence and judges both in very negative terms.

to re-establish what he felt was the Senate's traditional dominance in the Roman state.[79]

Chapters in This Volume

This volume approaches Sulla from two main angles: politics and reception. While the chapters by Catherine Steel, Sophia Zoumbaki, Cristina Rosillo-López, Alexander Thein and Arthur Keaveney work on different aspects of the political dimension, Federico Santangelo, Alison Rosenblitt, Inger Kuin and Alexandra Eckert investigate Sulla through the lens of reception.

Catherine Steel's chapter offers a detailed survey and analysis of the fragments of Sulla's speeches in senatorial, contional, diplomatic and military contexts. Sulla's use of public speech, it is argued, reveals his conception of the new political system created by the reforms of his dictatorship. Oratory was tightly controlled, and its function was not to persuade or to seek approval, but to justify, instruct, and inform. Sulla's instincts were autocratic, and his aim was to limit the scope for public speech to create unpredictability in politics. Sulla's own career is used to illustrate how public speaking was part of being a senior politician at Rome, even for those who did not claim to be great orators and had never spoken in the law courts.

Sophia Zoumbaki examines the social and economic impact of the First Mithridatic War on the *poleis* of central and southern Greece, focusing in particular on the evidence of coinage and epigraphy. Sulla billeted his soldiers in the Greek towns and requisitioned troops, supplies, and money to cover the cost of the war, thus establishing the later Roman practice of exploiting local resources to fund warfare. The war was highly disruptive, and there had also been a long period of stagnation in the half-century before Sulla. Further demands were made in the post-war settlement, and the most effective response, it is argued, was for local elites to use their personal wealth to support and revitalise their communities. Sulla's policies were a shock to the system which forced the *poleis* to adapt to the new realities of Roman Imperialism in the Greek East. The chapter also discusses the recently-discovered inscription and trophy monument from Orchomenus in the context of the commemoration of Sulla's victories in the East.

Cristina Rosillo-López investigates the impact and ambition of Sulla's electoral reforms, in particular the laws on electoral corruption and reintroduction of co-option in the selection of pontiffs. The chapter also examines the potential for Sulla, as dictator, to influence the outcome of elections, and it poses the question why he chose not to abolish the secret ballot. Sulla tends to be viewed as an all-powerful reformer, but

---

[79] Senatorial primacy: Badian (1970) 23–25; Seager (1994) 200–202; Keaveney (2005) ^{2}[1982] 145. Differently: Flower (2010) 131–132; Steel (2014a); (2014b).

there were limits to his power to change the workings of Roman politics, and also to his ambition. This chapter argues that Sulla's electoral reforms were limited, and that there was little scope for him, even as dictator, to use procedural mechanisms to ensure the election of his preferred candidates. It was the voters who enjoyed the ultimate power of choice, and this did not change until the transfer of elections from the people to the Senate in the reign of Tiberius.

Alexander Thein's contribution uses a problem of prosopography to explore the workings of politics within the Sullan faction after the civil war of 83–82. The starting point is a passage in Plutarch's synkrisis of Lysander and Sulla which notes how Sulla 'tried to take away from Dolabella the naval command which he had given him'.[80] One problem is the identity of Dolabella, either the consul or praetor of 81, and it is also unclear what is meant by the term 'naval command' (ναυαρχία). But the key point is that Sulla only *tried* to impose his will on Dolabella. Scholars have assumed the opposite, but Plutarch is clear that Sulla failed to revoke Dolabella's command, and elsewhere he gives other examples of individuals standing up to Sulla, some of them members of his own civil war faction. Sulla was the dominant figure in politics, but there were limits on his 'power to dictate'. This chapter also argues that unity within Sulla's faction broke down before his death.

Arthur Keaveney's chapter on Sulla's veteran settlement policy examines a problem passage of Sallust's speech of Lepidus which claims that many veterans were 'banished to marshes and forests' (*relegati in paludes et silvas*) where their reward was hatred and insults.[81] The chapter argues that the normal procedure of settling colonists on land with the potential to be cultivated was not always carried out in the Sullan settlement, for one of two reasons: muddle or fraud. The settlement programme was carried out in a short period of time, and settlers may have received poor land due to haste and unfamiliarity with the local regions, but a strong argument can also be made for fraudulent practices in which those in charge abused their right to designate portions of land as 'set aside' (*excepta*) for themselves. It was a common problem, and Augustus legislated against it, but it was arguably a particular characteristic of the Sullan settlement. It is important, for it highlights the conflict of interests between ordinary Sullan veterans and those in charge of the settlement process.

With the next chapter the volume turns to the field of Sulla's reception. Federico Santangelo analyses Sulla's early career and offers a close reading of his portrayal in Sallust's monograph on the war with Jugurtha. Due attenion is given to Sallust's well-known character sketch of Sulla at *BJ* 95–96, in particular the emphasis on Sulla's eloquence and intellect, but also his ambition and industry, and his virtues as an officer who built up a good rapport with his soldiers and used favours

---

80 Plut. *Comp. Lys. Sull.* 2.4.
81 Sall. *Hist.* 1.55.23 (Maurenbrecher) = 1.48.23 (McGushin) = 1.49.23 (Ramsey).

to make sure others were always in his debt. The chapter also offers a detailed commentary on the literary strategies employed by Sallust in his narrative of Sulla's role in the war, as he is brought from the periphery to the centre of the conflict in order to become the leading actor in the negotiations that lead to the capture of Jugurtha. The core premise is that any assessment of Sallust's text as a historical source has to rest on an appreciation of its literary dimension.

Alison Rosenblitt's chapter offers an intertextual reading of Tacitus' *Annals* and Sallust's *Histories* which argues that the way Tacitus' depicts Augustus' impact on the Imperial system closely reflects how Sallust described the effects of Sulla's dictatorship on the Late Republic. Tacitus uses military language in his narrative of Imperial politics, while Sallust, it is argued, portrays Sulla's legacy as a *res publica* in which the people and the elite view each other as enemies (*hostes*). The chapter's focus is on the speeches of Lepidus, Macer, and Cotta in Sallust's *Histories*, along with the speech of Percennius, one of the leaders of the mutinies on the northern frontiers in A.D. 14. One of the complaints in the speech (Tac. *Ann*. 1.17) is that on discharge soldiers were settled in swamps or on mountains, a clear echo of the charge levelled by Sallust's Lepidus (discussed in detail in Keaveney's chapter).

Inger Kuin examines Sulla's negative reception in Greek authors of the Imperial period, focusing on a passage of Aelian which poses the rhetorical question: What do a dolphin and an ox have in common, and what Sulla and philosophers? The proverb, it is argued, can be linked with Sulla's acquisition of Apellicon's philosophical library, and with the rapacity and violence of his conduct of the war in the Greek East, notably the sack of Athens, the destruction of the sacred groves of the Academy and Lyceum, and the appropriation of artworks and votive offerings from sanctuaries and other public places. Earlier writers such as Diodorus and Strabo focused on the military perspective, but in later authors like Plutarch and Pausanias the focus shifts to the destruction of cultural capital, and Sulla comes to be seen as the antithesis of a philhellene and an *exemplum* of excessive, even irrational violence.

Alexandra Eckert's chapter re-examines the 'Sulla myth', a cornerstone of modern scholarship on Sulla's reception in antiquity. It challenges the hypothesis put forward by Laffi and Hinard that Sulla was not viewed as an *exemplum* of cruelty and tyranny until thirty years after his death, in sources written in the aftermath of Caesar's civil war victory over Pompey. Cicero called Sulla a tyrant in one of the speeches of his consulship in 63, in his election campaign in the previous year he had drawn attention to the torture of M. Marius Gratidianus by Catiline, and in a speech delivered in 80, while Sulla was consul, he spoke of the cruelty inflicted on the Roman people in a continuing wave of violence. Sulla's image was already negative during his lifetime, and in the decades after his death, it is argued, there was a broad popular consensus in favour of repealing the key pillars of Sulla's reforms.

Part I: **Politics**

Catherine Steel
1 Sulla the Orator

Sulla is not normally considered to be a Roman orator. He is not included in Malcovati's edition of the fragments of the Roman orators; nor does Cicero include him in *Brutus*. His role in Roman history in the Late Republic is generally seen as a military commander, as an initiator of and participant in civil conflict and, above all, as a reshaper of the *res publica* as dictator. Insofar as the topic of oratory might arise in relation to Sulla, it would be through his assault on the role of oratory through his curtailing of the office of tribune of the plebs. Yet Sulla was a speaker, and not simply at the routine occasions, particularly in senatorial contexts, which no senior magistrate could avoid. Moreover, the way he used oratory was highly significant as evidence for his conception of the *res publica*. His absence from our conventional histories of oratory in Republican Rome is a reflection less of his abilities and activities than a politically slanted representation shaped by the priorities of the generation which came after him. Replacing him into the history of oratory not only gives a more accurate picture of Sulla; it also helps us to understand the transformations he imposed on Roman political life.

Sulla's Career Before his Consulship
L. Cornelius Sulla was born in 138 B.C. He was a member of the patrician Cornelii gens, but from a branch not recently prominent; he was not closely related to the Scipiones or the Nasicae.[1] He held the quaestorship in 107 and was assigned to the consul Marius; that position was prorogued into 106 and 105, during which time Sulla served with Marius in Numidia and led the negotiations with Bocchus which ended with the capture of Jugurtha.[2] His relationship with Marius continued in Gaul in 104 and 103, but in 102 and 101 he shifted to the forces of Catulus, perhaps indicating a breakdown of relationship with Marius.[3]

Up until this point Sulla's career had proceeded according to the expectations for those in public life in terms of tenure of offices. He held the quaestorship at the age of thirty. He had concentrated thereafter on military activity, rather than activity at Rome, and had not sought the aedileship with its opportunities to engage with the *populus* in Rome. This kind of specialisation is increasingly evident at this

---
[1] He may have been the grandson of the praetor of 186.
[2] Sall. *Iug.* 105–113.
[3] Plut. *Sull.* 4.1–2; cf. *Mar.* 25.4–5. Differently: Badian (1970).

period in career-building among members of the elite.⁴ The next stage was election to the praetorship and it was at this point Sulla's career ran into difficulty, with his failure to be elected on his first attempt at the office. Plutarch records Sulla's own explanation: that he was foiled by an electorate which wanted him first to hold the aedileship so that his African contacts could ensure spectacular shows; but he is rightly sceptical.⁵ Given the limited evidence for internal politics in the 90s it is not possible to explain Sulla's initial failure definitively, but a possible answer would be that he lacked a sufficiently high and favourable profile among voters in Rome because his overwhelmingly military trajectory up until that point had kept him away from Rome and from the kinds of activities which made a politician visible, known and therefore an attractive candidate to vote for. A complicating factor in the analysis is that neither the date of his unsuccessful attempt nor that of his successful campaign the following year is secure.⁶ He could have stood for the office in 93, which would place the unsuccessful campaign towards the end of 95 for tenure in 94; but a case has been made that he stood for the praetorship as early as 99, to hold it in 98 at the minimum age of 40.⁷ If that argument is held, his praetorship is to be dated to 97. Sulla held the urban praetorship, and then was sent as propraetor to Cilicia; he restored the exiled Ariobarzanes and engaged in the first diplomatic activity between Rome and Parthia.⁸ He had returned to Rome by the outbreak of the Social War, and his military experience ensured that he played a significant role in that conflict: initially as a legate attached to one of the consuls of 90, L. Iulius Caesar, and then in what appears to have been a more independent role in the fighting in Campania and Samnium.⁹ He was then elected to the consulship of 88 on his first attempt.

At forty-nine, he held this office at a relatively late age, after a career progression which is likely to have reached the consulship only because the Social War intervened and suddenly created an urgent demand for Sulla's particular set of skills.¹⁰ The focus of his public activities up until this point was outside Rome. This is reflected in his oratory. There is no evidence that he spoke as an advocate in the courts; and on this point, silence bears interpretation, since it seems unlikely that

---

4 Van der Blom (2016) 46–66; on forensic activity and careers, Steel (2016).
5 Plut. *Sull.* 5.1–2.
6 Plut. *Sull.* 5.2 confirms that the two campaigns were in consecutive years, and suggests, plausibly, that bribery explains the different outcomes.
7 *MRR* 3.14–16 opts for 93; Brennan (1992) sets out the argument for 97, which is accepted by Kallet-Marx (1995).
8 Kallet-Marx (1995).
9 He is only referred to as a *legatus* throughout the Social War, but his command may have been authorised by the Senate; *MRR* 3.38.
10 At the very least, the Social War gave Sulla an opportunity to show his abilities at a crisis of the *res publica*; it is perhaps possible, too, that his election reflected a fear that military activity in Italy would continue at a more demanding level of intensity than turned out to be the case.

any forensic activity would not have made some impact on the sources given his subsequent reputation.[11] He is not known to have addressed a *contio* (public meeting) up until this point, nor is that silence particularly surprising among men who did not hold the tribunate.[12] As urban praetor Sulla would have had to speak in the course of administering justice and may have on occasion presided over the Senate, but neither of these duties will have required lengthy speech or imposed any persuasive demands.[13]

Nonetheless, there is evidence for Sulla as an orator in a military context. In Sallust's *Jugurtha*, indeed, Sallust ascribes to him *facundia* (eloquence), in the context of the negotiations towards the end of that work between the Romans and Bocchus.[14] When Bocchus makes contact with Marius asking him to send envoys to negotiate, Marius chooses A. Manlius and Sulla; and it is Sulla who addresses Bocchus. Sallust gives him a speech as an envoy both at this point in his narrative (in direct statement) and a little later in indirect statement, the result of which is to secure Bocchus' cooperation in the capture of Jugurtha.[15] Sulla also appears in the *Jugurtha* as an orator at a military *contio*, addressing his men prior to what they expect will be a fight with Jugurtha's forces (though in fact no battle follows).[16] Sallust has his own purposes in giving Sulla a prominent position in the closing chapters of *Jugurtha*.[17] But these episodes may also derive from Sulla's own memoirs, and the possibility, or even the probability, that among the autobiographical material Sulla recorded were accounts of his own speeches.[18] If that were the case, then Sulla should be considered within the subset of Roman orators as one of those who recorded their own speeches; there is of course a generic difference between disseminating a speech as an independent text and including one in a work of historiography, but the crossover between the genres goes back to the beginning of the written record of Roman oratory with the elder Cato.

---

11 He was threatened with prosecution after his return from Cilicia by C. Marcius Censorinus (Plut. *Sull.* 5.6) but the case did not come to trial, and even if it had Sulla need not have spoken in his own defence.
12 The dispute between him and Marius in 91 over the display of Bocchus' gift of a statue group showing the moment of Jugurtha's surrender (Plut. *Mar.* 32.2–3; *Sull.* 6.1–2) is the kind of issue that could have been aired in a *contio*, but there is no evidence that it was, and even if it had been Marius is the more likely to have attempted to use his relationship with the people to put pressure on the Senate.
13 On the role of the urban praetor in this period, Brennan (2000) 441–453. If praetor in 98, Sulla was presumably enrolled in the Senate by the censors of 97, but will not have had the opportunity to speak as a senator until his return from Cilicia; it is possible that he then spoke in the context of the debate on Bocchus' gift (see above, n. 12).
14 Sall. *Iug.* 102.2–4.
15 Sall. *Iug.* 102.5–11; 111.1.
16 Sall. *Iug.* 107.1.
17 Levene (1992) 59–64.
18 See Smith (2009); Cornell (2013) 1.282–286.

Sulla and Public Speech During his Consulship

As consul in 88, Sulla and his colleague Q. Pompeius Rufus faced a domestic political crisis which blew up, apparently unexpectedly, as the Social War was coming to an end. It was triggered by the proposal from the tribune of the plebs P. Sulpicius to transfer to Marius the *prouincia* of Asia, and with it the war against Mithridates which had begun the previous year and which had been allotted by the Senate to Sulla. The consuls attempted to block the passage of Sulpicius' law by declaring the suspension of public business, but were forced by violent rioting to allow the vote to proceed. The measure passed; once stripped of his command, Sulla joined his army near Nola and persuaded it, though not its officers, to follow him to Rome. He seized the city by force, and initiated a purge aimed at Marius, Sulpicius and their closest followers, during which Sulpicius was killed and Marius escaped from Italy and took refuge in Africa.[19]

P. Sulpicius was an exceptional speaker, the greatest orator, with Cotta, in the generation immediately prior to Hortensius: that, at least, is Cicero's view (and Cicero had heard him speak).[20] He was notable for the quality of his voice, energetic delivery, and for his impressiveness as a speaker.[21] Cicero seems also to have been struck by Sulpicius' persuasive talents. In his speech *De Haruspicum Responsis*, he constructs a canon of radical tribunes to sustain the rather implausible argument that, whatever their nuisance value to the *res publica*, there was nonetheless 'a certain dignity' to the struggle with them – in contrast to that currently underway with Clodius. 'For what should I say about Sulpicius? His eloquence was characterised by such weight, charm and brevity that through his speech he could make the prudent go down the wrong path and good men hold less good views'.[22] Sulpicius could change minds.

The events of 88 not only pitched a brilliant speaker against a consul who was untested in the contional arena of Roman politics.[23] It was played out in that arena. Sulpicius presented his tribunician programme of activity, including the proposal on the Asian command, in frequent *contiones*.[24] The relationship that he built with the

---

19 On these events, App. *B Civ*. 1.56; Steel (2013) 87–97.
20 Cic. *Brut*. 203; 306.
21 Cicero's fullest descriptions are at *De or*. 3.31 and *Brut*. 202–204.
22 Cic. *Har. resp*. 41: *nam quid ego de Sulpicio loquar? cuius tanta in dicendo grauitas, tanta iucunditas, tanta breuitas fuit, ut posset uel ut prudentes errarent, uel ut boni minus bene sentirent perficere dicendo.*
23 Sulla's colleague Q. Pompeius was an orator of some ability, according to Cicero (*Brut*. 304). But Pompeius was not disadvantaged by Sulpicius' proposal to transfer the Mithridatic command to Marius.
24 Cic. *Brut*. 306 (of the year 88 B.C.): *tum P. Sulpici in tribunatu cottidie contionantis totum genus dicendi penitus cognouimus* ... ('At that time, I got to know the tribune Publius Sulpicius' oratorical style very well through his daily *contio* speeches'.)

people was the basis of the support it offered for his programme; indeed, the law on Asia may well have been a device to intensify that relationship with a view to furthering other elements in his programme, particularly that on the enrolment of new citizens, rather than an end in itself. His opponent Sulla did not have that relationship with the people or experience in dealing with it, and when the conflict between the two reached a *contio*, at the point at which Sulla and Pompeius announced the suspension of public business, Sulpicius prevailed. That *contio* collapsed into lethal violence: Pompeius' son was killed in the fracas, and Sulla was forced to run away to save his life. The consuls had failed to control events through the medium of public deliberation. A second *contio* followed, at which Sulla was forced to announce that the vote would go ahead. That particular day in the early summer of 88 encapsulated the tensions which existed between the framework of procedure according to which the *res publica* was expected to operate, the concept of popular sovereignty, and the reality of popular power when expressed through violence. Under normal circumstances, a consular declaration of a *iustitium* should have halted proceedings. But 'normal circumstances' prevailed only when the people, in the guise of those who were present, allowed them to do so. Sulpicius' relationship with the people, consolidated through his oratory, underpinned its refusal to accept the consuls' declaration; and Sulla had no corresponding claim on its adherence.[25]

Sulla was, however, an orator who could persuade an audience to undertake a controversial course of action. He persuaded his troops to follow him to Rome and, in effect, to capture it as though it were a hostile city. This was a far more radical act than the use of violence at a *contio*. The use of an army by a Roman commander to attack Rome was unprecedented. Both Plutarch's and Appian's accounts indicate that he secured his troops' loyalty at a military *contio*.[26] Neither includes a version of the speech itself, and Plutarch only records the outcome. But Appian notes that Sulla said that he was going to Rome in order to free it from those who were behaving tyrannically.[27] Appian's reference to tyrannical behaviour suggests that Sulla presented the situation which he, and his soldiers, were in as an attack on their *libertas*. An argument along the following lines can be hypothesised: Sulla's own position as consul had been the object of an illegal attack by those in Rome, who had sought to undermine the power of the people as those who elected consuls by bestowing *imperium* on a private individual. This attack was therefore not only an injury to Sulla himself; it was a direct affront to the rights of his audience as citizens whose vote bestowed the position of consul. In support of this suggestion is some evidence that Sulla's action in marching on Rome could be considered legitimate.

---

25 Whether or not what happened at the first *contio* was illegal was at the heart of the struggle between people and Senate, and the question never reached a decisive conclusion. See further Straumann (2016) 119–129.
26 Plut. *Mar.* 35.4; App. *B Civ.* 1.57. Plutarch's *Sulla* does not, however, include this episode.
27 App. *B Civ.* 1.57: ἐλευθερώσων αὐτὴν ἀπὸ τῶν τυραννούντων.

In a letter from Cicero to Atticus in March 49, when he was reflecting on his own decision not to follow Pompeius and leave Italy, he sketches a history of civil war at Rome to explain his reluctance to participate in the current conflict. He notes that it could be said that Sulla – as well as Marius and Cinna – acted rightly, and perhaps even legally; yet their victories were disastrous.[28] Cicero's description is very brief, but his argument indicates that there was a possible interpretation of Sulla's actions which accepted that his resort to military action could be justified, despite his behaviour after his victory.[29] It seems reasonable to conclude that Sulla's success as an orator when speaking to his troops depended not only on his talent as a speaker – though it can certainly be used as evidence for that – but also his popularity with them on the basis of his and their campaigning during the Social War. The existing relationship worked to support the persuasive capacity of speech, in which legitimate deliberation (involving Roman citizens who happen to be serving in the army) was set against illegitimate deliberation (orchestrated by Sulla's personal enemies and unrepresentative of the citizen body).[30]

Sulla's successful oratory as consul thus appears to involve a move that can be paralleled in other conservative politicians, of identifying their own careers and interests with those of the Roman people.[31] A fragment of Sulla's memoirs which Gellius quotes is worth notice in this context:

> If it can be that even now you have some concern for me, and you believe me worth treating like a citizen rather than an enemy, and someone worth fighting for you rather than against you, that does not happen to me without reference to my services and those of my ancestors.[32]

Gellius provides no contextual information beyond identifying the book from which it comes as the second (he quotes the passage because it illustrates the use of *nostri* instead of *nostrum*). The book number, if correct, is a major obstacle to placing this fragment in the context of the Social War or of Sulla's consulship: the only other fragment placed in Book 2 concerns his ancestor who held the position of *flamen Dialis* in the mid-third century. Nor is it certain that the speaker of this fragment, or author of the letter from which it came, was Sulla himself. Yet it is

---

28 Cic. *Att.* 9.10.3: *at Sulla, at Marius, at Cinna recte. immo iure fortasse; sed quid eorum uictoria cruidelius, quid funestius?* The use of *at* indicates that Cicero is presenting an argument that an opponent could put forward.
29 See further Morstein-Marx (2009).
30 What is less clear is how far an understanding among his troops that a change of commander in the fight against Mithridates was likely to involve a change of army affected their decision-making. Many modern interpretations include that as a factor, but it is worth noting that Appian does not.
31 Cicero offers frequent examples, particularly from the period after his return from exile.
32 Gell. 20.6.3: *quod si fieri potest, ut etiam nunc nostri uobis in mentem ueniat, nosque magis dignos credatis, quibus ciuibus quam hostibus utamini quique pro uobis potius quam contra uos pugnemus, neque nostro neque maiorum nostrorum immerito nobis id continget.* The final clause very strongly suggests that the first plural is being used for first singular.

certainly intriguing in this context to have an apparent fragment of Sulla's own memoirs in which the distinction between *ciuis* and *hostis* is potentially permeable and can be affected by someone's own identity and services to the state as well as that of his *maiores*.[33]

Once Sulla had taken control of Rome, he enacted a number of measures: some of these were directed at his opponents and at securing his own position, others appear to have addressed the running of the *res publica*. The precise sequence of events and details of his activity are not recoverable, but he appears to have worked through the Senate where possible; thus the decree through which twelve of his opponents were declared *hostes* was apparently ratified by the Senate.[34] It was presumably also the Senate which declared invalid legislation passed after the consuls' declaration of a *iustitium*. Sulla also seems to have strengthened the role of the Senate in relation to the people by insisting on senatorial discussion of legislative proposals before their presentation to the people and by restricting legislative voting to the centuriate assembly (which tribunes of the plebs could not summon).[35] Nonetheless, in the course of this programme both consuls addressed a *contio* at which they justified their activity on the grounds of saving the state from demagogues.[36] The parallel with the arguments that Sulla used to persuade his troops is clear. The move also demonstrates Sulla's recognition of the role of the people in the *res publica*, including the need for them to be informed of events by magistrates. The *contio* had its place in the Sullan *res publica*, a point to which I return below.

Sulla's Proconsulship Until his Return to Italy

The narratives of Sulla's campaigning during the Mithridatic war include a number of speeches, diplomatic negotiations as well as military *contiones* and battle exhortations. His attested speeches in this period are (i) during negotiations with Athenian envoys during the siege of Athens and in the aftermath of its capture[37]; (ii) an exhortation to his troops during the subsequent campaign in Greece[38]; (iii) an exhortation to his troops during the battle of Orchomenus[39]; (iv) a speech to his

---

[33] For discussion, see Keaveney (1981); Lewis (1991); Cornell (2013) 3.290.
[34] Val. Max. 3.8.5, noting the opposition to the measure of Q. Mucius Scaevola *augur*.
[35] Sandberg (2004). A methodological difficulty is that the evidence for these two innovations comes from the same passage of Appian (*B Civ.* 1.59) which also includes the much less plausible suggestion that Sulla enrolled new members of the Senate at this point.
[36] App. *B Civ.* 1.59.
[37] Plut. *Sull.* 13.4; 14.5.
[38] Plut. *Sull.* 16.6.
[39] Plut. *Sull.* 21.2; App. *Mith.* 49.

troops after Orchomenus[40]; (v) negotiations with Archelaus after Orchomenus[41]; (vi) talks about talks with envoys from Mithridates[42]; (vii) negotiations with Mithridates leading to the treaty of Dardanus[43]; (viii) a justification to his troops for negotiating peace with Mithridates[44]; (ix) a meeting with C. Flavius Fimbria[45]; and (x) an address delivered at Ephesus to delegates from the cities of Asia Minor threatening them with penalties for supporting Mithridates.[46]

These are the kinds of speeches which *imperium*-holders regularly gave in the course of campaigning. Their number may reflect Sulla's own record of his achievements.[47] Nonetheless, there are notable differences of emphasis between the two major accounts, those of Plutarch and of Appian, which suggest that his oratory has been shaped by the logic of each narrative. Plutarch uses speech to justify Sulla's actions[48]; it also illustrates Sulla's cultural self-presentation.[49] Appian gives Sulla two long speeches in direct statement, which can be interpreted as illustrations of the brutality of Roman imperialism and its capacity for self-delusion.[50] Sulla may have delivered speeches on the occasions which are recorded during his campaigns against Mithridates, but the fact that their existence was recorded seems to owe more to his subsequent notoriety within Roman political life and his own self-memorialisation than their inherent significance or quality.

Civil War and Dictatorship

Some negotiations took place between Sulla and his opponents before his final civil war victory in November 82.[51] Appian records that in Greece in 84, before crossing back to Italy, Sulla met envoys from the Senate and observed that his possession of a

---

40 App. *Mith.* 50.
41 Gran. Lic. 35.71 (Criniti); App. *Mith.* 54.
42 Plut. *Sull.* 23.3–4; App. *Mith.* 56.
43 App. *Mith.* 57–58.
44 Plut. *Sull.* 24.4.
45 App. *Mith.* 59.
46 App. *Mith.* 61–62.
47 Sulla's exhortation during the battle of Orchomenus (iii in the list above) is repeated in both Plutarch and Appian's accounts, suggesting a common source which may have been Sulla's own; and clearly it draws on tropes of how generals should behave at turning points during battles.
48 Plut. *Sull.* 24.4 (viii above).
49 Thus Sulla rejects overtures from the Athenians as being too reminiscent of great oratory from the past (13.4) and justifies his behaviour after the capture of the city by reference to Athens' history (14.5).
50 The speeches are at App. *Mith.* 57–58 and 61–62. On Appian's interpretative stance, and in particular the role of clemency, see Thein (2014).
51 In Greece in 84: App. *B Civ.* 1.79; with the consul Scipio near Teanum in 83: Cic. *Phil.* 12.27.

στρατὸν ... εὔνουν (an obedient army) meant he was well placed to protect the *res publica*. Appian observes that the remark indicated 'by this one sentence that he did not intend to disband his army but was already aiming at tyranny'.[52] Setting aside hindsight, however, the remark nonetheless fits its context as a reference to Cinna, who had been killed by his own troops earlier that year. Negotiations took place in 83 between Sulla and Scipio Asiagenes near Teanum in Campania; Cicero records that they talked 'about the authority of the Senate, the votes of the people, and the rights of citizenship' (*de auctoritate senatus, de suffragiis populi, de iure ciuitatis*) but does not record any details of what either man said. This evidence does not suggest extensive use of oratory by Sulla in the civil war's negotiating phase.

As Sulla took control of Italy, however, oratory started to play a more significant part. In Appian's account in the *Bellum Civile*, the most detailed narrative of Sulla's capture of Rome and activity in Rome as dictator (and only non-fragmentary historiography source), speeches to the people and to the Senate are both prominent. He describes a series of *contiones* at which Sulla articulated his record and vision for the future, which started even before he assumed the office of dictator.[53] There were four: (i) before the Colline Gate battle (but after the executions ordered by the praetor Damasippus and the departure of Carbo and others from Rome)[54]; (ii) shortly after the Colline Gate battle, in which he announced the proscriptions[55]; (iii) during the consular campaign in 81, after the death of Ofella[56]; and (iv) on demitting his dictatorship.[57]

The first is striking in part because it involved Sulla's entering Rome whilst the civil war was still ongoing (though after his opponents had departed the city). Appian does not give a precise location for the *contio*: Sulla may have spoken outside the *pomerium* rather than in the Forum, thus preserving his *imperium*.[58] It is also unclear who summoned the *contio* for Sulla, since on no understanding of Rome's *res publica* did a proconsul have such capacity. Nonetheless, Sulla's use of a *contio* at this point in events shows not only a confidence in his reception by an audience in Rome but also a commitment to the civil state. On Appian's telling, Sulla's message was ostensibly one of reassurance: current disturbances would soon come to an end and 'the country would return to its proper state'.[59] This first

---

[52] App. *B Civ*. 1.79: ἑνὶ ῥήματι τῷδε, οὐ διαλύσων τὸν στρατόν, ἀλλὰ τὴν τυραννίδα ἤδη διανοούμενος.
[53] On the chronological issues of this period, see Heftner (2006a); Eckert (2016a) 140–146.
[54] App. *B Civ*. 1.89.
[55] App. *B Civ*. 1.95.
[56] App. *B Civ*. 1.101.
[57] App. *B Civ*. 1.104.
[58] See, e.g., Fimbria's remark at App. *Mith*. 59. Appian's description of Sulla's going εἴσω need not undermine this interpretation, since Rome's urban area was not coterminous with that bounded by the *pomerium* (whose line had changed between the Republic and Appian's time).
[59] App. *B Civ*. 1.89: τῆς πολιτείας ἐς τὸ δέον ἐλευσομένης.

contio should be seen as the result of a choice by Sulla to seek to demonstrate that his conduct was justified and to raise the prospect of a restoration of proper civilian government. It is also significant that this was a *contio* to share information: there was no measure under discussion and it was not linked to a voting assembly.

In describing the content of the second contional speech Appian says that Sulla

> boasted a great deal about his achievements and made alarming statements to frighten them and added that he would lead the people to beneficial change, if they would follow him, but spare his opponents no penalty at all, but pursue in full force praetors, quaestors, military tribunes and anyone else who had collaborated with the enemy since the day when the consul Scipio had abandoned the agreement he had made with him.[60]

Here too is the idea of change at the level of the political community as a whole, but now combined with vengeance on his enemies (in Appian's narrative, the publication of the proscriptions list follows in the next sentence). The precise identification by office of those whom he intends to pursue (along with the potentially arbitrary 'others') suggests a distinction between a corrupt elite, who will suffer for their actions, and an innocent populace who will now benefit from the restoration of good government. There is nothing in the words which Appian reports which contradicts a Sullan stance of benevolence towards the people.

The third *contio* in Appian's narrative took place after Sulla had Lucretius Ofella, who was attempting to stand for the consulship, executed.[61] His speech, the only one in this series to be given in direct statement, justifies his action, with a parable about a farmer being driven finally to burn a lousy tunic to demonstrate that there were limits on his patience.[62] The existence of the *contio* confirms the idea that part of the point of the manner of Ofella's death was its publicity: and in this sequel to the death itself, Sulla not only seizes responsibility for it but also offers a blunt justification for it. Ofella was disobedient, and a similar punishment could be extended to others who are disobedient. Unlike the two earlier *contiones*, explicit menace is not limited to magistrates but potentially encompasses those who supported Ofella.[63]

The final *contio* occurred when Sulla demitted the dictatorship, and in Appian's narrative the *contio* itself is secondary to the encounter which follows it, in which a boy abuses Sulla once he has returned to private status, leading him to observe that, as a result, he will be the last man to give up power at Rome voluntarily. That

---

60 App. *B Civ.* 1.95: πόλλα ἐμεγαληγόρησεν ἐφ' ἑαυτῷ καὶ φοβερὰ ἐς κατάπληξιν εἶπεν ἔτερα καὶ ἐπήνεγκεν, ὅτι τὸν μὲν δῆμον ἐς χρηστὴν ἄξει μεταβολήν, εἰ πείθοιντο οἱ, τῶν δ' ἐχθρῶν οὐδενὸς ἐς ἔσχατον κακοῦ φείσεται, ἀλλὰ καὶ τοὺς στρατηγοὺς ἢ ταμίας ἢ χιλιάρχους ἢ ὅσοι τι συνέπραξαν ἄλλοι τοῖς πολεμίοις, μεθ' ἣν ἡμέραν Σκιπίων ὁ ὕπατος οὐκ ἐνέμεινε τοῖς πρὸς αὐτὸν ὡμολογημένοις, μετελεύσεσθαι κατὰ κράτος.
61 This *contio* also occurs in Plutarch's narrative (*Sull.* 33.4).
62 App. *B Civ.* 1.101.
63 On Ofella's campaign, see Keaveney (2003).

apophthegm could well be anecdotal, but there is no need to doubt the existence of a *contio* at which Sulla gave up his office and offered to give an account of his actions.

There are two other *contiones* not in Appian's narrative but recorded elsewhere. One is a speech in which Sulla announced that he was taking the cognomen 'Felix'.[64] The other is recorded by Cicero, and included by Plutarch in his comparison of the lives of Sulla and Lysander.[65] It took place in the context of property sales during the proscriptions, so chronologically it falls between Appian's third and fourth *contiones*. Sulla observed there that selling the property of the proscribed was *praedam suam uendere*, to sell his own booty. For Cicero, the point of the anecdote is to show the extent to which Sulla's position went beyond anything that could be conceptualised by the *res publica* at that point, by conflating the state with the individual and by turning citizens into *hostes*.[66]

Speeches to the *populus* can be set alongside Sulla's engagement with the Senate. The best documented occurrence is a meeting in the temple of Bellona at which Sulla addressed the Senate for the first time following the Colline Gate.[67] The meeting was within earshot of where prisoners of war were being kept; as Sulla began to address the Senate, they began to be executed, so that his speech took place to the accompaniment of the cries of dying men. Seneca and Plutarch do not include the substantive content of Sulla's address, though both record the substance of a comment Sulla apparently made, that what his audience was hearing was his punishment of some rebels (Seneca: *seditiosi*) or criminals (Plutarch: οἱ πονηροί). This was a carefully orchestrated demonstration of power to intimidate the Senate and ensure their absolute compliance with whatever he might then do.

Another significant senatorial meeting is one at which a senator asked Sulla how long the slaughter of his enemies was to continue and asking for clarity on those who were to be included as victims.[68] Plutarch identifies the questioner as a

---

64 Plut. *Sull.* 34.2. On Sulla's assumption of the name 'Felix', Eckert (2016a) 46–48. There is thematic overlap between this speech, linked by Plutarch with Sulla's triumph, and the one in Appian when he demitted the dictatorship: Thein (2009) 99–102.
65 Cic. *Verr.* 2.3.81–2; *Leg. agr.* 2.56; *Off.* 2.27; Plut. *Comp. Lys. Sull.* 3.3; see further the discussion in Eckert (2016b) 139; van der Blom (2017). Cicero uses the word *contio* in his account; it is an interesting question (though beyond the scope of this chapter) whether that should be taken as definitive evidence for a formally-summoned *contio* or whether Cicero's focus on communication between Sulla and his audience might explain his use of this term for words that were actually uttered in the context of an auction.
66 There may have been other *contiones*. Plutarch (*Sull.* 31.4) records a chilling anecdote in which Sulla tells the people he is proscribing those he can remember, and will add people as they come to him; but this could come from the same *contio* as the second in Appian's narrative.
67 Sen. *Clem.* 1.12.2; Plut. *Sull.* 30.2–3. Appian does not include the episode.
68 Plut. *Sull.* 31.1–3.

Gaius Metellus.[69] But he does note that some people ascribe the remark to a known associate of Sulla, Fufidius, raising the possibility that this question, so far from being oppositional, was arranged by Sulla to allow him to show a commitment to constitutional propriety through establishing a framework for violent reprisals.[70]

Alongside dramatic meetings of the Senate which were included in historiographical accounts of his dictatorship, the business of the Senate appears to have continued, with Sulla potentially in attendance. So, for example, on the 16th March 81 the Senate met, with Sulla as presiding magistrate, in the temple of Concord to listen to envoys from Stratoniceia ask for permission to dedicate a gold crown and sacrifice on the Capitol and for the Senate to confirm the political and legal status of their community and its privileges.[71]

As dictator Sulla communicated with both Senate and people, and in his speeches he did not privilege the Senate. It was the object of threats, whereas the message to the people, at least initially, was one of reassurance, albeit reassurance depending on an acceptance of Sulla's power. Sulla was deeply hostile to *popularis* behaviour, but it is important to acknowledge that that attitude did not imply that he saw no role for the people within the *res publica*. Sulla's speeches to the people demonstrate what that role should be: communication from magistrate to people is essential, but such communication does not seek, or require direct popular confirmation or approval for the acts which it describes. The use which Sulla himself made of oratory, both contional and senatorial, can be aligned with his view of the proper use of public speech as it emerges from his redesigned *res publica*. His changes to the role of the tribunes of the plebs and to the framework of legislative activity changed the place of the *contio*. If it was summoned in order to consider legislation, it was summoned by a consul or a praetor, and the legislation itself would have been considered by the Senate and thus, in theory, only proceed to a vote if it represented a consensus decision by the elite. Replays of, for example, Sulpicius' challenge to the authority of the people as embodied in their choice of consuls was impossible. The implication of such changes is that there was no need in the *res publica* for oratory which could change minds and thus lead to unpredictable outcomes; but oratory remained necessary to inform the people and to justify the decisions of magistrates and senators. Sulla's contional practice conforms to this pattern; he is the ideal orator of the Sullan *res publica*.

Another aspect to his new *res publica* is the role of forensic rhetoric. Sulla's system of *quaestiones* standardised and organised forensic oratory in cases of public

---

69 Metellus is described as a young man, so he is probably not the consul of 80 (identification with whom would require Plutarch to be wrong about the praenomen, as the consul of 80 was Quintus); this Metellus has an *RE* number (71) but no other attestation.
70 On the organisation of the proscriptions, see further Hinard (1985b). Fufidius is mentioned at Flor. 2.9.26 as a Sullan adviser; the remark recorded there may come from this debate.
71 *OGIS* 441. In 80 Sulla addressed envoys from Thasos in the Senate (*RDGE* 20).

significance. No longer was the politically motivated free-for-all of the *iudicia publica*, with their citizen audiences, to be the mechanism for judging members of the Roman elite. Instead, they would defend their actions in courts in front of their senatorial peers, presided over by praetors empowered to ensure proper and transparent procedure. Forensic rhetoric was now very clearly demarcated as different from deliberative rhetoric.

Flower has characterised Sulla's republic as 'a political constitution based on laws and their regular enforcement by a system of courts'.[72] As she argues, this kind of state was radically different from what had gone before at Rome in which deliberation and debate took centre stage. A direct reflection of this change can be seen in the changing role of oratory and the functions to which it could be put. But the nature of the change can be framed in a slightly different way. What Sulla was attempting to eliminate from the *res publica* was unpredictability and, above all, the unpredictability that took place when a particular group of people made a particular decision at a particular time and place, exposed to partial and uncontrolled public speech. Whilst oratory remained a key element in the management of his *res publica*, it did so now in a tightly controlled fashion that meant that the decisions it was implicated in were consonant with the organisation of the state as a whole. Hence, apparently paradoxically, there are examples of very free speech even before Sulla's death; it was acceptable provided that it took place in the right environment. Hence, too, the possibility of arguing that Sulla was – perhaps despite himself – a protector of the rights of the new citizens, insofar as he restricted the capacity of citizens who happened to be in Rome to reroute policy onto unexpected paths.

Conclusion

Sulla was an orator, by any reasonable definition of that term at Rome. His absence from the *Brutus* was a decision driven by the concept of oratory that Cicero wanted to put forward in the context of Caesar's dictatorship: it involved the editing out of both Sulla and Marius.[73] He spoke extensively in a variety of deliberative contexts whenever his career created the opportunities for him to do so; but he did not seek to make oratory an element in his appeal to the people for electoral support. He never spoke forensically, and for patricians – at least prior to Clodius – forensic oratory was the only significant opportunity for speech at Rome prior to the praetorship, given that the tribunate of the *plebs* was not open to them. But although forensic and tribunician oratory provided the majority of high profile and dramatic

---

72 Flower (2010) 129.
73 Steel (2003).

speeches at Rome which contributed to the reputation of those considered to be great speakers, they were not the only occasions on which speech was required by those in public life. Prior to his dictatorship, Sulla demonstrates how even those in public life who made no claims to great skill, expertise or talent as orators would nonetheless be speakers once they reached a certain seniority; that was the nature of the *res publica*. In his dictatorship, speech assumed a greater importance for Sulla and for new ends. He used speech to exemplify key aspects of the *res publica* as he reshaped it during his dictatorship and to model the appropriate use of oratory. The *contio* provided a venue for him to reconfigure the Roman people into an obedient audience of instruction from magistrates, and his senatorial oratory revealed his autocracy whilst also shaping the role of the Senate in his *res publica*. Oratory was a key medium through which Sulla demonstrated how the *res publica* could and should work, and in order to give it this value Sulla himself took on the role of orator.[74]

---

[74] The research presented in this chapter was conducted as part of the European Research Council funded project *The Fragments of the Republican Roman Orators* (St-G 283670) based at the University of Glasgow. I am extremely grateful to the volume editors for their comments on an earlier draft.

Sophia Zoumbaki
2 Sulla's Relations with the Poleis of Central and Southern Greece in a Period of Transitions

The star depicted on coins of Mithridates VI Eupator, king of Pontus, was said to be closely linked with the king's fate, as it shone in the years of his birth (135 B.C.) and coronation (120 B.C.). It appeared again in the sky in 87, this time to bode his defeat by L. Cornelius Sulla.[1] Even before astronomers studied the star and named it 'Halley's comet', it was viewed with awe as an omen of momentous events. The year 87 was to be a turning point for the towns of central and southern Greece due to Sulla's landing in Epirus and his subsequent actions in the first phase of the Mithridatic War. It was a shocking blow for the Greek towns, and a violent end to Mithridates' promises of liberation: Athens was besieged and sacked along with Piraeus,[2] Eretria was destroyed,[3] and other *poleis* were threatened or ravaged.[4]

What was the situation in the region before Sulla's arrival? In his landmark book on Sparta, Spawforth has remarked that 'between 146 BC and the outbreak of the First Mithridatic War in 88 BC, a period during which Greece as a whole enjoyed peace and prosperity, Spartan affairs are largely a blank.'[5] It is true that the period between 146 and 88 was a time of peace for the towns of central and southern Greece after a long period of political weakness and economic contraction due to warfare, shifting alliances, the establishment of foreign garrisons, and internal strife resulting in insecurity and the loss of human and economic resources. In the years after 146 no act of Roman brutality is reported on a par with the plundering of Ambracia by M. Fulvius Nobilior in 189, the plunder of 70 Epirote towns by L. Aemilius Paullus in 167, or the annihilation of Corinth by L. Mummius in 146. The suppression of any revolutionary ambition at Dyme by Q. Fabius Maximus in 144/143 was an effective warning to secessionist tensions in other towns.[6] Further, no economic demands on the part of Rome are reported, and no military activity took place in the region in the decades after 146. Whether peace brought prosperity is difficult to trace, however, as

---
1 Stephenson et al. (1985); Yeoman et al. (1986) esp. 71–72; Gurzadyan/Vardanyan (2004); Mayor (2010) 27–42.
2 Plut. *Sull.* 12.2, 14.1–7; App. *Mith.* 34–35, 38; Strabo 9.1.15; Paus. 1.20.7. Archaeological documentation for Athens: Geagan (1979); Camp (1986) 181; Hoff (1997); cf. Eckert (2016a) 86–102; for Piraeus: Grigoropoulos (2005) esp. 15–30.
3 Schmid (2000) 169–180; Kaltsas et al. (2010) 85–86.
4 Anthedon, Larymna and Halae: Plut. *Sull.* 26.4; cf. Santangelo (2007) 48 n. 66. For Daulis: Pomptow (1921) 181–182, no. 168 (*SEG* 1, 175); *FD* III 4, 69. Cf. Eckert (2016a) 102–110.
5 Cartledge/Spawforth (2002) [1989] 93.
6 Rizakis (2008) no. 5.

the lack of evidence, the 'blank', to use Spawforth's word, is not only a Spartan, but also a general phenomenon for central and southern Greece. A drastic reduction in public activity is indicated by the low volume of public texts produced between 146 and the Mithridatic Wars, as a survey of the epigraphic corpora shows, while archaeology documents public buildings left to collapse. Descriptions in the few available literary sources (e.g. Polyb. 36.17.5–6) and the portrait of miserable public finances in the few surviving inscriptions indicate that the second half of the 2nd century was not a prosperous period for the region.[7] The situation will have been better in some areas, at least during some periods, but the majority of the towns were in a state of stagnation or decay. As for coinage, beyond the Athenian silver tetradrachms and emissions of the Thessalian *koinon*, the situation in the south of Thessaly is not known with any certainty, as the civic mints have not been studied comprehensively and the dating is largely based on coin hoards of debated chronology. The traditional view that no silver coinage was produced after 146 has been challenged and several scholars accept that both federal and civic emissions existed, yet dating them no more precisely than to the period between 146 and the outbreak of the First Mithridatic War.[8] A more precise dating of the coinage and a thorough study of civic mints are required to shed light on this period. Minting activity is no proof of prosperity, just as its absence does not necessarily indicate poverty.[9] But limited production or the cessation of coinage may imply limited economic activity. Athens, which flourished thanks to its control over Delos, was certainly an exception in the second half of the 2nd century B.C. The declaration of Delos as a duty-free port resulted in the dissolution of a trade and transport network which was earlier centred on Corinth and certainly

---

7 Epigraphy: e.g. Augis' benefactions in Argos: Daux (1964) (*SEG* 22, 266); cf. Migeotte (1984) 84–86, no. 20.
8 Crawford (1985) 126–127 argued that bronze coins continued to be produced for local circulation 'on a vast scale in Greece towards the middle and end of the second century,' while as for silver 'after 146, Athens was the only mint active south of Thessaly, apart from a tiny issue of Chalkis.' Based on the hoard evidence Kremydi (2004) 251–256 shows that during the second half of the 2nd century the only silver coinage was that of Athens and the Thessalian *koinon*, both allies of Rome. Ashton (2012) 204 speaks of little silver coinage south of Thessaly and the revival of the Achaean federal mint around 90 B.C. Thonemann (2015) 173–174 points to new numismatic studies that place Peloponnesian civic silver triobols 'right down through the late second and into the early first century BC', especially Grandjean (2003) esp. 130–152 (who, in the absence of data from closed excavated contexts, offers only a vague dating for Messenian triobols to the periods 152–146 and 88–82 based on comparative evidence from hoards, stylistic elements, and onomastics) and Boehringer (2008). On the other hand, there is a tendency to ascribe these emissions to the lower date. See Cargill Thompson Warren (1997) 112–113; (1999a) 99–109; (1999b) 375–393; (2007) 111, 174–176, who argues for an almost complete cessation of coin production, both silver and bronze, in the Peloponnese in the second half of the 2nd century, suggesting that the Peloponnese reverted to an agrarian subsistence economy. On the prosperity of Athens and its gradual decline in the late 2nd century and especially in the 90s, see Antela-Bernárdez (2015) esp. 59–60 and n. 7.
9 Howgego (1990).

included the Peloponnese and part of central Greece north of the Corinthian Gulf (Strabo 10.5.4). These factors posed problems for many towns and limited their economic growth.

Sulla's arrival had consequences for various aspects of the towns' life. I do not intend to engage here with the question of possible political reforms which arose directly or indirectly as a consequence of his presence, such as a supposed reform of the Athenian constitution.[10] I will rather focus on the impact of Sulla's actions on the social and economic life of the towns, taking the literary sources into account but placing more emphasis on epigraphic and numismatic evidence. My investigation focuses first on the long-term impact of Sulla's interventions in the region, then on the reaction of the *poleis* to cope with the new realities.

Sulla's Wartime Requisitions

As soon as Sulla landed on the Greek mainland, he urgently and forcibly gathered troops and provisions from Rome's allies in Thessaly and Aetolia, as the literary sources report, since Rome supplied him with only limited military forces and finances.[11] An illustration can be found in a fragmentary inscription of the allied Aetolian *koinon* in honour of a man who had served in Sulla's army and was granted honours, possibly *dona militaria*.[12] Sulla may also have used allies from the Thracian kingdom of the Odryssae; this is indicated by a decree of Chaeronea in honour of Amatokos whose contingent was left there while Sulla was besieging Athens.[13] Perhaps Chaeroneans fought on the Sullan side as well, given that two locals, Anaxidamos and Homoloichos, played a decisive role in the outcome of the battle of Chaeronea.[14] While recruitment from Rome's allies in Greece is attested before Sulla,[15] it seems that he expanded this beyond allies, for on his return to Rome

---

10 On the Athenian post-Sullan 'constitution', see Geagan (1967); Kallet-Marx (1995) 212–219; Santangelo (2007) 41–44; Kuin (2018). On politics in Athens from the end of the 2nd century to the 80s, see Bernhardt (1985) 39–49, 181 and Antela-Bernárdez (2015).
11 App. *Mith.* 30; cf. Plut. *Sull.* 12.3–4 and 15.3.
12 *IG* IX 1² 1, 139. For the individual, see Grainger (2000) 15, 205 (Ladames no. 5). On the award of *dona militaria* to allies in the Republican period, see Maxfield (1981) 121; on rewards to soldiers, see Prag (2011) 23–27, especially for *dona militaria* to auxiliary troops (mentioning the Aetolian Ladas in n. 64).
13 Holleaux (1919) 320–337. Amatokos' contingent served with Q. Braetius Sura, legate of the governor of Macedonia, who defeated Archelaus at Chaeronea before Sulla's arrival (App. *Mith.* 29; Plut. *Sull.* 11.4–5).
14 Plut. *Sull.* 17.5–7.
15 E.g. in 104, when about 800 Thessalians, Bithynians and Acarnanians were recruited for the slave war in Sicily (Diod. Sic. 36.8.1). For recruitment in Greece before as well as after Sulla, see Strauch (1996) 45–46. In general, on levies in the Late Republic, see Prag (2010); (2011) 16–22, who

in 83 he took military forces from the Peloponnese and Macedonia.[16] Recruitment from locals is afterwards attested as standard.[17]

Further, Sulla's demands for financing the war and the sustenance of the army entailed a huge burden for local communities. Provisions of various types, from mules, wood and other supplies to precious metal for coins to pay soldiers were gathered from the region.[18] More generally, the stationing of Sulla's army also posed a major challenge for the area. There is no direct evidence that the inhabitants of the Greek mainland were ordered to billet Roman soldiers as later in Asia, where Sulla obliged each rich family to host a soldier (Plut. *Sull.* 25.2). However, the wintering of Sulla's army in Thessaly must have been a burden on local communities given Appian's testimony that right from the beginning Sulla did not hesitate to gather provisions for the maintenance of his army at the expense of the locals, and that he let his soldiers ravage Boeotia on the pretext that the region was continually changing sides.[19] From Asconius' commentary on Cicero's *In toga candida*, it seems that post-battle plundering by Sulla's army was commonplace during its time in Greece.[20] It is in any case noteworthy that the earliest attestation of billeting and requisitioning supplies for the Roman army in the East at the expense of the locals comes from Sulla's age.[21] Afterwards this practice was frequent. This is evident in inscriptions of the 70s, which offer vivid snapshots of the burden created by the presence of Roman soldiers both in central Greece[22] and in the Peloponnese at Epidaurus (*IG* IV² 1, 66), Gytheion (*IG* V 1, 1146), and perhaps Sparta (*IG* V 1, 11).

Sulla's demands had consequences for the economic life of the region, especially its bullion reserves. Metal for the currency to pay Sulla's troops was mainly derived from votive offerings removed from the panhellenic sanctuaries of Olympia, Epidaurus, and Delphi.[23] Sulla's treasurer, L. Licinius Lucullus, was responsible for collecting the precious metal and issuing the so-called 'Lucullan' coins. The identification of these coins is still debated. The 'Lucullan spread-flan coins' (πλάτη Λευκόλλεια) mentioned in an inscription from Delphi (*FD* III 3, 282, ll. 5–6) are usually identified with three series of the Athenian New Style tetradrachms which

---

highlights the difficulty of distinguishing recruitment from the flexible categories of allies and subject peoples.
16 App. *B Civ.* 1.79.
17 See e.g. *IG* IV² 1, 66; cf. *IG* V 1, 1433, l. 39. Messenians contributed to an unknown campaign by enrolling slaves as rowers.
18 App. *Mith.* 30; Plut. *Sull.* 12.2–3; cf. Roth (1999) 144.
19 App. *Mith.* 30, 51. Cf. Mackay (2000b) for Chaeronea's changing sides during this phase of the Mithridatic War.
20 Eckert (2016a) 104 and n. 14, argues for a negative impact on Orchomenus' economy based on Asc. 84, 88 (Clark).
21 Roth (1999) 143–144; Ma (2002) 119; Cagniart (2007) 83.
22 Graninger (2011) 40.
23 Plut. *Sull.* 12.3–4; App. *Mith.* 54; Paus. 9.7.5–6; Diod. Sic. 38/39.7.

Thompson dated to Sulla's age.[24] Other emissions strikingly similar to the Athenian tetradrachms, such as the didrachms of the *koinon* of the Aenianes, have also been considered by De Callataÿ as part of the Lucullan coin issue.[25] In addition, Cargill Thompson Warren argues that a further part of this coinage can be recognised in a group of silver triobols from Sparta, and Boehringer includes triobols struck in the format of the Achaean League coinage.[26]

As the issue of Lucullan coins is unsolved, only a few certain facts can be emphasised here. Firstly, according to Plutarch, the majority of this coinage was minted in the Peloponnese, and it remained in use for a long time.[27] This is confirmed by the late 1st-century inscription from Delphi mentioned above.[28] Secondly, the Lucullan coins will have been Greek types that were recognisable by the soldiers and acceptable to them, for example the Athenian New style, as was the rule for coins minted in Greece at the command of Roman magistrates for the payment of troops.[29] Finally, Plutarch's statement that *most* coins were minted in the Peloponnese seems to imply that minting was not conducted exclusively in the Peloponnese, or at one time or at a single place, but rather on a regional level. In this case, it is unclear if one specific type was used by all mints, or if different coin-types were adopted by each regional mint, all of them struck on Lucullus' orders.[30] The latter scenario would, however, mean that no specific coin type can be identified as 'Lucullan'.

Recruitment, demands for army supplies, and the removal of precious metal deprived the region of its human and economic resources. It was a logistical challenge for the *poleis* to meet Sulla's demands, and they will have had to utilise all their strength and any still-functioning mechanisms to coordinate the recruitment of soldiers and the supply of war material. It may be that the coordination of military recruitment was entrusted by Sulla to the *koina*: there are references in Appian to the collection of troops from the allied Thessalians and Aetolians, and one may also

---

24 Thompson (1961) esp. 425–439.
25 De Callataÿ (2004) 125–156 drew attention to the similarities of didrachms of the *koinon* of the Aenianes with the Athenian tetradrachms and connected them with Lucullus's presence in the region (cf. *IG* IX 2, 39 of 88/87, when Lucullus held the office of quaestor). Further similarities can be observed with Cretan emissions under Lucullus: Le Rider (1968) 313–335. De Callataÿ (2015) connects certain emissions of Leucas with the period under discussion.
26 Cargill Thompson Warren (1996). Traditionally Achaean silver triobols are dated to before the dissolution of the Achaean League in 146. Boehringer (1991) 163–170 placed them at the end of the 2nd or beginning of the 1st century B.C.; Cargill Thompson Warren (1997); (1999a); (1999b); (2007). For a summary of this controversy, see Zoumbaki (2010) 116 and notes 37–38.
27 Plut. *Luc.* 2.2: δι' ἐκείνου γὰρ ἐκόπη τὸ πλεῖστον ἐν Πελοποννήσῳ περὶ τὸν Μιθριδατικὸν πόλεμον, καὶ Λουκούλλειον ἀπ' ἐκείνου προσηγορεύθη καὶ διετέλεσεν ἐπὶ πλεῖστον.
28 *FD* III 3, 282, ll. 5–6; on the identification of πλάτη Λευκόλλεια with Lucullan coins, see Daux (1935) 1–9.
29 Sometimes the name of a Roman magistrate appears as well, e.g. Macedonian tetradrachms bearing the name of the quaestor Aesillas, see Bauslaugh (2000).
30 Boehringer (2008) 88–89. Differently: Assenmaker (2017).

note the aforementioned honorific inscription of the Aetolian *koinon* for Ladas who served under Sulla.³¹ The Thessalian *koinon* maintained its privileges after the military events of 168 and 146,³² as did the Aetolian *koinon*.³³ As for the other *koina*, Pausanias (7.16.10) states that they were dissolved in 146 and reinstated 'shortly afterwards', but the evidence is so fragmentary that any attempt to reconstruct a portrait of the *koina* of central and southern Greece in the late 2nd and early 1st centuries remains conjectural.³⁴ The Phocian *koinon* and the *koinon* of the Aenianes appear in inscriptions shortly after 146, if we can rely on mainly prosopographical or linguistic dating criteria, while other *koina* of central Greece are attested in a limited number of inscriptions of uncertain date.³⁵ The revival of the Boeotian *koinon* has been dated to between 140 and 120,³⁶ but this is challenged by Knoepfler, who dates it after 86,³⁷ while Müller argues for the last third of the 1st century B.C.³⁸ As for the Achaean *koinon*, the first epigraphic signs of its revival can be dated with relative accuracy (due to the mention of Roman magistrates) to shortly after the Mithridatic War.³⁹ Further, a fragmentary inscription from Aegium, the religious centre of the Achaean League, mentions *Sylleia* games which were perhaps established by the *koinon*.⁴⁰

The function and organisation of the reactivated *koina* are unknown, but one may assume that they were politically useful to Roman interests or at least not harmful. It is noteworthy that the reactivated *koina* of the Aenianes, Athamanes, and Achaeans erected honorific monuments in the period of the Mithridatic Wars or shortly afterwards for Roman magistrates involved in economic affairs: the *koinon* of the Aenianes honoured the *tamias* Lucullus (*IG* IX 2, 39), the Achaean *koinon* honoured the *proquaestor* Q. Ancharius (*IvO* 328), and the *koinon* of the Athamanes honoured Q. Braetius Sura (*IG* IX 2, 613), whose full title, *leg(atus) pro q(uaestore)*,

---

31 Cf. Ñaco del Hoyo et al. (2009) 42.
32 Harter-Uibopuu (2003) 211; Graninger (2011) esp. 37–39; Bouchon/Helly (2015).
33 Strauch (1996) 129–130 and n. 14 on earlier bibliography. Federal magistrates are still attested after 146: Grainger (2000) 172; but no federal coinage seems to have existed after this date: Tsangari (2007) 36, 254–255.
34 Martin (1975) 147, 587–590 argues for the dissolution of certain *koina* by the Romans, while Kallet-Marx (1995) 57–59, 76–82 argues that there was no Roman intervention, and that Pausanias generalises on the basis of the Achaean *koinon*.
35 Strauch (1996) 129–130 and n. 14 on earlier bibliography. On the Phocian *koinon*, see Zachos (2013) 115–118; Rousset (forthcoming); cf. e.g. the inscriptions Pomptow (1921) nos. 145, 146a; *IG* IX 1, 91; *CID* V 713; on the *koinon* of Aenianes, see e.g. the texts dated to *circa* 130 B.C.: *IG* IX 2, 6a (*SEG* 44, 447); 6b; 6d; 6e; 6f; *FD* III 4, 57 (91–68 B.C.).
36 Harter-Uibopuu (2003) 214.
37 Knoepfler (2008).
38 Müller (2014a).
39 Zoumbaki, (2010) 115–118, with earlier bibliography.
40 Rizakis (2008) no. 125, ll. 2–6.

appears in a coin series minted on Thasos.⁴¹ These documents seem to show that the *koina* cooperated with magistrates entrusted with tasks in the sphere of the economy, probably in connection with securing soldiers and supplies for the army, and perhaps the minting of coinage on the orders of Lucullus.⁴² Rome was not interested in reorganising the federations, but in exploiting convenient pre-existing structures which could coordinate common actions, such as recruitment and collection of material resources from individual *poleis*. *Koina* continued in this new guise until they assumed a different role in the Early Imperial period. The *koinon* of Asia also seems to have gained in significance in the period immediately after Sulla. Although it is not evident that Sulla intervened to reorganise it, such a network of towns was obviously useful for the implementation of his economic measures.⁴³ An alternative view holds that the *koinon* was reorganised between 85 and 80 by Lucullus when he was charged by Sulla with the organisation of Asia.⁴⁴ Either way, it is clear that neither Sulla nor Lucullus had any intention of resurrecting the *koinon* of Asia *per se*, but to use it to exploit the economic resources of the province. Similarly, *koina* of central and southern Greece may have been used by Sulla for the coordination of actions aiming at channelling human and material resources to cover the needs of his expedition.

Channelling human and material resources from provincials to the Roman army was not Sulla's invention, yet supplying the Roman war machine to such a large extent at the expense of locals inaugurated a new phase in the participation of Greek *poleis* in the Roman war economy. After a long period of low demands by the Romans, Sulla's requisitions were not only a challenge for the Greek towns, but would be established as a standard practice in the following years.

Sulla's Post-War Settlement

Sulla manifested his dominance after the victories over Mithridates with the imposition of punitive measures on the king's supporters. Thus he confiscated 10,000 *plethra* on Euboea, the base of Pontic forces during the war. The land was then donated to Sulla's old enemy Archelaus, Mithridates' general.⁴⁵ He also confiscated half the territory of Thebes (ἀποτέμνεσθαι, Plut. *Sull.* 19.6; Paus. 10.7.4–6), dedicated it to Apollo and Zeus, and ascribed its revenues to the sanctuaries of Delphi,

---

41 De Callataÿ (1998).
42 Cf. Ñaco del Hoyo et al. (2009) 42. See also notes 25–26 above.
43 Santangelo (2007) 125–133. Cf. Campanile (2007).
44 Ferrary (2001b) 29.
45 Plut. *Sull.* 23.2; cf. Hill (1946) 39–41; Kallet-Marx (1995) 63–64.

Epidaurus, and Olympia as compensation for the treasures he removed from them.⁴⁶ Further, Sulla attributed the islands Sciathos and Peparethos to Thasos as a reward for its pro-Roman stance during the First Mithridatic War.⁴⁷ Before the Mithridatic Wars, land confiscations are reported in the cases of Corinth (also confiscated were the private properties of the Achaean leader Diaeus and his supporters, Polyb. 39.4) and royal lands in Macedonia.⁴⁸ Delos and perhaps also Scyros, Imbros, and Lesbos were transferred to Athenian control after 167 in return for the latter's loyalty to Rome.⁴⁹ Sulla, once declared *hostis*, had no official authority, and so his confiscations and distributions of land to new beneficiaries were legitimised only by the law of war.

Loss of territory entailed a serious economic damage for the towns. Moreover, Appian reports that many regions in Greece and Macedonia, which previously did not pay tribute to Rome, were subjected to it in the aftermath of the Mithridatic Wars.⁵⁰ This is verified by the epigraphic evidence, where tributes in central and southern Greece are attested only after Sulla, yet without any indication that a regular system of taxation existed directly after the First Mithridatic War.⁵¹ When exactly tributes began to be levied on a regular basis is unknown. The situation in Greece in the preceding period, namely between the Achaean War and Sulla, is far from clear.⁵² It is believed that in this period Rome did not levy regular tributes,⁵³ despite Pausanias' statement (7.16.9) that φόρος τε ἐτάχθη τῇ Ἑλλάδι after 146.⁵⁴ It seems that *vectigalia* from certain state monopolies and custom duties were levied. Otherwise there is evidence only for extraordinary levies, indemnities, and war booty, but no solid evidence for regular and general taxation.

---

46 Cf. Hill (1946) 38–39 rejects the view that the territory of Boeotia was made *ager publicus* after the Achaean War, since in that case Sulla would not have confiscated it, as its revenues would be lost for the Roman state rather than Thebes. Cf. Kallet-Marx (1995) 62. Reinach's suggestion (1895) 197 that the land of Chalcis was already part of the *ager publicus* (based on Livy, *Per.* 52, that Chalcis had the same fate as Corinth), is disputed by Picard (1979) 295.
47 Dunant/Pouilloux (1958) no. 175, l. 18; Picard (1989).
48 Rizakis (2015) 5.
49 Bugh (1990) esp. 25. Sulla did not deprive Athens of these territories: Santangelo (2007) 41.
50 App. *Mith.* 118.
51 Kallet-Marx (1995) 59–76.
52 Cf. Ñaco del Hoyo (2011) with bibliography. In general on the status of Greece in this period: Kallet-Marx (1995) 42–96; Bouchon (2011); Müller (2014b) 200–201, 203.
53 Strauch (1996) 20–25; Kallet-Marx (1995) 59–65, both with earlier bibliography.
54 Pausanias' credibility in regard to earlier periods is doubtful, cf. Kallet-Marx (1995) 57–59, 65 on the ambiguity of the term φόρος in Polybius (who was perhaps Pausanias' source). Similarly, Strabo's (8.5.5) information on Sparta's taxation has to be placed in the right context. Kallet-Marx (1995) 63 n. 24 interprets the inscription *Syll.*³ 748 from Gytheion as an indication of *ad hoc* exactions not regular tributes.

The sources do not focus on Sulla's imposition of tributes, but rather his grants of exemption from tribute, along with other privileges to those who remained faithful to Rome. Elatea was declared 'free' and exempt from taxation (ἀτελῆ νέμεσθαι τὴν χώραν, Paus. 10.34.2–6), if one can trust Pausanias' credibility in this case.[55] Perhaps Chaeronea was granted this privilege as well.[56] Exemptions are also reported in two inscriptions: a *senatus consultum* of 78 B.C. which awards various privileges to three naval captains,[57] and an inscription from Oropus dated to 73 B.C. which offers a retrospective report of Sulla's grants to the sanctuary of Amphiaraus after the First Mithridatic War (later confirmed by the Senate).[58] Whether exemptions imply that a regular taxation system already existed or was imposed by Sulla cannot be answered with certainty.[59] First, during this period, Sulla was still officially an enemy of the Roman state, thus his decisions were not authorised by Rome. Moreover, regular taxation, even if it existed, is not attested in the wording of the two inscriptions. The grant to the Amphiareum did not concern an exemption from regular Roman tribute, but a declaration that the land of Oropus as well as the revenues from its territory and harbour were sacred to Amphiaraus and thus not liable to taxation. The legality of Sulla's measures was later challenged by the *publicani* on the grounds that Amphiaraus was not a god,[60] and that his land should not be exempt from taxation.[61] The sacred land of Amphiaraus, called ἡ ἐπ' Ἀμφιαράου, and its liability to taxation had been the subject of debate as early as the 4th century.[62] The aim of Oropus was to settle this long-standing dispute – apparently on the initiative of a prominent citizen, Hermodoros, a priest of Amphiaraus and member of the Oropian delegation to the Senate, who was able to redeem his good services to Rome and Sulla by securing favourable decisions both for his home town and his own estates.[63] The Latin and Greek bilingual *senatus*

---

55 On the privileges granted to Elatea, cf. Kallet-Marx (1995) 64; Zachos (2013) 118–122. On Pausanias' reliability, above n. 54.
56 Kallet-Marx (1995) 281.
57 *IGRom.* 118; *RDGE* 22; privileges are extensively analysed by Raggi (2001). On the status of *amici*, see Zack (2013).
58 *IG* VII 413; *Syll.*³ 747; *RDGE* 23; Rigsby (1996) 6; *IOropos* 308. On the reasons of Sulla's favourable treatment, see Cosmopoulos (2001) 79. Eckert (2016a) 132–133 stresses Sulla's connection with the oracle and the fact that part of the altar was devoted to Aphrodite. Kallet-Marx (1995) 267–273, esp. n. 32. Cf. Santangelo (2007) 105 n. 1. There were also revisions to Sulla's decisions on other issues, Thasos: Picard (1989); Maroneia: Clinton (2003); Chios: Marshall (1969).
59 Kallet-Marx (1995) 59–62 regards exemptions from tributes as a solid evidence for tribute after the Mithridatic War.
60 In the inscription Amphiaraus is referred to as θεός, but his divinity is still debated at Cic. *Nat. D.* 3.48. Cf. Pirenne-Delforge (2010) 381–382, 387.
61 Kallet-Marx (1995) 272–273; Bowman/Cooley (2008) 94–95, 113,114 (for the exemption of land set aside for sacred purposes).
62 *IG* II² 1672; *IEleusis* 177 (329/328 B.C.); Papazarkadas (2011) 48–50 with bibliography.
63 Kallet-Marx (1995) 272; Papazarkadas (2011) 50.

consultum of 78, preserved on a bronze tablet in the Capitoline Museum, awards three naval captains, two from towns in Asia Minor and one from Carystus on Euboea, along with their descendants, exemption from both local and Roman taxation as a reward for their military assistance to Rome. Kallet-Marx argues that a regular tribute existed in Carystus after this date.[64] The wording of the inscription (l. 23) merely implies, however, that Roman magistrates were authorised to impose tributes to be farmed out on a contract basis.[65] There is no sign either that Sulla's arrangements dealt with the *publicani*. The *senatus consultum* and the Oropus inscription attest their presence in the 70s, but the only reference to *publicani* in mainland Greece in the preceding period is derived from Livy (45.18), who reports that Aemilius Paullus excluded them from Macedonia as they were always the reason for the 'rights of the people to become a nonentity and for the freedom of the allies to be destroyed'. The *publicani* were active in Asia before Sulla, but their activities were limited by the proconsul Q. Mucius Scaevola (cos. 95) in the 90s, then they disappeared and reappeared at the same time as in mainland Greece.[66]

Given the lack of evidence, it is difficult to identify administrative and fiscal innovations brought in on Sulla's initiative, for example the regular or *ad hoc* imposition of tribute. Perhaps tributes or indemnities were imposed by Sulla as a punitive measure in certain regions. Boeotia which constantly changed sides according to Appian (*Mith.* 51) and where important battles took place, as was also the case with Phocis, could have been subjected to tribute or indemnities from which certain *poleis* were exempted. In any case, Appian's reference (*Mith.* 118) to the imposition of tributes on Greece after the Mithridatic Wars shows that Sulla's presence was remembered as a turning point in the relations of Greeks with Rome. Even if no substantial modification of the taxation system was initiated by Sulla, his actions during and after the war set the basis for a redefinition of Rome's control over the East. Sulla's speech at Ephesus to the representatives of the towns of Asia made reference to Rome's lenient treatment of Greeks, who had until then been left autonomous despite their secessionist tendencies, and this indirectly showed his conviction that it was time to deal with the Greeks with greater severity.[67] This is reflected in his behaviour towards certain towns on the Greek mainland, although the imposition of a fine, as in Asia, is not attested.

---

[64] Kallet-Marx (1995) 59–65, 278–282.
[65] Santangelo (2007) 56 suggests that it would be in addition to regular taxation.
[66] Santangelo (2007) 34; Ferriès/Delrieux (2011).
[67] Cf. Eckert (2016a) 97–98 on Sulla's attitude to Athens. On Sulla's clemency or cruelty in his treatment of Asia and the Greek mainland, see Thein (2014), with earlier bibliography, and Kallet-Marx (1995) 278–279. Sulla imposed a fine of 20,000 talents on the cities of Asia: Plut. *Sull.* 25.2; App. *Mith.* 62. Cf. Raggi (2001) 93; Santangelo (2007) 107–133; Ñaco del Hoyo et al. (2011) esp. 298–304.

Despite this, there is no evidence that Sulla engaged in a reorganisation of the region or planned a system of general taxation. Rather, he regulated certain issues *ad hoc*, as was the practice of Roman magistrates active in the Greek mainland before him. In some respects, the only exception was Aemilius Paullus who halved but maintained the tribute previously paid to the king in Macedonia, and avoided major administrative reforms aside from the division into four self-governing regions and the imposition of some economic restrictions (Livy 45. 29–30). In any case, these arrangements, although they are called *leges* by Livy (45.32.7), did not aim at a fundamental reorganisation of Macedonia, but mainly at the avoidance of unwelcome tensions, especially those that could arise from the local management of important economic resources such as the royal gold and silver mines. Sulla, therefore, was in the tradition of Roman generals who took some measures after the conquest of a territory, but not as part of a systematic plan. Sulla's interventions were of an *ad hoc* nature, concerning specific *poleis* or regions, and often defined punishment or reward depending on the towns' stance towards Rome. His grants of exemption from tributes need not imply fiscal innovations or the imposition of regular and general tributes. Instead they can refer either to indemnities imposed by him on certain regions, or to extraordinary tributes and *vectigalia* (above, notes 52–54) already levied in Greece before him. As it has been argued, even the 'Sullan constitution' of Athens was no more than the restoration of the situation before the war (above, n. 10).

Nevertheless, either deliberately or not, his actions signalled a new phase in Rome's treatment of the regions of the East by standardising or establishing certain practices. The billeting of troops and demands for recruits and provisions entailed a systematic integration of the East into the Roman war economy. Sulla also showed that it was time for Rome to integrate the eastern provinces firmly into its control leaving no space for secessionism, and in later years a general fiscal reorganisation would be an inevitable consequence of Sulla's reforms. As Santangelo (2007, 133) remarks, 'it is hard to deny that he did not know that his measures would inevitably bring about a new political climate'.

Trophies, Victory Games and Other Festivals
The aftermath of Sulla's victory in the first phase of the Mithridatic War was a critical moment at which he had to manage his victory over the defeated enemy as well as the Greeks who supported him. He had to decide how his personal image was to be defined, how his severity or mercy should be expressed, and how stability and peace could be restored. As a *hostis* of Rome, he also had to use his victory as a vehicle for his personal rehabilitation.

When Sulla was still at or near where the decisive battles took place he ordered the erection of trophies (the plural is used by Plutarch) in order to glorify his victories.[68] Of these trophies, only the impressive monument commemorating the victory at Orchomenus has been found *in situ*.[69]

Fig. 1: The orthostat base blocks of Sulla's trophy *in situ* (viewed from the south). Picture printed with the generous permission of E. Kountouri, N. Petrochilos, S. Zoumbaki, M. Magnisali and T. Billis (research team for the publication of the Orchomenus trophy).

It is an imposing monument which dominated the plain and was visible from a distance. A rectangular pedestal covered with local limestone plaques stood on a stepped base and bore relief decoration depicting military equipment such as pieces of armour and broken chariots – obviously of the defeated Mithridatic army. The pedestal was surmounted by an inscribed cornice which bore a tier decorated with ovoid shields and above it a prismatic plinth decorated with circular shields. The whole structure was crowned by a tree trunk adorned with armour, the reproduction in stone of the traditional Greek perishable trophy of the battlefield. The inscription commemorated Sulla as αὐτοκράτωρ and assigned his victory to the divine help of Ares, Nike, and Aphrodite:

---

68 The Chaeronean trophy mentioned by Plutarch (*Sull.* 19.5; *Mor.* 318d) and Pausanias (9.40.7) has not been found. On the problem of Sulla's trophies in the region, see Mackay (2000a) 170 n. 30 and 173; Kountouri et al. (forthcoming).
69 Kountouri (2001–2004) 193–194. The publication of the monument is being prepared by a team of archaeologists and architects. For a preliminary study, see Kountouri et al. (forthcoming).

L. Cornelius L.f. Sulla imperator
(who fought) against King Mithridates and his allies
(dedicated it) to Ares, Nike, Aphrodite.⁷⁰

Figs. 2–4: The inscribed crowning of Sulla's trophy near Orchomenus. Picture printed with the generous permission of E. Kountouri, N. Petrochilos, S. Zoumbaki, M. Magnisali and T. Billis (research team for the publication of the Orchomenus trophy).

---

70 [Λεύκιος Κ]ορνήλ[ιος Λευκίου υ]ἱὸς Σύλλας αὐτοκράτωρ | [κ]ατὰ βασιλέως Μιθραδάτου καὶ τῶν συμμάχων α[ὐτοῦ] | [Ἄ]ρ[ει] vac. Νί[κη]ι vac. Ἀφροδί[τηι]. On the triad of divinities: Assenmaker (2014) 216–218. Cf. Eckert (2016a) 76 for the connection of Tyche with Sulla's name 'Felix'.

The concept of the monument, the content of its inscription, and the traditional Greek *xoanon* on top, sent messages to various recipients: Mithridates, the Greek *poleis*, and Rome itself. Everything indicates that the concept was dictated by Sulla himself and expressed his deliberate choice to celebrate his victories using a Greek-style victory monument and a Greek inscription.[71]

The importance of victory monuments for Sulla is obvious in the depiction of two trophies on a series of coins minted by him in the style of the Athenian New Style tetradrachms, and also on the reverse of his gold coins with the legend *Imper(ator) Iterum*.[72] It is the first time that Roman coins bore the name of a magistrate defined as *imperator*. The use of the title *imperator* and its Greek equivalent, αὐτοκράτωρ, highlighted his connection with Mars/Ares, and it is attested in the two monuments erected by him in Greece during this period: the trophy of Orchomenus and his dedication to Mars in Sicyon, *L. Cornelius L. f. Sulla imper(ator) Martei*.[73] The title of *imperator*/αὐτοκράτωρ also appears in several inscriptions on monuments erected in Sulla's honour by the *poleis* of mainland Greece.[74] It is not surprising that Sulla used the title *imperator*/ αὐτοκράτωρ given to him by acclamation of his troops in preference to the official title of *proconsul* assigned to him by the Roman state, which had declared him an enemy.[75] Sulla's adoption of trophy-iconography on his coins and his self-presentation as *imperator* is understandable for the period of the First Mithridatic War, when his reputation rested on his victories on the battlefield and the loyalty of his troops.[76]

Beyond the erection of trophies, Sulla celebrated his victory over Mithridates by organising *epinikia*-games at Thebes where he put a stage near the fountain of Oedipus (Plut. *Sull.* 19.6). In order to humiliate the town, he did not appoint judges from Thebes to preside over the games, but invited Greeks from other places. It has been suggested that the organisation of a local form of victory celebration in the Hellenistic manner, as other Roman commanders had done as well, highlighted and rewarded the role of local troops.[77] Certainly, it was part of Sulla's personal strategy to promote his own victorious image. It is possible that Sulla played a role in the revival of agonistic festivals in Boeotia which is attested after the First

---

[71] Plut. *Sull.* 19.5: διὸ καὶ τοῖς τροπαίοις ἐπέγραψεν Ἄρη καὶ Νίκην καὶ Ἀφροδίτην … οὕτως ἀναγέγραπται; 34.2: παρ' ἡμῖν ἐν τοῖς τροπαίοις «Λεύκιος Κορνήλιος Σύλλας Ἐπαφρόδιτος».
[72] *RRC* 359, 367–368. Cf. Santangelo (2007) 204–207; Assenmaker (2013b) 248–277; (2014) 159–193; Eckert (2016a) 123–124.
[73] Orlandos (1938) 121–122; *CIL* I² 2828; *ILLRP* 224.
[74] Cf. Mayer (2008) 121–135. Thespiae: *IThesp.* 397; Acraephia: *ADelt* 23 (1968) 293–294; Messene: *SEG* 48, 496.
[75] Only the Latin inscriptions of monuments on Delos include his title of proconsul (*IDélos* 1850–1852).
[76] On Sulla's self-presentation, see Gisborne (2005) 105–123, esp. 112–116 on the title of *imperator*.
[77] Prag (2011) 25–26.

Mithridatic War.⁷⁸ The promotion of local festivals will have emphasised his close personal relationship with specific deities and his claims to divine support. A connection with Sulla is perhaps to be traced in the reorganisation of the Ἐρωτίδεια Ῥωμαῖα at Thespiae, in the trieteric *Soteria* at Acraephia perhaps named after the 'salvation' owed to Sulla's victory, and in the revival of the *Amphiaraeia* at Oropus as *Amphiaraeia Rhomaia*, which now included sacrifices ὑπὲρ τῆς νίκης καὶ τῆς ἡγεμονίας τοῦ δήμου τοῦ Ῥωμαίων (*IOropos* 308, ll. 47–49) and a contest named εὐαγγέλια τῆς Ῥωμαίων νίκης (*IOropos* 521, l. 62).⁷⁹ Even if Sulla did not himself engage in the (re)organisation of local festivals, perhaps he exploited this excellent opportunity to use religion as an instrument in his self-presentation, in order to promote his image as the undisputed victor who restored normality. Certainly, the regular celebration of local festivals signalled the return to stability, since during the war some festivals were apparently suspended.⁸⁰

Sulla even included the famous Olympic Games in his propaganda, as he decided to celebrate them in Rome,⁸¹ perhaps with the aim of representing Rome as the centre of an empire which embraced the whole Greek world.⁸² This striking action showed his ability to move material and immaterial treasures, mobile and immobile goods at will. He removed sacred objects from certain sanctuaries in order to dedicate them at others,⁸³ and he carried treasures and works of art from the Greek East back to Italy on his return in 83.⁸⁴ The Olympics were likewise 'transported' to Rome as an immaterial symbolic treasure.

All these actions aimed at defining Sulla's image as a victor who reinstated order, security, and stability, and had complete dominance over the region. On the one hand he adopted a punitive policy towards disobedient Greeks, and on the other hand he placed himself in a Greek tradition of trophies, *epinikia*-games, and the organisation of local festivals. Simultaneously, some titles of local

---

78 Gossage (1975).
79 Ἐρωτίδεια Ῥωμαῖα: Knoepfler (1997) 17–39 (*SEG* 47, 518, 521). *Soteria*: *IG* VII 2727 (*BÉ* (1959) 311; (1962) 58; *SEG* 32, 452 and 459; 43, 1253); cf. Chaniotis (1995) 165; Zoumbaki (2014) 211–212. Amphiaraeia: Schachter (1994) 26–27; Rigsby (1996) 77–81; Strasser (2001) (*SEG* 51, 585); Williamson/van Nijf (2016) 53–57; for a different view: Kalliontzis (2016).
80 On the suspension of celebrating certain festivals during the Mithridatic Wars, see Habicht (2003) 44–46.
81 Siewert (2002).
82 Santangelo (2007) 218.
83 Paus. 9.30.1, 9.33.6. Cf. Santangelo (2007) 201–202; Eckert (2016a) 109–110.
84 On booty from Athens, see e.g. App. *Mith.* 39 (gold and silver from the Acropolis), Plin. *HN* 36.45 (columns from the Olympieum), Paus. 10.21.6 (shields of Athenian heroes from the stoa of Zeus Eleutherios), Strabo 13.1.54 (library of Apellicon of Teos); Paus. 10.21.6 (treasures from Delphi); Lucian, *Zeux.* 3 (on a work of Zeuxis, which was lost in a shipwreck off Cape Malea). On Sulla's booty from the East: Arafat (1996) 100–104; Santangelo (2007) 200 n. 5 (with 168 on whether the shipwreck at Mahdia contained Sulla's booty from Athens); Miles (2008) 24, 75, 93–94, 157, 210.

festivals included epithets and clauses that recalled Roman victories and manifested Rome's image as a dominant saviour; this was a strategy of the Greek *poleis* to flatter Rome and its representatives, to show their gratitude and loyalty, and to cultivate links to the ruling power.[85] All these pre-existing elements now became standard strategies for the towns to negotiate their new place in the Roman *oikoumene*.

The *poleis* reactivate: Loans, Sales and Euergetism

The second half of the 2nd century is almost a dark age in the area under examination. The meagre evidence of the literary and epigraphic sources, as well as the dereliction of the archaeological remains, gives the impression of poverty and introversion.[86] It is, however, remarkable that after a long period of silence, texts related to public activity begin to proliferate in mainland Greece at the beginning of the 1st century. This does not imply an improvement in the economic situation of the towns. On the contrary, the epigraphic sources which offer the earliest evidence attest continuing hardship.[87] The image produced by the texts of the early 1st century is not one of economically strong communities which faced disruption due to the Mithridatic Wars, but one of exhausted towns unable to revitalise despite the long years of peace and the relatively modest Roman demands after 146 (which were limited mainly to the recruitment of soldiers from Rome's allies). Sulla's appearance inaugurated an era of requisitions which worsened an already difficult situation. Most towns were in need of resources to cope with a twin challenge: firstly, to promote their own internal recovery; secondly, to withstand new Roman demands (e.g. supplies of various kinds, tribute, recruitment, and the feeding and clothing of Roman soldiers).

Under these circumstances, towns again began to leave traces of public activity, and it is as if the events of the First Mithridatic War awoke them from lethargy. First, the *poleis* realised that there was no saviour to restore their freedom, as Mithridates had promised. They had to mobilise all their energies to negotiate their restored place in the new order. Further, the removal of precious metal from the sanctuaries to mint coins for Sulla's troops deprived the region of its economic reserves, though part of this currency will have circulated in local markets while Sulla's troops remained in Greece. This is indicated by an inscription of the late 1st century from Delphi (*FD* III 3, 282, ll. 5–6), where the cost of freeing slaves is assessed in πλάτη Λευκόλλεια, and by Plutarch's notice that Lucullan coins remained

---

85 On festivals as instruments of politics, see Chaniotis (1995).
86 Polyb. 36.17.5–6, see also n. 9.
87 E.g. *IG* IV² 65; 66; V 1, 11; 962; 1144–1146.

in use for a long time (*Luc.* 2.2). But economic difficulties remained, as is evident from inscriptions up to the age of Augustus. Written sources dating from the 1st century show the strategies adopted by the towns in order to deal with the new Roman demands for resources: borrowing, sale of public property, and euergetism.

Borrowing was a frequent choice, attested by honorific decrees for benefactors who made loans to some towns at a low or zero rate of interest.[88] The role of creditor was sometimes undertaken by Roman or Italian businessmen, such as the Cloatii brothers at Gytheion and Atticus at Athens.[89] Atticus was in Athens in the aftermath of the Sullan sack, and his benefactions included interest-free loans and the supply of corn. In other cases towns were obliged to sell public property. Thus Sicyon, which was indebted to Atticus and had difficulties in repaying its loan, was ultimately forced some years later to sell famous paintings in public ownership.[90] The main response to the problems of the period was the old tradition of euergetism. Honorific decrees indicate how private benefactors not only offered loans at low or zero interest, but also supplied grain at low prices in times of shortage, undertook costly liturgies, restored sanctuaries in a state of collapse, took up priesthoods of neglected cults, and hosted Roman magistrates at their own expense; we even hear of doctors who offered their services for free.[91]

The towns were 'compelled ... to react' (Santangelo 2007, 128) to adapt to the new Roman demands, and to this end they employed every mechanism, above all euergetism. The integration of the wealthiest Roman businessmen into the euergetic tradition proved very useful.

Roman 'Businessmen' in the East
Roman and Italian residents in mainland Greece were certainly terrified by hostilities against their compatriots in Asia and on Delos (App. *Mith.* 28) and experienced a period of insecurity as long as Pontic troops advanced and found supporters in Greek towns. No incidents of hostility against Italian and Roman settlers are recorded on the Greek mainland, as in Asia.[92] That said, the existence of these Roman nuclei could not prevent a philo-Mithridatic stance in several towns, even in Athens with its Delian connections and the relatively large Italian community whose members had

---

88 E.g. *IG* IV² 65, ll. 11–14 (Epidaurus); V 1, 962, ll. 9–12 (Kotyrta); 1370, l. 20 (Kalamai).
89 Kay (2014) 195–197. E.g. Cloatii at Gytheion: *IG* V 1, 1146; Atticus: Nep. *Att.* 2.3–5 and cf. Migeotte (1984) 34–35, no. 7.
90 Cic. *Att.* 1.13.1; cf. Migeotte (1984) 79–80, no. 18. On the sale, see Plin. *HN* 35.127.
91 *IG* V 1, 1445.
92 According to Bernhardt (1985) 137, their existence sufficed for Mithridates to order their annihilation.

begun to assimilate into Athenian society, for example as participants in the *ephebeia*.[93] It may be, however, that an Italian community in Thespiae influenced its decision to remain loyal to Rome (App. *Mith.* 29).[94] Sulla will no doubt have found support from Roman residents in Greece. One may note Plutarch's reference (*Sull.* 17.1–2) to a certain Q. Titius, described as an 'important man of business active in Greece' (Κόιντος Τίτιος, οὐκ ἀφανὴς ἀνὴρ τῶν ἐν τῇ Ἑλλάδι πραγματευομένων), who announced the prophecy of the god Trophonius for a second Sullan victory after Chaeronea.[95]

Sulla's victory no doubt gave them a sense of security and returned them to the fore. It is no coincidence that after Sulla they appear more prominently in the sources and take action collectively for the first time beyond Delos, notably as instigators of honorific monuments, sometimes in collaboration with the local authorities.[96] Their economic strength allowed them to undertake the role of benefactors in the towns or to hold expensive liturgies, and this led to their integration into local societies and to their greater visibility in the documents of the period. However, they were also motivated by profit and increased their wealth by assuming the role of moneylenders both to towns and individuals.[97] The prominence of Roman businessmen in the towns of the Greek mainland greatly increases after Sulla. They participate in local events such as festivals and contests, and their youth joins the local *ephebeia*. The importance of Rome's dominance for the consolidation of their position is obvious in the honorific monuments erected for Sulla, such as the statue erected in his honour by the Ἰταλικοὶ ἐν Λαρίσῃ[98] and the two monuments erected by the *Italici* of Delos who had survived the massacre of 88.[99]

Being on Good Terms with Rome

Sulla's victory revealed the permanence of the Roman conquest, extinguished hopes for the restoration of freedom, and made the Greeks realise that the fate of the towns and individual citizens depended on good relations with Rome and its local representatives. For them the victorious Sulla was not the *hostis* of Rome, but

---

[93] On Romans in Athens, see Zoumbaki (2015) with bibliography. On the involvement of resident Romans in the politics of Athens, see Antela-Bernárdez (2015).
[94] Cf. Bernhardt (1985) 57–58, 137, 263; Müller (1996).
[95] For an interesting identification of this individual, see Bouchon (2007).
[96] Zoumbaki (forthcoming).
[97] Bernhardt (1985) 263 n. 848.
[98] The unpublished inscription is mentioned in brief by Bouchon (2007) 271.
[99] *IDélos* 1850, 1852.

Rome's powerful agent. Honorific monuments for him and his wife[100] as well as for his generals[101] were erected at various places. Games named *Sylleia* were established at Athens and Aegium.[102] Festivities in honour of Roman magistrates – a practice that goes beyond a simple honorific distinction and assumes features reserved for heroes and deities – had earlier been established in *poleis* of mainland Greece and Asia Minor, such as the *Muceia* for Mucius Scaevola, or the *Titeia* in Argos and the *Eleutheria* in Larissa for Flamininus.[103] With the exception of the honours bestowed on Flamininus, the Roman who announced the freedom of Greeks, honorific statues for Sulla outnumber those for any other Roman magistrate before him.[104] Monuments in honour of Sulla and the organisation of festivals on the part of the *poleis* – the *Sylleia*-festivals at Athens and Aegium, the Ἐρωτίδεια Ῥωμαῖα at Thespiae, the *Amphiaraeia Rhomaia* at Oropus, and perhaps the *Soteria* at Acraephia – were part of a strategy to show loyalty to Rome and gratitude for Sulla's victories. The *poleis* of the Greek mainland did not establish a new chronological system taking their starting point from these victories, but the appearance of the phrase 'after the war' in inscriptions show that they recognised Sulla's victory as the dawn of a new era, e.g. the first celebration of the *Soteria* after the war, πρῶ

---

100 Athens: *IG* II² 4103 (*SEG* 24, 214) and *Agora* XVIII (2011) H407. Delos: *IDélos* 1850–1852. Oropus: *IG* VII 264; *IOropos* 442 and *IG* VII 371; *IOropos* 443 erected for Sulla and his wife Caecilia Metella. Acraephia: *ADelt* 23 (1968) 293–294. Thespiae: *IThesp.* 397, 398; cf. Plassart (1926) no. 73 and his comments. Messene: Themelis (1998) 100, no. 3 (*SEG* 48, 496). Larissa: Bouchon (2007) 271. The inscriptions call Sulla 'saviour' and 'benefactor' because he saved the towns from Mithridates. It was part of a strategy to avoid the fate of pro-Mithridatic towns: Kallet-Marx (1995) 60–61, 64–65; Meyer (2008) 77–78.
101 L. Licinius Lucullus: Delos: *ILS* 865 = *CIL* III 7237 = *IDélos* 1620. Hypata: *IG* IX 2, 38. Athens: *IG* II² 4104, 4105 (*SEG* 29, 179). Chaeronea: Plut. *Cim.* 2.2. C. Scribonius Curio: Oropus: *IG* VII 331; *IOropos* 444; with Ma (2013) 112. L. Munatius Plancus (identical with the Munatius in charge of Chalcis at App. *Mith.* 34): *IDélos* 1695–1696. A. Gabinius: honoured with his brother Publius on Delos (*IDélos* 2002) is perhaps to be identified with the tribune who testified to the bravery of Anaxidamos and Homoloichos at the battle of Chaeronea (Plut. *Sull.* 17.7). In Messene Sulla is honoured along with L. Licinius Murena and the otherwise unknown *legatus* Cn. Manlius Agrippa. Several inscribed blocks bearing their honorific inscriptions seem to belong to a large podium for bronze statues: (i) *IG* V 1, 1454 (*SEG* 48, 494); (ii) *SEG* 47, 401; 48, 495; (iii) *SEG* 48, 496. Cf. Dohnicht/Heil (2004).
102 Athens: *IG* II² 1039, ll. 56–58 (*SEG* 22, 110) and *SEG* 37, 135. Cf. Raubitschek (1951); Santangelo (2007) 218. Aegium: Rizakis (2008) no. 125, ll. 2–6.
103 Muceia: Ferriès/Delrieux (2011) 211. Cultic honours and games at Chalcis for T. Quinctius Flamininus: Plut. *Flam.* 16.3–4; honours at other towns: Plut. *Flam.* 17.1; cf. Eckstein (1990) 51 n. 22.
104 Polyb. 18.44–48 (esp. 46.5); Livy 33.30–35; Plut. *Flam.* 10.3–5. Cf. nos. 1–90 in the list given by Payne (1984) 367–389. Only central and southern Greece is taken into account. Beyond the special case of Delos with 35 attestations, only 15 honorific monuments for Roman magistrates are attested from 199/198 to the Sullan period. Santangelo (2007) 129–130 notes the spread of Roman patronage in Greek communities in this period.

[τον] ἀπὸ τοῦ πολέμου (above, n. 79) or the reference to ἀγωνοθετοῦντος [— ἀπὸ τοῦ πολέμου] πρῶτον ... in another Boeotian inscription.[105]

Not only *poleis* but also individuals realised the importance of being on good terms with Sulla. Conversely, Sulla knew that influential citizens could function as useful nuclei in their home communities in order to build his own network of supporters and to maintain order and loyalty.[106] Grants to individuals such as the priest of Amphiaraus or the Carystian captain were mutually beneficial.

Conclusion: The Revitalising Shock

Sulla's impact on mainland Greece, I would argue, can be characterised as a 'revitalising shock'. His appearance on the scene after a long absence of military action and a period of limited demands on the part of Rome was a violent caesura for the Greek *poleis* which marked the introduction of practices which in later periods would remain as constant features of Roman rule: the billeting of troops and their supply with all essentials at the expense of the local communities, military recruitment beyond Rome's allies, and other mechanisms of economic exploitation. Sulla, as a *hostis*, was not authorised to carry out a formal reorganisation, and thus he relied on *ad hoc* arrangements, but deliberately or not he took the first step towards a reorganisation of the subjected regions on the basis of measures which were later applied by the Roman authorities as a general and regular practice.

When Sulla arrived in central and southern Greece, most of the region was numbed by economic stagnation and immersed in an inward-looking silence defined by the limited production of public texts and perhaps the total cessation of mint activity. Sulla's presence was a shock which revitalised the towns, as it forced them to adapt to the new reality. The reason why the *poleis* reactivated at this time is not to be sought in a general economic recovery: much of the volume of epigraphic texts produced after the First Mithridatic War attests to continuing economic problems made worse by the post-war Roman settlement. But the new demands gave the towns no choice other than to rise to the challenge, and to this end they mobilised all existing mechanisms, above all the tradition of euergetism. Prominent individuals used private money to support their home towns, to increase their personal status, and cultivate links with Rome. Roman businessmen, more than before, used the opportunities of euergetism to integrate into local societies and even to increase their wealth. It is no accident that the bulk of our epigraphic

---

105 Knoepfler (1992) 476–477, no. 121 (*SEG* 42, 436).
106 For Sulla's role in the emergence of a pro-Roman Greek elite, see Santangelo (2007) esp. 218–219.

evidence is from honorific decrees which record benefactions by citizens of good economic standing.

It is possible that under these circumstances, regional *koina* – some of which still functioned yet in limited form – realised their new role. As centralised mechanisms, they seem to have been used under Sulla to coordinate the gathering of troops and precious metal for the needs of the army, and at the dawn of the Imperial period they continued in this role as collaborators in Rome's service. While Sulla's presence had a negative impact on civic life due to punitive measures and demands, it also accelerated the end to a long period of silent stagnation. All these developments evolved during the 'long' 1st century B.C., a period of transition which culminated in the stabilised form of the province Achaea dictated by Augustus.[107]

---

107 I am grateful to Charikleia Papageorgiadou, Sophia Kremydi and Panagiotis Doukellis for discussions on various aspects of the topic examined in this chapter.

Cristina Rosillo-López
3 Can a Dictator reform an Electoral System? A Reassessment of Sulla's Power over Institutions

Sulla's impact on Roman Republican history has not been neglected by scholars, and the 'age of Sulla' has been identified as a caesura in Roman history, either as the starting point for monarchical government or as the last opportunity for the reorganisation of the Republic.[1] Much attention has been bestowed on Sulla as the great reformer of the Late Republic, and Badian called him 'the deadly reformer'. However, a survey of the tangible impact of his reforms might also bestow upon him the nickname of 'the failed reformer'. Since the Gracchi, the necessity of reforming the Republic as a way of ensuring its survival was present in the minds of both conservative and more radical politicians, and one can ask if Sulla was the reformer that the Republic needed. But other questions can also be posed. To what extent did Sulla actually reform the political system? How powerful was one individual against established institutions and political processes, and could anyone in the second or first century map out a new political and constitutional framework? This study seeks to contribute to modern discussions about the possibility for reform in the Late Roman Republic, a fruitful field since Meier's view of the 'Krise ohne Alternative'.[2] More specifically, this chapter argues that in spite of the almost limitless powers of his dictatorship, Sulla's reforms were timid in conception, and, with only a few exceptions, of remarkably little consequence or long-term impact for the Republic.

My focus in this chapter is not on the legal aspects of Sulla's reforms, but on their political impact, and even on potential reforms that were not carried out. The specific issue I have chosen is the relationship between Sulla and the people, in particular the mechanics of elections, the moment at which the voters conferred legitimacy and political power upon the elite. The chapter will reassess to what extent Sulla could, and did, interfere with the structure of Roman politics to control the results of the elections, or at least to reduce uncertainty. It will examine the logic and scope of Sulla's reforms of the voting system, and it will also reflect on his ambition. Could his reforms have been more comprehensive, and did he even believe that a Roman autocrat could control the outcome of elections? As dictator, Sulla enjoyed unprecedented powers, but he was also shaped, I would argue, by the experience of popular dislike manifested in the

---

1 Hantos (1988) 13; cf. 165–167, for a positive evaluation of Sulla's reforms and their impact. All dates in this chapter are B.C. unless otherwise stated.
2 Meier (1997) ³[1966]. His view is that great men like Sulla, Pompey, or Caesar changed the *res publica* 'from the outside' in absence of pressure to change the status quo. For a critical reassessment see Winterling (2008).

aftermath of his march on Rome in 88. As consul he presided over the elections, but his nephew, Sextus Nonius Sufenas failed to secure election, and his preferred candidate for the consulship, P. Servilius Vatia, was also defeated, despite having recently celebrated a triumph. Sulla did manage to block Sertorius' election to the tribunate, on unknown grounds. But Marius Gratidianus, the nephew of Marius, was chosen as tribune of the plebs, and L. Cornelius Cinna, who did not support Sulla, was appointed consul. Sulla's only resort, ultimately fruitless, was to make the consuls swear to respect his legislative reforms.[3] Sulla then left the city and spent the next five years in Greece and Asia fighting Mithridates. The year 88 will have shown him the difficulty of controlling the results of elections, or even diminishing the possibility of unwanted outcomes. Neither his role as presiding magistrate nor his recent victory could guarantee him the election of magistrates who would not oppose his policies. We should not disregard this episode, and should set it in context alongside his proposals, five years later, in the negotiations with Scipio Asiagenes in 83. Sulla most likely still had his last electoral experience in mind.

In 83, Sulla returned to Italy and initiated a civil war that lasted until his victory at the Colline Gate in November 82. The first battle of the war was followed by a truce in which Sulla met the consul Scipio Asiagenes in an abortive attempt to negotiate terms of peace.[4] This failed negotiation was a turning-point for Sulla, and as civil war victor he announced in a *contio* that proscription was the punishment for anyone who had fought against him after the day on which the consul Scipio had broken their pact.[5] Cicero offers a summary of the discussions: *de auctoritate senatus, de suffragiis populi, de iure civitatis*.[6] The first topic was the authority of the Senate, a key pillar in the reforms of Sulla's dictatorship.[7] Another issue discussed were the rights of citizenship, a reference to the enfranchisement of the Italians and the modalities of their enrolment in the tribes after the Social War.[8] The second topic in Cicero's list is more enigmatic, but I would suggest that this reference to

---

3 Plut. *Sull.* 10.2–4; *Sert.* 4.3. Cf. Broughton (1991) 17, 46; Yakobson (1999) 161.
4 On these negotiations see Scardigli (1971) 237–238; Keaveney (2005a) ²[1982] 112–113. The praetor Q. Sertorius was sent by Scipio to communicate with the consul Norbanus, but decided on his own initiative to capture a town friendly to Sulla. The talks broke down due to Sertorius, and Scipio's army deserted him for Sulla. Scipio was proscribed (Oros. 5.21.3) but lived in exile in Massilia until at least 57 B.C. See Hinard (1985b) 344–346.
5 App. *B Civ.* 1.95. Hinard (1985b) 35 suggests that part of this speech was taken from the preamble of the edict of proscription. On the chronology of Appian's account and this *contio*, cf. Hinard (1985b) 107–109; Pina Polo (1989) 285 no. 228.
6 Cic. *Phil.* 12.27. Cf. Scardigli (1971) 237–238; Keaveney (2005a) ²[1982] 112–113.
7 On Sulla's reform of the Senate: Santangelo (2006); Steel (2014a); (2014b), with previous bibliography.
8 See Taylor (1966) 70–83; Wulff Alonso (2002) 113–178; Dart (2014) 171–204. *De suffragiis populi* cannot refer to the distribution of the Italians, since that was described by Cicero as *de novorum civium suffragiis* (Cic. *Phil.* 8.7).

the suffrage of the people alludes to future electoral reform. The question is this: what exactly were his plans, and how could he translate his ideas into practice?

In order to answer these questions, this chapter will examine the legislation of Sulla's dictatorship and review the reforms which had an impact on electoral practice and the mechanics of voting. The evidence is limited, and the scholarship has filled the gaps with hypotheses, in part to bolster the image of Sulla as an all-powerful dictator-reformer. A more cautious approach will highlight the limits of what Sulla was able to achieve.

Laws Against Electoral Corruption

Electoral corruption and malpractice was a recurrent issue in the Roman Republic, and the years before and after the Sullan *dominatio* were no exception. We do not know if Sulla passed a law on electoral corruption, but there is evidence which at least justifies the question. The Bobbio scholiast mentions a penalty imposed by a *lex Cornelia*, in which candidates condemned for electoral malpractice could not run for office again for ten years.[9] Taking into account that the source mentions a *lex Calpurnia* (probably that of 67) and describes it as *aliquanto postea* in comparison with the *lex Cornelia*, it is likely that the scholiast is referring to the *lex Cornelia Baebia de ambitu* of 181, passed in relation to the reorganisation of the *cursus honorum* after the Second Punic War.[10] If there was a *lex Cornelia de ambitu*, its contents are lost to us, but Sulla did reorganise the courts, and these included a permanent tribunal dealing with electoral corruption (*quaestio perpetua de ambitu*). Its effectiveness was relative, as with the other courts, but its existence did at least acknowledge the existence of the crime and facilitate its punishment.[11] Other measures addressed the issue tangentially. In 81 Sulla passed the *lex Cornelia sumptuaria*, which limited to three hundred sesterces the amount that could be spent on banquets during holidays, or on the Kalends, Ides, and Nones, while for the rest of the year costs could not exceed thirty sesterces.[12] Elections were moved to the summer. Before Sulla, elections took place at the end of the consular year, with no fixed date.[13] Furthermore, Sulla revived the *lex Villia*

---

9 *Schol. Bob.* 78 Stangl: *Nam superioribus <temporibus> damnati lege Cornelia hoc genus poenae ferebant, ut magistratuum petitione per decem annos abstinerent. Aliquanto postea severior lex Calpurnia* ...
10 Cf. Rosillo-López (2010) 55–57.
11 Mommsen (1899) 867; Rosillo-López (2010) 70–74.
12 Plut. *Sull.* 35.3; Cic. *Att.* 12.35.6. Wyetzner (2002) 28; 30–32 on this law as a means to reduce senatorial competition.
13 Pina Polo (2011) 198–199. It was a month or so before the elected magistrates took office: in winter after the war with Hannibal, and in the autumn after 153.

annalis and confirmed the fixed order of the magistracies in the *cursus honorum* and the minimum age requirements for each office. He also increased the number of praetors from six to eight, which increased competition for the consulship, and he specified a two-year gap (*biennium*) between the praetorship and the consulship.[14] However, the effectiveness of these measures was limited. Laws against corruption do not seem to have acted as a strong deterrent, and *ambitus* was not stopped or even limited in the following decades.[15]

Election of Pontiffs

Sulla altered the voting mechanisms for religious offices by repealing the *lex Domitia de sacerdotiis* of 104, which had put the election of the pontiffs in the hands of the people. From 81 these posts were filled through co-option by peers. However, the law proved short-lived, albeit with a longer lifespan than some other Sullan laws: in 63, a law passed by the tribune T. Atius Labienus returned the vote to the *comitia tributa*.[16] Sulla probably did not alter the procedure for the election of the *pontifex maximus*, a post that, unlike other religious appointments, had been elected by the people since the *lex Ogulnia* of 300.[17] Livy mentions the election of the *pontifex maximus* by the *comitia* in 212.[18] Such elections did not take place on

---

14 Cf. Astin (1958); Rögler (1962); Beck (2005); Keaveney (2005a) ²[1982] 143–146. For Brennan (2000) 391–394, these measures 'created a "winner takes all" atmosphere in the curule elections'.
15 Cf. Rosillo-López (2010) 234–236 on effectiveness.
16 *Lex Cornelia de sacerdotiis*. Livy, *Per.* 89; Cass. Dio 37.37.1. *Lex Atia de sacerdotiis:* Suet. *Iul.* 13; Vell. Pat. 2.12.3; Sall. *Cat.* 49; Plut. *Caes.* 7.1. In 63 Julius Caesar was elected *pontifex maximus* using bribery to defeat two distinguished *consulares*, and Taylor (1942a) 423 suggested that he supported the *lex Labiena* to promote his candidacy, just as Domitius Ahenobarbus had done in 104 (in 103 the latter was elected *pontifex maximus*). In the aftermath of Caesar's murder, Antony reinstated *cooptatio* for the election of Lepidus as *pontifex maximus* (Cass. Dio 44.53). Antony himself, as augur, inaugurated Lepidus. This move ensured Antony the support of Lepidus' army; supporters of the conspirators had already offered Lepidus the chief pontificate in exchange for his support (App. *B Civ.* 2.132). Lepidus' candidacy found a precedent in the case of his homonymous forefather (cos. 187), who had been *pontifex maximus* (180–152) and *princeps senatus* at the same time. It was considered an illegal move by Augustan historians, since there is no record of a law being passed (e.g. Livy, *Per.* 117), while Cicero accused Antony of engraving laws in bronze before anyone had heard of them (Cic. *Phil.* 2.97; 3.30; 5.11–12). Taylor (1942a) 424 proposed that Antony may have attributed the law to Caesar; Weigel (1992) 48–49 feels that in a fair election Lepidus would have been 'a most likely candidate' because of his prestigious record and seniority over other pontiffs.
17 Livy 10.6. The law also opened the priesthood to plebeians. The first plebeian *pontifex*, elected in 254, was Ti. Coruncanius, cos. 280, who defeated Pyrrhus in battle (Livy, *Per.* 18).
18 Livy 25.5: *comitia inde pontifici maximo creando sunt habita*. But Livy 40.42 states that co-option was used in 181. It is uncertain if the election of 181 was an exception.

an annual basis, since the appointment was for life, but a new *pontifex maximus* is attested every 10–15 years.[19]

It is worth reviewing developments before Sulla. In the second half of the 2nd century attempts were made by tribunes to end the practice of co-option. In 145, the tribune C. Licinius Crassus proposed a law to establish the election by the people of all pontiffs and augurs, not just the *pontifex maximus*. The proposal was rejected, and Nonius preserves a fragment of a speech of the praetor C. Laelius who argued against the law on the grounds that it posed a threat to the *pax deorum*.[20] In 104, the tribune Cn. Domitius Ahenobarbus succeeded in changing the procedure for the election of pontiffs and augurs.[21] Candidates were selected in the first instance by the *collegia* of priests, then there was an electoral campaign in which 17 out of 35 tribes were chosen by lot to make a decision.[22] The impetus for the *lex Domitia* was personal, for Ahenobarbus had failed to be co-opted into a priestly college at the death of his father in what had been a family tradition since 172.[23] In particular, he blamed M. Aemilius Scaurus, the *princeps senatus* and staunch conservative, who belonged to the college of augurs.[24] Rawson interpreted the *lex Domitia* and other religious initiatives of the final quarter of the 2nd century as popular attempts to abolish the optimate control of public religion.[25] Rüpke likewise sets the unsuccessful law of Licinius Crassus in the context of a wider political struggle: for him it was 'part of an older Licinian and plebeian-populist tradition of liberalizing the priesthood'.[26] After the defeat at Arausio, attributed to the obstinate incompetence of Q. Servilius Caepio, the aristocratic proconsul of 105, Marius was elected *in absentia* to his second consulship, for 104, and in that year the *lex Domitia* dealt a further blow to optimate leadership.[27] The abolition of the *lex Domitia* by Sulla is consistent with this interpretation. It should also be noted that he abolished a procedure that was only 23 years old.

Strasburger and Taylor have argued that Sulla's reforms did not affect the election of the *pontifex maximus*.[28] The key piece of evidence is a passage of Cicero's *De*

---

19 Lists of *pontifices maximi* in Münzer (1920) 414 and Rüpke (2008) 982–983.
20 On this failed *lex Licinia*: cf. Cic. *Amic.* 96; Non. 398.28M = 640L; cf. North (1989) 536; Rüpke (2012) 118–119. Not much of its content is known, but Cicero felt its aim had been fulfilled by the *lex Domitia*.
21 Dating to 104: *MRR* 1.559.
22 On the procedure, see Mommsen (1877) 2.26–30; Taylor (1942a); North (2011).
23 On this law: Linderski (1972); Hantos (1988) 120–125; North (1990); Rüpke (2012) 118–122. Ahenobarbus was elected *pontifex maximus* the year after the law passed.
24 Rüpke (2012) 120–121 lists the known conservative aristocrats in the colleges of priests.
25 Rawson (1974).
26 Rüpke (2012) 118.
27 Rüpke (2012) 120.
28 Strasburger (1938) 102 n. 30; Taylor (1942a); cf. Mommsen (1877) 2.29, who stated that a Sullan change in the election of the *pontifex maximus* cannot be proved with the existing evidence.

lege agraria: in a discussion of Rullus' agrarian proposal of late 64, Cicero suggests that the law proposed the *comitia pontificis maximi* as the method for choosing the agrarian commission.[29] It could be argued that Rullus' proposal referred to the new provisions of the *lex Labiena*, but Cicero was speaking in the first days of January 63, right after taking office, and at this point the *lex Labiena* could not yet have been passed, although it was proposed at the very start of the year.[30] Rüpke suggests that Rullus' proposal for the election of the agrarian commission alluded to the forthcoming proposal of Labienus.[31] The argument that Sulla only changed the mechanisms of the pontiffs, but not the *pontifex maximus*, is convincing, and it fits with the idea that Sulla's aim was to correct what he saw as the misguided drift of the Roman state during the previous decades, but not to remove a customary voting right enjoyed by the Roman people for 200 years. It is also worth noting that priesthoods were offices for life, and that no change was made to the elections for annual magistrates.

In conclusion, Sulla did carry out an electoral reform, restoring co-option to the college of pontiffs. It was repealed by the *lex Labiena* in 63, and the popularity of this measure points to the lack of support among voters for the reform carried out by Sulla in 81.

New Citizens

Sulla manumitted and gave Roman citizenship to more than ten thousand slaves of the proscribed, and Appian interprets this as a way of securing a large number of plebeians at his command among the citizens.[32] Sulla probably counted on their support in elections. As was the custom for *liberti*, they will have been enrolled in the urban tribes, thus diluting their impact, given that there were only four urban tribes in comparison with the 31 rural tribes. This measure seems not to have had any effect on the outcome of elections.[33]

Election of Tribunes of the Plebs

In his discussion of Sulla's reform of the tribunate, Appian suspends his judgment on the question of whether Sulla transferred the election of this office from

---

[29] Cic. *Leg. agr.* 2.18.
[30] Pina Polo (1989) 291 n. 258 proposes the 2nd January 63. On the afterlife of Sulla's reforms, cf. Laffi (1967).
[31] Rüpke (2008) 1642.
[32] App. *B Civ.* 1.100; they were the so-called Cornelii.
[33] Marino (1974) 130–133.

the people to the Senate.³⁴ Nicolet proposed that Sulla might have carried out an electoral reform, taking away from the people the power of electing the tribunes of the plebs and placing that task in the hands of the Senate.³⁵ In his view, an electoral measure that suppressed the *comitia tributa* was passed in 88 by Sulla and Pompeius Rufus, annulled by Cinna and Marius, and then reestablished by Sulla after 82. However, the evidence for this hypothesis, which rests on two ambiguous passages, is far from convincing and has generally been rejected.³⁶

Secret Ballot

In a recent survey of the 'Sullan Republic', Flower asks why Sulla did not abolish the secret ballot, or introduce mechanisms for a more active and direct involvement in elections: 'Meanwhile, it is interesting and suggestive that he did not do away with the secret ballot, or apparently introduce any reform into the actual mechanics of voting'.³⁷ Before turning to the broader question of controlling elections one must ask why Sulla did not abolish the secret ballot.

Our knowledge of how the written secret ballot was progressively introduced in electoral, legislative and judicial voting is quite limited.³⁸ In 139, the *lex Gabinia tabellaria* established the secret ballot in the elections of magistrates. Three tribunician *leges tabellariae* extended this to other voting contexts: to the *iudicia populi*, with the exception of cases of *perduellio*, by the *lex Cassia tabellaria* of 137; to the legislative assemblies by the *lex Papiria tabellaria* of 131; and finally to cases of *perduellio* by the *lex Caelia tabellaria* of 107.³⁹ Cicero's *De Legibus* is our main source for the introduction of the secret ballot. In one passage Quintus Cicero argues that it freed voters from the domination and power of the *optimates*. Later in the same discussion Atticus confirms the *popularis* character of the law.⁴⁰ Cicero's views cast some light upon this subject: for him the objective of the secret ballot was to curtail electoral corruption, or *ambitus*, but he was sceptical about its efficacy, and he conceded that

---

34 App. *B Civ.* 1.100.
35 Nicolet (1959).
36 The passages are Ps. Asc. 189 (Stangl) and Sall. *Hist.* 3.48.15 (Maurenbrecher) = 3.34.15 (McGushin) = 3.15.15 (Ramsey). Cf. Gabba (1967) 274–275; Marino (1974) 82–84; Keaveney (2005a) ²[1982] 141 n. 7.
37 Flower (2010) 125.
38 On the *leges tabellariae* cf. Bicknell (1969); Troiani (1981); Hall (1990); Vaahtera (1990); Jehne (1993); Yakobson (1995); Marshall (1997); Salerno (1999); Feig Vishnia (2008); Lundgreen (2009).
39 Cic. *Leg.* 3.34–36.
40 Cic. *Leg.* 3.34, 3.37. Cf. Millar (1984); (1986) 1.

for the people the secret ballot was a symbol of their liberty.[41] In what seems a purely theoretical exercise, Cicero proposed that the ballot should be shown in public before being put into the box: this procedure would give the appearance of liberty while maintaining the authority of the elite.[42] Nicolet has proposed that this mixed system was taken from a passage in Plato's *Laws*.[43] The main bone of contention for modern scholars is to what degree the secret ballot was viewed as a menace by conservative politicians, given the fact that Sulla did not propose that it should be reformed. Yakobson argues that a repeal of the secret ballot would not have been politically feasible, and that Sulla probably considered the rest of his reforms sufficient to reduce the danger of undesirable candidates winning elections.[44] Meier and Feig Vishnia offer the opposing view that before Sulla the secret ballot was not seen as a threat.[45] But this is an interpretation which relies on the lack of any Sullan reform: Feig Vishnia does not consider it plausible that Sulla 'would have left such a loophole in his reform program'.[46] It is preferable in my view to think that Sulla's aim was to strengthen the Senate, not simply to oppose the people. Cicero reveals that the people saw the secret ballot as a symbol of their liberty. Any politician who opposed it would probably have faced a heavy price.

But even if the secret ballot was removed, could senators control how the people voted? Patronage ties were not as strong as they had been, the enfranchisement of the Italians had changed the electorate, and electoral corruption was increasingly endemic. The *lex Maria tabellaria* had narrowed the *pontes* that led to the voting boxes, so it was no longer easy to intimidate voters on the spot.[47] The only option for senators to impose their will on the people was through their *auctoritas*, or by persuasion in a *contio*. Taking all this into account, the elimination of the secret ballot would not have provided Sulla with any practical means of controlling the result of the elections.

---

41 Cic. *Leg.* 3.39; with Arena (2012) 58–60. Atticus' and Quintus' interpretation has found support from Yakobson and Millar, who claim that the *leges tabellariae* aimed to reduce the influence of the patronage system and the relationship between generals and their soldiers: Yakobson (1995) 427; Millar (1998) 26–27. Others suggest that these laws strengthened oligarchic tendencies and did not weaken the influence in the elections of patron-client relationships: Hall (1990) 194–199; Jehne (1993); Mouritsen (2001) 75–76. Jehne (1993) has also proposed that the secret ballot may have hidden the fact that the patronage system was defined at the time by competing layers of patronage ties and that electors were conflicted in their choices. These modern interpretations should not be considered as opposing views, as the aims of the laws, despite the intentions of the lawgivers, are not always consistent with their consequences.
42 Cic. *Leg.* 3.39.
43 Nicolet (1970) 59–60; with Pl. *Leg.* 753c-d.
44 Yakobson (1995) 429; (1999) 128.
45 Meier (1997) ³[1966] 128–129; Feig Vishnia (2008).
46 Feig Vishnia (2008) 336.
47 Plut. *Mar.* 4; Cic. *Leg.* 3.38.

Intervention in Elections

Canvassing for a candidate or recommending him to the people was the conventional way in which politicians showed their support for friends, family, or allies at elections. The effectiveness of such tactics depended, of course, on the status and popularity of both the recommender and the candidate. Having retired from politics, Sulla looked on with alarm when M. Aemilius Lepidus canvassed for the consulship of 78 with the explicit intent of repealing Sulla's laws. Sulla went back to Rome to campaign actively for Catulus, but with mixed results. His candidate was elected consul in second place, while Lepidus won first place.[48]

Acting as the presiding magistrate allowed for a more active intervention in the elections.[49] The *professio*, or declaration of candidacy, remains the subject of debate: for Astin it was a necessary step in an election, required by law from the 2nd century, while for Levick it was optional.[50] Either way, the presiding magistrate, one of the consuls, had to approve the names of the candidates.[51] After the elections, he also announced the results and proclaimed the winners (*renuntiatio*). In 67, the consul C. Calpurnius Piso declared in a *contio* that he would refuse to proclaim Palicanus as consul if the latter won, but in practice, it is doubtful if he would have been able, or would have dared, to do so.[52] The presiding magistrate had some influence in the electoral proceedings, and Vervaet has suggested that Sulla may have presided over the consular elections for 81 to ensure the right men were elected.[53] In 88, however, Sulla had presided over the elections and at that time, even though he had an army outside the city walls, he was unable to prevent the election of candidates who opposed him. The post of presiding magistrate did not offer complete control of elections, and in any case it could not be secured on a long-term basis. It was generally assigned to one of the consuls, but there was no fixed rule: it could be decided by drawing lots (*sortitio*), by previous agreement between the consuls (*comparatio*), by the Senate, or it could depend on proximity to Rome (especially in the pre-Sullan age, when consuls spent long periods away from the city with their armies).[54]

Let us now examine the possibility that Sulla exercised a more active control of elections after his appointment as dictator in 82. At the time of Sulla's civil war victory at the Colline Gate, on 1st November 82, the elections for 81 had not yet been held by the consuls, Marius the Younger and Cn. Papirius Carbo, or by any other

---

48 Plut. *Sull.* 34.4–5; *Pomp.* 15.1–2.
49 Cf. Rilinger (1976).
50 Astin (1962); Levick (1981).
51 On the role of the presiding magistrate in the elections, cf. Rilinger (1976).
52 Val. Max. 3.8.3.
53 Vervaet (2004) 41 n. 14.
54 Pina Polo (2011) 192–207 (pre-Sullan period); 287–290 (post-Sullan period).

magistrate.⁵⁵ Despite his dominant position, Sulla attempted to follow legal procedure as much as possible.⁵⁶ Elections were not considered until both consuls were dead. An *interrex* was created to preside over the elections: he was L. Valerius Flaccus, *princeps senatus*, a senior figure. Sulla then wrote him a letter, suggesting the revival of the dictatorship and proposing himself for the job. The people, with Flaccus presiding, voted for the *lex Valeria* that conferred these powers onto Sulla. Sulla appointed afterwards Flaccus as his *magister equitum*.⁵⁷

Mommsen argued that the *lex Valeria* gave Sulla the right to appoint magistrates without the involvement of the *comitia*, but this is refuted by the sources which attest elections on a regular basis.⁵⁸ Our main source, Appian, viewed Sulla as a forerunner of the emperors and described his rule as an absolute tyranny (τυραννὶς ἐντελής).⁵⁹ In his view, elections under Sulla served only to maintain a semblance of Republican liberty.⁶⁰ Sulla's second consulship, in 80, is offered as a precedent for Imperial *designatio*, the practice by which emperors appoint consuls, sometimes holding the office themselves in conjunction with the supreme power.⁶¹ In 80 he was elected consul for the following year, according to Appian, but refused the office and 'designated' the consuls. Vervaet interprets this to mean simply that Sulla was the presiding magistrate who announced the *consules designati*, not that he actually nominated or appointed them.⁶² In general, Appian's narrative is factually reliable, but there is an agenda, and one has to be aware of distortions and anachronisms.⁶³

Elections were held for the year 81 while Sulla and Valerius Flaccus held the offices of dictator and master of the horse, and the consuls elected were M. Tullius Decula and Cn. Cornelius Dolabella. Broughton lists nine praetors and five quaestors but no tribune of the plebs.⁶⁴ Keaveney, following Appian, has suggested that Sulla's powers were so far-reaching that, although elections were held, no one of substance put himself forward.⁶⁵ This might explain the election to the consulship of Cornelius Dolabella, a mid-ranking follower of Sulla, or Tullius Decula, of whom

---

55 Elections before Sulla were not held on a fixed date; they took place at the end of the consular year, so one of the consuls usually went back to Rome to preside over them. See Pina Polo (2011) 193–207.
56 Hurlet (1993).
57 Sources in *MRR* 2.65–66.
58 Detailed refutation in Vervaet (2004) 47–48.
59 E.g. App. *B Civ.* 1.99. On Sulla's negative image after his death, see Seidl Steed (2008); Eckert (2016a).
60 App. *B Civ.* 1.100.
61 App. *B Civ.* 1.103.
62 App. *B Civ.* 1.103; Vervaet (2004) 47–48.
63 Cf. Keaveney (2003) 85 suggests dismissing Appian's interpretative glosses.
64 *MRR* 2.74–78; Hurlet (1993) 135–143.
65 Keaveney (2005a) ²[1982] 164, with App. *B Civ.* 1.100.

almost nothing is known.⁶⁶ However, the silence of the sources about Tullius Decula should not be regarded as a conclusive argument on his lack of political stature or the degree of Sulla's control over the voting.

The consuls elected for the year 80, following Sulla's abdication as dictator, were Sulla himself and one of his partisans, Q. Caecilius Metellus Pius, who had already been rewarded with the chief pontificate.⁶⁷ Only three praetors are known (plus two of doubtful attribution), one tribune of the plebs (C. Herennius) and one quaestor (C. Malleolus, who died while serving in Cilicia under Cn. Cornelius Dolabella, praetor of 81). However, the elections were not a smooth affair, with Sulla attempting to prevent his former legate Q. Lucretius Ofella (or Afella) from standing for the consulship.⁶⁸ A Marian partisan who had defected to Sulla's camp, Ofella had distinguished himself in command of the siege against Marius' son in Praeneste, a major event in the outcome of the war.⁶⁹ He probably counted on his military exploits to curry favour with the voters, and in this he seems to have been successful; Cicero praised his skills in *contiones*, that is, speaking before the people.⁷⁰ Sulla's opposition to his candidacy did not stem from political reasons, but from the fact that he was still an *eques* and had not even held the office of quaestor.⁷¹ Sulla's method of dealing with this problem was decisive: after an initial warning, Sulla dispatched a centurion who murdered Ofella in the middle of the Forum, while the latter was canvassing with a full retinue.⁷² The people dragged the soldier before Sulla, who was in the temple of Castor, and demanded punishment; his refusal was accompanied with a threatening parable of a farmer who, unable to shake the lice off his shirt twice, burned it the third time.⁷³ Vervaet has

---

66 On the consuls of 81, cf. Thein in this volume. On Decula, cf. Münzer (1948).
67 Metellus Pius is said to have left for the Iberian peninsula to fight Sertorius, leaving Sulla as consul in Rome for part of the year: App. *B Civ*. 1.97, 1.103; Pina Polo (2011) 231, 239.
68 On Ofella: Münzer (1927); Lanzani (1936) 270–272; Keaveney (2003). On the variants of his name: Badian (1967) 227–228; Keaveney (2003) 84. Plutarch and Appian give Ofella, while the Latin sources prefer Afella. No epigraphic evidence has been found. On the dating problem, Hinard (1985a) 239–240 and Keaveney (2003) 90–92 have argued convincingly that he was murdered in 81 while canvassing for the consulship of 80. Discussion with bibliography in Hurlet (1993) 161 n. 128.
69 Vell. Pat. 2.27.6; App. *B Civ*. 1.94.
70 Cic. *Brut*. 178.
71 Lundgreen (2011) 81 on the irregularity of Ofella's candidacy. Velleius (2.27.6) states that he had been *praetor* with the Marians. Broughton, in *MRR*, did not include him in his prosopography. Sumner (1973) 106–107 and Brennan (2000) 384, 748 argue that he may have been praetor in 83 or 82, and that he was seeking an exemption to the *biennium* between magistracies prescribed by the *lex Cornelia annalis*. Keaveney (2003) 85–86 argues that Velleius uses *praetor* to mean 'general' or 'commander'. The evidence, in my opinion, does not allow us to reach a categorical conclusion. Moreover, whether or not Ofella had been praetor is ultimately unimportant, since either way his candidacy violated the *lex Cornelia annalis*.
72 The assassin was tried and condemned in 64 in the *quaestio inter sicarios* (Cass. Dio 37.10.2).
73 Plut. *Sull*. 33.4; App. *B Civ*. 1.101 includes the parable.

argued that Sulla was a *dictator sine provocatione*, which granted the legal grounds for Afella's murder. Hurlet bases it on the *lex Cornelia de magistratibus*.[74]

Sulla's intervention in the elections of 81 for 80 was direct and violent, and Vervaet, for instance, has stated that the murder of Ofella 'shows that it was the dictator who really decided who was to be chosen consul by the *comitia centuriata*'.[75] Yet the fact that he resorted to such an extreme measure attests to Sulla's failure to control the elections: neither his unprecedented powers as dictator, which exceeded those of all other magistrates, nor even a direct instruction seem to have deterred Ofella and his supporters from canvassing. It is not known who presided over the elections, and the sources do not specify if there was a *professio* (it is not even clear if such a step was compulsory at the time), at which point the presiding magistrate could have refused to accept Ofella's candidacy on legal grounds.[76] Vervaet has proposed that Sulla wished to act as the presiding magistrate over the elections for 81 to ensure that his preferred candidates were chosen.[77] However, the murder of Lucretius Ofella clearly reflects his failure to do so, since he had to resort to assassination instead of using his authority or legal measures.

Sulla's actions had the potential for popular disturbances, for Appian tells us that Ofella stood for the consulship, in contravention of an unspecified new law, 'counting on the greatness of his services, according to the traditional custom, and appealing to the populace'.[78] In the past there had been several cases of candidates who did not fulfil all the requirements for their candidacy but were nevertheless elected by the people, with the necessary confirmation from the Senate afterwards. Scipio Aemilianus, for instance, was elected consul for 147 when he was only 38 years old, below the minimum age, and had not previously held either the aedileship or praetorship. The people regarded it as one of their prerogatives to choose the candidate they deemed to be most suitable, and on occasion even those who had not presented themselves as candidates were elected.[79] Sulla could not legislate against electoral irregularities of this kind, even by passing a *lex annalis* of his own.[80] Any irregular elections had to be confirmed by a vote of the Senate, and it is unlikely that the Sullan Senate, which included several hundred people who owed their seat to the dictator, would have endorsed a popular choice that displeased the

---

74 Vervaet (2004) 51–56; Hurlet (1993) 161.
75 Vervaet (2004) 47–48.
76 See above, n. 50.
77 Vervaet (2004) 41 n. 14.
78 App. *B Civ.* 1.101. If the murder occurred in mid-81, the *lex Cornelia annalis* will have applied: Keaveney (2003) 90.
79 Lundgreen (2011) 62–73 for a list and analysis of irregularities in candidacies.
80 In a clear case of double standards, Sulla did not oppose Lucullus' candidacy *in absentia* for the aedileship of 79, in contravention of his own laws. See Cic. *Acad.* 2.1; Plut. *Luc.* 1.6; Lundgreen (2011) 101. Keaveney (2009a) 34 suggests that Sulla may have been among the friends that canvassed for Lucullus in his absence.

dictator.[81] But there was a risk of violence if the Senate did not yield to the pressure of a popular vote. In 99, Saturninus attempted to be re-elected as tribune and his ally C. Servilius Glaucia canvassed for the consulship in the year after his praetorship without having waited the prescribed *biennium*. The Senate accused them of aiming at tyranny, passed a *senatus consultum ultimum* and both were murdered. Irregularities at elections could be a pretext for violence.[82]

The people voted the *lex Valeria* that made Sulla dictator, but they also voted for their preferred candidates in an electoral system based on a written and secret ballot, and in 81 they showed their support for Ofella just as in 88 they had voted for men like Cinna. There is also a telling example in a non-electoral context in which the people did not vote according to Sulla's wishes. In 81, Sulla decided to punish the people of Volaterrae and Arretium, who had long and actively resisted his armies, by depriving them of Roman citizenship, but when he put this measure to the vote, the Roman people rejected it.[83] The fact that the people rejected Sulla's measures or voted for candidates to whom he was opposed need not be understood as anti-Sullan opposition, but rather as evidence of the political unfeasibility of a dictator like Sulla controlling the votes of the Roman people. Sulla may have wanted to control elections, but ultimately it was the people who chose the winning candidates, and no *lex annalis* could stop them selecting whom they pleased.

In summary, Sulla's only electoral reform, for the election of pontiffs, involved a *comitia* that did not meet on a regular annual basis. Nicolet's hypothesis of a transfer of the election of the tribunes to the Senate is doubtful, but there was perhaps a law, and certainly a permanent tribunal dealing with electoral corruption, and there was also a *lex Cornelia annalis* which regulated progression, with prerequisites and minimum age requirements, along the *cursus honorum*. The elimination of the secret ballot might have provided satisfaction to some staunch conservatives, but it would probably not have changed much in practice, and a survey of other potential Sullan electoral reforms leads to a similar conclusion. Direct intervention in elections was effective, but at the risk of conflict with voters.

Conclusions

Sulla was not a new Servius Tullius: his initiatives did not solve the important issues of the time, and in spite of his almost unlimited powers his changes were

---

[81] On the Sullan Senate, see Santangelo (2006).
[82] Cf. the forthcoming article by F. Pina Polo entitled 'Transgression and Tradition in the Roman Republic: Some Reflections'.
[83] Cic. *Dom.* 79. *Pace* Santangelo (2007) 174 n. 12, who argues that the passage does not state explicitly that the Roman people voted against it.

timid and of little consequence (with two exceptions: the functions of the tribunes of the plebs and, in the longer term, the exclusion from political life of the children of the proscribed).[84] This chapter has focused not on the laws, but on the impact of these laws in practice.[85] Sulla's attempts to reform the political system did not take into account the complexity and reality of the system and, thus, were not effective enough, only a drop in the ocean; a revealing drop, but a drop nonetheless. Taking Sulla and electoral reforms as a proxy for this hypothesis, this chapter has argued that (i) despite having a previous plan, none of Sulla's electoral initiatives had a lasting effect; (ii) taking into account the complex interactions in elections in the first century, nothing that Sulla could have done would have helped him to reduce uncertainty in the electoral results, nor control them in any way, and (iii) his reforms did not even enable his followers to control or win elections. Nicolet, drawing on Appian, offers the following analysis: 'Il est bien certain – toutes nos sources sont d'accord – que Sylla enleva, par sa toute-puissance, toute signification aux élections, durant sa dictature'.[86] This chapter has shown instead that the mechanics of the Roman political system, even after Sulla's reforms, prevented him from assuming direct control of the elections and, thus, of controlling who was elected as magistrates. That said, his intentions may have been very different. The negotiations with Scipio Asiagenes suggest that Sulla had some kind of electoral reform in mind in 83, in part to avoid a repetition of his frustrations in the elections of 88, but the silence of the sources only allows for speculation.

Meier argued that Sulla was a reformer whose attempt to stabilise the Roman political system resulted instead in destabilisation; in his opinion, the problems were too big to tackle and the cure too exhausting.[87] Leaving aside the scale of the problems, did Sulla have any realistic chance of effecting deep and lasting reforms? Augustus managed it, creating another form of *res publica*, but what of those who came before him? It is useful to consider parallels for Sulla's difficulties, despite being dictator, in controlling the outcome of elections. In 44, Caesar was given the right to appoint half the magistrates, but this did not eliminate the

---

[84] In 63 there was a failed attempt to restore the rights of the descendants of the proscribed: Vell. Pat. 2.43.4, on Caesar's initiative; Cass. Dio 37.25.3. Cicero delivered a speech *De proscriptorum liberi*, a fragment of which survives, sympathising with the cause but opposing reform on the grounds of potential political instability: Quint. *Inst.* 11.1.85; cf. Crawford (1994) 205–211, at 209 n. 19 arguing against the scholarly view that Quintilian did not give Cicero's words. The *ius honorum* was restored by the *lex Antonia de proscriptorum liberis* of 49 (Suet. *Iul.* 41.2). For the children of the proscribed see also Eckert in this volume.
[85] Leaving aside Mommsen's analysis of magistracy-Senate-assemblies of the people only as institutions and not as constitutive bases for Sulla's reforms, as suggested by Hantos (1988) 18.
[86] Nicolet (1959) 220.
[87] Meier (1997) ³[1966] 266: 'Die Probleme waren zu groß, die Ärzte überzeugten nicht recht, und daher war die Kur zu anstrengend, sie griff mehr an, als daß sie nützte'.

normal problems in electing the rest of them.[88] Mark Antony also experienced difficulties in influencing voter behaviour. After Caesar's murder, in 44, one of the tribunes of the plebs died, and faced with the prospect of having Octavian as candidate, Antony threatened to use his full authority as consul against him. According to Appian, the people felt insulted and grew angry; Octavian's chances of winning the election increased as a result, and finally, to defuse the situation, Mark Antony annulled the *comitia*, arguing that the number of tribunes was sufficient.[89] This example illustrates two points that have been emphasised in this chapter: firstly, that from time to time the people deliberately ignored the *leges annales* and reacted intensely against interference from above; and secondly, that the choice of the voters was difficult to control. Antony's power as consul did not impress them and only the cancelling of the election solved the situation.

In conclusion, let us focus briefly on Augustus as *princeps*. From 28, magistrates were again elected by the vote of the people, and the sources mention intense electoral competition.[90] Augustus' lack of consular *imperium* prevented him having any control before the vote.[91] In 21, two candidates canvassed strongly for the consulship that was left vacant when Augustus refused to accept the consulship that had been reserved for him. There were disturbances in Rome, and the *princeps* wanted the two candidates not to be present in Rome on the day of the elections. The intervention was to no avail, however, and the unrest in Rome persisted until one of the two, Q. Aemilius Lepidus, was elected consul.[92] Augustus' role in elections in the latter part of his reign is well documented thanks to the reference to the electoral reform of the *lex Valeria Cornelia* in the *Tabula Hebana* of A.D. 5. Ten new centuries of senators and knights were created and charged with the election of consuls and praetors, and their *designatio* was communicated to the *comitia centuriata* for the final vote.[93] Augustus might communicate his preferences to the assemblies, his influence, once he was no longer consul, resting on his *auctoritas*.[94] He also canvassed personally each year until he stopped for health reasons in A.D. 8. But as Jones concludes, he found it 'impracticable or impolitic to exercise strong pressure on the elections'.[95]

This chapter has argued that the question of impracticability was a reality faced even by reformers with almost unlimited powers like Sulla, and it was a problem

---

88 Cf. Jehne (2010) 198–201. Caesar relied on *suffragatio* and *commendatio*, i.e. oral and written recommendations for candidates.
89 App. *B Civ*. 3.31.
90 Suet. *Aug*. 40.2; Cass. Dio 53.21.6.
91 Ferrary (2001a) 128 n. 103.
92 Cass. Dio 54.6.3; Hollard (2010) 216–221; Courrier (2014) 851–852.
93 On elections under Augustus cf. Jones (1955); Frei-Stolba (1967); Levick (1967); Hollard (2010) 151–226.
94 Ferrary (2001a) 127–128.
95 Jones (1955) 20.

solved only Tiberius' transfer of the elections from the people to the Senate. Caligula lamented that the Roman people did not have a single throat to slit. Neither did Republican voters have a single ballot. Reducing the uncertainty of elections was a task of socio-political and constitutional reform arguably far too complex for any reformer working within the constraints of the Republican system.[96]

---

[96] This research has been financed by the project 'Opinión pública y comunicación política en la República Romana (siglos II-I a de C.)' (2013-43496-P, Ministerio de Economía y Competitividad, Spain) and the Humboldt Research Fellowship for Experienced Researchers of the Alexander von Humboldt Foundation.

Alexander Thein
4 Dolabella's Naval Command

In his *synkrisis* of Lysander and Sulla, Plutarch offers his opinion that Lysander acted unjustly only to promote the interests of his friends, whereas the acts of injustice committed by Sulla were sometimes directed against his friends.[1] The antithesis is then developed in more detail. First there is an allusion to the proxy-rulers established by Lysander in the cities freed from Athenian control at the end of the Peloponnesian War.[2] Then Plutarch offers three examples in which Sulla used his power to thwart the ambitions of three men.

> For it is generally agreed that Lysander committed the most of his transgressions for the sake of his comrades, and that most of his massacres were perpetrated to maintain their power and sovereignty; but Sulla cut down the number of Pompey's soldiers out of jealousy, and tried to take away from Dolabella the naval command which he had given him, and when Lucretius Ofella sued for the consulship as a reward for many great services, ordered him to be slain before his eyes, causing all men to regard him with fear and horror because of his murdering his dearest friends.[3]

Plutarch offers a detailed description of the death of Q. Lucretius Ofella in a section of his biography of Sulla in which he depicts his subject as a tyrant and highlights his arbitrary exercise of power after his assumption of the dictatorship.[4] There is a detailed treatment, in Plutarch's *Pompey*, of Sulla's order to Pompey to send the bulk of his legions back to Italy after his victories over the Marian remnant in Sicily and Africa.[5] But the story of Sulla reducing the size of Pompey's army does not feature in the main narrative of Plutarch's *Sulla*, and there is no mention in any ancient source, except the passage quoted above, of Sulla's attempt to deprive Dolabella of a naval command (ναυαρχία). It is an isolated testimony and it has therefore received little comment. One problem is the identity of Dolabella: he is either Cn. Cornelius Dolabella, consul of 81, or his cousin of the

---

[1] Plut. *Comp. Lys. Sull.* 2.3. Interestingly, the biography ends with the epitaph on Sulla's tumulus tomb which proclaimed that no-one had surpassed him in harming his enemies *or helping his friends* (Plut. *Sull.* 38.4).
[2] Plut. *Comp. Lys. Sull.* 2.3.
[3] Plut. *Comp. Lys. Sull.* 2.3–4: Λύσανδρος μὲν γὰρ ὁμολογεῖται τὰ πλεῖστα διὰ τοὺς ἑταίρους ἐξαμαρτεῖν καὶ τὰς πλείστας σφαγὰς ὑπὲρ τῆς ἐκείνων ἀπεργάσασθαι δυναστείας καὶ τυραννίδος· Σύλλας δὲ καὶ Πομπηΐου περιέκοψε τὸ στρατιωτικὸν φθονήσας, καὶ Δολοβέλλα τὴν ναυαρχίαν ἐπεχείρησε δοὺς ἀφελέσθαι, καὶ Λουκρήτιον Ὀφέλλαν ἀντὶ πολλῶν καὶ μεγάλων ὑπατείαν μνώμενον ἐν ὀφθαλμοῖς ἀποσφάξαι προσέταξε, φρίκην καὶ δέος ἐμποιῶν πρὸς αὐτὸν ἀνθρώποις ἅπασι διὰ τῆς τῶν φιλτάτων ἀναιρέσεως (main text, above: Loeb trans.).
[4] Plut. *Sull.* 33.4; cf. App. *B Civ.* 1.101. The main treatment of this episode is Keaveney (2003) 88–93, cf. 84 for discussion of the alternative name Afella.
[5] Plut. *Pomp.* 13.1–7.

same name, praetor in 81. A related problem is the date and scope of Dolabella's naval command: the standard view is that Plutarch refers to the command of a fleet by the consul of 81 during the civil war of 83–82, but an alternative reading proposes that the term ναυαρχία refers to the Cilician *provincia* of the praetor of 81.[6] It is my aim in this chapter to explore these problems and to emphasize that if Sulla only *tried* to deprive Dolabella of his command, then he must have failed in his attempt. Plutarch uses the episode to present Sulla as a capricious tyrant who removes *imperium* at will, but read 'against the grain' the passage reveals limits on Sulla's 'power to dictate'.

The key treatment of Sulla and the Dolabellae to date is an article by Gruen which focuses on two extortion trials that took place at around the time of Sulla's death in 78: the acquittal of the consul of 81 when prosecuted by the young Julius Caesar on his return from his province of Macedonia in 77, and the conviction of the praetor of 81 when prosecuted by Sulla's stepson M. Aemilius Scaurus on his return from Cilicia in 78. Gruen argues that the Sullan oligarchy acquiesced in the conviction of the praetor of 81, a Marian turncoat and associate of the consul Lepidus, but rallied to the defence of the consul of 81, a committed Sullan. This trial, for Gruen, demonstrates the strength of the Sullan regime in the aftermath of Sulla's death: the uprising of Lepidus was defeated on the battlefield, opposition in the courts was suppressed, and it was not until the end of the decade that the oligarchy was forced into a fundamental reform of the Sullan system.[7] It is not obvious, however, that Caesar's motives were anti-Sullan, or that the Dolabella prosecuted by Sulla's stepson had a Marian past. It is also problematic, in my view, to adopt a narrative in which the weaknesses in the Sullan system emerged only in the years after his death.[8] There are sources, in particular Appian, which portray Sulla as an all-powerful tyrant, and scholars tend to assume that Sulla faced no dissent or constraints on his power while he held the dictatorship and consulship in the period 82–80.[9] But there is also evidence which points to the limits of Sulla's 'power to dictate'. An important example is Sulla's failure to complete his veteran settlement programme, in particular at

---

6 Consul of 81, civil war fleet: Münzer (1901a), 1297; *MRR* 2.65, 2.71; Gruen (1966a) 386; less explicit on date: Drumann (1902) 561; Carcopino (1931) 131; Lanzani (1936) 81–82; Vervaet (2004) 57; Steel (2013) 107; Syme (2016) 58; treated as undatable: Keaveney (1984) 139. Praetor of 81, Cilicia: Brennan (2000) 572. Cousins several times removed: Badian (1965) 51; cf. Gruen (1966a) 389.
7 Gruen (1966a) 388–389, 398–399. Important re-evaluations of the logic of Sulla's reforms and the post-Sullan decade: Santangelo (2014); Steel (2014a); (2014b).
8 The strength of Sulla's dictatorship and the failure of the Sullani are stressed by Badian (1970) 29–32; cf. Syme (1939) 22–23; (2016) 64; Flower (2010) 130–131, 137–138. Mediocrity and sterile conformism as hallmarks of the post-Sullan era: Seager (1994) 202. Compromise: Paterson (1985) 26–27.
9 App. *B Civ.* 1.3, 1.99–101, 104; cf. Cic. *Verr.* 2.3.81; *Leg. agr.* 3.5; *Har. resp.* 54; further sources: Santangelo (2014) 1–2. Dissent only after Sulla's retirement: e.g. Badian (1962) 61; Gruen (1974) 42; Keaveney (1984) 146; (2005a) ²[1982] 171; (2005b) 435. Elements of weakness in Sulla's regime: Thein (2006).

Volaterrae and Arretium where not all confiscated land was distributed to veterans.[10] One may also note the anecdotes in which individuals are said to have taken a moral stand against Sulla or defied his requests.[11] The risks of opposition find an extreme illustration in the fate of Q. Lucretius Ofella, who was killed in the Forum by a Sullan centurion after he ignored Sulla's order to give up his candidacy for the consulship.[12] But there is also the case of P. Cornelius Lentulus who was called to account in the Senate for wasting public money as quaestor during Sulla's dictatorship in 81. Sulla is said to have been angry, but Lentulus refused to give an answer and insolently offered the calf of his leg in imitation of a gesture, Plutarch tells us, made by those who miss the ball in a boy's game. The incident was remembered, and Lentulus assumed the *agnomen* Sura, the Latin word for the calf of the leg.[13] Sulla was in this case impotent in the face of a challenge from a junior magistrate guilty of corruption or malpractice, and Plutarch tells us that he also had problems with men he had appointed to military commands: he faced a near-mutiny when he recalled Pompey from Africa, he was forced to drop his opposition to Pompey's triumph, and he failed to remove Dolabella from a naval command.[14] This testimony is at odds with the standard image in which Sulla is strong and only his legacy is weak, and in Gruen's article on the Dolabellae the result is a rewriting of Plutarch in which Sulla's failure to impose his will on Dolabella is conflated with his alleged envy towards Pompey and the reduction of his army: 'That Sulla at one point reduced the number of ships under Dolabella's command was probably not due to envy as Plutarch suggests. Strategical (*sic*) considerations may have been involved'.[15]

Sulla tends to be viewed as an all-powerful dictator who was able to impose his will on Roman politics and maintain a position of unchallenged strength until his voluntary decision to abdicate from the dictatorship.[16] But there is almost no source

---

10 Cic. *Att.* 1.19.4; with Thein (2010) 85–86.
11 The following sources and episodes are listed by Keaveney (2005b) 435: Catulus (cos. 78) criticising the violence of Sulla's victory (Oros. 5.21.2); Pompey returning from Africa with his army contrary to orders (Plut. *Pomp.* 13); Ofella's bid for the consulship (App. *B Civ.* 1.101); Caesar refusing to divorce Cinna's daughter (Suet. *Iul.* 1.1); Granius of Puteoli refusing to pay a public debt (Plut. *Sull.* 37.3). In addition one may note, for example, the boy who abused Sulla in the streets after his abdication (App. *B Civ.* 1.104).
12 The episode is often used to argue that Sulla's power was absolute: e.g. Ridley (2000) 220; Keaveney (2005b) 435. There are, however, no other examples in which opposition to Sulla from his own faction resulted in death.
13 Plut. *Cic.* 17.2–3; with Keaveney (2005b) 434–435. Cicero notes that Lentulus was twice acquitted (*Att.* 1.1.9), and one view holds that Plutarch offers a distorted account of a Sullan period trial *de peculatu*: Drumann (1902) 529–30.
14 Pompey's recall and triumph: Plut. *Pomp.* 13.1–7, 14.1–3.
15 Gruen (1966a) 386 n. 4.
16 Standard view: e.g. Meier (1997) ³[1966] 248–253, 261; Gruen (1968) 277; Flower (2010) 132–134; Syme (2016) 62–64, 77–78. Internal opposition and forced retirement: Carcopino (1931) 186–211; Worthington (1992) 190–191.

material for politics in the period of the dictatorship, and it is known that Sulla's civil war faction was a heterogeneous group motivated by self-interest and ambition of office rather than personal loyalty to Sulla or an ideological commitment to conservative politics.[17] Sulla gave them the unity of purpose required to win the civil war, but it should not be taken for granted, in my view, that this coalition survived into the post-war period as a monolithic block in which there was no room for internal power struggles and occasional acts of defiance towards Sulla. This chapter examines one example and begins with two questions: who was Dolabella, and what was his ναυαρχία?

The Consul of 81

One of the consuls of 81 was the otherwise unknown M. Tullius Decula. His colleague, Cn. Cornelius Dolabella, was from an old patrician family which had fallen from prominence and had not supplied a consul since 159.[18] Plutarch mentions a Dolabella who was one of Sulla's commanders in the civil war. He was encamped 'at some distance' from Sulla's army at the battle of Sacriportus in the spring of 82, but Marius prevented a junction of the two forces, and Sulla was thus forced to fight and win the battle without assistance.[19] Dolabella also makes an appearance in Plutarch's narrative of the decisive Sullan victory at the Colline Gate: the army was ordered to form up for battle after a forced march and only a short meal, and two of Sulla's officers, Dolabella and Torquatus, appealed to him to give the men more time to rest, but he ignored their advice and ordered the trumpets to sound the attack, even though it was already late in the afternoon.[20] It is generally assumed, no doubt correctly, that the Dolabella who appears in Plutarch's accounts of the Sullan victories at Sacriportus and the Colline Gate is the consul of 81. Scholars also feel certain that he was elected with Sulla's blessing, as a reward for his services in the civil war.[21] No doubt he was a loyal and effective commander, but this did not give him a unique claim on Sulla's gratitude, nor should it be assumed that his patrician status was sufficient to make him Sulla's

---

17 Heterogeneity: Badian (1962) 59–60; Gruen (1968) 236–238, 249–250; (1974) 7, 38; Keaveney (1984) 141–142, 144; Paterson (1985) 23–25; Seager (1994) 202; Keaveney (2005a) ²[1982] 170. Careerism: Keaveney (1984) 144–146; Paterson (1985) 24–25. Unity in civil war from common enemy: Seager (1994) 202; Keaveney (2005a) ²[1982] 170–171.
18 *MRR* 2.74. The consuls of 81 are named by App. *B Civ.* 1.100; cf. Cic. *Leg. agr.* 2.35; Gell. *NA* 15.28.2. The consul of 159 was not a direct ancestor of the consul of 81. See Badian (1965) 49, 51.
19 Plut. *Sull.* 28.4–6.
20 Plut. *Sull.* 29.4. A Sullan coin minted in 82 attests L. Manlius Torquatus as *proquaestor* (*RRC* 367).
21 Münzer (1901a) 1297; Gruen (1966a) 385, 386; Keaveney (2005a) ²[1982] 164.

choice as consul for 81.²² Certainly, there is no basis to the view that he 'joined Sulla early, not as a last-minute deserter'.²³ The evidence does not let us even guess when he decided to join the Sullan ranks.²⁴

Dolabella was allotted Macedonia as his consular *provincia*, and it may be that he left Rome for the East during his year of office, in order to take charge from the *legati* whom Sulla had appointed to govern the province at the outbreak of the civil war in 83. Certainly, he is attested in his province in 80.²⁵ He remained there until the arrival of his successor, Ap. Claudius Pulcher, consul of 79, at some point in 77.²⁶ On his return to Rome he celebrated a triumph, probably for campaigns on the northern frontiers.²⁷ The young Julius Caesar had also been in the East, serving with M. Minucius Thermus in Asia from 81 to 80, then with P. Servilius Vatia in Cilicia in 78.²⁸ In 77, he made a high-profile debut in the courts and brought Dolabella to trial for extortion. The defence was conducted by Q. Hortensius and C. Aurelius Cotta, and the result was an acquittal, but Caesar was able to establish a reputation as an eloquent orator.²⁹ In 76, he conducted a second prosecution for extortion in the Roman province of Macedonia: the case was heard by the peregrine praetor, M. Terentius Varro Lucullus, and the accused was C. Antonius Hybrida, a Sullan cavalry officer whose rapacity in his treatment of the Greek civilian population was notorious; his guilt was manifest, but he made a successful appeal to the tribunes and the case was dismissed on a technicality.³⁰ Gruen has argued that both trials were highly political, and that Caesar's aim was to challenge the Sullan system, not just to promote his own career as an up-and-coming politician: Antonius had a Sullan past, while Dolabella was a Sullan defended by two men with close links to the Sullan regime. For Gruen, opposition to Caesar was an imperative for the supporters of the Sullan oligarchy.³¹

---

22 *Contra*: Gruen (1966a) 386.
23 Gruen (1966a) 386; cf. (1966b) 55; (1968) 237.
24 Dolabella's career prior to the civil war is unknown, hence Keaveney does no more than place him in the category of neutrals who joined Sulla on his return to Italy and received their due rewards in the hour of victory. See Keaveney (1984) 137–140, cf. 147 n. 234; (2005a) ²[1982] 164.
25 Brennan (2000) 528–529.
26 Damon/Mackay (1995) 54 n. 71; Brennan (2000) 530.
27 Cic. *Pis*. 44; Suet. *Iul*. 4.1; with Münzer (1901a) 1297.
28 Suet. *Iul*. 2.1, 3.1. Dates of commands: Brennan (2000) 557, 572. It is likely that Caesar remained in the east when C. Claudius Nero assumed control of Asia early in 80 (before he joined Servilius Vatia in 78).
29 Suetonius places the trial in a period of quiet after the sedition of Lepidus (*Iul*. 4.1). It is dated to 77 (or 76). Defence by C. Aurelius Cotta and Q. Hortensius: Cic. *Brut*. 317; cf. Val. Max. 8.9.3. Acquittal: Asc. 26 (Clark); Plut. *Caes*. 4.1; Suet. *Iul*. 4.1. Caesar's speeches were still read in the time of Tacitus (*Dial*. 34).
30 Asc. 84 (Clark); cf. Cicero, *Comment. pet*. 8; Plut. *Caes*. 4.2; with Damon/Mackay (1995).
31 Gruen (1966a) 388–389. Similarly: Drumann (1906) 134 (Groebe's edition of a work written in 1837). *Contra*: Strasburger (1938) 91, 131, arguing against a black-and-white political reading.

It is preferable to think, however, that the young Caesar had already reached a compromise with the new regime: he rejected Sulla's demand to divorce Cinna's daughter and fled to the Sabine hills in fear of his life, but then he was pardoned after an intercession by the Vestals and two of his relatives, and on his return he pursued a military career on the staffs of two men who served the new regime as proconsuls of Asia and Cilicia.[32] Everyone in politics in Rome could be defined to a greater or lesser extent as a *Sullanus*, so it is a mistake to assume that the prosecution of two men with a Sullan past was an attack on the system as a whole.[33] Caesar's actions were calculated and above all self-interested. He wanted to cause a stir in order to announce his arrival in politics, but his aim was also to strengthen his family's existing client base in the East: he had established a close relationship with Nicomedes of Bithynia, and he used his debut in the courts to champion the rights of oppressed Greek civilians.[34] In my view, little credence should be placed in Suetonius' claims that Caesar returned to Rome after Sulla's death because he was tempted to join the revolt of Lepidus, or that he left Rome to spend time learning rhetoric in Rhodes because his activities in the courts had made him a *persona non grata*.[35] Caesar maintained good relations with members of Sulla's faction, and in 74 or 73 he was co-opted into the college of pontiffs.[36]

Let us now return to the problem of Dolabella's naval command. It is generally assumed that Dolabella is the consul of 81, and that he was in command of a fleet in the early stages of the civil war, before his involvement in the campaigns on the Italian mainland which led to the Sullan victories at Sacriportus and at the Colline Gate.[37] There has been no scholarly comment, however, on the possible size and composition of this fleet, its theatre of operations, or its strategic function. Nor has there been any comment on the limitations on Sulla's 'power to dictate' implied in Plutarch's statement that Sulla only *tried* to remove Dolabella from his command. It has been assumed instead that Sulla was able to impose his will without any protest, and that Dolabella was a loyal partisan who would not have dared to stand up

---

[32] Thus: Taylor (1941) 117–118; (1942b) 5; (1957) 12–13; Ridley (2000) 226–229. The narrative of compromise is accepted by Gruen (1974) 38 but rejected at (1966a) 387–388.
[33] Everyone a Sullan: Gruen (1974) 11; Keaveney (1984) 144; with the caveat that some individuals, e.g. Lepidus with an exiled son, did maintain links with members of the defeated faction: Rosenblitt (2014) 437.
[34] Caesar as a typical young man using a high-profile prosecution to make his name: Taylor (1941) 119; (1942b) 7. Caesar's father had been governor of Asia in the 90s: Brennan (2000) 553, 555. Caesar's aim was to build patronage links with Nicomedes and with the victims of Dolabella and Antonius Hybrida: Osgood (2008) 690; (2010) 332.
[35] *Contra*: Suet. *Iul.* 3, 4.1; accepted by Gruen (1966a) 387–388, 389, 399. Analysis of how the rumour of involvement with Lepidus might have been invented: Strasburger (1938) 90–91.
[36] Vell. Pat. 2.43.1 (to replace his relative C. Aurelius Cotta, cos. 75). Analysis: Taylor (1941) 117–119, 132; (1942b) 7–9; (1957) 13–14.
[37] Stated explicitly: Münzer (1901a) 1297; *MRR* 2.65, 2.71; Gruen (1966a) 386.

to Sulla. In Carcopino's view, Dolabella was an officer schooled in discipline but lacking in initiative: he was quietly removed from his command of a fleet because he had achieved nothing; he then served as a subordinate officer in Sulla's army, but he was incapable of executing the manoeuvre assigned to him at Sacriportus, and he exhibited excessive caution in pressing Sulla to delay the start of the battle at the Colline Gate.[38] Carcopino's conclusion is that Dolabella, like his consular colleague M. Tullius Decula, was a docile nonentity, and that it had been Sulla's intention to secure the election of pliant consuls in order to bolster his own power and authority in the first year of his dictatorship.[39] Carcopino was open to the possibility that there were tensions within the Sullan regime at a later date, and this led him to argue that a coalition of the nobility led by the Metelli forced Sulla to abdicate from the dictatorship, in 79.[40] But he insisted that Sulla was initially able to rule as an autocrat, and thus he refused to accept that one of the nobles who stood up to Sulla might have been Dolabella, the consul of 81. More recently, the focus has shifted from the dynamics of Sulla's dictatorship to the stability of the 'regime' in the decades after Sulla's death. It is known that Sulla's civil war faction was by no means a homogeneous group, but it is assumed that Sulla's victory gave them unity of purpose, and that they understood their obligation to defend his political legacy, and their own collective dominance, in the years after his death. Gruen, one of the proponents of this view, offers a portrait in which the Sullan regime united against the uprising of Lepidus and then rallied to the defence of Dolabella when he was prosecuted by Caesar on his return from Macedonia. The trial, for Gruen, was an attack on the Sullan system, and so he presents Caesar as a Marian sympathizer and Dolabella as a Sullan loyalist.[41] One of the core assumptions in this model is that Sulla did not face opposition from his own faction, at least not from the military men whom he himself had promoted to key commands and sponsored for high office. It is this conviction that has led some to claim that Sulla *did* in fact remove Dolabella from his naval command.[42]

The standard view is that the Dolabella whom Plutarch mentions in his *synkrisis* of Sulla and Lysander and in his accounts of the civil war battles at Sacriportus and the Colline Gate is the consul of 81. Dolabella's ναυαρχία is understood to have been the command of a fleet during the civil war of 83–82, and there are scholars

---

38 Carcopino (1931) 131; with Plut. *Sull.* 28.4–5 and 29.4 (where Dolabella is in fact presented not as a yes-man, but as a loyal officer who speaks his mind).
39 Carcopino (1931) 131. Similarly: e.g. Meier (1997) ³[1966] 248–249; Keaveney (1984) 147, 149; (2005a) ²[1982] 164; Steel (2013) 107–108; Syme (2016) 58.
40 Carcopino (1931) 186–211.
41 Gruen (1966a) 386–389, 398–399.
42 Carcopino (1931) 131; Lanzani (1936) 82; Gruen (1966a) 386 n. 4 (quoted above n. 14). Sulla's failure is noted, but with no comment: Keaveney (1984) 139; Syme (2016) 72; identified as a temporary dispute: Vervaet (2004) 57 n. 80.

who argue that Sulla relieved Dolabella of his command or reduced the number of ships in his fleet. The problem, of course, is that these readings contradict the testimony of Plutarch, who states that Sulla reduced the size of *Pompey's* army and only *tried* to remove Dolabella's naval command. But if the consul of 81 was not removed from his command of a civil war fleet, how is it possible that he was in command of an army in operating in Latium at the battles of Sacriportus and the Colline Gate? Clearly it is problematic to identify the consul of 81 with the Dolabella mentioned by Plutarch in his *synkrisis* of Sulla and Lysander, but there is another Dolabella who held high office under Sulla, as praetor in 81, and there is a solid basis to link his career with Plutarch's reference to a ναυαρχία.

The Praetor of 81

Cn. Cornelius Dolabella, the consul of 81, had a cousin of the same name who was praetor in the same year.[43] In mid-March, he issued a ruling in a property dispute between Sex. Naevius and P. Quinctius, and when the case came to trial later in the year Cicero insisted that the decision was prejudicial to the interests of his client.[44] Cicero was also critical, in his speech in defence of C. Cornelius in 65 B.C., of a contentious decision made by Dolabella against C. Volcacius in another civil law case.[45] It is probable, but not certain, that Dolabella held the urban praetorship.[46] After his year in office he was sent out to govern Cilicia, where he remained until the arrival of P. Servilius Vatia, consul of 79, early in 78 B.C.[47] On his return he was prosecuted on a charge of extortion brought by the young M. Aemilius Scaurus, son of Sulla's wife Caecilia Metella. The result was a conviction, and Dolabella was forced into exile.[48] Details of the case against Dolabella are known from Cicero's speeches against Verres, who joined the governor's staff as a *legatus* and then assumed the duties of quaestor after the death of C. Malleolus.[49] Verres cooperated with the prosecution in return for immunity, and he supplied an exact figure for the large quantity of gold removed from the temple of Athena when Dolabella stopped at Athens en route for Cilicia. Cicero insists that this act was ordered by Verres, and he makes the point that Dolabella saw to the return of several high-quality antique

---

[43] *MRR* 2.76.
[44] Cic. *Quinct.* 30–31.
[45] Asc. 74 (Clark).
[46] Gruen (1966a) 392; Brennan (2000) 444.
[47] Gruen (1966a) 395; Brennan (2000) 571–572.
[48] Prosecution: Asc. 26 (Clark). Verres enlisted as witness: Cic. *Verr.* 2.1.41, 2.1.97–98. Dolabella's exile: Cic. *Verr.* 2.1.77. Financial penalties: Cic. *Verr.* 2.1.99–100.
[49] Cic. *Verr.* 2.1.41, 44, 90.

statues stolen by Verres from the sanctuary of Apollo on Delos.[50] Cicero also refers to the depredations carried out by Verres in Cilicia, and as evidence he cites the assessment of damages submitted at Dolabella's trial.[51] Dolabella's reputation was defined by his conviction and in later generations he became a byword for corruption. In a moralising passage on the rapacity of Roman imperialism Juvenal refers to ships loaded with secret spoils by Dolabella, Verres, and an Antonius who has been identified with C. Antonius Hybrida, Cicero's fellow-consul of 63.[52]

Cilicia was established as a province, or created as a military zone attached to the province of Asia, after the campaign by M. Antonius, praetor of 102, to eliminate piracy in the region.[53] Dolabella was sent out to Cilicia, by now certainly an independent province, at a time when piracy again posed a threat to the security of the eastern Mediterranean: the Cilician pirates had allegedly acted as allies of Mithridates, and after the war they continued to menace the islands and coastal cities of the Aegean.[54] Appian attests that booty to the value of 1,000 talents was plundered from a temple on Samothrace while Sulla was on the island, in 85 or 84, and in his account of the Sullan dictatorship he comments on how piracy, the war with Mithridates, and Roman taxation had impacted on the peoples beyond the borders of Italy.[55] Campaigns against the pirates were conducted by L. Licinius Murena, Sulla's lieutenant in Asia from 84 to 81, and by P. Servilius Vatia Isauricus, Dolabella's successor as governor of Cilicia from 78 to 74, but piracy remained a problem until Pompey cleared the seas and carried out a resettlement policy after the campaign of 67–66.[56] Plutarch uses the term ναυαρχία with reference to Pompey's command, and in Roman contexts he otherwise uses the word only once, in the *synkrisis* of Sulla and Lysander.[57] Brennan notes this and argues that the latter passage refers to the Dolabella who governed Cilicia *ex praetura* from 80 to 79. The term ναυαρχία is usually understood to mean the command of a fleet, but

---

50 Cic. *Verr.* 2.1.45–46.
51 Cic. *Verr.* 2.1.95–96. Emphasis on Verres' guilt: cf. Cic. *Verr.* 1.11, 2.1.41, 2.1.97, 2.3.177.
52 Juv. 8.105–107; cf. Asc. 84, 88 (Clark), on the rapacity of C. Antonius Hybrida in Greece, also in the Sullan period. Identification of Dolabella: Münzer (1901b) 1298.
53 Province: Brennan (2000) 357–359; Ferrary (2000) 167–170. Military zone attached to the province of Asia, with province of Cilicia established in the reforms of Sulla's dictatorship: Sherwin-White (1976) 6–11; (1984) 152–153; Kreiler (2007) 124. Cilicia as independent *ad hoc* command in 102 and 100; province from 81: De Souza (1999) 103–106, 109–115, 124. Incremental and gradual process: Kallet-Marx (1995) 293.
54 Plut. *Pomp.* 24.1–2; App. *Mith.* 63, 93; cf. Flor. 1.41.1–2. Overview on Cilician piracy: De Souza (1999) 97–178.
55 App. *Mith.* 63; *B Civ.* 1.102; cf. Cic. *Leg. Man.* 32–33.
56 Murena: App. *Mith.* 93; Cic. *Verr.* 2.1.89–90. P. Servilius Vatia, cos. 79, triumphed in 74 and took the *cognomen* Isauricus: Livy, *Per.* 93; App. *Mith.* 93; Flor. 1.41.4–5. Pompey: e.g. Cic. *Leg. Man.* 34–35; Plut. *Pomp.* 25–28.
57 Lex Gabinia: Plut. *Pomp.* 25.2, with Brennan (2000) 572. Brennan's further citation of Plut. *Mor.* 779a is to be ignored: this passage refers not to a ναυαρχία but to a ναυαρχίς, which means 'admiral's flagship' (*LSJ* 1161).

Brennan makes the point that it could equally apply to the province of Cilicia. It was set up to combat piracy, there are frequent references to Roman fleets operating in its waters, and thus it can aptly be described as a 'naval command'.[58] In my view, this is a persuasive solution to the problem of Plutarch's testimony: it was the praetor of 81, not the consul of 81, whom Sulla tried to remove from a ναυαρχία.

Dolabella was appointed to Cilicia with the title *pro praetore*, and Brennan argues that it was an anomaly for a governor of Cilicia, in the post-Sullan period, not to receive enhanced *imperium* and the title *pro consule*.[59] His solution to the problem draws on Plutarch's testimony that Sulla tried and failed to revoke Dolabella's ναυαρχία: 'Sulla for some reason interfered with the younger Dolabella's *ex praetura* command, eventually letting him have Cilicia, but refusing him the same grade of *imperium* that all the other territorial governors in his system had'.[60] According to this view, Sulla was thwarted in his attempt to block the allotment of Cilicia to the praetor of 81, but he was able to salvage his pride and have the last word by ensuring that Dolabella was only appointed *pro praetore*, not *pro consule*. One problem lies in the premise that it was the norm in this period for governors of Cilicia to receive enhanced *imperium*. It is not universally agreed that Cilicia was a province before Sulla, and there are scholars who argue that the first governor was Dolabella, the praetor of 81.[61] And even if it is accepted that Cilicia was set up as a province two decades earlier, the fact remains that the rank of *pro consule* is attested only for Q. Oppius, the military commander in southern Asia Minor at the start of the war with Mithridates in 89, and for M. Antonius, who campaigned against the pirates from 102 to 100. The title is not attested for Sulla, who was sent to the region of Cilicia *ex praetura* in the mid-90s, and it is not certain that Cilicia was the destination of L. Gellius and L. Cornelius Lentulus, both of whom were sent to the East in this period with the rank of *pro consule*.[62] It is not obvious, therefore, that it was an anomaly for Dolabella to be appointed *pro praetore*, nor need it be assumed that he clashed with Sulla before his departure for his province. Dolabella was governor for two years, so it could be that Sulla made an attempt, as consul in 80, to recall him from his province before his *imperium* was extended. Brennan's premise is that Sulla tried to block Dolabella's initial appointment to Cilicia, but this dating solution relies on the hypothesis that it was an anomaly for Dolabella to be appointed *pro praetore*, and that it was Sulla who denied him the rank of *pro consule*. Plutarch's

---

58 Brennan (2000) 572. Naval warfare is mentioned, for example, in connection with P. Servilius Vatia: Flor. 1.41.4–5. The word ναυαρχία means both 'command of a fleet' and 'period of such command' (*LSJ* 1161).
59 Dolabella: Cic. *Verr.* 2.1.99 'pr. et pro pr.' (attested in the title of a court document from his trial). Cf. Brennan (2000) 444, 572, 630.
60 Brennan (2000) 572, cf. 444.
61 Sherwin-White (1976) 10; (1984) 152–153; Kreiler (2007) 124.
62 Titulatures: Brennan (2000) 357–359. Alternatively, Sulla's praetorian province is identified as Asia; likewise for Q. Oppius, L. Gellius, and L. Cornelius Lentulus: Kreiler (2007) 119–123; cf. Sherwin-White (1976) 8–9; De Souza (1999) 115 (on Sulla).

testimony, moreover, is taken by Brennan to mean that Sulla assigned Cilicia to Dolabella having first opposed his appointment. But what Plutarch actually states is that Sulla turned on his friends and tried to 'take away from Dolabella the naval command *which he had given him*'.[63] If this testimony is taken literally, it would mean that the praetor of 81 received Cilicia through Sulla's patronage before falling out of Sulla's favour, perhaps when an attempt was made to recall him from his province. In my view it is thus best to date Sulla's failure to dictate Roman policy in Cilicia to the year of his consulship in 80, not to his dictatorship in 81.[64]

Plutarch does not offer a reason for Sulla's opposition to Dolabella, and Brennan works on the assumption that it was rooted in a personal enmity which stretched back to the period before the civil war. In doing so, he relies on Gruen's analysis of the limited evidence for Dolabella's political career in the decade before his praetorship.[65] The one known fact is that Dolabella participated with his relative Q. Servilius Caepio in a prosecution of M. Aemilius Scaurus, the *princeps Senatus*, in 91.[66] Within two years this influential establishment figure was dead, and his widow, Caecilia Metella, was married to Sulla, consul elect for 88.[67] Gruen highlights Sulla's prominence in the circle of the Metelli and argues that Dolabella, having attacked Scaurus in the courts, 'was not a man likely to become a trusted follower or confidante of Sulla'.[68] He also posits that Dolabella was one of Pompeius Strabo's junior staff officers in the Social War, and that this 'would lead him on a path sharply diverging from that of Sulla'.[69] Sulla found Strabo to be a formidable rival after his march on Rome in 88.[70] But there is no reason to think that Dolabella shared Strabo's politics, nor is it even certain that he served under Strabo in the Social War. The inscription which lists the members of Strabo's *consilium* at the siege of Asculum includes a 'Cn. Cornelius Cn. f. Pal.' along with a '[...]ilius Q. f. Pal.' who is identified as M. Aemilius Lepidus, the consul of 78.[71]

---

63 Plut. *Comp. Lys. Sull.* 2.4: καὶ Δολοβέλλα τὴν ναυαρχίαν ἐπεχείρησε δοὺς ἀφελέσθαι.
64 The date of Sulla's abdication is debated, but I follow the view that it occurred before the end of 81: e.g. Seager (1994) 205; Hinard (1999); Keaveney (2005a) ^{2}[1982] 165–166; (2005b) 438–439. *Contra*: e.g. Vervaet (2004) 60–68, arguing for a staged return to normality leading up to Sulla's abdication early in 79.
65 Brennan (2000) 887 n. 8, citing Gruen (1966a) 389–398. An alternative explanation made by Brennan (2000) 444 is that Sulla was displeased by Dolabella's arbitrary conduct of his praetorship. Elsewhere (2000) 630 he refers simply to Sulla's 'personal pique'.
66 Asc. 26 (Clark). On the trial: Gruen (1966b) 55–59; (1968) 206.
67 Sulla's marriage: Plut. *Sull.* 6.10.
68 Gruen (1966a) 391.
69 Gruen (1966a) 391–392. One may note, of course, that Pompey Strabo's son became one of the leading Sullani.
70 See App. *B Civ.* 1.63–64.
71 *CIL* VI 37045 = *ILS* 8888 = *ILLRP* 515. Identification of Lepidus: Cichorius (1922) 147; Gruen (1966a) 391. The Palatina tribe suggests patrician status for Cn. Cornelius: Taylor (1960) 206.

The inscription lists names in order of seniority, and this lets us infer that Lepidus and Cn. Cornelius were both junior officers. Lepidus was praetor in 81, as was Cn. Cornelius Dolabella. It is this coincidence which leads Gruen and others to identify Dolabella, the praetor of 81, with the Cn. Cornelius on Strabo's staff.[72] A further argument is that there were family ties between the praetors of 81. Lepidus is known to have married an Appuleia who was perhaps the daughter of Saturninus, while Dolabella may have been the son of a Cn. Dolabella who is attested as a *frater*, perhaps a half-brother, of the tribune of 100. Orosius attests the relationship and states that he was killed as he fled through the Forum Holitorium.[73] M. Aemilius Scaurus played a key role in the repression of Saturninus, and it is thus argued that vengeance for the death of his father motivated the future praetor of 81 to take part in the prosecution of the *princeps Senatus* in 91.[74] The problem with these speculations is that the filiation of the praetor of 81 is not attested. It is not *known* that he was a 'son of Gnaeus', so it can only be a conjecture that he was a nephew of Saturninus or an officer in Strabo's army.[75] One must note, in addition, that Dolabella is not the only individual who can be identified with the Cn. Cornelius Cn.f. on Strabo's staff. Taylor, for example, proposes that he was an unknown son of Cn. Cornelius Cn. f. Cn. n. Lentulus, consul of 97.[76]

Nothing is known of Dolabella's career in the decade before his praetorship, yet it is assumed that he remained in Rome during Sulla's absence in the East and advanced his career under Cinna.[77] It is also assumed that he was elected to the praetorship with Sulla's support after defecting from the Marians at a late stage in the civil war once it became clear that a Sullan victory was inevitable.[78] But the sources are silent, and so it is equally valid to conjecture that he joined Sulla from the start, or that he was an opportunist who remained neutral before taking sides. All that is known about Dolabella, aside from his praetorship in 81, is that he took part in the prosecution of M. Aemilius Scaurus in 91, and that the latter's son secured his conviction on his return from Cilicia in 78. There is no evidence that he

---

[72] Gruen (1966a) 391, citing Cichorius (1922) 148. The latter's argument that Cn. Cornelius is the praetor of 81 rests on the weak premise that he was the same age as Lepidus and so reached the praetorship in the same year. It is accepted with caution by Criniti (1970) 108–110. Similarly: *MRR* 2.35, with n. 11.
[73] Lepidus and Appuleia: Plin. *HN* 7.122; with Gruen (1966a) 392–393. Dolabella *frater* of Saturninus: Oros. 5.17.10, with Badian (1965) 49; Gruen (1966a) 389–90, 392; (1966b) 55.
[74] Badian (1965) 49; Gruen (1966a) 392; (1966b) 55–56. On Scaurus in 100: Cic. *Rab. perd.* 21; *De vir. ill.* 72.9.
[75] It is circular for Gruen (1966a) 392 to argue that the filiation of the praetor of 81 can be established on the basis of his identification with the Cn. Cornelius Cn.f. on the Asculum inscription (or as the son of the Cn. Cornelius killed in 100).
[76] Taylor (1960) 206, 208; cf. *MRR* 3.62; *ILLRP* 2.31. Other suggestions: Cichorius (1922) 147–148.
[77] Gruen (1966a) 392; (1968) 243; (1974) 39; Hinard (1985a) 226, 247; Keaveney (2005a) ²[1982] 170.
[78] Gruen (1966a) 394–399; (1968) 250, 254; (1974) 39; Keaveney (1984) 142; Hinard (1985a) 178.

was anti-Sullan, but this is what Gruen claims in order to promote the idea that the trials of the Dolabellae reveal the strength of the Sullan regime in the aftermath of Sulla's death. The consul of 81, in his view, was a Sullan loyalist whose prosecution by the young Caesar was a calculated attack on the new system. The Sullan oligarchy therefore rallied to his defence, and he was acquitted.[79] The praetor of 81 was in contrast an ex-Marian who defected late to the Sullan cause, and thus no effort was made to prevent his conviction. The trial took place in 78, at a time when the consul Lepidus was starting to challenge the Sullan system, and the establishment therefore decided 'to make an example of another ex-Marian of doubtful loyalty'.[80] The Sullan oligarchy had the strength and will to protect its own, in Gruen's reconstruction of events, and so Dolabella is imagined as an old enemy of Sulla opposed to the new regime.

The key point to note about the trial of the praetor of 81 is that the prosecution was brought by the young M. Aemilius Scaurus, son of the *princeps Senatus* whom Dolabella had prosecuted in 91. It is clear that the motive of Sulla's stepson was to make his name in the courts and settle an old family score.[81] It is also important to note that the prosecution was able to enlist the support of Verres, who had been Dolabella's quaestor and was thus able to provide testimony which was decisive in securing a conviction.[82] No defence counsel is recorded, and Gruen interprets this silence in the sources to mean that Dolabella 'had difficulty in attracting distinguished advocates for his cause' and even that he was 'abandoned on all sides'.[83] But it is unlikely that Dolabella had literally no-one to defend him, and in my view it is also wrong to use the absence of evidence in the sources to argue that Dolabella was a committed Marian who betrayed his principles to defect to Sulla in the civil war. The problem is that Gruen assumes the trial to have been political, and thus he is forced to construct a career path for the praetorian Dolabella which explains how he could be convicted when only a year later his cousin was acquitted.

Standing up to Sulla
Plutarch cites the examples of Dolabella, Pompey, and Ofella to illustrate the theme of Sulla's injustice towards his friends: he reduced Pompey's army, he tried to

---

79 Gruen (1966a) 388–389, 398–399.
80 Gruen (1966a) 398, cf. 399; the attribution of the Dolabellae to opposing political camps is explicitly rejected by Twyman (1972) 856.
81 It is estimated that he was about 19 years old. See Henderson (1958) 196.
82 Arguably the chief factor in the trial's outcome: Münzer (1901b) 1298; Hinard (1985a) 247.
83 Gruen (1966a) 397, 398; cf. (1974) 39. *Contra*: Twyman (1972) 856, who conjectures that the defence was undertaken by Hortensius.

revoke Dolabella's naval command, and he killed Ofella for seeking the consulship against his wishes.⁸⁴ The standard view is that Dolabella is the consul of 81, but there is no satisfactory historical context for when he might have held the command of a fleet. One must therefore accept the alternative hypothesis, proposed by Brennan, that Dolabella is the praetor of 81, and that his ναυαρχία is the province of Cilicia. A further argument of Brennan is that Sulla tried to block Dolabella's appointment, and that he used his influence to ensure that the new governor of Cilicia was not elevated to the rank of *pro consule*.⁸⁵ But Plutarch highlights the paradox that Sulla first granted then tried to remove Dolabella's command. I have suggested, therefore, that it was not Dolabella's initial appointment to Cilicia which Sulla failed to prevent, but the extension of his *imperium* for a second year. Sulla's motives cannot be known. It is obvious, however, that the praetor of 81 will have opposed his recall: it is known that he abused his tenure of Cilicia for material gain, and it may be that he had ambitions for a triumph. Sulla was unable to impose his will, and it makes sense to assume that the praetor of 81 had the support of political allies at Rome who could overrule Sulla in the Senate. Plutarch's testimony is limited, but it attests that Sulla was thwarted in a clash with his 'friend' Dolabella, and thus it reveals that there were limits on Sulla's ability to impose his will on his adherents.

Plutarch cites numerous examples of individuals who stood up to Sulla, and he mentions two of them, Pompey and Ofella, in conjunction with Dolabella and his ναυαρχία.⁸⁶ Ofella refused to back down when Sulla tried to persuade him not to stand for the consulship of 81: his candidacy was invalid because he had not yet entered the Senate or held public office, but he argued for an exemption on the grounds that he had ended the civil war with his capture of Praeneste.⁸⁷ One of Sulla's centurions, acting on his own initiative, murdered Ofella when he came to the Forum to announce his candidacy, and Sulla chose to claim that he had ordered the killing.⁸⁸ Pompey stood up to Sulla twice following his victories over the Marians in Sicily and Africa in the winter of 82/1. He was ordered to send his army home and remain in Africa with one legion until the arrival of a new commander.

---

84 Plut. *Comp. Lys. Sull.* 2.4.
85 Brennan (2000) 444, 572.
86 The following episodes are discussed above; Caesar: Plut. *Caes*. 1.1–2; Lentulus Sura: Plut. *Cic.* 17.2–3; Granius of Puteoli: Plut. *Sull.* 37.3. Note in addition; C. Metellus, criticising the violence of Sulla's victory: Plut. *Sull.* 31.1–2; Cato the Younger in Sulla's house asking his pedagogue why no-one could be found to kill the tyrant: Plut. *Cat. min.* 3.2–4; cf. Val. Max. 3.1.2b; with Thein (2006) 244; a freedman executed for harbouring one of the proscribed, reminding Sulla of his former poverty: Plut. *Sull.* 1.4; with Thein (2015) 184–185.
87 App. *B Civ.* 1.101. It is best assumed that he stood for the consulship of 81, at the end of 82, or early in 81. Cf. Seager (1994) 200; Steel (2013) 108. *Contra*: Keaveney (2003) 90–92; (2005a) ²[1982] 164 (elections of 81 for 80).
88 Plut. *Sull.* 33.4.

Instead, he returned to Italy with his army and demanded a triumph for subduing the client kings of Numidia. Sulla was opposed, on the grounds that only a consul or a praetor should receive this honour – Pompey was not even a member of the Senate, and Sulla sought to persuade him that a triumph would reflect badly on both of them.[89] Pompey, refusing to be cowed, muttered under his breath that men worship the rising not the setting sun. Sulla was astonished when he discovered what Pompey had said, but he recovered his composure and exclaimed: 'Let him triumph, let him triumph'.[90] Sulla had also backed down when he learned of Pompey's return from Africa with his army: the urban plebs prepared a grand welcome, so Sulla went out to meet Pompey on the road, hailing him as Magnus, 'the Great', in recognition of his popularity in the city of Rome.[91] Pompey and Ofella were not the only generals who stood up to Sulla in the year of his dictatorship. In Asia, L. Licinius Murena initiated a border war with the forces of Mithridates, and he was ordered to desist by two envoys sent by Sulla and the Senate. He ignored the first envoy, Calidius, and only ceased hostilities, after he had been defeated by Mithridates in the field, when a second envoy, A. Gabinius, rebuked him for his failure to comply with the Senate's orders. But there were no repercussions and on his return to Rome he was rewarded with a triumph.[92] Sulla was opposed as dictator by three men he had himself promoted to military commands, and twice he was forced to back down. It is no surprise that Sulla was again thwarted as consul when he opposed Dolabella.

Dolabella had sufficient support within the Sullan elite to ensure that his tenure of Cilicia was prorogued in spite of Sulla's opposition, but he was unable to escape conviction when he was charged with extortion on his return to Rome. The prosecution was brought by the young M. Aemilius Scaurus, whose father had been taken to court by Q. Servilius Caepio, in collaboration with Dolabella, in 91. He was motivated by a desire to make a name for himself and settle an old family score, but Sulla would no doubt have discouraged his stepson from undertaking the prosecution if, at the time, Dolabella had still been a member of his inner circle of adherents. The praetor of 81 scored a victory over Sulla, but it came at a cost.

---

89 Plut. *Pomp.* 13.1–3, 14.1–2; cf. *Mor.* 203e. Pompey's opposition to Sulla is downplayed by Keaveney (1982) 128–131; (2005a) ²[1982] 160–161; Hillman (1997) 99–104.
90 Plut. *Pomp.* 14.3, cf. *Mor.* 203e. The context must have been a meeting of the Senate. Cf. Vervaet (2004) 57–58. The triumph took place on the 12th March, probably in 81. See Badian (1961).
91 Plut. *Pomp.* 13.4; cf. *Mor.* 203e. Pompey received a hero's welcome from the urban plebs because he had captured Sicily and Africa and secured Rome's grain supply.
92 App. *Mith.* 65–66; cf. Cic. *Leg. Man.* 8; *Mur.* 11. Note the idea put forward by Kallet-Marx (1995) 263, that Sulla's triumph over Mithridates (in January 81) was dependent on an end to Murena's war in the East.

Conclusion

Gruen uses the example of the Dolabellae to illustrate the pitfall of assuming political alliances on the basis of family connections: both reached high office in 81, allegedly with Sulla's support or approval, and both were attacked in the courts in the early 70s, but one was convicted and the other acquitted, and this leads Gruen to develop the hypothesis that the consul of 81 was a committed Sullan whereas his cousin of the same name, the praetor of 81, was a Marian defector of doubtful loyalty. In doing so, he assumes that the two trials were political, and thus he imagines that the praetorian Dolabella was abandoned to his fate, whereas his consular cousin was backed by the establishment and acquitted. Sulla's stepson was thus able to resume a family feud and win his case, but Caesar was unsuccessful in two anti-Sullan trials because the regime was too strong.[93] Gruen has since changed his views on the trials of the 70s, arguing that Caesar, while no friend of Sulla, was working within the system, and that the prosecution of a Sullan adherent was not an attack on the Sullan constitution or the ruling class as a whole.[94] In fact, he argues that the civil war cleavages of 'Sullani' and 'democrats' no longer applied in the 70s, 'when all had become part of the new order'.[95] Yet he still insists that the praetor of 81 was left to his fate because he was a late-comer to the Sullan cause who had collaborated with the opposite faction.[96] The unstated premise is that a loyal Sullan could not have been convicted for corruption in 78.

The Sullani were a heterogeneous group, and scholars accept that internal politics resumed in the 70s, but it is still the norm to assume that all were united during Sulla's dictatorship, and to think that this was a period in which Sulla acted as an all-powerful autocrat, even to the extent of controlling elections.[97] There is little evidence for politics in the period of Sulla's dictatorship, and the problem is that the vacuum has been filled using Appian, whose agenda is to highlight the monarchical nature of Sulla's rule.[98] But if it is accepted that Sulla's civil war coalition was

---

93 Gruen (1966a) 385–386, 389, cf. 398–399.
94 Gruen (1974) 11, 38, cf. 15. On Caesar, *contra*: Gruen (1966a) 388–389, 398–399.
95 Gruen (1974) 11–12. In this model there was scope for internal feuds within the ranks of the Sullani, but unity in the face of serious threats to the system such as the Lepidus uprising. Cf. Gruen (1974) 8–11.
96 Gruen (1974) 39. Cf. Santangelo (2012) 191 for the observation that *Sullanus* and *Sullani* are attested in the sources only with reference to the civil war and its immediate aftermath.
97 The consuls of 81 are assumed to have been chosen by Sulla, or at least elected with his consent: e.g. Carcopino (1931) 130–131, 200; Gruen (1966a) 385–386 (cf. 390, 393 for praetors); Meier (1997) ³[1966] 248–249, 251; Keaveney (1984) 146; Syme (2016) 58. Allegedly only two candidates in the elections for the consuls of 79 and 78: Syme (1964) 185; (2016) 61, 75. Sulla's influence on elections decisive, but limited to public endorsements: Vervaet (2004) 47–48.
98 App. *B Civ*. 1.98–101, 1.105. Appian's analysis of Sulla's political strength (*B Civ*. 1.100, 1.104) is treated as fact, e.g. Meier (1997) ³[1966] 247; Syme (2016) 62.

motivated by self-interest rather than political ideology, why should it be assumed that Sulla could rely on their blind obedience after the profits of victory had been disbursed, and the *cursus honorum* reopened to men who had seen no future under the old regime? My aim is to challenge the view that the Sullan dictatorship was a hiatus from normal politics, and to highlight evidence which suggests that there were limits to Sulla's 'power to dictate'.[99] Sulla's failure to recall Dolabella from his Cilician command offers an example from his consulship, while Pompey and Murena offer examples of generals in the provinces who stood up to Sulla during his dictatorship. Most striking, however, is the story of the quaestor P. Cornelius Lentulus who acted with insolent defiance when asked by an angry Sulla to respond to the charge of wasting or losing public money. At this point it will have been apparent to all that Sulla's power was in decline.[100] Carcopino is one scholar who has taken the evidence for internal opposition to Sulla seriously, but he also argued that Sulla was aiming at monarchy, and the scholarly response has been to reject his thesis in its entirety, and to promote the paradoxical idea that Sulla was a Republican who enjoyed absolute power.[101] In my view, this is a mistake. Carcopino was wrong to think of Sulla as a would-be monarch, and there are also problems with his argument that Pompey and the Metelli forced Sulla to abdicate, but he was right to consider the constraints on Sulla's power and think about politics within the Sullan elite.[102] There is evidence for internal dissent and opposition to Sulla, and it is wrong for scholars like Syme to reject this source material in order to maintain the established image of Sulla the all-powerful dictator.[103]

As a final point one may note that the case of Dolabella offers evidence not just for the limits of Sulla's power, but also for shifting loyalties within the Sullan elite. The praetor of 81 was a friend of Sulla who fell out of favour, and at his trial he lost the support of his quaestor, C. Verres, who supplied evidence to the prosecution. The case was brought by M. Aemilius Scaurus, son of Sulla's wife Metella, and it is

---

99 An extreme position is that Sulla's aim was to create a political system in which law and the courts took the place of normal politics focused on debate in the Senate and the Forum: Flower (2010) 129; cf. Gruen (1968) 254.
100 The episode is dated by Keaveney (2005a) ²[1982] 171 and (2005b) 434–436 to Sulla's consulship in 80, on the grounds that Sulla did not act unilaterally but called Lentulus to account in the Senate. In my view this does not exclude a date during Sulla's dictatorship.
101 In particular, Syme (2016) 56–78: Sulla as dictator from 82 to 79, designating the consuls four years in a row, and abdicating from a position of unimpaired strength. One must note that even Carcopino's Sulla abdicates from a position of considerable strength, retiring to his villa in what is imagined to be his personal fiefdom, an area of Campania garrisoned by veterans and detached from the rest of Italy. See Carcopino (1931) 205–209, 212–214.
102 Sympathetic criticism: Meier (1997) ³[1966] 247–248, 260–261; cf. Syme (2016) 66–77.
103 Plutarch's testimony that Sulla opposed Lepidus' candidacy in the consular elections for 78 (*Sull.* 34.4–5; *Pomp.* 15.1–2) is rejected by Syme (1964) 184–185 and (2016) 74–77 on the basis that Lepidus cannot have run for office without Sulla's support.

worth noting that Cicero, at a later date, was able to describe Verres as a friend and kinsman of the Metelli.[104] It may be that Verres supplied evidence at the trial because he was already a client of the Metelli, or perhaps they persuaded him to switch allegiance with the promise of patronage. Either way, the trial of Dolabella reveals an episode of political intrigue in which Sulla was not involved. Sulla was the dominant figure in Roman politics until his retirement and death, but not everything revolved around him.

---

104 Cic. *Verr.* 2.2.64, 2.2.138 (Verres described as an *amicus* and *cognatus*). Cf. Henderson (1958) 196 for the speculation that Verres was a distant cousin of the younger Scaurus.

Arthur Keaveney
5 *Paludes et Silvae*: The Ruin of the Veteran

Often the source material available to the ancient historian is scant in comparison to his modern counterpart. Sometimes, indeed, all that is available to us is a passing remark or fragmentary reference which, by its very nature, may admit of more than one interpretation. In this chapter, I wish to consider one such passing remark which is the only piece of evidence we possess concerning a particular aspect of Sulla's veteran settlement policy at the end of Rome's first civil war.[1] The passage in question comes from a speech Sallust puts into the mouth of M. Aemilius Lepidus in his consulship in 78. Here he is made to claim that Sulla's veterans were 'richly rewarded, no doubt, when, banished to swamps and woods, they find that insult and hatred are their portion' (*egregia scilicet mercede, cum relegati in paludes et silvas contumeliam atque invidiam suam ... intellegerent*).[2] This immediately provokes certain questions. What does Lepidus mean by *paludes et silvas*? Is he speaking of whole regions or of individual portions of a given settlement? It might also be asked, whence comes the *invidia* and *contumelia*? Again we may wonder at how it was that victorious *Sullani* found themselves in this plight?[3]

In an effort to answer these questions, I propose, first of all, to look at some of what Cicero had to say in 63 B.C. in three speeches (*De lege agraria*) he made against the tribune P. Servilius Rullus who was introducing a land bill. In these

---

[1] I would like to thank Alexander Thein for giving me the chance to expound in more detail an aspect of the Sullan settlement I touched on many years ago and for commenting on an earlier draft. I must also thank Brian Campbell for answering a query. However, I myself am responsible for this version and such imperfections as it may contain. Citations from the *Agrimensores* are from the editions of Campbell (2000) = C and Lachmann = L in Blume et al. (1967) [1848]: Translations are from Campbell.

The most recent detailed discussions of the Sullan settlement all come independently to broadly similar conclusions. See Keaveney (1982b); Santangelo (2007) 147–182; Krawczuk (2008) 59–92. A radical reassessment will be found in Thein (2010).

[2] Sall. *Hist*. 1.55.23 (Maurenbrecher) = 1.48.23 (McGushin) = 1.49.23 (Ramsey). Quotation above: Loeb translation. Dating: Keaveney (2005a) ²[1982] 217 n. 9.

[3] The fact that two other passages of the speech of Lepidus can be verified by reference to other sources serves to demonstrate that this is unlikely to be mere rhetoric. As we shall demonstrate fully below, the claim that innocents were proscribed (§17) is certainly true. Again, the declaration in §12 that a number of *socii* and the people of Latium were deprived of the citizenship receives support from Cicero who speaks of diminution of the citizenship of Arretium and Volaterrae: *Caecin*. 97, 102; *Dom*. 79; with Harris (1971) 265–266, 274–283; Sherwin-White (1973) ²[1939] 102–104; Krawczuk (2008) 37–53, 99. Some, e.g. Harris and Krawczuk, suppose other cities may have suffered in the same way and there is some support for this in Cicero's use of the plural and a somewhat vague notice in Ps. Asc. p. 189 (Stangl). See notes 55, 62. We shall, in another context, return to the essential veracity of the contemporary allusions in the speech of Lepidus. See notes 90–93.

speeches we often find mentioned a class of individuals who are dubbed *possessores*.[4] As Drummond pointed out, these, from a legal viewpoint, fall into a number of different categories which Cicero sometimes elides but which Drummond's own careful analysis clarifies.[5] A detailed treatment of all these categories is not necessary here but certain observations are relevant. In the *De lege agraria* we hear at 1.15 that certain *possessores* have earned *invidia*. From 2.68–70 we learn more. *Invidia* is the direct result either of holding land granted by Sulla, or encroaching on the *ager publicus* or, it would appear, elsewhere. This theme of *invidia* is also met with at 2.98. The issue of encroachment is found again in 3.8 and 3.12–13, while at 3.14 we find Valgus the encroacher with his uncertain title.[6] Moreover, as Drummond has convincingly demonstrated, Cicero is not speaking here of veterans with small plots but of *latifondisti*.[7] It is also tolerably clear where the *invidia* comes from: possession of land legitimately conferred by Sulla and equally from holding land acquired by dubious means. I hold also it is not unreasonable to believe that when people of this type encroached upon what was not theirs, they had three targets: land made public by Sulla, estates of fellow magnates, and the plots of veterans.[8] I shall return again to this last point but first I wish to examine more closely what Cicero has to say about worthless land.

It has long been recognised that Cicero draws a distinction between worthless lands and those of value.[9] What has not, perhaps, received sufficient emphasis is that Cicero, addressing the masses and not the few, not only speaks of individual worthless holdings but also of whole settlements.[10] He suggests that, thanks to Rullus, people could wind up in the *siccitas* of the colony of Sipontum or in the *pestilentia* of Salapia where there had been a Gracchan settlement.[11] On the basis of this it might be possible to argue that Cicero, in an oblique fashion, is reminding his hearers that whole Sullan settlements had been set up in unsuitable places. On the other

---

4 On the technical meaning of *possessio* see Drummond (2000) 133–139.
5 Drummond (2000) 133–141.
6 Valgus was Rullus' father-in-law and Cicero also mentions him in *Leg. agr.* 2.69; 3.8, 13. On him see further Hardy (1913) 246–247; Harvey (1973); Keaveney (1982b) 525–526, 531 n. 215 and the remarks in n. 81 below. In general on the problem of encroachment in Roman history see Harvey (1975) 34 n. 3 and Brunt (1986) 315–316.
7 Drummond (2000) 134. Note that Cic. *Leg. agr.* 2.78 specifically says Praeneste is in the hands of a few. Discussion: Harvey (1975).
8 Cic. *Leg. agr.* 3.12 specifies that land made public by Sulla is in private hands, while 3.14 shows private estates seized by dubious means. *Leg. agr.* 2.70 might be pressed to mean the same while, as Drummond (2000) 136 n. 39 pointed out, *Leg. agr.* 2.78 indicates that veterans suffered at the hands of these people.
9 See, for example, Hardy (1913) 246.
10 On the holdings, see below.
11 Cic. *Leg. agr.* 2.71. Sipontum: Salmon (1970) 99, 185 n. 67. Salapia: *Lib. colon.* 164.27–29 (C) = 210.10–13 (L). Cf. Campbell (2000) 44 n. 14; Brunt (1986) 366, 368.

hand, bearing in mind what I said about the multiple interpretations ancient evidence may often offer, an entirely different explanation could be entered. Cicero is not invoking the Sullan settlement at all but is referring to another established feature of Roman history: an occasional tendency for a colony, planted in the wrong place, to fail. Sipontum is, in fact, one such and, by way of further illustration, we might also point to the case of Liternum.[12] Again, under the Empire we shall discover that Emona was not established in a particularly benign environment.[13]

Now, from the proposed colonies of Rullus and their implications for our thesis we turn to reality in the shape of individual tracts and their owners. In *De lege agraria* 1.15 Cicero contrasts those lands which cause *invidia* with those which are characterised by their *pestilentia*. This contrast is found again in 2.70 and 2.98, while in 3.14 Cicero personalises the issue and blends the two types. Valgus has land *nullo iure* but he also holds *desertos atque longinquos*. This evidence may not be as easy to interpret as might appear on the surface. While it is not difficult to envisage that veterans with small holdings which were worthless or provoked *invidia* might be glad to be rid of them, the general thrust of the orations, along with the mention of Valgus strongly suggests that it is great magnates who are chiefly in question here.[14] Further, for all his concern with the legal status of *possessores*, Cicero says nothing about the status of this worthless land. In making his contrast he only describes the motivation for wanting to sell up: some to be rid of land because of *invidia*, others because of *pestilentia*. This immediately raises a question. If I am right in assuming that we are mostly speaking of magnates then how did they come to own land afflicted by *pestilentia*? I think we can safely claim that very few had estates which consisted only of useless acres. After that, any answer must have an element of speculation in it but we can envisage the situation arising in two ways. It could be that some people had bad land to start with as it formed part of their own (or, if you will, ancestral) domain. But, seeing how the categories of *invidia* and *pestilentia* intersect in the case of Valgus, a known encroacher, it might not be straining credulity to argue that, when people grabbed what was not lawfully theirs, they were not in a position to complain about its overall quality. As so often in life, they had to take the bad along with the good.[15]

---

12 Liternum: Val. Max. 5.3.2, cf. Livy 38.52.1. See further Salmon (1970) 99.
13 Wilkes (1963) 270.
14 Note especially that in *Leg. agr.* 2.98 Cicero accuses Rullus of wanting to plant land *a vestris necessariis et a vobismet emptos*, 'bought from kinsfolk and even yourselves' (Loeb translation) which, I think, points to a small number of individuals.
15 This modifies a suggestion of Brunt (1986) 311 n. 1 who thought the magnates might have acquired such wastelands; this was rejected by Gruen (1974) 424 n. 78; followed by Drummond (2000) 127 n. 7. It is, I believe, absurd to argue, as Brunt seems to do, that *latifondisti* would set out to acquire useless lands.

At this point it may be useful to pause for a moment to summarise what we have learnt from Cicero that is of relevance to our attempt to elucidate Lepidus' remark. The root cause of *invidia* emerges with great clarity. A Sullan proprietor, whether he held his land by legitimate grant from the dictator or whether he held it unlawfully, would equally awaken this emotion. There is a clear link between what Lepidus is representing as saying in 78 and Cicero says in 63. So to be a Sullan landowner, whatever your social standing, would attract *invidia*.[16]

Tracking down the *paludes et silvae* of the veteran is not as easy. As we noted, Cicero's remarks on the unsuitability of the places where Rullus intended to plant colonies could be pressed to mean that Sullan veterans had received poor lands in the past. It may also be that some veterans are to be numbered among those who wanted to get rid of worthless land. For the rest, one of the main issues Cicero addresses is the illegal acquisition of land by the great (and this could mean they, in the process, acquired some that was worthless) some of which belonged to the veteran. Drummond postulates how land grabbing most likely was carried out: 'direct purchase, voluntary surrender, seizure or retention of a surety, forcible eviction where the plot had fallen vacant on the death of the previous owner'.[17] From the point of view of our enquiries there is a difficulty here.[18] The process outlined by Drummond self-evidently extended over a period of time from the end of the Sullan settlement down to 63 B.C. Thus, equally self-evidently, it cannot account for the *paludes et silvas* of Lepidus which stemmed immediately and directly from Sulla's own planting which had finished at the latest by 79.[19] In fact, during the Sullan period there were two ways for a man to acquire an estate. He could in the first instance buy or receive as a gift from Sulla the property of the proscribed. What is in question here is large estates of which few, or any, were broken up. We are looking at the substitution of one set of magnates for another.[20] Thus, our only concern with this will be to illustrate the criminal venality of some of the Sullans.[21] The other way to acquire property was by becoming an *auctor divisionis et assignationis*. In this position, as we shall see, advantage could be taken of the veteran.

Cicero, in the first instance, provides a clue as to what went on. He says (*Leg. agr.* 2.67) that Rullus aims to settle people on land *quod arari aut coli possit* ('which can be ploughed or cultivated'). Scholarly opinion on this statement seems to be

---

[16] The attack on Faesulae in 78 shows how high feelings could run: Gran. Lic. 28 (Criniti). Note also Caesar's charge (App. *B Civ.* 2.94) that Sulla had made people living in the same community enemies to each other.
[17] Drummond (2000) 136.
[18] And it was seen by Drummond (2000) 136 n. 39.
[19] For the dating see below.
[20] Plut. *Sull.* 33; *Comp. Lys. Sull.* 3; Cic. *Leg. agr.* 2.56; *Arch.* 25; *Quinct.* 76; *Rosc. Am.* 6; with Brunt (1986) 303–304; Keaveney (1982b) 534; Thein (2010) 80. Change of ownership could be swift. See Cic. *Rosc. Am.* 23.
[21] See below.

unanimous. Rullus had in mind land which had the potential to be cultivated.[22] Likewise, it appears Rullus here was proposing to follow what was standard procedure, just as Sulla had done.[23] Augustus, too, seems to have followed this same procedure when, as we learn from the *Agrimensores*, he decreed by means of a *lex data*[24] that land should be planted *qua falx et arater ierit* ('as far as the scythe and the plough shall have gone').[25] He, too, was anxious that only productive land should be used.[26] I would argue that, in some instances during the Sullan settlement, these procedures were not properly carried out.[27] But, before we can divine how it happened, we need to find out why. Muddle or fraud seem the most obvious reasons and the one need not exclude the other.

Muddle, in my opinion, is most likely to come from haste. I hold that the Sullan programme was carried out quickly even though there is a widespread scholarly view that land settlement could be a lengthy business.[28] A glance at some specific instances shows this view may be in need of modification. So, for example, the settlements of 197–194 were delayed because the triumvirs were also serving in other offices, while in 183–181 the local population proved troublesome. It is well known, too, that the Gracchan programme was slowed down by problems in determining who owned the land and resistance from the Italians.[29] In the case of Caesar the settlement extended from 47 to 44 and even after the dictator's death because he needed for his campaigns men earmarked for retirement.[30] Conversely, when Saturninus passed a bill giving land in Africa to Marian veterans of the Jugurthine War those not required for the German wars were settled immediately.[31] In 83, when the Cinnan tribune M. Iunius Brutus passed a measure to

---

22 Hardy (1913) 246; Brunt (1986) 297; Ferrary (1988b) 157–158; Campbell (2000) 357 n. 4.
23 Brunt (1986) 297.
24 It has been pointed out to me that his *auctoritas* would mean that this was the norm in all foundations.
25 Hyginus 1.78.2–3 (C) = 112.24 (L); 2.158.11–12 (C) = 201.7–8 (L); 2.160.6–7 (C) = 203.14–16 (L). Cf. also 242.8–9 (C) = 246.19 (L). It has been pointed out to me that the *falx* would be used to clear scrubland.
26 Hyginus 2.160.6–12 (C) = 203.14–204.4 (L). We shall be returning later to this important passage.
27 Perhaps Cicero (*Leg. agr.* 2.67) was recalling the Sullan settlement in words which to me have an ominous ring: *quod solum tam exile et macrum est quod arato perstringi non possit, aut quod est tam asperum saxetum, in quo agricolorum cultus non elaboret*, 'what soil is so poor and then that it cannot be broken up by the plough, or what stony ground is so rough that a man cannot spend his labour in cultivating it' (Loeb translation).
28 Keppie (1983) 87; Brunt (1986) 296; Thein (2010) 86 n. 37.
29 Gargola (1995) 62, 67, 69; Brunt (1986) 79–80.
30 Keppie (1983) 49–52.
31 Keaveney (2007) 24–25. Others will have followed by 100 at latest: Brunt (1986) 580. See *MRR* 3.21.

colonise Capua – apparently for strategic reasons – it was immediately put into effect.³² Finally, the Bononia agreement of 43, put on hold for the Philippi campaign, when it properly began in 41, was carried out rapidly. Octavian's troops saw to that and, in the summer of that year, when the Perusine War broke out, it was already well advanced.³³ From this survey I draw two conclusions. We cannot speak of a specific set time for an agrarian settlement.³⁴ Each case must be scrutinised separately and due weight given to the particular circumstances in which it was carried out.³⁵

Bearing this in mind, we cannot envisage Sulla being constrained by a particular timeframe. There are, I believe, a number of factors to be considered which point to him proceeding swiftly: his character, his previous actions and those now, and his current constitutional position. With regard to the first, we should not underestimate his capacity for ruthlessness.³⁶ We should never forget this was the man who chastised the cities of Asia and set the proscriptions afoot.³⁷ And that chastisement had been carried out in a single winter. Previous to this, in all of the troubles of 88 Sulla had found time to bring in a number of constitutional reforms which foreshadow those of the dictatorship and then he even seems to have envisaged some kind of colonial programme. All of this will have been hurried.³⁸

Now, in 82, the enabling legislation of the *lex Valeria* had conferred dictatorial powers on Sulla and it was in virtue of these that he passed the *leges Corneliae*.³⁹ Though the powers were of the widest, he was bound by the nature of the Roman magistracy. Sulla is the last figure in an age of reform which began with Tiberius

---

32 Cic. *Leg. agr.* 2.89, 92–93, 98 with Gabba (1976) 56–59 and Harvey (1982).
33 App. *B Civ.* 5.13–15 with Keaveney (2007) 61, 64 and Keppie (1983) 58–61, against Thein (2010) 86 n. 37.
34 It should be noted that only in Livy 32.29.4 and 34.53.2 do we hear of the *triumviri* in a colony having a three-year *imperium*. Salmon (1970) 19 thought this was the norm and was unquestioningly followed by Briscoe (1973) 226. Keppie (1983) 87 is more cautious: 'could take up to three years'. See also Gargola (1995) 69.
35 On the procedures followed in founding colonies, see Salmon (1970) 19–28 and Keppie (1983) 87–100, the latter with especial reference to the Late Republic and Early Empire.
36 Here I agree with Brunt (1986) 445.
37 Proscriptions: Hinard (1985b) 18–223. Asia: Keaveney (2005a) ²[1982] 91–97, 190–193.
38 Keaveney (2005a) ²[1982] 56–57. The only notice we have of colonies is Livy, *Per.* 77: *colonias deduxit*. Rejecting the contention of Schneider (1977) 131–132 that this is a doublet of the dictatorial programme, we may interpret the passage as follows. Sulla may have been inspired by the programme of M. Livius Drusus (tr. pl. 91) but, given the contemporary situation, no colonies were actually founded. They were mooted or, at best, the first steps (cf. n. 35) to found them were taken: Gabba (1976) 136; Keaveney (1983a) 73–74; Brunt (1986) 300; Thein (2010) 84. It is worth noting that the Cinnan M. Brutus was more fortunate in fraught circumstances some years later, see n. 32.
39 This seems to be the natural interpretation of Cic. *Leg. agr.* 3.5–6 where he mentions the *lex Valeria* and the Cornelian law confiscating land. See Hurlet (1993) 15–16, 33–36 and Keaveney (2005a) ²[1982] 135–136. Cf. Santangelo (2007) 82–83 for a similar interpretation of Cic. *Rosc. Am.* 125.

Gracchus and it should not be forgotten that such reformers were constrained by the year-long tenure of Roman magistracies.[40] In Sulla's own case he had two years to implement his work, a dictatorship running from sometime before the end of 82 to before the end of 81 and then a consulship in 80.[41] The other two issues he elected to deal with were disposed of quickly. The amendments to the constitution were carried out in the dictatorial year and the proscription lists were closed on the 1st June 81.[42] Thus, there is no reason why Sulla should not also have wished to begin planting quickly and striven to bring it to a rapid conclusion.[43]

A close examination of our sources will support this notion of a swift beginning and a swift end for the agrarian programme.[44] Our first source is the Livian epitome, which narrates the events of 82–79. A notice there reads: 'he took the legions to captured territory, and divided it among them' (*legiones in agros captos deduxit et eos his divisit*).[45] From its position in the epitome it could be dated prima facie to either 80 or 79 B.C.[46] The year in question must, however, be 80. Consular activity

---

40 See Keaveney (2009b).
41 See Keaveney (2005b). I would suggest that Sulla consciously worked within this timeframe. See further n. 43 for some other possible considerations which may have weighed with him.
42 Proscriptions: Keaveney (2005a) ²[1982] 125–126. It might be argued that some of the proscribed got away but this is to miss the point. The purpose of the proscription was to publicise the names of all adjudged *hostes* and by the 1st June that work of adjudication was complete – a work of some six months. In the land programme Arretium and Volaterrae provide a rough parallel. Their lands were confiscated and earmarked for settlement in 81, but thanks to their continuing resistance that could not take place until 79 (see further below).
43 We recall the speed of 88 (n. 38). How far he feared resistance now is a moot point but we do know that, even as dictator he was defied in the assemblies when he tried to deprive Arretium and Volaterrae of the citizenship: Cic. *Dom.* 79; *Caecin.* 79, 102 (see n. 3 above) and in his consulship defiance also grew: Keaveney (2005b) 433–438. One wonders, therefore, how far he anticipated or feared such recalcitrance.
44 So far as I am aware, such an examination has never been carried out. In consequence, a variety of different dates for start and finish have been proposed. Schneider (1977) 131 thought it started as early as 83 with the bulk of the work carried out from 82 to 80, while Harvey (1975) 48 n. 42 thought it only began in the latter year. Thein (2010) 85–86 argues that it was still incomplete on Sulla's death in 78. Krawczuk (using App. *B Civ.* 1.104) envisaged a programme of two years but with the work at Arretium and Volaterrae incomplete at Sulla's death: Krawczuk (2008) 11, 35–36, 96. We shall say about these theories below.
45 Livy, *Per.* 89 (Loeb translation). The wording here speaks of an actual act in contrast with the *colonias deduxit* of *Per.* 77, which refers only to an intended or aborted project (n. 38).
46 The sequence is as follows:
  (a) Pompey's campaigns in Sicily (82): Seager (2002) ²[1979] 27; *MRR* 2.70.
  (b) Sulla appointed dictator (82) and passes the *leges Corneliae* (81): Keaveney (2005a) ²[1982] 135–155.
  (c) Murder of Afella (81): Keaveney (2003) 88–92.
  (d) Pompey's African campaign (82–81?) and triumph (81): Badian (1955), (1961); Keaveney (1982a) 131–132, 137–138. Cf. Seager (2002) ²[1979] 174, *contra MRR* 3.161.

is well attested then and by 79 Sulla was a *privatus*.⁴⁷ Now, *deduxit* might appear to refer to a work completed in 80, but, bearing in mind the loose phrasing of the epitome, it may mask something just begun then or still in progress at the year's end.⁴⁸ Our next source is Granius Licinianus. His version of Lepidus' speech contains the following: 'and with nobody opposing him he supported a corn law whereby five *modii* of grain should be given to the people. And he was promising many other things: to bring back the exiles, to annul what had been enacted by Sulla, to restore those into whose lands Sulla had led his soldiers'.⁴⁹ As we can see, the threat to dismantle the land settlement – found also in Exuperantius⁵⁰ – is included with other features of the Sullan programme which were definitely established by 78. In other words, the natural inference is that it too had been completed by then at the latest. Thematically there are other resemblances to Lepidus' speech as recorded by Sallust,⁵¹ but both versions are plainly speaking of events prior to 78 and so the *paludes et silvas* must be located prior to them.⁵²

Thus, our Latin evidence seems to point to a settlement being carried out in 80 and completed by the end of 79 at the very latest. A consideration of our Greek source Appian enables us to develop and refine this conclusion. Four passages concern us. In *Bellum Civile* 1.96 which deals with the years 82 and 81 he tells us Sulla established colonies in Italy.⁵³ The events of *B Civ*. 1.100 are dated by consular dating to 81 and in it are narrated the Sullan constitutional reforms as well as the settlement programme. At 1.104 we have Sulla in retirement in 79 with his men established on the land. Finally at 1.107 we have Lepidus' agitation in 78. According to Appian he promised the

---

   (e) Suicide of Norbanus (81): Gabba (1967) 244. True if taken with (d) but it could conceivably go with (f) and so could be 80.
   (f) Suicide of the Samnite C. Papius Mutilus (80): Gran. Lic. 25 (Criniti).
   (g) Sulla takes Nola and possibly Aesernia (80): Keaveney/Strachan (1981) 365–366.
   (h) *legiones . . . divisit*. If taken with (g) to be dated to 80. If with (i) to 79.
   (i) Surrender of Volaterrae (79): Gran. Lic. 25 (Criniti).
   (j) The fall of Mytilene (79): Keaveney (2009a) 245–253.

47 Keaveney (2005a) ²[1982] 164–166; (2005b) 436–438; Krawczuk (2008) 63. Care must be exercised with the language of the epitome which as we saw (n. 38 and n. 45) may be loose. Thus (j) in n. 46 cannot refer to Sulla himself but to another *Sullanus* or even two, the consuls of 79: Gran. Lic. 25 (Criniti). This point has been overlooked by Kendall (2013) 628.
48 See notes 38, 45, 47.
49 Gran. Lic. 25 (Criniti): *et legem frumentariam nullo resistente tutatus est, ut annonae quinqui modii populo darentur, et alia multa pollicebatur: exules reducere, res gestas a Sulla rescindere, in quorum agros milites deduxerat, restituere.*
50 Exup. 6. As we shall see in a moment it is also found in the Greek authority.
51 On the main themes of the speech see below notes 90, 91, 92, 93.
52 We observe that Livy, *Per*. 90 and Flor. 2.11.2–3 speak of an attack on the whole of Sulla's *acta* and the latter specifically singles out the fate of the proscribed.
53 The mention of Pompey's contemporary campaigns helps with the dating. See n. 46 (a) (d).

restoration of confiscated lands.⁵⁴ It would thus appear that our Latin and Greek authorities are in broad general agreement. From Appian we learn that settling was in progress in 81, and both he and the Livian epitome show it continuing in 80. For Appian planting was concluded in 80 but, as we saw, the Latin authors can be pressed to suggest there was still activity in 79. In fact, we know of two places of which this was true, the *municipium* of Volaterrae and, as I shall argue, the *colonia* of Arretium.⁵⁵

Recently, some scholars have given emphasis to the fact that in both these places not all of the land confiscated received veterans.⁵⁶ We must now seek to divine the significance of this. We know that Volaterrae fell in 79.⁵⁷ But prior to this Sulla had shown an especial hostility to the place, for, as we know, as dictator, while it was still resisting, he confiscated its land and attempted to deprive it of citizenship.⁵⁸ Moreover, in that same year 81, he personally took charge of its siege.⁵⁹ However, as we have seen, it was not until 79 that settlers arrived. Arretium is more problematical.⁶⁰ But the resemblance of its situation to that of Volaterrae – an attempt to take away its citizenship in Sulla's dictatorship and partial settlement – points to a dating like that of the latter.⁶¹ But why was there only a partial settlement in these two places?⁶² So far as I am aware, only Krawczuk has attempted to answer this question. He envisaged that Lepidus' rebellion interfered with the programme, or that Sulla's waning influence may have caused his plans to be upset.⁶³ Against the first hypothesis some arguments may be deployed. A rebellion in 78

---

54 Gabba (1967) 293 thought that this repeal was 'l'argomento principale'.
55 There would seem to be no reason to accept Harvey's very tentative suggestion, (1975) 37 n. 13, that there were other places like these.
56 Santangelo (2007) 179; Krawczuk (2008) 36, 96; Thein (2010) 86. Arretium: Keaveney (1982b) 523; Volaterrae: Harris (1971) 264; Keaveney (1982b) 525. Some, e.g. Gabba (1976) 46 and Krawzcuk (2008) 96, have wondered if Cic. *Leg.* 3.12 with its few men might be relevant but other explanations are possible. See n. 8.
57 See n. 46.
58 See n. 3. Both acts are specifically dictatorial (Cic. *Dom.* 79) and thus predate the city's surrender by two years. Sulla's land settlement had its benign aspects. See Keaveney (1982b) 544, (2005a) ²[1982] 155. But this is plainly an example of its punitive side, for which see Keaveney (2005a) ² [1982] 151–152 and Santangelo (2007) 190.
59 Cic. *Rosc. Am.* 20.
60 On the basis of an emendation in App. *B Civ.* 1.91 and the archaeological evidence for fire and destruction, Harris (1971) 257 n. 4, 263 supposes it was captured late but emendation is not necessary, see Keaveney (1982b) 523 n. 155, and the fire and destruction need not indicate lateness. Norba was destroyed by fire (App. *B Civ.* 1.94) either in late 82 or possibly 81: Gabba (1967) 252; *MRR* 2.71.
61 In other words, Sulla as dictator had established the status of both towns but it was left to others to carry out the actual plantation since he was a *privatus* in 79. Cf. Santangelo (2007) 186.
62 I do not think that any other places will have been affected in the same way. If they had, we might expect land left unsettled to be subject to later attempts at appropriation which, as we shall now see, happened to these two cities alone.
63 Krawczuk (2008) 36, 96. See n. 44 above.

does not, I would argue, point to disruption in 79. We might indeed further add that we have no evidence of any kind of disturbance to the settlers.⁶⁴ And, for good measure, we have no reason to suppose the settlers were not marched out in a body at the start of the settlement as was usual Roman practice.⁶⁵ In sum, if some could be settled there is no reason to suppose that, in the conditions of the time, more could not have been, and so we must reject the suggestion that Lepidus had anything to do with this state of affairs. Krawczuk's other suggestion, that Sulla's waning influence in 79 had something to do with it, seems more attractive. It is just possible that powerful friends intervened on behalf of these places. We know of individuals in these times who had such friends. This was how Caesar escaped. The younger Roscius was helped by the Metelli.⁶⁶ It may just be that Arretium and Volaterrae also enjoyed such patronage now. They certainly had it later, especially when attempts were made to settle the undistributed land.⁶⁷ If that is so they will have benefited by a practice described by Siculus Flaccus: 'But not all conquered peoples were deprived of their lands; for the status, or influence, or friendship of some persuaded the victorious commander to grant their own lands to them'.⁶⁸ There is, however, a weakness here. The people of Arretium and Volaterrae did not enjoy security of tenure. This is clearly shown in the later attempts to resume the land which had not been settled.⁶⁹ These attempts at resuming the land very clearly show that the lands of Arretium and Volaterrae fell into the category of *subseciva* which might be appropriated. We have this on the authority of Hyginus: 'we should make a ledger recording all *subseciva*, so that whenever the emperor wishes he can find out how many men can be settled in that area'.⁷⁰ So how, then, do we account for this state of affairs? I believe the solution may be in a suggestion made

---

64 There seem to have been many veterans at the time of Catiline's conspiracy: Cic. *Cat.* 3.14; *Mur.* 46; Sall. *Cat.* 36. There is no evidence it suffered an attack such as that on Faesulae: Gran. Lic. 28 (Criniti).
65 See Salmon (1970) 24.
66 Caesar: Suet. *Iul.* 1. Roscius: Badian (1958) 249–251; Ward (1977) 67. Berry (2000) vi–ix has some reservations.
67 Cic. *Caecin.* 97, 101; *Dom.* 79; *Att.* 1.19.4; *Fam.* 13.4, 5.2; with Harris (1971) 281–283 and Terrenato (1998) 106–108 who analyses in depth Cicero's relations with the Caecina family in Volaterrae. I think it unlikely that any advantage accrued to Volaterrae by expelling the proscribed. What the guarantee in Strabo 5.2.6 was worth may be seen from Gran. Lic. 25 (Criniti). Similar useless agreements are attested at Nola: Livy, *Per.* 89; Gran. Lic. 25 (Criniti); and Praeneste: Val. Max. 9.2.1.
68 Siculus Flaccus 120.35–36 (C) = 155.6–8 (L): *nec tamen omnibus personis victis ablati sunt agri; nam quorundam dignitas aut gratia aut amicitia victorem ducem movit ut eis concederet agros suos.* See further Campbell (2000) 394 n. 40. Thein (2010) 92 highlights the importance of patronage in the Sullan settlement.
69 See n. 67.
70 Hyginus 2.158.22–23 (C) = 202.5–7 (L): *subsecivorum omnium librum facere [scire] debebimus, ut quando voluerit imperator sciat quot in eum locum homines deduci possint.* Augustus is recorded as buying surplus land: Hyginus 2.154.31–32 (C) = 197.18–19 (L). Sometimes surplus land was given to

independently by Harris and Santangelo, both of whom think there was more land in Volaterrae and Arretium than veterans to occupy it.[71] To me the logical conclusion to draw from this is that fewer men were now available because the bulk had already been settled in 81–80 and this, I would further submit, is in harmony with the evidence we examined earlier.[72]

We can see that juridically there is nothing exceptional about the Sullan settlement. It would appear to follow normal Roman procedures. The main part of the settlement was carried out in two years. As we noted earlier, each act of settlement must be judged by its peculiar circumstances and in this case the resistance of Arretium and Volaterrae with their consequent late and partial planting may form the peculiar circumstances of the Sullan. In my opinion, Santangelo has recognised a likely result of this haste. Speaking of Etruria he says, 'unfamiliarity with the territory, and perhaps haste, may have led some of the newcomers to settle in not very productive land'.[73] I would merely add that the phenomenon was most likely not just confined to Etruria but was more widespread.[74] I readily concede that the evidence here is circumstantial and may not admit of absolute proof. Nevertheless it strongly points towards muddle and confusion.[75]

But, if the case for administrative incompetence is circumstantial, there is abundant evidence for a more sinister phenomenon – fraud. As is well known, after the Colline Gate victory, the *Sullani* turned on their defeated enemies and the proscriptions were soon set afoot. A detailed treatment of this situation is not necessary here.[76] However, we may observe that, if in meting out retribution, genuine mistakes may sometimes have been made, there is evidence – and this is important for the point I wish to establish – that the innocent were sometimes killed purely because people wanted to get a hold of their property. Even if not all of them were guilty of murder, we are looking at the mindset which informed those *possessores*

---

a colony as commonage: Hyginus 2.158.15–18 (C) = 201.14–18 (L). See Brunt (1986) 299; Campbell (2000) 396 n. 47 and further n. 85.

71 Harris (1971) 262; Santangelo (2007) 188 although he was previously, 178–179, agnostic.

72 Plainly this is not the place to discuss in detail the revisionist thesis of Thein (2010) but one observation seems pertinent. Shortage of veterans by 79 would offer support to his thesis, 93–95, that fewer men than is generally supposed were actually settled.

73 Santangelo (2007) 186.

74 See below on the question of numbers and note here that throughout Roman history boundary disputes were a feature of Roman settlement: Dilke (1971) 44–46, 105 and there is also some evidence for lack of care in measuring: Dilke (1971) 85. It is not, I believe, beyond the realm of possibility that Sullan boundaries had not been accurately set either.

75 Here I should like to invoke for purposes of comparison, as I did for fraud in Keaveney (1982b) 539 n. 526, the Cromwellian settlement of Ireland. In that settlement we find confusion due to what Santangelo postulates for the Sullan, namely unfamiliarity with the land and a lack of proper surveys. See Corish (1976) 361–368.

76 It is treated fully in Keaveney (2005a) [2][1982] 125–131.

of dubious title we considered earlier in this chapter. We first of all have two instances where the victims seem to have had little or no connection with the Cinnans. In Bruttium Crassus had a man's name put on a proscription list because he coveted his estate.[77] Seeing his name on a proscription list an apolitical *eques* Q. Aurelius exclaimed that he had been destroyed by his Alban estate.[78] We have also another three occasions where people, already engaged in feuds with family and neighbours, took advantage of the situation to liquidate opponents and appropriate their property. The most famous of these victims is, of course, the elder Roscius, who had a longstanding familial quarrel and, although a Sullan partisan, was murdered and had his name posthumously added to a proscription list.[79] At Larinum, Oppianicus, who was feuding with other locals, fled to the Sullan Metellus Pius and eventually used proscription as a weapon against his foes and then seized their land.[80] Finally we come again to Valgus who built up a large estate at Casinum by proscribing his neighbours.[81]

Now, it is my contention that the sort of people who would do this kind of thing against their peers would not, given the chance, hesitate to rob veterans of their land if it meant they could add to their own holdings. Furthermore, as we have suggested, the way this was done was by misapplying the usual mechanism of settlement.[82] Three passages from the *Agrimensores* provide the clue as to how it was done. The first is from Hyginus: 'on the map you must note separately "areas cultivated and uncultivated", "woods"'.[83] The second is from Siculus Flaccus: 'some places are listed as "set aside" (*excepta*), which the man who conducted the division and allocation either reserved for himself or granted to someone else'.[84] The third is a longer passage of Hyginus:

---

[77] Plut. *Crass.* 6 with Keaveney (1982b) 516–514. There is a half-hearted attempt at defence in Ward (1977) 66–67. Cf. his remarks, 62 n. 19, on Crassus' appropriation of the booty of Tuder. Interestingly, Sallust's Lepidus is represented as promising to restore the goods of the proscribed which he claims he bought out of fear: Sall. *Hist.* 1.55.18 (Maurenbrecher) = 1.48.18 (McGushin) = 1.49.18 (Ramsey). In *Cat.* 33, Sallust's Caesar complains that people were made away with for their property. See also *Cat.* 11.
[78] Plut. *Sull.* 31. Status: Keaveney (2005a) ²[1982] 210 n. 8. *Contra* Hinard (1985b) 334–335.
[79] Cic. *Rosc. Am.* 15–22.
[80] Cic. *Clu.* 20–25 with Keaveney (1982b) 531.
[81] Cic. *Leg. agr.* 3.14. In view of what was said earlier, it looks as if Valgus went on as he had begun. In laying the foundation of his fortune in this way he may be compared to Crassus (Plut. *Crass.* 2).
[82] See notes 22–26. It has been suggested to me that bribery may have facilitated the process I am about to describe. There is no direct evidence of this but, given the well attested venality of many Sullans, it is not improbable. It certainly occurred in the Cromwellian settlement: Corish (1976) 366.
[83] Hyginus I.78.3–4 (C) = 112.25–26 (L): *In forma generatim enotari debebit LOCA CULTA et INCULTA, SILVAE*, reading *SILVAE* (Campbell) rather than *VILLAE* (Lachmann).
[84] Siculus Flaccus 124.3–6 (C) = 157.7–8 (L): *Inscribuntur quaedam EXCEPTA, quae aut sibi reservavit auctor divisionis et assignationis, aut alii concessit.*

We shall allocate this land according to the law issued (*lex data*), or if we like, the law of the divine Augustus, as far as 'the scythe and the plough have gone'. This law is open to interpretation. Some think that it refers only to cultivated land. In my opinion, it says that it is correct to allocate usable land. The purpose of this is to prevent the allocation to a recipient of a plot consisting entirely of woods or pasture. But a man who receives cultivable land as the larger part of his allocation will, according to the law, properly receive some woodland to make up the area. So, it will happen that some receive woodland adjoining their allocation, while others receive woodland on mountains, perhaps more than four neighbouring properties away.[85]

From these passages it is tolerably easy to divine what seems to have happened. The *auctor divisionis* kept as much *excepta* for himself and his friends as possible. Naturally this was of good quality and some of it should have gone to the veteran who was then fobbed off with worthless land. Augustus recognised the problem and took specific measures to see that land was distributed fairly.[86] It may very well be that he was being innovative here but, as we saw above, on the balance of probabilities, he was merely seeing to it that age old procedures were being correctly followed.[87] In doing this, Augustus may have reacted against an abuse characteristic of the Sullan settlement. Again, it might not be rash to claim he remembered what happened when he was implementing the Bononia agreement. Then soldiers grabbed other people's land, took more than was lawfully theirs and kept the best lands for themselves.[88] The author of an extensive settlement programme would want to see all went well.[89]

But how widespread was this abuse? Unfortunately we have no figures but two circumstances suggest it must be considered serious. Firstly, it is significant that Sallust in the speech of Lepidus elected to include it as one of the features of the Sullan regime. It takes its place alongside a number of well-attested phenomena: the dictatorial power over laws, courts, the treasury and the provinces is absolute[90]; the rights of the people have been curbed and specifically disabilities have been placed

---

85 Hyginus 2.160.6–12 (C) = 203.14–204.4 (L): *Hunc agrum secundum datam legem aut si placebit secundum divi Augusti adsignabimus eatemus QUA FALX ET ARATER IERIT. haec lex habet suam interpretationem. quidam putant tantum cultum nominari: ut mihi videtur, utile\<m\> ait agrum adsignare oportere. hoc erit ne accipienti silvae universus modus adsignetur aut pascui. qui vero maiorem modum acceperit culti, optime secundum legem accipiet aliquid [et] silvae ad inplendum [acceptae] modum. ita fiet ut alii sibi iunctas silvas accipiant, alii in montibus ultra quartum forte vicinum.* Note that *pasqua* could, of course, sometimes be assigned to the *ordo*: Hyginus 2.156.3–5, 158.15–21 (C) = 198.3–6, 201.14–202.4 (L).
86 Keaveney (1982b) 538–539.
87 See above and Salmon (1970) 20, 24; Campbell (2000) 358.
88 App. *B Civ.* 5.13.
89 On Augustus' settlements see Keppie (1983) 58–82, 208–209.
90 §13.

on the tribunate and the courts, along with an abolition of the corn dole[91]; people have been proscribed and their goods are seized, often winding up in the hands of those of low degree, while their descendants face civic disabilities[92]; some have been deprived of citizenship and land has been confiscated.[93] As these are prominent features and of great moment, so to number *paludes et silvae* among them would seem to indicate that they, too, were significant. My second argument may be stated more briefly. If I am right in the hypothesis made above that Augustus was reacting against an abuse in the Sullan system with legislation, then it was clearly a matter of some importance.

Upon his death in A.D. 14 we have evidence that not everything went as Augustus planned it. The Pannonian legions mutinied.[94] In this we see a return, however briefly, to how things had been under Caesar and the triumvirs. In that time, with fractured authority, the troops had asserted themselves and made demands. Now, with Tiberius' position doubtful and some thinking Germanicus should be emperor, the troops once more made demands.[95] The soldiers complained about the number of years they were kept with the colours, the harshness of military discipline, the poor pay and at discharge receiving 'some boggy marsh or hilly desert as so-called "farmland"' (*per nomen agrorum uligines paludum et inculta montium*).[96] In the last of these complaints we have a situation akin to that Lepidus described all those years before. As so often happens, two separate explanations of the situation may be entered. The first we owe to Wilkes. He thought the soldiers' reaction could be tied to a single event, the foundation of a colony at nearby Emona in A.D. 14. There was a good deal of poor land, and the soldiers could see they were about to be short changed.[97] But the date of the foundation of Emona is disputed and, so far as I am aware, there is no scholarly consensus on the matter.[98] Thus, Wilkes' suggestion could only be accepted if his proposed date were securely established. On another interpretation, the complaint may refer to

---

91 §11, 23.
92 §6, 17–18, 21.
93 §12, 24.
94 Tac. *Ann*. 1.16–17. In *Ann*. 1.31.1 Tacitus says that, at about the same time, the German legions also mutinied, see Goodyear (1972) 241.
95 Situation in A.D. 14: Tac. *Ann*. 1.7.6; 16–17; 31.1 with Goodyear (1972) 203 n. 2, 242; Vell. Pat. 2.125.1–2 with Woodman (1977) 228–229. Situation in Caesarian and triumviral times: Keaveney (2007) 42–54, 82–90, cf. also 63–67.
96 Tac. *Ann*. 1.17 (translation: Yardley, Oxford World's Classics) where the proposed remedies are also listed: properly fixed terms of service with good pay and a cash gratuity on discharge. Goodyear (1972) 203 wonders if Tacitus is merely echoing the phraseology of Sallust's speech of Lepidus (§23) and if historical truth could be imbedded in a speech, both of which notions I find unpersuasive. For Sallust in Tacitus see Rosenblitt in this volume.
97 Wilkes (1963) esp. 269–270. It will be recalled (see above) that, on one interpretation of Cic. *Leg. agr.* 2.71 there might have been whole Sullan settlements of this type.
98 Wells (1974).

many places across the empire. Campbell was prepared to envisage a situation where Augustus' wishes were not always implemented whether through carelessness, lack of scruple on the part of officials, or the difficulty of finding enough suitable land.[99] A problem arises when we search for such places. In 13 B.C. Augustus substituted a gratuity for land, and after 14 B.C. there is virtually no evidence of provincial settlement aside from Emona (whose foundation date, as we saw, is disputed) and the possibility that some colonies in Pisidia belong after 13 B.C. It has, however, been observed that Augustus would surely settle on newly conquered land which would cost him nothing.[100] On the other hand, I would urge in favour of Campbell's view that the other two main grievances of the Pannonian mutineers were of long standing and thus it may very well be so was that concerning land.[101] Therefore, it could that there were some other settlements we do not know of, but the hazards of making such a guess are obvious if we keep in mind that less than fifty colonies are known for the period A.D. 14–117 and yet about three hundred would have been required to cater for the numbers discharged.[102] At base, all we really can say is that a complaint made against Sulla surfaced again in the case of Augustus.[103]

Our search for an explanation of Lepidus' accusation in 78 has taken us over a wide area. It is proper, therefore, that, by way of conclusion, we briefly sum up our findings. From Cicero's orations against Rullus we catch what may be a glimpse of veterans on poor land and this could possibly include whole colonies. We also encounter magnates who have added to their holdings, certainly at the expense of their peers and maybe of the veteran. Furthermore, the mere fact of being a *Sullanus* awoke *invidia*. Sulla's settlement, I argued, was carried out quickly and this could have led to confusion. We also know of the dubious character of many *Sullani* and this could have led to outright fraud. A study of the relevant Roman practices in land settlements and their perversion shows how this might have been carried out. We know Augustus was aware of the problem and made provisions to counter it. An incident after his death (however we interpret it) shows it could recur.

---

99 Campbell (2000) 358. The resemblance to my conclusions about Sulla need not be laboured. Wilkes (1963) 268 did wonder if the soldiers' complaints had a wider application but dismissed the notion.
100 Keppie (1983) 208–209.
101 Pay had been set in the time of Caesar: Watson (1969) 90–91 and length of service in A.D. 5: Cass. Dio 55.23.1.
102 Campbell (1994) 211.
103 The problem may not have entirely gone away afterwards. Dilke (1971) 44 draws attention to penalties imposed by Constantine on judges in a boundary dispute who claimed disputed territory for themselves. However, to pursue this matter further is beyond the scope of this chapter.

Part II: **Reception**

Federico Santangelo
6 Sulla in the *Bellum* Jugurthinum

The brief of this chapter is to provide a close reading of the sections of Sallust's *Bellum Jugurthinum* (henceforth *BJ*) in which Sulla features as a character, and his actions are described and commented upon. It is therefore important to stress what this chapter does *not* set out to do: providing a general discussion of Sallust's views on Sulla, a topic that has received a number of modern treatments, and also features prominently in Alison Rosenblitt's contribution to this volume.[1] On the contrary, the focus will be firmly on the monograph on the Jugurthine War, and the underlying premise is that an assessment of its value as an historical source has to rest upon an appreciation of its literary dimension. Detailed discussions of specific passages have of course been provided, especially within existing commentaries, but a holistic and discursive exploration of Sallust's portrayal and assessment of Sulla in *BJ* has not yet been offered.[2] No other extant source gives a fuller account of Sulla's involvement in the Jugurthine War: Velleius is emphatically clear on the extent of Sulla's contribution to the victory over the king, but has no detail to offer (2.12.1); Plutarch is chiefly interested in the impact that the capture of Jugurtha had on the relationship between Sulla and Marius, and on later developments in Rome (*Sull.* 3.4; see also *Mar.* 10.5–6), as well as in the displays of remarkable courage and rising arrogance that Sulla gave at the time. A central aim of the present discussion is to make a contribution to our understanding of the early phase of Sulla's career, but some implications of wider import will also be drawn.

Sulla makes a sudden appearance in *BJ*: he enters the narrative at a crucial juncture of the conflict, in 107 B.C., after Marius' conquest of Capsa and his lucky capture of the fort of Moluccha, where his foresight and ability had shown all their striking limitations, and the contribution of an unnamed Ligurian from the auxiliary troops had played a central role in enabling the Romans to seize the site.[3] As those events are unfolding, Sallust resorts to a device that he has been employing throughout the monograph, and opens up the narrative to another level of action: from Marius and the events at Moluccha he directs the reader to the developments that follow the arrival of Sulla. *Ceterum*, a connective he often employs in battle narratives, marks the start of a

---

1 Zecchini (2002) offers a useful discussion and full doxography. For ease of reference this chapter uses the abbreviations *BJ* and *BC* (instead of the usual *Iug.* and *Cat.*) for Sallust's two monographs, the *Bellum Jugurthinum* and *Bellum Catilinae*. In this chapter Metellus is always Metellus Numidicus.
2 The most thorough study is Dijkstra-Parker (2007), which also provides detailed bibliographical guidance.
3 Capsa: *BJ* 91–92; Ligurian soldier: *BJ* 93–94. On Sallust's assessment of the capture of Moluccha see Gilbert (1973) 105, who offers a useful inventory of the evidence for a tradition on Marius' association 'with fortune and the gods' (107). Brescia (1997) has a close reading of the account of the deed of the Ligurian.

new chain of events. Sulla is introduced without his gentilician, as is customary in Sallust, and is right away presented in his official capacity as quaestor. He joins Marius' camp with a contingent of new cavalry forces, which he has himself recruited in Italy. His connection with the cavalry remains a distinctive aspect of his involvement in the campaign until the end of the conflict. The arrival of fresh forces, which can bring an element of dynamism to the management of the campaign, further corroborates the idea of a moment in which a new phase of the war is about to unfold. Sallust stresses that Sulla had conducted the levy of that contingent, and had recruited contingents from Latium and from allied communities, probably Italian (at 105.2 mention is made of a Paelignian cohort). That is a task that, whilst not being unusual in itself, requires a considerable degree of expertise, and is not immediately easy to reconcile with Sallust's later claim that by that time Sulla had virtually no military experience. We shall come back to that point in a moment; what is worth stressing for now is that Sulla was entrusted with that task, and therefore must have developed a relationship with Marius before his departure for Africa.

At this stage of the narrative, Sallust makes a remarkable choice, which he does not make for other major characters of his work: he takes a brief digression to comment on Sulla's character and achievements, right after introducing him. Most strikingly, Marius had not received such a treatment. His early mentions in *BJ* (46.7; 55.5; 55.8; 56.5; 57.1) just show his involvement in military operations, in a clearly subordinate position to Metellus. He only receives close discussion when he decides to stand for the consulship (63). Metellus, whose leadership receives frequent and close attention throughout the central part of the work, is not granted a lengthy introduction: we are told about his election to the consulship, a brief mention is made to his strength of character and political allegiance, and a discussion of his approach to the conduct of the war is offered (43.1–4). At 95, on the contrary, Sallust immediately recognises that the greatness of Sulla imposes a brief assessment of his background: notably, of his character and his upbringing (*natura* and *cultus*). This could legitimately be read as an instance of Sallust's keen interest in Sulla, and of his willingness to recognise him as an historical problem: both themes are apparent from other aspects of his work. Sallust cannot help but reflect on a figure that he regards as central, and whose importance is strongly evoked by the events under discussion (*res admonuit*). It may also have to do with a more contingent set of preoccupations: Sulla appears in the final section of the work, and there will hardly be scope for a discussion at a later stage. His importance has to be confronted right away. Moreover, Sallust makes clear that the monograph will not include a treatment of Sulla's later success. It has been argued that this passage already presupposes that he does not intend to discuss these events anywhere else in his work, and that the periodisation underlying the *Historiae* has not been decided yet. This may be an overly rigid reading, and in fact the Latin suggests a different interpretation: Sallust's *scripturus* does not refer to his future body of work, but to the monograph on the Numidian war – to the work at hand.⁴ One point is reasonably clear: Sallust claims to be engaging critically with the author who had produced the fullest assessment of Sulla's age to date, L. Cornelius Sisenna. His work is here given a famously complex assessment: he is an effective and thorough student of this period, but has not shown sufficient intellectual independence.⁵ The factors that prevented him from discussing this period as freely as it could have been possible are not made clear.⁶ Although Sallust does not intend to speak about Sulla at any length, and will avoid any overlap with the work of Sisenna, he promises to bring a corrective to his assessment of Sulla. On the other hand, the actual terms of his disagreement with him are not spelled out.

The subsequent portrait of Sulla has rightly received much attention, and its sharp differences with that of Marius have not failed to attract many a reader.⁷ Unlike his consul, Sulla hails from a patrician family; his ancestors have failed to reach senior magistracies since the praetorship of P. Cornelius Sulla in 186 B.C., and their *ignauia* appears to assimilate them to the members of the *nobilitas* that Marius criticises elsewhere in *BJ* for failing to live up to the standards of their forebears.⁸ Sulla appears to have come full circle, and to have effectively overcome the shortcomings and underachievement of his ancestors. There is, however, another revealing difference between him and Marius: his literary training, which has also enabled him to become fluent in Greek. Sulla is a political player with a robust intellectual hinterland. We are also presented with the suggestion that he is at home in different cultural and linguistic contexts, that there is an ambidexterity to him which will prove a major and valuable facet of his involvement in the war. His significant contribution to the Roman success involved dealing with foreign counterparts and finding common ground with them. It is predicated on an effective transition from being a military leader who commands the obedience and respect of the Romans to standing out as a skillful diplomat who effectively deals with enemies and allies.

The wealth and complexity of Sulla's interests is matched by what follows. He is led by a tension between quest for pleasure and pursuit of glory, in which the latter has the upper hand (95.4: 'a man of great ambition, craving pleasure, but craving glory more', *animo ingenti, cupidus uoluptatum, sed gloriae cupidior*). Sulla's commitment to a value that is central in the moral horizon of the Roman nobility is unquestionable.

---

4 See Levene (1992) 58. Cf. Syme (1964) 177 ('Sallust proved unable to shake off the obsession and break loose from Sulla'); Paul (1984) 235. I am much indebted to Jaap Wisse for illuminating discussion of this problem.
5 *BJ* 95.3: *L. Sisenna, optume et diligentissime omnium, qui eas res dixere, persecutus, parum mihi libero ore locutus uidetur* ('Lucius Sisenna, who of all those who have written about those matters dealt with them best and with the greatest diligence, seems to me to have spoken with little intellectual freedom').
6 Paul (1984) 236 invokes *BC* 4.2 (*quod mihi a spe, metu, partibus rei publicae animus liber erat*) as a possible blueprint of the criticism that Sallust might have levelled at Sisenna.
7 See e.g. Earl (1961) 79; La Penna (1968) 226–232; Dench (2005) 148.
8 Sall. *BJ* 85.5, 14.

Ingens animus is not a neutral expression in Sallust: it has been applied to Marius, with a crucial qualification (63.2: *animus belli ingens domi modicus*), and a similar judgement was reserved to young Jugurtha (8.1: *non mediocrem animum*). The following sentence is partly corrupt, and it is not quite possible to follow Sallust's argument here. It is sufficiently clear, however, that Sulla's tendency to resort to *luxuria* in his leisure time alerts us to an area of tension in his relationship with wealth, which becomes clearer in what follows, but also takes us beyond *BJ*: in *Catiline's War* (henceforth *BC*) Sulla's conduct towards his army is regarded as the crucial factor in the onset of unbridled *luxuria* and moral decline in Late Republican Rome.[9] This passage, however, deals with a much earlier phase in Sulla's career, and to a different context. Moreover, it is doubtful whether *BJ* should be explained by cross-references to *BC*, and the degree to which readers of *BJ* may be encouraged, or indeed well advised, to be looking at connections with Sallust's previous monograph is at least debatable.

When the text resumes, another major thematic area is drawn out: Sulla's eloquence. His *facundia*, 'eloquence', is singled out as a fundamental aspect of his public persona.[10] The earlier point on his bilingualism is here corroborated and expanded by further references to his use of words: Sulla is shrewd, and equally capable of simulation and dissimulation.[11] The spoken word is a tool of persuasion as much as it is a tool to negotiate his way through the complexity of politics and of life at the camp, or indeed beyond it, as his later dealings with the Mauretanian dynast Bocchus will make apparent. Sallust establishes a clear link between Sulla's use of the spoken word and his intellectual qualities. He speaks of his *altitudo ingeni*, an intellectual depth that strongly qualifies the earlier comment on his *ingens animus*; this adjectival use of *incredibilis* is unparalleled in what survives of Sallust, and strongly conveys the exceptional degree of the talent of Sulla that the historian intends to single out. The last term of the sentence, however, introduces a further element that takes us back to the earlier comment on *luxuria*: Sulla's readiness to make gifts to others – especially, but not exclusively, of a monetary kind. The comment on *luxuria* and its impact is suitably narrowed down, and a greater sense of urgency is conveyed. The gifts that Sulla uses have a considerable destabilising potential, and put the economic and financial order into question. *Largitio* is negatively connoted in the Roman political vocabulary.[12] More specifically, Sallust explicitly singles it out as the prime method employed by Jugurtha in his dealings with Rome. Early on in the narrative, his envoys are confident that the Senate will not heed Adherbal's call for help because of the gifts they have made, rather than

---

9 Sall. *BC* 11.5.
10 On this aspect cf. Catherine Steel's contribution to this volume.
11 On this 'paradoxical' portrait' see La Penna (1978) 208–211. Dijkstra/Parker (2007) 143 note that Sulla shares the ability to dissimulate with M. Aemilius Scaurus (*BJ* 15.4); the same also applies to Metellus (*BJ* 47.9–48.1).
12 Hellegouarc'h (1963) 219–221.

because of the cause they are advocating (15.1: *largitione magis quam causa freti*, 'relying on bribery, rather than on their argument'); a few lines below, Sallust speaks of 'the notorious and shameless bribery of the king' (15.5: *regis largitionem famosam inpudentemque*). The word *largitio* does not occur again until Sulla comes into play.

The opening portrait is then compounded by a comment that has received much discussion, as it is one of the earliest surviving comments on what makes him *felix*: its main point of interest is the way in which Sallust sets it within a wider framework of reference. On the one hand, it identifies a watershed in Sulla's life and in the manifestation of his good fortune: the victory in the civil war. Until then, he was indisputably the most fortunate (*felicissimus*) of all the Romans, but *felicitas* was not his only distinctive attribute: his *industria* was a match to his good luck (*fortuna*), and his strength was regarded by some as his distinctive quality.[13] The time-honoured debate on the balance between fortune and virtue finds a further application here. Sulla's *felicitas* therefore receives two important qualifications: one chronological and one qualitative. It is, however, recognised as a meaningful aspect to the understanding of Sulla, which Sallust can acknowledge even without expressing approval for his conduct after seizing supreme power, which is in fact unreservedly condemned. This is an impressive instance of the pattern that D. Levene has convincingly identified throughout *BJ*: an historical monograph that is also a fragmentary work, and gains much of its significance and depth from the issues that it points towards, but does not quite cover.[14]

Sulla's industry finds powerful confirmation in the events that follow his arrival, and which are discussed as the narrative resumes, with the connective *igitur* that Sallust customarily employs when a new section of an evenemential account is introduced. Sulla and his cavalry contingent reach Marius' camp near Moluccha after a long journey from Italy through Africa, and that movement through space enables an even more significant transition: when Sulla came to Africa he was a recently elected quaestor, and – most importantly – was not yet equipped with the necessary knowledge and skill in warfare. In a short space of time he readily proved the most effective member of the whole army. Ridley has persuasively questioned the reliability of the first part of this account. It is indeed hard to accept that Marius entrusted the levy of his cavalry contingent to a quaestor who did not have any military experience, and it is at least plausible that Sulla developed it on one of the overseas campaigns that Rome led between the late 120s and the 110s.[15] Ridley has also suggested that this

---

[13] *BJ* 95.5: *multique dubitauere, fortior an felicior esset*. Cf. Eckert (2016a) 64–65, setting Sallust at the beginning of a tradition on Sulla's change for the worse.
[14] Levene (1992).
[15] Ridley (2010) esp. 109–111. Schietinger (2013) argues that Sulla had an early connection with the Metelli and owed his rise through the *cursus honorum* to them (see 212–213 on the election to the quaestorship); the evidence is at best slight.

image derives straight from Sulla's autobiography, and is intended to demonstrate that his success depended on innate abilities verging on genius. It is indeed likely that Sallust had direct knowledge of Sulla's extensive account of his *res gestae* and that he found plenty of valuable material in that work. For the purposes of this discussion, however, it seems prudent not to envisage direct reliance on, or use of, that text in *BJ*, not least because Sallust does not make any reference whatsoever to it; nor should we assume that Sisenna merely presented a condensed version of Sulla's account of the campaign.

To go back to Sallust's portrayal: what makes Sulla such an effective and remarkable presence in the Roman camp is not just his ability to exert himself. His leadership qualities also become apparent. He establishes a warm and close relationship with his soldiers, standing out as a commander who seeks the company of his men and deals with them benevolently (*milites benigne appellare*). He is also ready to answer the many requests for assistance that he receives. We are suddenly presented with a picture of the Roman camp as a place where words matter as much as deeds, and indeed enable the performance of further feats that will have a major impact on the unfolding of the campaign. This is not an unprecedented development in the context of this campaign: both Metellus (54.1) and Marius (92.1–2) had shown remarkable ability to attend to the needs of their soldiers, reward their merits, and forge an effective relationship with them. Sulla establishes his credentials as a military leader by his skill in answering the requests he receives, and by his wider ability to fit into an economy of favours and benefactions that is largely, but not exclusively, monetary. Sallust's prose neatly conveys the impression of a method devised *more geometrico*: Sulla is always ready to give favours, but does not willingly consent to receive any. When he is forced to accept one, he pays it back even more quickly than he would pay back a debt. At the same time, he would pointedly refuse to expect people to return his favours (*ab nullo repetente*), whilst always striving to have as many people as possible in debt to him. The *arcanum imperii* that Sulla reportedly spelled out on his gravestone – that no friend surpassed him in generosity, and no enemy in causing harm – was not in the open yet.[16] What is in the open, though, is Sulla's willingness to be, and be seen to be, close to his men. Sallust implicitly draws attention to the complexity of this pattern of behaviour, by showing that he fostered his connection with the soldiers through words (exchanging banter and having earnest conversations, even with the humblest), through deeds (taking part in marches and guard duty), and even through his silence: he never undermines the consul by questioning his authority or criticising his actions. Sallust singles out this conduct in especially approving terms: showing disrespect towards people in a position of authority is a symptom of *praua ambitio*. In the prologue to *BC* (4.2) Sallust speaks of the *ambitio mala* that had led him to covet political success and disregard his intellectual pursuits; Sulla is here depicted as someone who has not yet

---

[16] Plut. *Sull.* 38.4.

been corrupted by the dominant ways of political competition. The reward of Sulla's conduct is an explicitly old-fashioned one: concord. The clever combination of deeds (*rebus*) and personal abilities (*artibus*) that he displays earns him the favour of consuls and soldiers alike, and Sallust stresses how quickly (*breui*) that was achieved. The language that Sallust uses here, however, is not so much reminiscent of what happens in *BC* as it is of previous sections of this monograph: there are striking, and indeed meaningful, connections between this portrayal of Sulla and the account of the behaviour of young Jugurtha in the Roman camp at Numantia.[17] Their promising beginnings also serve as disturbing warnings to anyone who has the benefit of hindsight.

Having set the scene in these terms, Sallust then moves back to the Numidian front, and to Jugurtha's joining forces with Bocchus, with a view to launching a counter-offensive on Marius, who was making his way back to the winter quarters (97.4). Sulla is of course with the consul, but his presence is not mentioned until the two armies come to an open clash, and Marius, at the end of the first day of hostilities, instructs him to quarter the cavalry by a water spring for the night, waiting for hostilities to resume. This casual detail strongly suggests that Sulla has been in charge of the cavalry throughout the operations: he has, after all, been responsible for the recruitment of most of it. Sallust's account shows Marius as firmly in charge of operations; Sulla is, at this point, offering valuable assistance on the fringes of the action, securing control over a valuable strategic location while the consul is rallying the bulk of his forces that have been scattered across the battlefield (98.4). Marius then orders his soldiers to regroup in silence and let the night pass, while the opponents set their camp and spend most of the night dancing and celebrating. There is a stark tension between silence and noise, which is suddenly reversed when the Romans launch their counter-attack from the position of strength that they have gained: by then the Numidians and their allies have just fallen asleep, and are overwhelmed by an attack that the Romans launch with a sudden outburst of force and noise (99.3–5). There is a striking parallel between this action and a major incident in the preceding narrative, when Jugurtha's soldiers attack Adherbal's troops in the vicinity of Cirta when the greater part of the night has passed but it is still dark (21.2: *obscuro etiam lumine*). They storm the camp finding some of them half-asleep (*semisomnos*) and some hastily fetching their weapons, and end up obtaining a comprehensive victory. In that account the emphasis is placed on visual details, notably the dim light in which the attack takes place and the sign that the soldiers receive before launching their attack; here the focus is on the contrast between sound and silence that leads to the attack and accompanies its unfolding.

The surprise offensive launched by Marius shows an army that is at last in control of the overall strategic situation and can rely on increasingly strong local knowledge: that offensive proves the most remarkable success of the Romans (99.3)

---

17 Sall. *BJ* 7.4–7.

and a turning point in the conflict. Sallust leaves us in no doubt that Marius is to be credited with that breakthrough, and stresses that he kept the same standards of discipline and vigour even in the following hours. His priority is to keep the ranks tight, and his lieutenants play a crucial part in helping him secure that aim: Sulla is again in charge of the cavalry, on the right flank of the army, while A. Manlius takes the lead of the archers and an auxiliary cohort of Ligurians on the right. His involvement is therefore marginal from a spatial point of view, but quite central to the brief that Marius has set himself. Nothing suggests that Marius was losing confidence in his quaestor; what makes this aspect of his running of the campaign stand out, however, is his ability to behave by setting himself the highest standards, and by acting 'as if he had not set a brief to anyone' (*quasi nullo inposito*). His conduct is closely reminiscent of that of Metellus, who repeatedly shows a keen willingness to address his soldiers directly as military operations are unfolding (49.6; 51.4; 54.1) and to be closely and meticulously involved with the action (46.7; 55.5; 57.2). We are also reminded, however, of the conduct of Sulla and of his own willingness to share in the toil and labour of the soldiers. Sallust insists at some length on this aspect of Marius' leadership, and notably on his ability to build a meaningful bond with his men. No reference is made to a willingness to trade jokes with them, as was the case with Sulla, but a clear link is again established between his readiness to make considerable personal efforts and his ability to obtain obedience from them. As Sallust makes clear, far from undermining the work of his advisors and soldiers, Marius' hands-on leadership becomes a source of inspiration and confidence.

On the fringes of the formation arranged by Marius there are clusters of Numidian deserters, who are entrusted with what would be termed in modern parlance a 'high risk, high gain' task: they are spying the movements of the enemy, making the most of their superior local knowledge. Their contribution proves crucial, as it enables Marius to receive some warning before the arrival of the Numidians. Marius' reaction turns out to be the correct one, albeit somewhat fortuitously: since he is uncertain on how to rearrange the army, he decides not to move it, and that choice ends up throwing Jugurtha's plans into disarray. Hope is a central theme throughout *BJ*, and a driving force behind the actions of most of the protagonists of the conflict.[18] In this instance, Marius' inaction, caused by a lack of strategic clarity and knowledge, ends up crushing Jugurtha's hopes. The Numidian king was expecting to find a divided enemy front, and to catch at least a part of it by surprise from behind; that was not to be.

---

18 See esp. 7.2 (Micipsa); 13.5 (Jugurtha); 14.10; 23.2 (Adherbal); 24.5; 25.9 (Jugurtha); 28.1; 29.3; 33.4 (Jugurtha); 28.4 (L. Calpurnius Bestia); 31.23 (the Roman people); 33.4 (Jugurtha); 37.3 (A. Postumius Albinus); 44.1 (Metellus); 48.2; 55.1 (Jugurtha); 60.1 (the Roman soldiers); 74.1 (Jugurtha); 84.3 (the Senate); 85.4 (Marius); 87.4 (Jugurtha); 88.1 (Metellus); 105.4 (Sulla's soldiers); 107.4 (Jugurtha); 113.2 (Sulla and Jugurtha's envoy).

Sulla's contingent is the first section of the army to face the brunt of the attack. Sallust does not explain Jugurtha's choice: whether it was dictated by contingent considerations, or was deliberate, and perhaps encouraged by Sulla's alleged lack of experience. At any rate, the response of the quaestor is as swift as it is consistent with the instructions and example set by Marius. The bulk of the cavalry is told to keep its ranks tight and hold on to its position; Sulla leads a small avant-garde contingent to attack the Moors, taking a direct involvement in a daring action, and trying to keep his attack front as compact as possible (101.4: *turmatim*, 'in a squadron'). The focus of the battle then suddenly expands, with Bocchus and Jugurtha taking a direct part in the attack and expanding it with the infantry towards the rear-guard of the Romans. Marius takes on the front line, and his involvement prompts the king to attempt a trick that turns the strategy from the military to the psychological domain: he quickly moves aside, and shouts in Latin that he has just killed Marius, showing a bloodstained sword. The current expression 'fake news' springs to mind: the impact of that ruse on Sulla's men is immediate, and potentially devastating. The Roman soldiers, unable to see where their consul is, are thrown into disarray.[19] It is at this point that Sulla makes a crucial intervention: having carried out his foray successfully, he is now ready to get back into the thick of the battle, quickly repelling the attack of Bocchus and, after somewhat stauncher opposition, of Jugurtha too, whose prospects of victory had begun to look fairly realistic. Sulla's military contribution to the success of the campaign proves crucial. In the confrontation in which Numidians and Moors are launching the last resort attack on the Romans, he is the factor that tips the balance in favour of the Romans. As the battle unfolds, he gains a central position, effectively leaving Marius with the task of completing a victory that others have in fact gained on his behalf.

Even after these events, however, Sallust leaves no room for ambiguity: the victory may have been made possible by Sulla's actions, but it belongs to the consul. The war has, at any rate, come to a crucial turning point. Bocchus' swift withdrawal upon Sulla's attack was not just a move dictated by a military emergency: it was the first, tentative step of a repositioning strategy. Five days after the battle, Marius is reached by a request for talks from the Mauretanian monarch. Manlius and Sulla are entrusted with the task. Their recent victory enables them to set the agenda and disregard usual conventions. They decide to address the king before hearing his requests, effectively framing the talks on their own terms. Jugurtha's fraudulent words had nearly tipped the balance of the battle in his favour; the Roman envoys are now hoping to use the manipulative power of words to complete the progress enabled by the Roman victory, and persuade the main ally of the king to switch sides. Sallust makes clear that it will be either a matter of 'influencing' (*flectere*) or 'to fire up' (*adcendere*) the spirit of the interlocutor. Manlius is older than Sulla; however, the quaestor is entrusted with the

---

19 Bilingualism is another quality that Jugurtha and Sulla share: cf. *BJ* 95.3.

speech in which the Roman expectations and demands to Bocchus are set.[20] The reader was alerted straight away to the eloquence, *facundia*, of Sulla (95.4, and above): we are now given full demonstration of it, although the summary of Sulla's speech is introduced by the customary proviso, 'a few words to this effect' (*pauca uerba huiusce modi*). The arguments he deployed are surely a reflection of the task he was given by Marius; what must be attributed to Sulla is the subsequent handling of the negotiations.

The main brief of the speech is to set the terms of the relationship with Bocchus. With a remarkable combination of oppositions, the Moor's change of attitude is saluted as a choice for peace instead of war, and Jugurtha is unreservedly singled out as the worst of all men (*cum pessumo omnium*), with whom no accommodation is possible.[21] Bocchus' earlier conduct is constructed as a mistake (*te errantem*) for which he is expected to make amends: Rome had the chance to inflict upon him the same kind of punishment (*pariter*), and indeed that would have been a necessary if harsh development (*acerbam necessitudinem*), which Bocchus' change of attitude can now avert. The prospect of enjoying the friendship of the Roman people is still open to him, provided that he takes concrete steps. The whole speech is framed around some stark alternatives, which are set out through a potted *archaiologia* of sorts: since the beginning of the empire Rome always favoured having friends rather than slaves, and conveying orders to people who offered their consent (*uolentibus*) rather than being coerced (*coacti*); the opposition between *parentis* and *amici* is also noteworthy. A further opposition is set out in geographical terms: under normal circumstances Rome will be a distant friend, and will not interfere much, but will offer as many rewards as to those who are physically close. Lastly, a contrast is established between the extent of Bocchus' suffering at the hands of the Romans and the rewards that he can still hope to achieve if he were to prove his loyalty to Rome (102.8: *multo plura bona accepisses, quam mala perpessus es*): the 'punishments and rewards' theme that was spelled out on Sulla's gravestone (see above) finds a further, different development here. The speech opens with a reference to the gods and the role that they had in showing Bocchus the need to approach Rome; that is later changed into a reference to *fortuna*. It ends with another opposition between the *beneficia* of the Roman people and ability in war. Bocchus' brief reply is reported in indirect speech, and revolves around a brief justification for his involvement in the conflict in light of his concerns over the safety of his realm, which he had also entertained about Jugurtha in the past. The tone of his riposte, however, is favourable, and is

---

20 Chlup (2013) offers a close reading of the two conferences between Sulla and Bocchus in *BJ* and views them as reflective pieces on the parameters of Roman hegemony. See Chlup (2013) 196–199 on the first meeting. The relation he posits with Thucydides' Melian Dialogue is not compelling.
21 Cf. the fragment of a lost speech of Gaius Gracchus in which he sets up his 'excellent' brother against the 'awful' men that killed him (Charisius, *GL* 1.240 = *ORF*[4] F 16: *pessumi Tiberium fratrem meum optimum interfecerunt*).

compounded by the stated intention to gloss over any previous disagreements he might have had with Rome (*uetera omittere*). The only purpose of his reply is to seek permission to send envoys to the Roman Senate, with the explicit task of holding formal negotiations on alliance and friendship. Sulla's speech has persuaded Bocchus that there is a margin to pursue appeasement towards Rome. The permission to seek an audience with the Senate is granted on Marius's behalf. Bocchus, however, soon changes his mind on this count: Sallust blames the role of some fraudulent advisors, bribed by Jugurtha, in persuading him not to seek a formal arrangement with Rome. In giving this factual detail, Sallust refers to Bocchus as *barbarus*; he also alerts his readers that Jugurtha may have met a major military defeat, but is still in a position to follow and influence the moves of his faltering ally.

Upon his return from the talks with Bocchus, Sulla is entrusted with the oversight of the winter quarters, while Marius leads a contingent against a stronghold of Jugurtha in the desert. Tellingly, the focus of the narrative is kept on Sulla, rather than on the consul: the dealings between Sulla, Bocchus, and his envoys are regarded as the most significant aspect of the terminal phase of the war. Sulla's transition from the periphery to the core of the conflict is now complete. It is enabled, not unlike what had been the case in the previous battle, by a fortuitous turn of events. The five envoys that Bocchus had sent to Rome are attacked and robbed by some Gaetulian raiders; in fear and disarray, they seek shelter in the Roman camp, which Marius has by now left, and are received by Sulla. He makes a decision that reveals great political foresight: although he was entitled to treat them like fickle enemies (it is implied that reports of Bocchus' temporary change of heart must have reached him), he chose to attend to them with care and generosity. The consequences were far-reaching. The envoys had no direct familiarity with the Romans and had only heard reports about their greed. Sulla's generosity (*largitio*) is a complete surprise to them: they mistake it for a demonstration of friendship, and immediately revisit their preconception of the Romans. It does not come as a surprise to Sallust's readers, who (quite apart from what they know about Sulla *beyond* the Jugurthine war) have been alerted right away to his generosity and his ability to dissimulate. Sallust takes the opportunity for a brief moralising point on the place that was accorded to generosity in the distant past (103.6). The difference between actual gifts and promised ones becomes hazy. The Moors are prompted by Sulla's generosity to seek his endorsement and support in the talks with the Roman Senate that they intend to initiate; he freely promises them assistance (promises are a typical device of Jugurtha, and the reader is surely intended to take notice of that further similarity), and does indeed give them instructions on how best to address Marius and the Senate. His dexterity in the use of the spoken word finds further confirmation, and is a centrepiece of Sulla's increasingly apparent ability as a political operator.

Sulla, however, is not establishing a personal bond with the envoys: he is facilitating a political process that will continue with their visit to Marius, in which they set out their requests, and during which they are accompanied by Sulla himself.

The encounter does not just involve the consul and the quaestor; all the members of the senatorial order who are taking part in the campaign are consulted, as Metellus had also done at a similarly important time (62.3). The authorisation to the envoys to leave for Rome is granted only after some debate, in which the prevailing view (argued by Sulla and by others) is countered by some who are in favour of a harsher treatment. When the group of envoys breaks up, and two of them return to Bocchus, they report back on Sulla's conduct in the warmest terms.[22] That, in turn, elicits a further political development. When the Senate makes clear that the friendship and alliance of the Romans will not come Bocchus' way unless he acquires further merits towards them, he immediately asks Marius to let him have a further, direct contact with Sulla.

Bocchus regards the quaestor as a fair broker (105.1: *cuius arbitratu communibus negotiis consuleretur*), but the overall context remains one of considerable tension and lingering mistrust. Sulla turns up for the talks with Bocchus with a robust military contingent. Sallust does not explain that remarkable display of military might: it was surely intended to avoid bad surprises had the talks taken an unfavourable turn, but might have also been done with a view to a forthcoming action against Jugurtha. Still, when the son of Bocchus, Volux, comes towards the Romans with a contingent of about a thousand knights, the prevailing sense among Sulla's men is at first one of fear (105.3: *hostilem metum*), and that feeling affects Sulla too. Only shortly afterwards does hope set in, this time with a firmly positive connotation: the Romans are quite aware that they defeated the Moors before. As Volux and his men approach, the tension gradually subsides: first the spies report that they are not in an attacking mode, then Volux declares that his only intention is to escort the Romans on the final leg of their march towards Bocchus' camp. On the following day, though, a further twist intervenes. Volux gathers that Jugurtha is approaching, and shares his fears with Sulla, inviting him to take flight.

Sulla's response reveals a resolve and a clarity of thinking that Sallust has not quite credited him with before: it is at this stage of the narrative that he firmly emerges as a lucid, capable, and independent military leader. The prospect of an escape is firmly ruled out, not least in light of the previous successes against Jugurtha; a flight would have amounted to a betrayal towards his men. Sulla firmly restates his loyalty to his soldiers, and further adds a surprising comment on the possibility of him meeting a premature death by disease: saving his life through a treacherous act would have made no sense (106.3). This remark is surely best read as a general comment on the vulnerability of the human condition, rather than as an oblique reference to a long-standing illness of Sulla.

Notwithstanding these emphatic claims, Sulla shows some willingness to readjust his strategy in light of the intelligence he has received. While escape is not an option,

---

22 Cf. *benignitatem et studium Sullae* at 104.5, echoing *milites*.

complicating Jugurtha's pursuit is, and Sulla gets the army to move and march overnight, whilst misleading the enemy by lighting up torches at the camp. This move, however, does not pay off. At dawn, when Sulla stops the army and starts drawing up a new camp, news comes that Jugurtha is about two miles away. For the second time within a few hours, Sulla shows considerable composure: while some of his soldiers accuse Volux of having betrayed them and urge punishment on him, Sulla orders that Volux not be harmed and urges the soldiers to conduct themselves bravely. Unlike on other occasions, Sulla does not dissimulate his emotions: he bases his actions on a cold assessment of the needs of the war and on the need not to precipitate matters (107.1). It is also based on the unspoken assumption that someone who had been fighting as an ally of the Roman people should not be harmed. As ever in these matters, religious considerations are also at play. Relations with foreign parties – not just with friends and allies – impinge on the dealings between the city and the gods. Invoking Jupiter as a witness when a counterpart was failing to meet the terms of an agreement or a request laid at its door by Rome was a central feature of fetial law. The call to the god could be issued by a magistrate, and not just by a priest. It would usually precede the outbreak of an armed conflict, or even the beginning of a phase that will lead to conflict: in this case Sulla invokes Jupiter to witness the devious and hostile behaviour of Volux in order to justify his imminent expulsion from the Roman camp. Sallust does not suggest that this was for show. The impact of the invocation, however, is immediate, and one wonders if the decision not to kill the prince was part of a ploy to establish his actual intentions. The point is left for the reader to establish. Volux, for whom rekindling ties with Jugurtha is clearly not an option, begs (*orare*) Sulla not to expel him, and squarely puts the blame on Jugurtha's ability to trace their movements: the familiar notions of 'cunning' (*dolum*) and 'craftiness' (*calliditas*), which have already been applied to the king, are now evoked by the son of his key ally (107.4). That bond, in fact, is formally not severed. Jugurtha's prospects still hinge heavily on Bocchus' support. Volux, therefore, proposes to disprove his duplicity to Sulla by exploiting his loyalty to Jugurtha: his bet is that he will be able to march through the camp without being harmed. The gamble appears sustainable to Sulla. The narrative is heavily compressed: Jugurtha is surprised by the arrival of the Roman and the Moor, and fails to mount a suitable response. It is unclear what caused Jugurtha's astonishment, since nothing suggests that his camp was not quite set. The very openness of the march of Volux and Sulla – an ally and an enemy proceeding together – seems to throw Jugurtha into disarray.[23]

---

23 Paul (1984) 252–253 suggests that this section of *BJ* heavily relies on Sulla's autobiography and notes that it does not provide a satisfactory explanation for the conduct of Sulla and Volux: emphasis on divine favour may have been central to Sulla's account of the episode. It is debatable whether the perceived deficiencies of Sallust's account should be explained by the possible flaws of his source material.

Jugurtha, as Sallust makes clear, is not in a position to mount a military response to Sulla's movements at this stage of the campaign, but is still prepared to pursue other options. We have already seen the impact of corrupt advisors of Bocchus that Jugurtha has effectively bribed. He now takes another step by sending Aspar, a mutual friend of Bocchus and himself, to keep his ally's actions under check. At any rate, the circle of Bocchus' advisers, as Sallust has already made clear (102.15; 103.2), is far from compact: some unnamed friends had persuaded him to pursue a direct contact with Rome, and the most influential pro-Roman advisor is now Dabar, who is significantly a descendant of Masinissa, a long-time ally of the Romans. Bocchus chooses him as chief intermediary with Sulla, and uses him to convey the request of a meeting to be kept secret from the envoy of Jugurtha. The situation, however, is immediately problematized further: Sallust cites a version of unspecified origin in which Bocchus made the same offers to the Numidians and the Romans alike: in his view, that was not a strategy of dissimulation driven by a clear commitment to the cause of Rome, but the symptom of a combination of indecisiveness and disloyalty.[24] His African background is, in Sallust's view, a factor of irrepressible strength: that is where Bocchus' instincts, his *lubido*, would have taken him. The prevailing consideration was not a political consideration either: it was fear.

Sulla shows the same willingness to wait for the opportune moment, and not to probe the motives of his interlocutors too hard, that he showed in dealing with Volux. He also confirms his proclivity to dissimulation, and his ability to manipulate his interlocutor in contexts where fraud is necessary. He does not just accept Bocchus' offer, but instructs him on how to respond to the address that he will make to him in the presence of Jugurtha's envoy. On Sulla's instigation Bocchus pledges to give him a firm response to his demands within ten days, only to summon him to a secret meeting shortly afterwards. Bocchus' *Punica fides* has been stressed; the whole development of the events puts the framework of *fides* under strain, with the decisive conference taking place at night and at a secret location (*occulte*). Yet, the conversation requires a framework of trust to bring the two men close to one another: they require interpreters, and of the trustworthy kind (*fidi*), and resort to the political mediation of their mutual friend Dabar, for whom Sallust has remarkably favourable words (*sanctus uir*).

The speeches exchanged by the two protagonists are then reported, in a format that mirrors chiastically the account of the previous conversation between Bocchus and Sulla: the king's address is reported in direct speech, while Sulla's response is summarised in *oratio obliqua*.[25] Bocchus frames his statement around his personal

---

24 *BJ* 108.3: *magis Punica fide quam ob ea, quae praedicabat*. Cf. 107.3: *ut sceleris atque perfidiae Bocchi testis adesset*.
25 Sall. *BJ* 110–111; cf. 102. See Chlup (2013) 199–202; cf. the sobering comment of Dijkstra/Parker (2007) 158: 'no-one really knew what Bocchus and Sulla had said to each other in that final interview'.

loyalty to Sulla and the proofs of the friendship that he is keen to offer. Although Sulla had publicly stated that he was coming on behalf of the consul, Bocchus presents his willingness to serve the interests of the *res publica* as an afterthought, and he pointedly opens his speech by referring to him as a private individual, effectively removing the fact that Sulla is the representative of a foreign power. He offers to withdraw beyond the Moluccha river, and compounds that offer with an expression of his willingness to satisfy whatever other requests 'worthy of him and of them' (*meque uobisque dignum*) that the Romans might make. That is a shrewd role-assignment strategy, to use the terms that Ma deploys in his discussion of the dealings between Antiochus III and the Greek cities of Asia Minor: drawing attention to the moral standards of the Romans is a way to restrain their behaviour within acceptable bounds.[26]

Sulla's response is measured and brief, in clear opposition to a speech that is as flattering as it is politically insidious. It is also opened by a point that Bocchus has deliberately overlooked: he has been defeated, and his withdrawal is not a favour he is offering to the Romans, but the logical response to recent military developments. He then reminds Bocchus (cf. 104.5) of the difference between the non-belligerence of the Romans and their friendship, which may in turn lead to the drafting of a treaty and the eventual conquest of a portion of Numidia. In order to secure the latter, Bocchus will have to perform a service that will enable the Romans to achieve something they have not yet attained. That deed is explicitly identified as the capture of Jugurtha and his rendition to the Romans.

Bocchus' initial response is firmly hostile: an array of legal and political arguments is invoked. Predictably enough, *fides* is again at the forefront. The surrender of the king would bring the betrayal of Bocchus into the open and undermine his standing among his fellow-countrymen, who tend to side with Jugurtha, rather than with Rome – this isolated comment does not clarify what impact (if any) that attitude had on the development of the conflict (111.2). Sulla, however, labours the point further, and his case is apparently echoed by others (possibly Dabar? See 111.3: *denique saepius fatigatus lenitur*, 'in the end, he was prevailed upon more often'). Bocchus has a change of heart, but his reasons are not explained. The crucial moment in the campaign – Bocchus' decision to betray Jugurtha – is not made clear: the reader is only told that it is taking place within a secret conference. Fatigue is invoked as a factor behind Bocchus' choice. Agency, however, is firmly with Sulla: the only point on which Sallust is unequivocal is that his will is prevailing, and that Bocchus is acting 'in accordance with Sulla's wishes' (*ex uoluntate Sullae*). The transition of the quaestor from the fringes to the very core of the conflict is now complete. As we shall see, the shift is not irreversible.

---

26 Ma (1999) 214.

The upshot of Bocchus' agreement to Sulla's request is further dissimulation: Jugurtha will be misled into thinking that peace with Rome is forthcoming. Sallust is unambiguous about the fraudulent nature of this arrangement: the ablative absolute *composito dolo* ('having perfected the fraud') makes clear that Jugurtha is being harmed with the very device to which he has often resorted, fraud, and that its use is the outcome of a premeditated measure involving both Sulla and Bocchus, who both know his weakness and his appetite for peace: the use of the adjective *auidissimus* ('most greedy') is significant, and no doubt ironic, as it refers to someone who has ruthlessly used his wealth in establishing his political and strategic position.

The ruse is then carried out swiftly. Any suspicion of dealings between Bocchus and Sulla is removed by the claim that the prospect of peace has been mooted by Sulla via Dabar, effectively denying that direct conversations have taken place. Jugurtha's response is inherently contradictory: he expresses a willingness to comply with Roman 'orders' (*omnia quae imperarentur facere*), while setting a further condition to Bocchus. He asks him to summon a conference involving Sulla and himself, with a view to taking Sulla hostage and using him as a bargaining chip with the Senate.[27] Quite apart from that fraudulent aim, there is a political reasoning behind this option: Jugurtha does not trust the ability of individual Roman magistrates to conclude an agreement that will prove lasting, and intends to negotiate a treaty directly with the Senate and the people. We are now at a stage of the conflict in which establishing the difference between truth and make-believe is increasingly hard. It is doubtful that Jugurtha felt that Rome would be willing to negotiate a settlement under duress.

Sallust acknowledges the difficulty in establishing the motives of the characters at this point in the narrative. He has been distinctly non-committal about Bocchus, and restates the point in his account of his reaction to Jugurtha's offer (113.1–4). Ostensibly, Bocchus is following through with the plan he agreed with Sulla, keeping communications with Jugurtha open whilst restating his loyalty to Rome. However, Sallust adds a further level of factual information: the night before the encounter with Sulla and Jugurtha, Bocchus summoned his closest friends, but ordered them to leave before actually meeting them. The event proves nothing in itself, nor does the troubled look that the dynast allegedly had. *Dicitur* has a twofold effect: it introduces an element of distance between Sallust and his subject matter, and at the same time conveys the image of an author that is close to his evidence, and has been gathering information even about events on which someone can reasonably claim to have any knowledge. Bocchus' hesitation is exploited as a symptom of his potential disloyalty, and is of course also turned into a formidable narrative tool in the final section of the monograph. The literary motif whereby the intentions of kings are by definition hard to sound out is also evoked, and Bocchus'

---

[27] Cf. the comments of Dijkstra/Parker (2007) 138 on the dubious value of this strategy.

silence (113.3: *tacente ipso occulta pectoris patefacisse*, 'despite his silence, the secrets of his heart were revealed') marks a clear contrast with the previous phase of the war in which the spoken word has played a major role. His decision to summon Sulla for a final conversation the night before the conference is therefore presented as the moment in which Bocchus makes his final choice, rather than a conversation in which the plans for the bold operation of the following day are gone through.

This narrative framework has a further implication, which also serves as a conclusion to the present discussion. The agency of Sulla, which has become increasingly prominent and focused in the preceding chapters and has reached its peak when Bocchus was first persuaded to deliver Jugurtha (111.4), has now faded away. The capture of the king is carried out by Bocchus: the crucial step is his movement towards Jugurtha, under the false pretence of paying homage, which takes the king to a spot where he will be easily visible to those who are about to capture him. The combination of silence and hiding, which has already played a central role in the depiction of Bocchus (cf. above, 113.3), is now given further significance. The war is solved by the intervention of armed men who are hiding in silence at a concealed location, and succeed in overpowering a king that had turned up unarmed for peace talks. Sulla is at the scene (113.5), but the subject of the action is Bocchus. The crucial step – the sign that is given to prompt the capturers into action – is not attributed to anyone. The capture of the king does not have a designated perpetrator: we are not told who laid hands on him, whether Moor or Roman. Sulla receives his final mention as Jugurtha is being delivered to him in chains (*uinctus*); he then carries out his duty to carry him to Marius.

There is no place for Sulla in the final chapter of the monograph: the focus is back on Marius and on the threat presented to Italy by the Cimbri and the Teutons, which leads to his re-election to the consulship and to a new imminent campaign. The fragmentary nature of the monograph is further confirmed, most emphatically by the final reference to the hopes and resources of the city (114.5: *spes atque opes ciuitatis*), eerily pointing to the crushing disappointments that Marius will have in store for his fellow-citizens. However, a brief, implicit reference to Sulla's achievement is perhaps to be seen in the restatement that Jugurtha was led to Rome in chains, *uinctus*. He had been put in chains under Sulla's watch, as is made clear at 113.6, and the depiction of Jugurtha in chains would soon afterwards make its way into the thick of political competition and rival claims over military distinction in Late Republican Rome. Sulla used it on his signet ring, much to Marius' unspoken dismay.[28] More controversially, it featured prominently in the monument that Bocchus put up for Sulla in Rome in the 90s, causing an open rift between Marius and his former quaestor. The significance of that monument to Sulla's self-

---

28 Plut. *Mar.* 10.5–6; *Sull.* 3.4–4.1.

representation, and indeed to his enduring memory in the years immediately following his death, is powerfully displayed in the *denarius* struck by his son Faustus Sulla in 56 B.C. (*RRC* 426/1), where the monument is reproduced.[29] That association will have hardly escaped Sallust's readers: Sulla may have behaved impeccably towards Marius during the campaign, but the consequences of his signal achievement in Numidia for the later development of his career and the destructive dynamics of political competition in Rome are made to loom large on the horizon through that visual association. The impending catastrophe of the civil wars of the 80s is there to be foreseen in the closing lines of *BJ*. We are not meant to miss it.[30]

---

29 Plut. *Sull.* 6.1–2. For a recent discussion see Assenmaker (2014) 131–134 and Stein-Hölkeskamp (2015) 224–226, where the identification of the Sant'Omobono reliefs with the Bocchus monument is still propounded. Giardina (2012) 338–343 and Kuttner (2013) 248–272 have independently brought compelling arguments against that view; for a 2nd-century B.C. dating of the reliefs see also Meyer (1991/1992) 19–22.
30 This piece stems from a collaborative commentary project that I am currently pursuing with my colleague Jaap Wisse, and I am very grateful to him for extensive discussion and invaluable advice on things Sallustian; he should of course not be held to be responsible for any of the views put forward here. I should also like to thank the audience at the Dublin panel for their reactions to aspects of my argument, and Alexander Thein for his comments on an early draft.

J. Alison Rosenblitt
7 Sulla's Long Shadow: Sallust in Tacitus and Tacitus in Sallust

Tacitus was, and will always remain, Sallust's greatest reader. Moreover, Tacitus – unlike us – had access to the complete text of Sallust's *Historiae*.[1] There can be no doubt that Sallust's *Historiae* inform Tacitus' *Annales*. When Syme looked at Tacitus' relationship to Sallust, he knew that the *Historiae* were 'incomparably richer than the monographs'.[2] But the fragmentary state of Sallust's *magnum opus* renders the relationship between Tacitus and Sallust's *Historiae* far harder to unpick than the various relationships between Tacitus' texts and Sallust's monographs. In spite of the copious scholarship on Sallust and Tacitus, there is (relatively speaking) only limited discussion of Tacitus' reception of Sallust's *Historiae*.[3]

Looking at Tacitus' *Annales* and Sallust's *Historiae* raises broader questions about reception theory and related approaches to intertextuality in ancient literature. In his classic study of intertextuality, Hinds distinguishes between attempts to observe 'local contact' and 'systematic contact' between texts. In the latter case, studies 'have tended to be unidirectional'. 'Either the *incorporating* text is read systematically, with the incorporated text fragmented into discrete events "alluded to", or the *incorporated* text is read systematically, with the incorporating text fragmented into discrete acts of allusive gesturing' (Hinds'

---

[1] For clarity: except where otherwise specified, all references to the *Historiae* are references to the work of Sallust (not to Tacitus' *Historiae*). Text of the *Historiae*: Ramsey (2015), an excellent new Loeb edition and translation which should now supersede Maurenbrecher (1891), Reynolds' *Oxford Classical Texts* edition, and the fragment numbering of McGushin (1992/1994); text of Tacitus' *Annales*: Heubner (1983), Teubner edition. Translations are my own.

[2] Syme (1958) 353; see further 196–199, 340–342, 353–356, 728–732. Syme draws out in particular the influence on the *Annales* of the geographical and ethnographical material of Sallust's *Historiae* (353–354).

[3] For some points of interaction specifically with Sallust's *Historiae*, see Heraeus (1905). In general, for Tacitus' relationship to Sallust, Ducroux (1978) 295 n. 12 presents a useful bibliography. To Ducroux's list, add Furneaux (1896) 72–73; Martin (1969) 125–131, 134–141; Cugusi (1974) 39–74; and more recent bibliography: Ginsburg (1986); Woodman (1988) 164–168, 180; (1992a); Epstein (1992); O'Gorman (1995); Ash (1997); Woodman (1998), with new material at 231–236 as well as reprinted papers, esp. 'History and Alternative Histories', 104–141; Parker (2008); Oakley (2009); Ash (2010); Keitel (2010) 351; Krebs (2012) (esp. 341, on the speech of Lepidus in Sallust's *Historiae*); Low (2013) esp. 129–180; Master (2014); Spielberg (2017). The most famous allusions to Sallust in Tacitus' *Annales* are probably the allusions made in Tacitus' preface. See Woodman (1988) 167–168 and (1992a) and the evocation of Catiline in Tacitus' portrait of Sejanus, on which see Martin (1969) 135–136; (1981) 106–107; Cugusi (1974) 66–67; Ducroux (1978) 303; Keitel (1984) 322–323; Pelling (2013) 7; Low (2013) esp. 131–132, 154–155, 166–180.

emphasis).⁴ The difficulties in keeping sight of both texts, evoked and evoking, may arise from the fragmentary survival of texts, from the differing prestige of the texts, or indeed – as particularly interests Hinds – from the inevitability of the reader taking a fixed position as required by the act of reading and interpreting.⁵ In this case, we can approach the third of these difficulties by varying our positions as readers; it is the first difficulty to which we return. When looking at the fragmentary *Historiae*, it is a considerable challenge to keep both the evoked *Historiae* and the evoking *Annales* equally in view or to construct a holistic sense of the relationship between these texts.

The problems might seem intractable; but that, I think, is pessimistic. If we are willing to use Tacitus as a reader of Sallust in order to read Sallust ourselves, we can find a Tacitean reading of Sallust's *Historiae* through Sallust's presence in Tacitus' *Annales*.⁶ Such an approach builds on a renewed confidence and intellectual flexibility shown recently in approaching other challenging aspects of Tacitean intertextuality – for example, Levene's study of Tacitus' allusive engagement with the Augustan author Pompeius Trogus, where the particular challenge originates in the circumstance of Trogus' survival only in later (post-Tacitean) epitome.⁷ My approach also builds on recent work on Sallust's *Historiae* and on a growing willingness to venture bolder thematic studies of the *Historiae* in spite of its fragmentary state of survival.⁸

One of the principal thrusts of my own work on Sallust's *Historiae* concerns his presentation of a 'hostile politics', whereby the Roman people and the powerful few (*pauci*) are constructed as foreign enemies of each other (*hostes*). The people have been conquered, enslaved, and despoiled; the only remaining form of effective political action is, therefore, to achieve their political will by inflicting fear.⁹ To readers of Tacitus elements of this must sound familiar. In classic works of scholarship,

---

4 Hinds (1998) 100–104 (quotes at 101). There is a vast further scholarship on intertextuality in classical studies. To focus on intertextuality in historiographical writing, see Woodman (1979) 148–149; O'Gorman (2006); (2009); Levene (2010); Marincola (2010); Damon (2010a); Shannon (2011) 276–279; Pelling (2013).
5 Drawing on Hinds, the second of these reasons is particularly well phrased by Wray (2001) 48: 'So, for example, until recently, in critical accounts of the intertextual presence of Apollonius' *Argonautica* in the *Aeneid*, the prestige of the (central) Virgilian text in large measure overpowered the (extracanonical) Apollonian intertext, disintegrating it into fragments placed in *Aeneid* commentaries'.
6 Hands (1959) 58–59, on *dissimulatio*, offers a kind of precedent for using Tacitus as a reader of Sallust in order to clarify Sallust.
7 Levene (2010).
8 To avoid swelling the list of works cited, I refer the reader to the extensive bibliographies on Sallust's *Historiae* in Rosenblitt (2011); (2013); (2016); (2019).
9 Rosenblitt (2016) and (2019); and, in my own mind, I always intended Rosenblitt (2011), on the specious *devotio* of Sallust's Cotta, as a step towards these ideas, as I aim to make more clear below.

Keitel and Woodman explored Tacitus' use of a recognisable imagery taken from the *topos* of the *urbs capta*, the captured city, and his use of the language of siege and warfare to characterise the political relationship between a series of *principes* and the city under their rule and care.[10] 'Through graphic descriptions and similes', Keitel observes, 'the historian implied that the princeps was waging a kind of war in peacetime against his own people'.[11] Keitel traced this imagery back to the political discourse of the Late Republic and to the idea of *stasis* in Sallust and Thucydides, and she argued that Tacitus' *urbs capta* motif serves to undercut the notion of the *pax Augusta*, implying instead a continuity between the civil wars of the 40s and 30s which brought Augustus to power and the subsequent functioning of the principate. While Keitel emphasises the *urbs capta* motif and the continuity with the civil wars of the 40s-30s, I wish to focus on the transfer of a language of warfare onto civic politics as a discourse arising in the 70s, in direct response to the civil wars of the 80s and to the impact of the Sullan dictatorship on Roman political culture. It was, after all, Sulla's explicit position after the civil war that the confiscated goods of Roman citizens were sold as his war booty (*spolia, praeda*).[12] It was a transgressive language which left its mark on our sources. However, it may be of even greater significance that in the 80s, probably for the first time in Roman history, political enemies were dealt with via an official declaration that certain named individuals were to be considered as *hostes*. This action was taken in 88, repeated in 87, and then recurred at further times of civic struggle. Scholars generally refer to this political innovation as the *hostis* decree, although to be exact there may have been some variability as to whether it was enacted as a senatorial decree or as a *lex* passed by the people.[13] A political rhetoric in which the enemy are figured as *hostes* can be understood as a direct response to the shocking new political occurrence in which exactly this understanding of political conflict was enacted via the *hostis* decree. I say more below in section two about the Sullan context for this shift in political language.

In this chapter, I start with Tacitus' text and argue that Tacitus' account of the mutinies on the northern frontier evokes Sallust's presentation of urban populist rhetoric. I will then offer a few observations about Sallust's presence in Tacitus – the easier job. However, bearing in mind the challenge of keeping evoked and evoking text equally in view, section two comments in the other direction, examining

---

10 Keitel (1984); Woodman (1988) 180–190; cf. (1992b); Sailor (2008) 190–191, 205–218, esp. 209–210; Low (2013).
11 Keitel (1984) 306.
12 Cic. *Off.* 2.27; *Verr.* 2.3.81; *Leg. agr.* 2.56; Plut. *Crass.* 2.3; *Comp. Lys. Sull.* 3.3; see also Thein (2016).
13 Generally: Lintott (1999) ²[1968] 155; Allély (2007); Appel (2013). *SC* or *lex* in 88 B.C.: Lintott (1999) ²[1968] 155; Allély (2007) 177–182; Appel (2013) 30–31. *SC* or *lex* in 87 B.C.: Morstein-Marx (2011) 265 n. 30, 266 n. 33.

what Tacitus' *Annales* might suggest about Sallust's *Historiae* and, specifically, about the way in which Sallust's *Historiae* understood and represented Sulla's effect on the *res publica*. By looking at Tacitus' intertextual engagement with Sallust in his narrative of the mutinies, and by appreciating the significance of this engagement in establishing the thematic structure of the *Annales* and its relationship to Republican history, it becomes possible to venture wider comments on the structural and thematic relationship between the *Annales* and the *Historiae*. This relationship offers a chance to use the Tacitean imagery of *urbs capta* to understand better how the rhetoric of hostile politics, which can be observed in Sallust's set speeches and traced in fragments of his narrative, may have functioned in Sallust's *Historiae* as comment on Sulla and his legacy.

Sallust in Tacitus

In A.D. 14, news of the death of Augustus and the accession of Tiberius triggered mutiny in the Pannonian and German armies. In Book 1 of the *Annales*, immediately after he relates the events of Tiberius' accession, Tacitus turns from Rome to the narrative of these mutinies on the northern frontier. Troublemaker in chief among the Pannonian legions is Percennius, the theatre claqueur turned *gregarius miles* (that is, a common soldier, 1.16.3). His subversive nocturnal conferences culminate in an open and rabble-rousing set speech, in indirect construction, of moderate length.[14]

> At last, when the men were prepared and some were aiding the sedition, as if holding a proper assembly, he began to probe why in the manner of slaves they would obey a few centurions, fewer tribunes. When would they dare to demand remedies, if they would not approach a new and still stumbling princeps either with prayers or with arms? It was enough to have erred through cowardice for so many years, that they each bore thirty or forty seasons, old men – and most of them at that with bodies mutilated from wounds. Nor indeed when they were demobbed was there any end to military life, but rather, retained under the colours, they ever bore the same tasks under a different title. And those who survived so many misfortunes were scattered to distant lands where they received, under the name of fields, wet expanses of swamp or the inhospitable terrain of mountains. Indeed it was a harsh, profitless service: breath and body were valued at ten asses a day. Demit from that clothes, arms, tents, and the buying off of the savagery of centurions and the price of exemptions from duty. By god, lashes and wounds, the hard winter, exhausting summers, savage war or sterile peace were endless. Nor would relief come unless military service was entered into upon fixed laws: that they would earn a denarius a day, that the sixteenth year of campaigning would bring an end, nor

---

14 On Tacitus' liking for *oratio obliqua*, see Miller (1964) 293. The distinction between direct and indirect speech may be predominantly literary or relevant to the characterisation of speakers. It may establish different tones or emphasis: see, e.g., Ginsburg (1986) 536–538. It may affect the level of authorial intrusion into the speech (e.g., with reference to Segestes and Arminius: see Pagán (2000) 360–361). The differences do not affect the argument presented here and I treat as 'speech' both *oratio recta* and *oratio obliqua*. More generally, see Marincola (2010); Laird (1999); van den Berg (2012).

would they be held back further under the colours; they would receive in camp itself the reward of decommissioning paid in money. Or did the praetorian cohorts who received two denarii a day, who were restored to their own hearths after sixteen years, face more danger? It was not for them to disparage the duties of urban guard: nonetheless, posted among frightful peoples, they themselves spy the enemy from their tents.[15]

I suggest that this speech, which is delivered 'as if holding a proper assembly' (*velut contionabundus*, 1.17.1), evokes Sallust's urban, Republican world of contional oratory and would-be popular champions. And in particular, I will suggest that it has a relationship with Sallust's speech of C. Licinius Macer, from his *Historiae*.

Percennius begins with the question, 'why in the manner of slaves they would obey a few centurions, fewer tribunes' (1.17.1). This aggressive opening distils the essence of the Sallustian popular complaint: the slavery of people to *pauci*.[16] Tacitus' rhetorically ascending *paucis centurionibus, paucioribus tribunis* foregrounds *pauci* in a way which draws attention to a term strongly associated with Sallust, both in Sallust's own voice and in the voice of his would-be popular champions, in reference to those limited few who hold real power.[17] Thus Percennius' first words summon a rhetoric which a reader might associate with Sallust. But the speech of Sallust's Macer is particularly relevant. The whole economy of Macer's speech is directed towards the argument that the enslaved plebs must regain their freedom by ceasing to obey voluntarily the despotic orders of magistrates. Sallust's Macer urges the plebs to exert pressure on the powerful few by refusing military

---

15 Tac. *Ann*. 1.17.1–6: *postremo promptis iam et aliis seditionis ministris velut contionabundus interrogabat, cur paucis centurionibus, paucioribus tribunis in modum servorum oboedirent. Quando ausuros exposcere remedia, nisi novum et nutantem adhuc principem precibus vel armis adirent? Satis per tot annos ignavia peccatum, quod tricena aut quadragena stipendia senes et plerique truncato ex vulneribus corpore tolerent. Ne dimissis quidem finem esse militiae, sed apud vexillum tendentes alio vocabulo eosdem labores perferre. Ac si quis tot casus vita superaverit, trahi adhuc diversas in terras, ubi per nomen agrorum uligines paludum vel inculta montium accipiant. Enimvero militiam ipsam gravem, infructuosam: denis in diem assibus animam et corpus aestimari: hinc vestem arma tentoria, hinc saevitiam centurionum et vacationes munerum redimi. At hercule verbera et vulnera, duram hiemem, exercitas aestates, bellum atrox aut sterilem pacem sempiterna. Nec aliud levamentum quam si certis sub legibus militia iniretur: ut singulos denarios mererent, sextus decimus stipendii annus finem adferret, ne ultra sub vexillis tenerentur, sed isdem in castris praemium pecunia solveretur. An praetorias cohortes, quae binos denarios acceperint, quae post sedecim annos penatibus suis reddantur, plus periculorum suscipere? Non obtrectari a se urbanas excubias: sibi tamen apud horridas gentis e contuberniis hostem aspici.*
16 Complaints voiced by the tribune Memmius (*Iug*. 31.11, 20, 22) and in the *Historiae* by Lepidus (1.49R), §§2, 6, 10–11 and by Macer (3.15R) throughout his speech, esp. at §§1, 6, 9, 11, 13, 15–17. In Sallust's first monograph, this theme is twisted by Catiline in a speech which generally parodies popular tropes (*Cat*. 20.17): see La Penna (1959) 151–152.
17 On Sallust's terminology, see esp. Syme (1964) 17–19.

service. It lies in their own hands to execute or refuse the commands of magistrates, and what purpose is there, he asks, in undergoing danger when there is no share of the rewards? Percennius' speech follows a very similar logic, urging that the soldiers cease to enact their own servitude by voluntarily obeying their officers. Like Macer, Percennius then proceeds to outline the miserable and abused state of his audience. And like Macer, Percennius concludes by asking why they should continue to obey when they face the dangers of battle without reaping their fair share of the rewards.

Percennius and Macer both implore and incite their audience as men who are cruelly exploited and themselves permit that situation to continue: it is only their listeners' continued obedience to orders which makes the exploitation tenable.[18] Both speakers construct their audience as slaves who obey just a few powerful men; and those men mislead and deceive. Such deception is accomplished in part, say both, by manipulation and misuse of language. Percennius protests that old men retained in reserve service are made to perform 'the same tasks under a different title': *alio vocabulo eosdem labores* (1.17.3). Veterans receive worthless land, 'under the name of fields, wet expanses of swamp or the inhospitable terrain of mountains': *per nomen agrorum uligines paludum vel inculta montium* (1.17.3). Here Percennius incorporates into his complaints the notion of the misuse of language in the service of political deceit which Sallust inherited from Thucydides' famous description of *stasis*. In Sallust's corpus, ideas of language misused are voiced both by Cato in the *Bellum Catilinae* and by Macer in the *Historiae*. Cato chastises his audience with the observation: *Iam pridem equidem nos vera vocabula rerum amisimus* ('Indeed we have long since lost the true names of things', *Cat.* 52.11) and Macer pleads: *Quod ego vos moneo quaesoque ut animadvortatis neu nomina rerum ad ignaviam mutantes otium pro servitio adpelletis* ('Of this I warn you and I beseech you to take care lest, changing the names of things to suit slothfulness, you call leisure what is slavery', 3.15R, §13).[19] Cato's formulation is more famous for the modern reader, but there is no reason that Macer's should not have been equally prominent for ancient readers.

To pause and clarify: I am suggesting that Percennius' speech has both a broad relationship with Sallust's corpus, and a close, more particular relationship with the speech of Macer. On that first point – the relationship more generally with Sallust's

---

18 On the construction of authority and oratorical *personae*, including the pose of the orator who reveals truths to his audience, see Burnand (2000).
19 For distortion of language, see also Sall. *Hist.* 1.12R; *Cat.* 38, 52.11. Sallust's formulation of this Thucydidean idea had considerable impact on Tacitus. Fletcher (1945) 46 detects an allusion to Macer's words at *Ann.* 3.34.4: *Frustra nostram ignaviam alia ad vocabula transferri*. Ducroux (1978) 306–309, 314 provides further examples and discussion of Tacitus' interaction with Sallustian ideas about the corruption of language; see now also Spielberg (2017).

corpus – I have already noted that the complaint about *pauci*, the few, evokes an idea which would be associated with Sallust's ideas (Macer being one among those who draw on it) and that the misuse of language is a Sallustian motif which appears in Sallust's authorial voice, in the voice of Sallust's Cato, and in the voice of Sallust's Macer. To add to these points, a connection can also be found between Percennius' speech and the Sallustian speech of M. Aemilius Lepidus, which is the first set speech of Sallust's *Historiae*. Goodyear, in his commentary on the *Annales*, tentatively suggested that Percennius' complaint of poor land for the veterans at discharge – swamps and mountainous terrain – might recall the description by Sallust's Lepidus of the poor rewards assigned to Sulla's veterans, 'dismissed to swamps and woodlands' (*relegati in paludes et silvas*, 1.49R, §23).[20] Goodyear suggested this connection cautiously because on this particular point Tacitus' phrasing is not especially close in language to Sallust's phrasing. It was the similar substance of complaint, and not any verbal echo, that triggered the connection for Goodyear. Indeed, taken on its own, the connection would seem a little stretched. However, it affects the reader differently in the wider context, which I have been proposing, of the dense relationship of Percennius' speech to Sallust's work. For the well-read ancient reader, Sallust is heavily present in this speech, and such a reader is far more likely to think of Lepidus' complaint when reading Percennius' complaint, given how strongly Sallust has been signalled at this point in the text.

I have paused over this broader relationship between Tacitus' Percennius and Sallust's corpus because I am not suggesting that Tacitus aims to draw sharp limits in his evocation of Sallust; I am not suggesting that the textual relationship is exclusive to the speech of Macer. I only suggest that there is a particularly strong and dense relationship with Macer's speech – one which is sustained, moreover, by a light, verbal echo which draws attention to Macer. Percennius complains about the legionaries' miserable pay: *Enimvero militiam ipsam gravem, infructuosam: denis in diem assibus animam et corpus aestimari* ('Indeed it is itself a harsh, profitless service: breath and body are valued at ten asses a day', *Ann.* 1.17.4). Here is an echo of Macer's description of the corn dole: *Nisi forte repentina ista frumentaria lege munia vostra pensantur; qua tamen quinis modiis libertatem omnium aestumavere* ('unless perhaps your services are recompensed by that hasty corn law; by this they have valued the liberty of all at five *modii*', §19).[21] As Ducroux has remarked, Tacitus

---

20 Goodyear (1972) 1.203 n. 1. He concludes: 'The similarity is not close enough to prove T. is here influenced by Sallust'. He does suggest, however, that Tacitus' *luxum et otium cupere, disciplinam et laborem aspernari* (1.16.2) holds 'a remote echo of Sallust's explanation of the decadence of Rome ... ' (1972) 199 and Malloch (2004) 202 also sees a Sallustian *otium* at work in *Ann.* 1.16. On Sallust's *paludes et silvae*, cf. Keaveney in this volume.
21 In these turns of phrase, the idea, word order, ablative of price, and choice of *aestimo* / *aestumo* are identical. The appearance of *anima et corpus* (Tacitus) and *libertas* (Sallust) in the accusative reflects different grammatical constructions, since one is the subject of a passive infinitive in indirect speech

often uses such verbal echoes to cue the reader in to a broader dialogue between his own text and an evoked text.[22] (And, of course, other ancient writers also used that strategy of verbal echo to signal a deeper relationship.) For the reader sufficiently versed in Sallust to summon the exact original to mind, it may seem a sign of Imperial times that Percennius substitutes the struggle for *anima et corpus* (breath and body) in place of Macer's call to *libertas*. Nor is it unreasonable to imagine such a reader: Seneca could quote the speeches from Sallust's *Historiae* from memory.[23] Perhaps Tacitus even enjoys a joke at Sallust's expense, puncturing Sallust's somewhat heavy-handed use of *animus* and *corpus* in the prefaces to both of his monographs.[24]

To return to Percennius' speech: military pay, ten asses a day, is miserable. The solution for the soldiery, says Percennius, is enlistment *certis sub legibus* on conditions of increased pay with full and fair discharge (1.17.5). *Sub legibus*, according to laws, is a marked way to call for regularised conditions of service since Percennius knows full well, when he urges his audience at the outset of the speech to challenge a new and unsteady princeps, that it is the Imperial will which determines the reality of life for the soldiery. Indeed, as the mutinies develop in Tacitus' narrative, what the soldiers desire is the Imperial guarantee. Percennius' call to enlist *certis sub legibus* is something of a misfit in his Imperial context, and it is at odds with Tacitus' own representation of the significance of the mutinies within the Imperial system. However, its resonance emerges if it is read as yet another detail which evokes the rhetoric of Sallust's popular champions and popular cries throughout the Late Republic. Sallust's Macer seeks the return of the legislative prerogatives of the tribunate, while Sallust's Lepidus asks what was defended against Pyrrhus, Hannibal, Philip, and Antiochus, other than liberty and hearths, 'and that we should obey no one but only the laws?' (*neu quoi nisi legibus pareremus?* §4). Enlistment *certis sub legibus* evokes the past, and the people's assertion of their right to live in a political community determined by

---

and the other is the object of a finite active form. However, the shared accusative case enhances a subjective impression of similarity. Indeed, Tacitus' *oratio obliqua* enables a more elegant and interesting echo than otherwise possible: the less straightforward the borrowing, the more the artistry. It is not possible of course to 'prove' that this phrase evokes Sallust, but such a requirement would take us in the wrong direction – a direction aptly challenged by Hinds (1998) 17–51, who exposes the problems with what he terms 'philological fundamentalism'. See esp. Hinds (1998) 26 on the preference for 'isolability and one-to-one specificity': 'the philologist's working assumption (elevated in the fundamentalist version to dogma) is that the interpretability of an allusion *depends* upon its nearest possible approach to this kind of isolability' (Hinds' emphasis).

22 Ducroux (1978) 296 on Tacitus' general approach to creating dialogue between texts: 'la récurrence verbale est le *signe* que Tacite a voulu donner à son propre lecteur, afin qu'à son tour il poursuivre cette méditation'.

23 With a small error: indeed, otherwise we should not know that the text had been quoted from memory. The speech in question is that of Lepidus: see Guilbert (1957) 296.

24 *Cat.* 1.2, 1.5 and *Iug.* 1.1–2.4. A nice touch suggested to me by Tim Rood.

sovereign law. Finally, Percennius' plea for fair pay is couched in terms of the dangers faced by the legions on the northern frontier, on which thought he closes his speech. Both Percennius and Macer protest that their listeners undergo dangers in battle but are robbed of the rewards which such dangers ought to bring. Percennius compares the position of the Pannonian legions to that of the pampered Praetorian Guard: 'Or did the praetorian cohorts who received two denarii a day face more danger? It was not for them to disparage the duties of urban guard: nonetheless, posted among frightful peoples, they themselves spy the enemy from their tents' (*Ann.* 1.17.6). Likewise when Macer urges his audience to withdraw military service, he suggests sarcastically that the powerful few who benefit from foreign wars can lead their own *imagines* into battle, but 'let those abstain from danger and labour, who do not share any part of the reward' (*absit periculum et labos, quibus nulla pars fructus est*, §18).

Thus almost every aspect of Percennius' speech from opening to closing words finds its precedent in Sallust's popular rhetoric in general and in Macer's speech in particular: his complaints about the few, about servitude and voluntary obedience, about the possibility of remedy if his audience will only act, about the misuse of language and deceitful rewards, his sarcasm about the valuation of the soldier's body and breath, desire for enlistment *certis sub legibus*, and complaint of the injustice in dangers undertaken without a fair share of the fruits of such labour. The evocation of Sallust's speech of Macer is the backbone of this relationship. However, the broader Sallustian framework and the intrusion of Lepidus' speech means that the individual Macer cedes some prominence and Percennius is seen more to encapsulate a Sallustian type: the demagogue or popular champion. Specific connections between the Pannonian mutiny and Sallust's narrative of the year 73 B.C. (during which Macer speaks) are, therefore, likely to be less important than the role of these evocations in signalling the kind of political activity in which Percennius is engaged.

Tacitus introduces Percennius as a practised rabble-rouser: *Erat in castris Percennius quidam, dux olim theatralium operarum, dein gregarius miles, procax lingua et miscere coetus histrionali studio doctus* ('In the camp there was a certain Percennius, once a leader of a theatrical claque, then a common soldier, insolent in his speech and a man who had learned from thespian partisanship how to rouse a crowd', 1.16.3). It is appropriate – in particular to the idea that Percennius is *doctus*, learned in troublemaking – that his speech should borrow from the great rabble-rousing oratory of Sallust. Percennius' demagoguery is emphasised and heightened by this evocation, but there is also more occurring here than this rich indirect characterisation. Percennius' speech is the first extended speech of the *Annales* and occurs in only the second chapter of the long narrative span devoted to the mutiny. The dialogue with Sallustian ideas offered in this speech affects the whole ensuing narrative of the mutinies and also the re-evaluation of the accession which the mutinies provoke.

Tacitus continues that relationship when his second mutinous rabble-rouser speaks. The despatch of Blaesus' son as an envoy to Rome brings temporary relief. However, the mutiny is reawakened by the return of disorderly troops from road, bridge, and similar duties (1.20), and at this point a certain Vibulenus, described (like Percennius) as *gregarius miles*, a common soldier (1.22.1), emerges with his sensational and false claims of a brother murdered by the legionary commander, Blaesus. Vibulenus accuses Blaesus in a brief and melodramatic speech which bewails the death of this fictitious brother (1.22.1–2). He challenges the commander to produce his brother's body and then to finish him off as well: *Cum osculis, cum lacrimis dolorem meum implevero, me quoque trucidari iube, dum interfectos nullum ob scelus, sed quia utilitati legionum consulebamus hi sepeliant* ('When I have completed my grieving with kisses, with tears, give the order that I too should be cut down; so long as – since we have been killed for no crime, but because we looked to the interest of the legions – they should bury us', 1.22.2).

The speech of Vibulenus follows hard upon the speech of Percennius, which, I have argued, is saturated with allusions to Sallust. The interval between the two Tacitean speeches is brief, and the speakers are established in parallel, both specifically described as common soldiers and both inflaming the mutinous crowd. Vibulenus' fabricated *cri de coeur* might not seem noticeably Sallustian in a neutral context, but in this context little is needed to indicate Sallustian readings. With Sallust's *Historiae* already on the mind, the reader may recollect the words of the Sallustian C. Aurelius Cotta, consul of 75 B.C., who speaks to calm the urban plebs during a corn riot and offers to that purpose his own life in the form of a *devotio*. Having made his profession (*voveo dedoque me*, 'I vow and give myself', 2.43R, §10), Sallust's Cotta continues: *Tantum modo in animis habetote non me ob scelus aut avaritiam caesum, sed volentem pro maxumis beneficiis animam dono dedisse.* ('Only hold in your memories that I was not killed for crime or greed, but I gave my life voluntarily as a gift in exchange for your greatest benefactions', §12). The Tacitean Vibulenus and the Sallustian Cotta each invite death, whilst protesting that this death is undeserved. The real cause of death for each man will be his concern for the welfare of those who constitute his audience. Each speaker pleads for attention to posthumous matters – respectively burial and reputation. The two passages share a similar construction, *non me ob scelus aut avaritiam caesum* and *interfectos nullum ob scelus*, with the perfect passive participle and the prepositional *ob scelus*. The real cause of death is introduced as a new contention (*sed*). Tacitus has twisted the thought into a more sophisticated and disjunctive syntax, which has repeatedly attracted the attention of scholars and commentators.[25] His heightened and attention-grabbing construction can be read

---

[25] Koestermann (1963) 130 finds parallels at *Ann.* 4.15.3 and 6.39.3; see also Martin (1953) 93, cited by Goodyear (1972) 217. Adams (1973) 125 also remarks on *interficio*, 'a word from the archaic register at this period'.

as the kind of competitive literary display which, as we know, often accompanies evocation of a great predecessor.[26]

The Sallustian recollection is apt. Cotta's offer of self-immolation in Sallust's *Historiae* is both specious and fatuous.[27] It is a pleasing scene to evoke in the presentation of Vibulenus' similarly fatuous pretence of grief for a non-existent brother. On the other hand, considered from the perspective of circumstance rather than character, the evocation may seem surprising, since the aims of Cotta and of Vibulenus diverge: Vibulenus speaks to inflame his audience where Cotta sought to calm. But elsewhere Tacitus can be seen to alter or reverse aspects of an evoked text. For example, Ginsburg argues that when Tacitus causes M. Aemilius Lepidus (that is, the Lepidus of Tacitus' own narrative in the *Annales*) to evoke Caesar's speech from Sallust's *Bellum Catilinae*, he introduces an ironic contrast between the great dangers posed by the events of 63 B.C. and the triviality of the accusation against Clutorius Priscus in a case where Lepidus sought in vain to mitigate the penalty.[28] In the case of Vibulenus and Cotta, perhaps the ease with which an audience can be manipulated is highlighted by an ironic reversal of the end to which it is bent.

Thus Tacitus injects into his narrative of the mutinies a recollection of the descent of Rome into political chaos, as documented in the *magnum opus* of the Republican historian he most admired. In doing so, he stakes his own claim to the grand, traditional themes of the *res internae* of Republican history.

In Book 4 of the *Annales*, Tacitus complains – in what is probably his most famous digression – of the limited possibilities afforded by his own subject matter in contrast to the topics which occupied the great Republican historians (4.32–33). There are many layers of irony in Tacitus' superficially unfavourable comparison of his own *in arto et inglorius labor* (4.32.2) to the richly-veined histories of the past. The Republican historians, he says, were privileged to record wars, sieges, and defeated kings, and to count among their domestic themes the 'discords of consuls against tribunes, agrarian and corn laws, and struggles of plebs and *optimates*' (4.32.1). Needless to say, scholarship has not taken this digression at face value.[29] While Tacitus laments the dearth of worthy material within the confines of the history which he is writing, no reader can take his complaint as a straightforward assessment of the *Annales*. However, previous discussion of this famous digression

---

[26] Stylistic improvement in literary imitation: Chausserie-Laprée (1980); competitiveness: Russell (1979).
[27] See Perl (1965); McGushin (1992) 211–217; Rosenblitt (2011). *Contra* such a reading of Cotta's speech: Büchner (1982) 216–219; (1973).
[28] Ginsburg (1986) 529–530.
[29] Martin (1981) 136–138; Woodman (1988) 180–190; Martin/Woodman (1989) 169–176; Moles (1998) with a survey of previous scholarship to date, 101–105, and comments on the digression and Sallust, 122–123, 135–136, 141, 146–147, 150–151; Clarke (2002); Sailor (2008) 259–275; Levene (2009); Damon (2010b); Low (2013) 185–195 with, at 193–194, consideration of the domestic side of this claim, which is overlooked in many discussions; Spielberg (2017) 365–366.

has laid comparatively more emphasis upon the great themes of *res externae* which Tacitus claims to lack – the wars, sieges, and kings – and their place in the *Annales*. Tacitus' narrative is not, in fact, lacking in wars. In particular, it has been remarked that the German war dominates the first two books.[30] Tacitus' digressive complaint is not a simple reflection of available subject matter: rather, his complaint is bent to his political, historiographical, and literary purposes. As a political judgement, Griffin argues that it constitutes a barb at Tiberius' unexpansionist military policy (*princeps proferendi imperi incuriosus erat*, 'the *princeps* was unmotivated to extend the empire', 4.32.2).[31] Moreover, in historiographical terms, as Keitel and Woodman have shown, Tacitus' complaint about the absence of grand wars and sieges relates to one of the principal and most daring inversions in his text, whereby the language and imagery of war is applied not to the foreign field but to internal relations between the rulers of the Roman world and Rome itself, and the relationship between successive *principes* and the city and people of Rome is portrayed in terms of siege and warfare.[32] The digression in Book 4 is a linchpin in this portrayal of *principes* and Rome, since it is the supposed absence of wars worth narrating which cements the displacement of language: the *principes*' war on Rome substitutes for the traditional military material.[33]

But what of the other, domestic portion of the Republican subject matter? At first glance, quarrels between consuls and tribunes or between plebs and *optimates* over corn and agrarian distributions might appear to be obsolete topics by A.D. 14. But Tacitus no more cedes his claim to these topics than to the military topics. Sallust's clashes of consuls and tribunes find their place again. The superficially obsolete topics of agrarian and corn laws recur in Percennius' complaints about the dispersal to swamps and mountainous terrain rather than suitable arable fields and in his evocation of Macer's reference to the corn dole in his own description of military pay.

Tacitus' treatment of Republican *res internae* is characterised by the same kind of appropriation and inversion which characterises his use of Republican *res externae*. Tacitus makes a point of describing Percennius as a theatre claqueur and informing the reader that the mutinous legions on the Rhine were packed with city

---

30 On the other hand, Martin/Woodman (1989) 170 read the Book 4 digression as a comment particularly on that section of the narrative, i.e. Tiberius' later years, with their comparative lack of suitable military material; see also Woodman (1988) 185. Cf. Malloch (2009) 119–123 on the structure of the Claudian books and the Book 4 digression. Levene (2009) reconciles the claims made in the digression with the military material covered in the *Annales* by proposing that Tacitus recounts warfare in a 'perfunctory' and 'simple' manner (229), deliberately rendering it 'unattractive by conventional historiographical criteria' (231).
31 Griffin (1999) 153.
32 See n. 10.
33 Woodman (1988) 180–190, esp. 190; see also Moles (1998) 170, 174; Keitel (2010) 333, 340; Levene (2010) 307–308.

recruits.³⁴ Percennius speaks *velut contionabundus* – a very unusual, long and slow word which draws attention to itself. (The word is an emendation, but an uncontroversial one which has stood for centuries.³⁵) The tone is sarcastic: 'as if speaking at a proper *contio*'.³⁶ When Tacitus evokes the urban quarrels of Sallust's Late Republic, he imports a civic frame of reference which highlights the intrusion of city behaviour into military discipline.³⁷ At the same time, the Tacitean text mimetically violates boundaries of form. Tacitus lays claim to the central subject matter of Sallust's account of *res internae*, but transfers that matter to his own account of developments outside of the *urbs*. As so often in Tacitus, apparent boundaries and inherited historiographical conventions are undermined. Although Tacitus appears at *Ann.* 1.16.1 to move from *res internae* to *res externae*, from the accession at Rome to mutinies in the provinces, the evocation of Sallust's account of urban affairs subverts the Livian organisation of *domi militiaeque* to which Tacitus superficially adheres – a subversion which is all the more elegant for the evocations of Livy (identified by Woodman) which the reader encounters as the narrative of the mutiny continues.³⁸

Thus Tacitus lays claim to the themes and historiographical legacy of Sallust, his most estimable Republican predecessor. He applies Sallust's urban material, his demagogues, his quarrels of consuls and tribunes, *optimates* and plebs, to the Imperial army. And in Book 4, he complains that he has not the material afforded to those earlier historians, whom – we might say – he has in every way surpassed.

---

34 *Ann.* 1.16.3 and 1.31.4; cf. Malloch (2004) 202 on the Rhine recruits.
35 An uncontroversial emendation (Beroaldus) of *conditionabundus*. Koestermann (1963) 120: the word is 'nur hier (vgl. die Liste SYME, Tac. II 719) und Liv. 3,47,2. 5,29,10. 21,53,5 *prope contionabundus* (in allen Fällen aber mit *haec* verbunden)'. The additional examples offered by Fletcher (1964) 8 are of dubious relevance. Cf. Furneaux (1896) 206 and Goodyear (1972) 201.
36 Goodyear (1972) 201: the force of adjectives ending in *-bundus* must be determined from immediate context. The context here renders the tone readable. For Tacitean sarcasm over the semblance of a *contio* in an inappropriate context, compare 1.44.2: *stabant pro contione legiones destrictis gladiis*. This latter passage has caused interpretative problems, on which see Furneaux (1896) 239, and textual problems, summarised in Watt (1998) 264. Watt proposes *stabant pro <tribunali uelut in> contione*. His solution (if accepted) only makes more explicit the meaning which anyhow has been generally agreed. Furneaux (1896) 239: 'after the fashion of an assembly'; Goodyear (1972) 298: 'Perhaps ... to indicate that this was not a proper *contio* but a travesty of one'. Cf. O'Gorman (2000) 36.
37 Rowe (2002) argues that the army had always shared with urban, civilian life an essential similarity of political culture built around the *contio* and that, in the Imperial era, the army assimilated further accoutrements of urban political culture including civic-style monuments and spectacles (154–163; discussion of *contiones* in the mutinies at 162–163). Rowe shows that there is a normality to this. However, Tacitus' presentation emphasises inversion of military and civilian spheres.
38 Woodman (2006). For Tacitus' relationship to *domi militiaeque*, see Ginsburg (1981), esp. 53–79.

Tacitus in Sallust

But what do these Tacitean evocations and inversions of Sallust tell us about the mostly lost Sallustian work? Clearly, it is not as simple as merely flipping the intertextual relationship: we cannot simply reverse the direction and recreate lost Sallustian text. However, since we are clearly looking at an intertextual relationship which engages the thematic structures of the two works, there may be ways to build on this relationship and, by understanding more of Tacitus as a reader of Sallust, to venture observations about Sallust's *Historiae* through Tacitus' *Annales*.

The evocation of Sallust at the outbreak of the Pannonian mutiny places Tacitus' engagement with Sallust at one of the critical moments for Tacitus' exploration of the nature of power in the Imperial system. Tacitus' treatment of the mutinies is disproportionately lengthy and detailed. Although a minority of scholars would attribute this to literary purposes alone, most scholars argue that Tacitus affords the mutinies such disproportionate treatment because they reveal Tacitean truths about the Imperial system, about the essential bargain of *pax et princeps*, and the foundations and vulnerabilities of Imperial power.[39] Thus Tacitus brings Sallust right into the heart of his political analysis. Moreover, this evocation of Sallust relates, I have been arguing, to Tacitus' digression in Book 4, which is a or perhaps *the* central textual moment for the historiographical self-positioning of the *Annales*. This intertextual relationship also builds on long-recognised allusions to Sallust in the opening chapter of the *Annales*.[40] Indeed, the parallel between Sallust's *Historiae* and Tacitus' *Annales* is structurally fundamental. Both works begin with the death of the man, Sulla and Augustus respectively, whose shadow hangs over the entire narrative to come.[41] Both narratives are framed at the outset by the politically loaded question of funeral arrangements for the late autocrat

---

39 The length and prominence of Tacitus' account of the mutinies has provoked considerable discussion. On the literary opportunities afforded by the topic, see Goodyear (1972) 194–196; Martin (1981) 115. For the thematic and programmatic importance of the material, notably the use of the mutinies to underline the atmosphere of threats and discontents which menaced Tiberius upon his accession, see Williams (1997) 44; Devillers (1993) 230–232; Keitel (1984) 318 n. 27; Malloch (2004) 200–201, cf. 199–200 for an exploration of the mutinies as a comment on the nature of the Imperial system; in particular, the power of the legions constitutes an *arcanum imperii* parallel to that revealed by Sallustius Crispus upon the death of Agrippa Postumus. On the significance of the mutinies for establishing the roles of Germanicus and Drusus: Woodman (2006).
40 See above, n. 3, and below, n. 41.
41 The starting point of the *Annales* is an old chestnut. See Syme (1958) 364–377; Shotter (1967); (1991) 3285–3287; Griffin (1995); O'Gorman (1995); Clarke (2002) 84–85. Specifically for discussion of the opening of the *Annales* with respect to Livy and Sallust: O'Gorman (1995), esp. 95–96 on the *Annales* and Sallust's *Historiae*. O'Gorman (1995) 105 remarks on the 'omnipresence' of Augustus both for Tacitus' narrative and for Tiberius as *princeps*; for a fuller discussion of the role of Augustus in the Tiberian era historically and historiographically in Tacitus' text, see Cowan (2009).

and both offer an assessment, of Sulla and Augustus respectively, at the point of death.[42] The fragmentary state of Sallust's *Historiae* makes it harder to explore in what sense, and with what effects, Sulla's legacy hangs over Sallust's narrative of the 70s (and beyond). I would argue, however, that we can piece together from speeches and fragments of the *Historiae* certain threads in Sallust's thinking, upon which Tacitus' engagements with the *Historiae* in the *Annales* may shed valuable light.

Sallust's popular champions espouse a political philosophy of hostile politics: that is, a construction of politics in which internal political opponents are understood as *hostes*, foreign enemies. In the hostile understanding of politics, the people are enslaved, they have been despoiled, and treated as if they were war captives. They must realise, however, that they are the stronger party; the only way to achieve their political will is by inflicting fear. Sallust's Lepidus is the first speaker in the *Historiae* to give voice to this hostile understanding of politics (1.49R). Lepidus describes his audience, the Roman people, as war captives under the tyranny of Sulla. Sulla behaves abominably, the better to enforce that slavery: *quo captis libertatis curam miseria eximat*; 'so that, for you as captives, wretchedness should remove all thought of liberty' (§1). Sulla, *scaevos iste Romulus* ('that twisted Romulus'), holds what belongs to the Roman people *quasi ab externis rapta*, 'as if seized from foreign nations' (§5).[43] The people, deprived of their liberty, are controlled through fear: *dum vos metu gravioris serviti a repetunda libertate terremini*; 'while you are frightened off the recovery of liberty by fear of a yet heavier slavery' (§6). The language of spoliation continues. Sulla and his *satellites* hold *spolia vostra* ('your spoils', §7) – a compressed phrase which builds directly on the earlier *quasi ab externis rapta*, and which therefore means 'your own property (and rights, etc.) held as (if) the seized spoils of war'. Likewise Sulla and his connections benefit from *praemia turbarum* ('the rewards of upheavals', §16). Sulla is described as having sacked Rome: *vastam urbem fuga et caedibus, bona civium miserorum quasi Cimbricam praedam venum aut dono datam*; 'the city wasted from flight and murders, the goods of wretched citizens as if Cimbric booty sold or given as a gift' (§17). Lepidus argues that there can be no further consensual government, no *concordia*: the people and the powerful are alienated from each other and can only interact as enemies. Thus he offers the political advice which stands at the centre of his speech: *hac tempestate serviundum aut imperitandum, habendus metus est aut faciundus, Quirites*. 'in this time, it is a case of slaving or ruling, living in fear or inflicting it, Quirites' (§10).

---

[42] We get a fuller version of the political clash over Sulla's funeral from Appian (*B Civ.* 1.105) and Plutarch (*Sull.* 38.1; *Pomp.* 15.3) while Sall. *Hist.* 1.50R–1.53R probably belong to Sallust's narrative of the funeral.

[43] On *scaevos iste Romulus*: Verdière (1957); Reggiani (1994).

In the speech of Sallust's Macer (3.15R), it is a given that the people have been enslaved by Sulla and by his more cruel successors (§1). The rich 'hold a fortress' – the language of war – 'made of your spoils': *arcem habent ex spoliis vostris* (§6). Macer openly endorses fear as the route to political success. If the people will unite and act, will the powerful resist them, *quos languidos socordesque pertimuere?* '(you) whom, though you are sluggish and apathetic, they feared nonetheless?' (§8). It was nothing other than fear, he says, which wrung concessions on tribunician rights from Cotta (§8). Macer describes the tribunician power as a weapon (§12). Although Macer claims not to advise violence, he repeatedly urges the plebs to realise that they are the stronger party. When he tells his audience, *vis omnis, Quirites, in vobis sit*; 'all force, Quirites, lies with you', this is the language of threat (§15). When he demands the rights of the plebs *iure gentium*, 'by the law of nations', echoing the Fetial formula for war, he makes it clear that the people and the powerful now negotiate with one another as hostile powers (§17). Macer closes his speech by explicitly likening the position of the plebs to a conquered enemy: *plebes, quodcumque accidit, pro victis est*; 'whatever happens, the plebs are treated as men who have been conquered' (§27).[44]

The construction of the political world voiced in these speeches directly reflects the history of the 80s and the traumas suffered in the Roman world and within the city of Rome itself. I trailed, at the outset of this chapter, two aspects of the politics and civil wars of the 80s which must have a direct bearing on the construction of politics along a hostile model: first, the political innovation of the *hostis* decree passed in 88 (and again in 87 and beyond) and, secondly, Sulla's open reference to the goods of the proscribed as *spolia* or *praeda*. In addition, there is Sulla's own direct demand for obedience in a *contio* held after his victory at the Colline Gate (Appian, *B Civ*. 1.95), a demand that implicitly positions the Roman *Quirites* as slaves, from whom obedience can be exacted, rather than as free citizens and sovereign decision makers in the *res publica*. Finally, Sulla's triumph – though almost certainly couched as a celebration of victory over Mithridates – offered a spectacle which could not be neatly separated from his victory in civil war. Roman exiles who owed their restoration to Sulla's victory in the civil war paraded in his triumph, and the subsequent *ludi Victoriae* further blurred Sulla's foreign victories with his new pose as a second Romulus, a new re-founder of Rome – a persona also predicated on his victory in the civil war.[45]

---

44 For a full-length discussion of this construction of politics by Sallust's speakers, see Rosenblitt (2016), esp. 664–673. I have borrowed the phrasing of these two paragraphs (in condensed form) from that article.

45 See Rosenblitt (2016) 677–683, and argued in more detail: Rosenblitt (2019) 115–130. Regarding the triumph: for the majority view that the triumph was only officially a celebration of victory over Mithridates, see Keaveney (1983b) 188 and Lange (2016) 95–103. For the connection between the *ludi Victoriae* and the image as re-founder of Rome: Santangelo (2007) 216–218.

While the speeches assigned to Lepidus and to Macer offer a direct (and, of course, partisan) response to the legacy of civil war and Sullan power, Sallust also explores hostile politics more thematically in his authorial voice, in his representation of his speakers, and in the ways in which he sets up his speakers to act and interact.[46] Sallust's Cotta provides one of the most potent examples. Cotta speaks *ad Quirites* in 75 B.C., in the midst of serious rioting occasioned by a shortage of corn, and he chastises his audience for their attitude and behaviour.[47] In the context of this emergency, Cotta offers his life. He makes his offer in the present tense, without conditional phrasing, in words that ought therefore to initiate this action: *voveo dedoque me* ('I vow and devote myself', 2.43R §10). Nonetheless, it is clear that there will be no follow-through in the form of a devoted death.[48] Cotta's problematically unfulfilled *devotio* promises a military act in the Roman Forum. Indeed, Sallust goes out of his way to foreground the military aspect of *devotio*. Cotta is made to specify that his *devotio* is modelled on the *exempla* of Roman generals in battle: *Facio quod saepe maiores asperis bellis fecere*; 'I do what our ancestors often did in taxing battles' (§10). Cotta, however, is not speaking or acting in the midst of a battle. There is no enemy line offering the opportunity to complete his *devotio* by rushing onto enemy spears and swords. Here, in the Forum, a devoted death could only come at the hands of his audience itself. Rioters had already attacked Cotta and his consular colleague days before as they escorted Q. Metellus (Creticus) to the Forum during his canvass for the praetorship (Sall. *Hist.* 2.41R). Sallust's Cotta toys in his speech with embracing death at the hands of a rioting mob, in a scenario which positions his audience, the Roman *Quirites*, as a battle-line of enemy soldiers.

The hostile *devotio* of Sallust's Cotta extends Sallust's portrayal of hostile relations in civic politics beyond the rhetoric of his speeches of Lepidus and Macer. There are other indications (beyond the scope of this piece) that Sallust thematises hostile politics in the narrative of his *Historiae*, including his foregrounding of the Struggle of the Orders (1.10R), his further explorations of the role of threat and fear in eliciting action (e.g. 2.86[D]R, §§11–12), and other indications of inverted language which may hint at elements of war penetrating urban politics (*inc*.14*R). However, it is difficult to get a sense of how Sallust's exploration of hostile politics *feels* to the reader when we have only such a fragmented text. On the other hand, as readers informed by the work of Keitel and Woodman, we *can* feel that theme in Tacitus' *Annales*. Indeed,

---

[46] See Rosenblitt (2019) 131–139.
[47] Previous work on Sallust's Cotta and his speech: Ullmann (1927) 43–44; Paladini (1957) 109–115; Earl (1961) 108–109; La Penna (1963) 245–246; Syme (1964) 200, 207, 208, 210; Perl (1965); Perl (1967); Malitz (1972); Büchner (1973); (1982) 216–219; Pasoli (1974) 91–104; (1976) 106–107; McGushin (1992) 211–217; Sträterhoff (1997); Perl (2005) 185–186; Sapere (2011), though her textual reconstruction overlooks Perl (1975); Gärtner (2011); Rosenblitt (2011).
[48] See Rosenblitt (2011). For *devotio*, see Versnel (1976); Versnel (1981); Janssen (1981); Beard, North, and Price (1998) 1.35–36, 111.

Cotta's inverted *devotio*-scenario surely feels very Tacitean (and it has been suggested that Tacitus plays extensively with a *devotio* topos in his own *Historiae*).[49]

Conclusion

Tacitus' intertextual relationship with Sallust's *Historiae* suggests that when we read Tacitus' *Annales*, sensitised as we are to his use of the *urbs capta* motif, we are also reading Tacitus as a reader of Sallust's *Historiae* and, specifically, as a reader of Sallust's exploration of hostile politics in the urban political environment. This is not to say that Sallust's hostile politics should be equated to Tacitus' *urbs capta*. Fire and wailing of captives are, for example, more central to the latter whereas the former places more emphasis on the use of fear to exert political will and on the possibility of fluctuation in the matter of who rules and who is ruled. Closer work on Sallust's *Historiae* can draw out such differences. However, work on the fragmentary *Historiae* can never give us the experience as readers that is open to us in reading the *Annales*.

The various threads explored in this piece have been intended to support the case that Tacitus' *Annales* offers an insight into the experience of reading hostile politics in Sallust's *Historiae*. This conclusion reflects Tacitus' engagement with the Sallustian speeches of Macer and Cotta (and, to a lesser extent, Lepidus) – speeches which offer key moments in Sallust's own exploration of hostile politics. It also reflects the importance of these intertextual moments in Tacitus' exploration of the Imperial system, their relevance to Tacitus' historiographical project and to the famous Book 4 digression, and the broad structural parallels between Tacitus' *Annales*, taken up from the death of Augustus, and Sallust's *Historiae*, taken up from the death of Sulla. Just as Tacitus explored the consequences of Augustan power for the Roman Imperial system, Sallust's *Historiae* were an exploration of the consequences of Sullan power for the Roman *res publica*. Tacitus' use of the *urbs capta* motif can help us to read Sallust's understanding of the ruptures caused in Rome after the Sullan civil wars: the legacy of Sulla, as understood in Sallust's *Historiae*, is a polity in which the people and the powerful construed each other as *hostes*.[50]

---

49 Edwards (2012).
50 I would like to thank Alexandra Eckert and Alexander Thein for their very kind invitation to the Sulla panel at the Celtic Classics Conference (2016) which was the seed of this edited volume. I also owe thanks to all the Sulla panel members, and to mentors and colleagues who talked with me about these ideas, mostly many years ago, including Miriam Griffin, Katherine Clarke, and Tim Rood.

Inger N. I. Kuin

8 Sulla and the Philosophers: The Cultural History of the Sack of Athens

The city of Athens had an alliance with Rome from the early 2nd century onwards which was still intact at the beginning of the 1st century B.C.[1] At this time Mithridates Eupator began increasing Pontic territory in the Crimea and Asia Minor, and in 89 the Romans incited King Nicomedes of Bithynia to invade Pontus, leading to the outbreak of the First Mithridatic War.[2] The following year Athens elected Athenion hoplite general, an Aristotelian philosopher loyal to Mithridates Eupator, and this probably meant the end of Athens' alliance with Rome.[3] Mithridates' general Archelaus replaced Athenion with the Athenian Aristion soon afterwards. The king sent Pontic troops to Athens in 87, and Sulla arrived in Greece in the summer of the same year. In the winter of 87/86 he besieged both the city and the Piraeus from Eleusis, finally storming Athens in March 86. Aristion capitulated on the Acropolis and was later executed. Sulla gave Athens some type of settlement, and pardoned the remaining Athenians.[4] After more fighting in Boeotia and Asia Minor the First Mithridatic War ended when Sulla and Mithridates Eupator made peace at Dardanus in 85. Mithridates Eupator and the Romans were to fight two more wars, but Athens would not be involved again.

Various accounts of the fall of Athens in 86 have been preserved. Plutarch's *Life of Sulla* and Appian's *Mithridatic Wars*, respectively, offer the most detail. There was clearly strong interest in Sulla's sack of Athens in Imperial Greek historiography, and there are indications that this event was important in Greek discourse of the period more broadly.[5] In this chapter I will examine a joke preserved in Aelian: I will argue that this witticism is connected with Sulla's siege of the city, and as such is one of the ways in which the memory of the event persisted for many centuries afterwards. The evolving perception of Sulla's relationship with Greek culture is an important aspect of this memory. The structure of this article will be as follows: in the first section the Aelian-passage that is at the core of this chapter will be discussed in detail. In the following section I look at the various links between

---

1 The precise nature and start date of the relationship are contested. Kallet-Marx (1995) 200–201 and Habicht (1997) [1995] 212–213 give good overviews of the debate.
2 McGing (1986) 86–88; cf. Habicht (1997) [1995] 298–300.
3 *BNJ* 87 F 36 (Posidon.); cf. Habicht (1997) [1995] 300–301, *contra* Kallet-Marx (1995) 209–211, who thinks Athens did not commit itself irreversibly to Mithridates until Aristion.
4 Whether or not Sulla intervened in the laws of Athens at this point (as reported by Appian in *Mith.* 39) is contested, see e.g. Kallet-Marx (1995) 213–219; cf. Kuin (2017).
5 Pausanias, for instance, also refers to the event repeatedly (see below). See Lamberton (1997) on the role of Athens in the 1st and 2nd centuries A.D.

this passage and the sack of Athens, and in the final section the wider context of Sulla's relation to Greek literature and art is considered.

Sulla in Aelian

The Byzantine encyclopedia Suda records a saying about Sulla that has traditionally been attributed to the 3rd century A.D. author Claudius Aelian, a Roman writing in Greek. Aelian identifies himself as a Roman in his *Variae Historiae* on several occasions, and Philostratus even writes that the author boasted of never having left Italy. Aelian's ethnic background and the related question of how his family acquired Roman citizenship have been subjects of debate. It is clear from his works, however, that he aligned himself strongly with Greek intellectual culture, not least through his careful and sophisticated Greek prose style. Philostratus writes that Aelian studied with Pausanias at one point, and that he was an admirer of Herodes Atticus.[6] Aelian's works must be situated, then, at least as much in a Greek cultural context as in Roman culture and society.

The comment on Sulla reported by Aelian is actually a set of two questions. I cite it in its reconstructed context, following the text of the fragments of Domingo-Forasté (fr. 56a-f), which is identical to Hercher's (fr. 53)

> (1) Alalcomenae is a city and I hear that it is not located on the top of a mountain or on an unyielding ledge, (2) nor does it have a circumference of walls strong enough to keep out and repulse enemies by force. (3) That murderer and oppressor[7] demanded to take the cognomen 'the Fortunate'. (4) For what do a dolphin and an ox have in common, they say, and what Sulla and philosophers? (5) Yet he did not enjoy it [good fortune] at all, but while still alive he seethed with nasty creatures; some [say] with worms; others [say] not with these but rather with lice. (6) After breaking out in lice and being, little by little, both consumed and liquefied, he died.[8]

The editors of Aelian's fragments have here connected the phrase about Sulla and the philosophers to other Aelian passages in the Suda concerning Sulla. These passages appear to be linked by the theme of Sulla's misfortune standing in stark

---

6 Ael. *VH* 2.38, 12.25, 14.45; Philostr. *VS* 624–625; for the debate on Aelian's background see Smith (2014) 11–28.
7 See *LSJ* A s.v. λευστήρ; cf. Ael. *NA* 5.15.
8 [1. Suda α3205] Ἀλαλκομεναί πόλις ἐστὶ καὶ ἀκούω αὐτὴν μήτ'ἐφ' ὑψηλοῦ κεῖσθαι καὶ ἀπιθοῦς λόφου, [2. α3550] μήτε μὴν τειχῶν ἔχειν περίβολον, οἷον ἀποστέγειν καὶ ἀναστέλλειν τοὺς πολεμίους καρτερόν. [3. λ344] ὁ δὲ παλαμναῖος καὶ λευστὴρ ἐκεῖνος ᾔτησεν ἐπωνυμίαν λαβεῖν Εὐτυχής. [4. τ556] τί γὰρ δὴ δελφῖνι καὶ βοΐ φασιν κοινὸν εἶναι, Σύλλᾳ τε καὶ φιλοσόφοις; [5. α3674] οὐ μὴν ἀπώνητο οὐδέν, ἀλλὰ ἐξέζεσε ζῶν κακοῖς θηρίοις, οἳ μὲν εὐλαῖς, οἱ δὲ ὅτι οὐ ταύταις, φθειρσί γε μήν. [6. λ358] ὃ δὲ φθειρσὶν ἐκζέσας ἐσθιόμενός τε καὶ κατὰ μικρὰ λειβόμενος ἀποθνήσκει. The translation in the main text above is my own.

contrast with his adoption of the cognomen *Felix* (*Eutychēs*). The first two fragments refer to Sulla's capture of Alalcomenae in Boeotia, where, according to Pausanias, he stole a statue of Athena (9.33.6). The third fragment focuses on the theme of Sulla calling himself Felix, while acting in ways that contradict the notion of *felicitas*. The fifth and sixth fragments are also clear illustrations of *infelicitas*, while the fourth passage, to which we turn now in some detail, may be connected to this theme through the notion that true *felicitas* is available only to the philosopher.[9] The fragments, then, cohere as a discussion of Sulla's *(in)felicitas* in Aelian, but we cannot exclude the possibility that these individual phrases were separated by additional comments on the topic.

The joke about dolphins, oxen, Sulla, and philosophers consists of two rhetorical questions, and the answer in both cases, it appears, should be 'not much'. The point of the expression seems to be that Sulla had very little in common with philosophers: as little as dolphins and oxen share with one another. Another occurrence of the saying about dolphins and oxen in Aelian's *Natura Animalium* might confirm such a reading.[10] In his discussion of sea creatures, Aelian tells the reader what he knows of the fishing practices of the Mysians living near the Black Sea. They use a yoke of oxen or horses to pull large fish out of the Ister. The author, once he has mentioned the yoke, imagines that the reader may now be thinking of agriculture, but he assures us that this is not at all what he means: 'for, as the saying goes, an ox and a dolphin have nothing in common, so in the same way, from where could any friendship arise between the hands of fishermen and a plough?'[11] In this iteration the saying explicitly asserts that oxen and dolphins have nothing in common; by analogy the hands of a fisherman and a plough have nothing in common either.

If we compare the passage in *Natura Animalium* to the fragment about Sulla, it becomes clear that the saying about dolphins and oxen could be adapted at will to other unlikely pairings. There are no occurrences of the saying except in Aelian, but it is possible that the proverb of the dolphin and the oxen was used in vernacular, spoken language. A passage from the 11th-century A.D. bishop and biblical commentator Theophylact of Ohrid juxtaposes three elements from the proverb of *Natura Animalium*: dolphin, plough, and oxen. In close proximity both the pairing of ploughman (ἀροτήρ) and dolphin, and the pairing of dolphin and oxen are used

---

9 In Aelian this notion is exemplified in the story of Timotheus, an Athenian general who at the height of his good fortune (εὐτυχία) thought that only Plato was living a life of 'true happiness' (ὄντως εὐδαιμονία, *VH* 2.10). For earlier instances see e.g. Arist. *Eth. Nic.* 10.7–8; the idea was later developed particularly in Stoic philosophy, cf. Annas (1993).
10 Tosi already connected the two phrases: 'Elien poursuivait ensuite en soulignant qu'il n'y avait rien de commun non plus entre Sylla et les philosophes' (2010) [1991] 1018 no. 1372.
11 Ael. *NA* 14.25: ὥσπερ γάρ φησιν ὁ λόγος, μηδὲν εἶναι βοῒ κοινὸν καὶ δελφῖνι, οὕτω τοι φιλία χερσὶν ἁλιέων καὶ ἀροτρῳ πόθεν ἂν γένοιτο. The translation in the main text above is my own.

as examples of extreme opposites.[12] This suggests to me that variations on the entire phrase about dolphins, oxen, ploughs and fishermen may have circulated in spoken Greek for several centuries after Aelian's lifetime.

The recurrence of the oxen and dolphins as a pairing of opposites in Aelian's *Natura Animalium* implies that the point of the passage about Sulla is that he does not share anything with philosophers. It is difficult to know if the full phrase with dolphins, oxen, Sulla, and philosophers, or the Sulla and philosophers part independently, had a life outside of Aelian's writings, as did the phrase about ploughs. (The comparison of Sulla and philosophers does not occur elsewhere in *TLG*; I will return to this issue below.) However, the double oxymoron about dolphins, oxen, Sulla, and philosophers can be compared with a saying following the same pattern in the works of Lucian of Samosata. In a diatribe against a book collector the speaker says that seeing someone buying many books who is as uneducated as the target of the piece will prompt people to ask: 'What do a dog and a bath have in common?' The analogy is implied: ignorant people have as little to do with books as dirty dogs with baths. This phrase functions in a similar way to the dolphins and oxen proverb, and is equally flexible; Lucian applies it elsewhere (ironically) to philosophers and the symposium.[13]

Finally, we need to briefly consider an alternative interpretation: Eckert has proposed that both pairs of opposites, dolphins and oxen and philosophers and Sulla, *do* have something in common, namely lice or parasites, and that the expression can be linked with Aelian's comments on the well-known story that Sulla died after being afflicted with lice, a fate also attributed to several philosophers. The Greek word for lice (φθείρ) can refer to suckerfish which infest dolphins as parasites; oxen can be afflicted with lice, so they too share the φθείρ with dolphins. Eckert thus argues that the phrase is a reference to the 'unfortunate' disease that plagued Sulla Felix at the end of his life, functioning as a riddle that a learned Greek speaker might be able to solve.[14] We can perhaps imagine, then, a scenario in which there was an everyday understanding of Aelian's saying – Sulla and philosophers have as little in common as dolphins and oxen – and a more sophisticated reading which exploited the different meanings of φθείρ and the existing association between lice and philosophers.

In the remainder of this chapter I will explore how it was possible to think of Sulla and philosophers as an equally oxymoronic pair as dolphins and oxen. In

---

12 Tosi does not mention this passage; it comes from a letter to Theophylact's brother on liturgy: Gautier (1980) 335.
13 Lucian, *Ind.* 5: τί κυνὶ καὶ βαλανείῳ; Cf. Lucian, *Par.* 51. The dog and bath saying is also mentioned by the 6th century A.D. medical writer Aëtius (6.24), and it is included in several collections of ancient proverbs, e.g. Suda τ584, Chrysocephalus 8.34, Arsenius 16.60a. Hopkinson (2008) 124 also compares this saying to the oxen and dolphins phrase.
14 Eckert (2016a) 3–4; cf. Eckert (forthcoming [a]). On Sulla's disease see also Bahmer/Eckert (2015).

order to do so I will connect the saying to Sulla's sack of Athens in 86, a context already invoked by the first two elements of the reconstructed text for the fragment about Alalcomenae. The application of the proverb on oxen and dolphins to Sulla can be linked, I will suggest, to the dealings he had with the philosophers residing in Athens at the time, and, specifically, their books.

From Aristotle to Aristion

In the 1st century B.C. Athens was still of great importance as a centre of education; many young members of the Roman elite spent time in the city in order to train with the resident philosophers and orators.[15] Apellicon, Athenion, and Aristion are all attested as playing important military roles at Athens during the First Mithridatic War *and* being actively engaged in philosophy.[16] Athenion asked Apellicon to lead a campaign to recapture Delos, which had stayed loyal to Rome. Apellicon fulfilled his task negligently and poorly. The Romans repelled the attack, and Apellicon fled in secret.[17] It is reported that later, after seizing the city, Sulla captured Apellicon's philosophical library.

In Lucian's *The Ignorant Book Collector*, mentioned above, an uneducated tycoon is ridiculed for his desire to own famous, rare books. The anonymous speaker of the diatribe offers the following sarcastic advice:

> Along the same lines, go ahead, have all the books of Demosthenes, the ones the orator wrote in his own hand, and the Thucydides volumes written also by Demosthenes – he copied them eight times – that have been found, and all the books that Sulla sent from Athens to Italy![18]

The point of this joke is that the uneducated book collector is likely to fall prey to sellers peddling fake copies, because he can be tricked into believing, for example, that there *are* eight copies of Thucydides in Demosthenes' hand.[19] It would be equally unlikely, according to the speaker, for the collector to be able to lay his

---

15 Some notable examples include Cicero, Brutus (Plut. *Brut.* 24), M. Valerius Messalla Corvinus, and L. Calpurnius Bibulus (Cic. *Att.* 12.32), cf. Bonner (1977) 90–91; Scholz (2011) 158–160. The milieu of young Romans studying in Athens can be gleaned most clearly from Cicero's correspondence with Atticus about his son Marcus' education, e.g. *ad Att.* 12.24; 12.32; 13.47; 14.7; 14.11; 14.16.
16 Athenion and Apellicon: Posidon. *ap.* Ath. 5.48–53 = *BNJ* 87 F 36; Euseb. *Praec. evang.* 15.2, cf. Barnes (1997) 10; Aristion: App. *Mith.* 28.
17 Posidon. *ap.* Ath. 5.53 = *BNJ* 87 F 36.
18 Lucian, *Ind.* 4: κατὰ δὴ ταῦτα, ἐκεῖνα ἔχε συλλαβὼν τὰ τοῦ Δημοσθένους ὅσα τῇ χειρὶ τῇ αὐτοῦ ὁ ῥήτωρ ἔγραψε, καὶ τὰ τοῦ Θουκυδίδου ὅσα παρὰ τοῦ Δημοσθένους καὶ αὐτὰ ὀκτάκις μεταγεγραμμένα εὑρέθη, καὶ ὅλως ἅπαντα ἐκεῖνα ὅσα ὁ Σύλλας Ἀθήνηθεν εἰς Ἰταλίαν ἐξέπεμψε. I have adapted the translation from Harmon's Loeb edition.
19 Cf. Johnson (2010) 167. The Greek here is difficult; Johnson translates 'into eight volumes', but 'copied eight times' fits better with the joke about the gullibility of the collector.

hands on 'all the books that Sulla sent from Athens to Italy', yet he may just be foolish enough to try. Hopkinson in his commentary on *The Ignorant Book Collector* explains this passage as referring to Sulla taking Apellicon's library from Athens in the First Mithridatic War.[20] He adds: 'The contrast between his violent action and its cultured object gave rise to the proverb τί γὰρ [κοινὸν] Σύλλαι καὶ φιλοσόφοις;'[21] Hopkinson supposes that in this phrase the word 'philosophers' stands for the philosophical texts in Apellicon's library, while the name Sulla represents the theft of the library, which is assumed to have been a violent action. But it is worth noting that violence is not implied in the Lucian passage: the books have simply been 'sent' to Italy by Sulla. The philosophical books from Apellicon's library form the third part of a tricolon, with oratory and historiography being supplied by the Demosthenes copies. To contextualise Lucian's joke we must consider how other ancient sources write about the transfer of Apellicon's books from Athens to Rome after the First Mithridatic War.

The earliest source to mention Sulla taking Apellicon's library to Rome is Strabo. In his *Geography* he discusses the history of the library at some length. One Neleus inherited the library of Theophrastus, which included Aristotle's library, and bequeathed it to his heirs. They hid the books underground to prevent the Attalid kings from taking them for their library at Pergamum; the family sold the books, damaged by moisture and moths, to Apellicon much later. Strabo calls Apellicon 'more a lover of books than a lover of wisdom' (φιλόβιβλος μᾶλλον ἢ φιλόσοφος, 13.1.54), because he had new copies made of the text with many incorrect emendations. On account of these mistakes the Hellenistic Peripatetics had to 'call many of their statements probabilities' (τὰ πολλὰ εἰκότα λέγειν, 13.1.54), and with Roman involvement things only got worse, says Strabo:

> Rome also contributed much to this: for, right after the death of Apellicon Sulla took the library of Apellicon when he seized Athens; once it had been brought to Rome the grammarian Tyrannio, who loved Aristotle's works, got his hands on it by paying court to the librarian, and so did some book sellers who used bad copyists and did not collate the texts.[22]

---

20 Hopkinson (2008) 123; cf. Barnes (1997) 16 n. 75.
21 Hopkinson (2008) 124. Hopkinson assumes that the phrase about Sulla and the philosophers was a proverb, in other words, that it was used by others than Aelian, but the Sulla and the philosophers saying is not otherwise attested in the *TLG*. Tosi (2010) [1991] 1018 no. 1372, not cited by Hopkinson, understands only the oxen and dolphins part as proverbial, treating the Sulla and the philosophers part as an addition by Aelian; similarly, in the Suda the Sulla and the philosophers part is not listed among the *paroemia*.
22 Strabo 13.1.54: πολὺ δὲ εἰς τοῦτο καὶ ἡ Ῥώμη προσελάβετο· εὐθὺς γὰρ μετὰ τὴν Ἀπελλικῶντος τελευτὴν Σύλλας ἦρε τὴν Ἀπελλικῶντος βιβλιοθήκην ὁ τὰς Ἀθήνας ἑλών, δεῦρο δὲ κομισθεῖσαν Τυραννίων τε ὁ γραμματικὸς διεχειρίσατο φιλαριστοτέλης ὤν, θεραπεύσας τὸν ἐπὶ τῆς βιβλιοθήκης, καὶ βιβλιοπῶλαί τινες γραφεῦσι φαύλοις χρώμενοι καὶ οὐκ ἀντιβάλλοντες. Translation adapted from Jones' Loeb edition.

Strabo contextualises Sulla's acquisition of the books in the library's longer, ill-fated history, which he, a scholar himself, laments. The violence done to the books started before Sulla, and continued after they were transferred to Rome. Strabo notes that Sulla took the books after Apellicon had died, and this in a way minimises any suggestion of theft or violence.²³

We find another account of Apellicon's library in Plutarch's *Life of Sulla* (26.1–2). His narrative aligns with Strabo's, but there are some differences in emphasis.²⁴ Plutarch does not mention if Apellicon was alive or dead when Sulla seized his library, and he writes that Sulla took the library 'for himself' (ἐξεῖλεν ἑαυτῷ, 26.1). Like Strabo he laments the treatment that the books received from Neleus and his family, but he does not criticise Apellicon. Plutarch appears to approve of Tyrannio's handling of the books, and adds that Andronicus of Rhodes received copies of the books from him, which were then used for new publications of the texts and to draw up 'a catalogue' of the library (πίνακας, 26.1). He dates the transfer of the books to Rome to Sulla's visit two years after the city's capture, the same visit when Sulla was reportedly initiated into the Eleusinian mysteries. Since we have no secure date for Apellicon's death, we cannot be certain if both authors had the same date in mind for the transfer of the library.²⁵ The fact that Plutarch omits Apellicon's death from his narrative has the effect of placing the appropriation of the library in a more negative light in comparison with Strabo, and the same applies to his addition of the comment 'for himself'.²⁶ At Rome Tyrannio and Andronicus contributed to the preservation of the library, but Plutarch does not credit this to Sulla at all. If anything this silver lining to the transfer of the books in his view came about in spite of Sulla. In any case, Tyrannio and Andronicus worked on the texts long after Sulla had died, possibly more than three decades later.²⁷

A third source which has been cited for Sulla's involvement with Apellicon's library are Cicero's letters. He writes to his friend Atticus from Cumae in 55 B.C. that he

---

23 Strabo generally puts Sulla in a positive light: Engels (1999) 316; Dowling (2000) 330; Pretzler (2005) 157; Thein (2014) 183–184.
24 Plutarch cites Strabo's lost *Histories* after mentioning the library of Apellicon (*Sull.* 26.3), thus it has been suggested that his information about the latter also derived from the *Histories*, but this is an open question. Düring (1957) 394–395; Chroust (1962) 51 n.6; Düring (1966) 40 n. 250; and Gottschalk (1972) 338–339 argue for Strabo as a source. Barnes (1997) 3 prefers to think that Strabo and Plutarch had a common source.
25 On Sulla's visit to Athens in 84 see also Santangelo (2007) 215. On Sulla's initiation see further n. 40. The last datable event from Apellicon's life is his serving as one of the two magistrates in charge of the mint, cf. Habicht (1997) [1995] 103. Some scholars argue that he survived the siege and died during Sulla's visit in 84, see Habicht (1997) [1995] 313; cf. Engels (1999) 317.
26 Compare Plutarch's Aemilius Paullus, who takes nothing for himself but allows his sons to have Perseus' books: *Aem.* 28.11; cf. Bremer (2005) 260. Lucullus obtained libraries in Pontus and Asia Minor primarily to allow others to use the books, according to Plut. *Luc.* 42.1–2.
27 Barnes (1997) 17–24; cf. Hatzimichali (2013) 16.

is 'living on the library of Faustus' (*ego hic pascor bibliotheca Fausti, Att.* 4.10), the son of Sulla Felix. Shackleton-Bailey suggests that 'Faustus Sulla may have sold his books to Cicero or Cicero may have been reading them in his villa'.[28] Scholars have connected Cicero's remark to his repeated mentions of dealings with Tyrannio (*Att.* 4.4a; 4.8.2; *Q Fr.* 3.4.5; 3.5.6), on the one hand, and a quip Plutarch ascribes to Cicero about Faustus having to sell his possessions to pay his debts (*Cic.* 27.3), on the other, to suggest that Tyrannio sold Cicero (parts of) Apellicon's library which Faustus had inherited from his father.[29] But the sparse evidence can be interpreted in other ways, and Cicero nowhere mentions Tyrannio's handling of the Aristotelian texts.[30]

The picture painted by Plutarch and Strabo of Hellenistic Aristotelians lacking texts until the various publications based on Apellicon's collection has inspired a heated debate among historians and philosophers. The state of Aristotelian philosophy before the 1st century is at stake, as well as the influence of Andronicus on Aristotelianism from then onwards. A possible challenge to the narrative of Strabo and Plutarch comes from Athenaeus, who writes that Ptolemy Philadelphus bought from Neleus all the books that Aristotle and Theophrastus had entrusted to his care, and sent them to Alexandria.[31] This account may be corroborated by the medieval Aristotelian scholar Al-Farabi, who writes that Augustus found manuscripts of Aristotle's works in the library of Alexandria after defeating Cleopatra.[32] Conversely, Posidonius' comment that Apellicon 'bought the library of Aristotle' supports the account of Plutarch and Strabo,[33] as does an entry in an Arabic catalogue of Aristotle's works that reads 'his books which were found in the library of a man called Apellicon'.[34] The accounts of Athenaeus and Strabo are mutually exclusive because the former writes that *all* the books went to Alexandria. I follow Barnes in preferring the version of Strabo et al. Al-Farabi's remark need not contradict Strabo, since (some of) Apellicon's books may have later ended up in Alexandria; this leaves only Athenaeus to support the alternative tradition, while Posidonius and Strabo lived and wrote much sooner after the events in question than he did.[35]

Even if we trust Strabo on Apellicon's acquisition of the books and Sulla's transfer of them to Rome, his claim that there were no Aristotelian texts available until Apellicon's library surfaced strains credibility. It has been suggested that

---

28 Shackleton-Bailey (1999) 324.
29 Chroust (1962) 52–53; cf. Lindsay (1997) 294–295.
30 Cf. Gottschalk (1972) 338 n.1; Barnes (1997) 16–17.
31 Ath. 1.4: Ἀριστοτέλην τε τὸν φιλόσοφον καὶ Θεόφραστον καὶ τὸν τὰ τούτων διατηρήσαντα βιβλία Νηλέα.
32 Fortenbaugh et al. (1992) 1.94–95; cf. Barnes (1997) 6.
33 *BNJ* 87 F 36 (Posidon.).
34 Translation in Düring (1957) 221–231, at 230.
35 Barnes (1997) 8–12.

Strabo wanted both to explain the decline of the Peripatetic school in the Hellenistic period, and to highlight the importance of his teacher Tyrannio in helping to make these texts available again, which is why he overstated the rarity of Apellicon's texts.[36] It is beyond the scope of this article to discuss the influence of Andronicus and of Apellicon's collection on the Aristotelian corpus, but we can safely say this much: Apellicon bought a collection of supposed autographs of Aristotle and Theophrastus, the rediscovery of which coincided with a resurgence of the Peripatos, but we do not need to assume a causal relation. It is inevitable that other copies of Aristotle's texts were available before Apellicon's collection was copied and disseminated.[37]

It is time to return to Sulla. How do the accounts of Sulla and Apellicon's library that we find in Strabo and Plutarch compare to the saying from Aelian and Hopkinson's interpretation of it? Both Strabo and Plutarch omit any mention of violence in connection with the capture of the library. If we follow Plutarch's dating of the event, there is even some temporal distance between Sulla's sack of the city and the transfer of the books, and it is likely that Apellicon had already died when Sulla appropriated the library. According to Strabo the books fared as badly at Rome as they had at Athens, with Sulla's actions indirectly contributing to the further deterioration of the texts. In Plutarch the books do better at Rome than at Athens. However, this is due not to Sulla but to the scholars who gained access to the texts after he died. We have no indication that Sulla or even his son took any interest in the contents of Apellicon's library. I propose, therefore, that the saying about Sulla and the philosophers draws attention, in fact, to a contrast between Sulla's disposition and the philosophical writings the library contained.

The saying from Aelian could be rephrased, I suggest, as 'what does a man like Sulla need books of philosophy for?' On this reading the Greek cultural discourse from which the phrase arose held a dim view of Sulla's intellectual accomplishments, thinking it unlikely that he would ever sit down with a book of philosophy.[38] But how would such a characterisation compare to other accounts of Sulla's relation to Greek culture and education?

---

36 Chroust (1962); cf. Lindsay (1997). Strabo calls Tyrannio his teacher at 12.3.16.
37 For a full discussion of these issues see Barnes (1997) 24–66; for a less sceptical view see Hatzimichali (2013).
38 I am omitting the possibility that the antithesis is between Sulla and the philosopher-generals of 1st-century Athens, i.e. Apellicon and Athenion (Posidon. *ap*. Ath. 5.48–53 = *BNJ* 87 F 36; Euseb. *Praec. evang.* 15.2, cf. Barnes (1997) 10), as well as Aristion (App. *Mith.* 28). Such a reading diverges from the other sayings on the dolphins and oxen model: the reason that dolphins and oxen, ploughs and fishermen, or dogs and baths have nothing in common is not dislike. Rather, in each case, there is a fundamental incongruity.

Sulla and *paideia*

Keaveney in his biography refers to Sulla repeatedly as a philhellene.[39] It seems that this might be an argument against interpreting the Sulla and the philosophers saying in the manner I propose: if Sulla is a philhellene, then why would it be so unlikely for him to take an interest in books of Greek philosophy? Keaveney cites several pieces of evidence to support his characterisation: Sallust writes that Sulla was skilled as much in Greek as in Latin literature (*BJ* 95.3), he is reported to have worn a Greek style short cloak when he was in Naples (Cic. *Rab. Post.* 27; Val. Max. 3.6.3), he was initiated into the Eleusinian mysteries (Plut. *Sull.* 26.1),[40] when he was at Athens he spent time with Atticus (Nep. *Att.* 4), and he brought back from Greece (or at least tried to) more than just Apellicon's library – in Lucian we find the remark that a ship carrying paintings by Zeuxis sank en route from Athens to Rome before reaching its destination,[41] and Pliny writes that Sulla brought columns of the still unfinished temple of Olympian Zeus to Rome to be used for temples on the Capitol.[42]

In considering Sulla's philhellenism it is worthwhile to distinguish how Romans treat this topic from how Roman Greeks approach it. Nepos, Cicero, Valerius Maximus, Sallust, and Pliny depict Sulla as a Roman who has a philhellenic attitude that is entirely appropriate for a member of the Roman elite during the Late Republic. Nepos' account of the friendship of Sulla and Atticus is particularly interesting because it emphasises that Atticus' Greek was so good that he *seemed* to have been born in Athens, while it was clear from his Latin that he was Roman born.[43] This is why Sulla was so fond of him: a companion in Athens who was beyond reproach Roman. Gruen has shown how to be a philhellene in the right way was a balancing act. For instance, knowing Greek and some Greek literature was a good thing, as long as traditional Roman education (legal and military) was not neglected. Philhellenism always needed to promote, not harm Roman interests.[44] Sulla, by knowing Greek and Latin literature equally well, by using columns

---

39 Keaveney (2005a) ²[1982] 105, 161, 181.
40 Plutarch's notice about Sulla's initiation into the Eleusinian mysteries has been called into question; he writes only μυηθείς without specifying the Eleusinian mysteries, as he does in other cases, and the verb is odd within the sentence. Clinton (1989) 1503: 'The suspicion arises that μυηθείς either is not exactly what Plutarch wrote or does not refer to the Eleusinian mysteries'. If he was initiated he would be in the company of other Romans of the Late Republic, e.g. Cicero and Atticus: Clinton (1989) 1504–1507.
41 Lucian, *Zeux.* 3.
42 Plin. *HN* 36.5: *Sic est inchoatum Athenis templum Iovis Olympii, ex quo Sulla Capitolinis aedibus advexerat columnas.*
43 Nep. *Att.* 4.1: *sic enim Graece loquebatur, ut Athenis natus videretur; tanta autem suavitas erat sermonis Latini, ut appareret in eo nativum quendam leporem esse, non ascitum.*
44 Gruen (1992) 223–271; cf. Rawson (1985) 3–18; Ferrary (1988a) esp. Part 3; Scholz (2011) 132–141; Eckert (2016a) 25–26. For the Imperial period see Woolf (1994); (2006).

from Athens for use in Roman temples, and by wearing a Greek cloak to win over locals in Naples is presented in Roman authors as having mastered this balancing act quite well.

In the Roman understanding of philhellenism there need not be any contradiction between being a lover of Greece and using violence in conquering Greek cities.[45] I want to propose, however, that from a Greek perspective the combination of Roman philhellenism, Roman violence in the east, and Roman appropriation of objects of Greek culture *could* be seen as problematic, also in the case of Sulla. I have argued elsewhere that in Greek writers the representation of Sulla's capture of Athens changed over time: in earlier authors (e.g. Strabo and Diodorus) the siege is presented primarily from a military perspective, while in later authors (e.g. Plutarch and Pausanias) the emphasis shifts to Sulla's destruction of cultural capital, and his treatment of Athens comes to be understood as excessive and even irrational. This change can be explained, I suggest, as a product of the growing Athenocentrism of the first two centuries A.D., in Rome as well as in Greece. Athens increasingly came to be seen as the symbol of Greek culture, and in response to this an image of Athens as cultural symbol was retrojected onto the 1st century B.C. Sulla's sack of Athens gained in significance, and Plutarch and Pausanias foreground the memories of the destruction and appropriation of temples, statues, and books during the war. In Greek discourse Sulla's reputation comes to be defined to an important degree by his sack of Athens, and the violence and looting it entailed.[46] The representation of Sulla as a looter of Greece and destroyer of Athens in authors such as Plutarch, Pausanias, and Lucian, I suggest, provided the basis for Aelian's saying about Sulla and the philosophers. The memories of Sulla's rapacity and violence in Athens make it an absurd joke that he would actually be *reading* the books from Apellicon's philosophical library.

One indication of the image of Sulla as looter in Athens is that improbable thefts or acts of destruction come to be attributed to him on top of the violence that is securely attested. For instance, the Zeuxis painting that, according to Lucian, Sulla stole from Athens might, it is argued, never have existed. Remarkably, aside from his comment on Apellicon's library, this is the only time Lucian mentions Sulla.[47] Another example may be Pausanias' account of Pericles' Odeion, located near the theatre of Dionysus at the foot of the Acropolis: 'Close to the temple of Dionysus and the theatre is a structure that is said to have been made to imitate the tent of Xerxes:

---

45 Sulla as 'the conquering general anxious to show his respect and affection for the superior culture of the conquered race': Keaveney (2005a) ²[1982] 105. For Sulla, philhellenism, and conquest see also Thein (2014) 179–183. Dmitriev (2011) 159–160 has argued that there was little to no connection between Roman philhellenism and Roman politics towards Greece.
46 Kuin (2018).
47 Pretzler (2009); *contra* Miles (2008) 24.

a second one has been made though, because the Roman general Sulla burned the old one when he took Athens'.[48] Pericles' Odeion was modelled on Xerxes' tent, and it was part of the architectural programme commemorating the Persian Wars at Athens. Pausanias' comment is noteworthy because it contradicts Appian's statement that Aristion and the Athenians burned the Odeion themselves, to prevent Sulla from using the timber for war machines (*Mith.* 38). Modern scholars generally side with Appian.[49] If Pausanias is indeed wrong to charge Sulla instead of Aristion with the burning of the Odeion, his 'mistake' can be explained in terms of his generally negative representation of Sulla's actions in Greece.[50] As mentioned, Pausanias condemns Sulla for stealing a statue of Athena from Alalcomenae (9.33.6), appropriating half the territory of Thebes to compensate the sanctuaries (at Delphi, Olympia, and Epidaurus) for the treasures he took from them (9.7.5–6), stealing and then rededicating a statue of Dionysus at Orchomenus made by the sculptor Myron (9.30.1), and removing the shields dedicated in the Stoa of Zeus Eleutherios in Athens, 'among other possessions of the Athenians' (10.21.5–6).[51] Perhaps there were competing oral traditions about the burning of the Odeion at Athens, with Pausanias choosing the one that best suited his narrative agenda.

In Plutarch's account of the fall of Athens, finally, we also find information that may contradict other sources, though not as clearly as in the case of Pericles' Odeion. Plutarch writes that during the siege of Athens Sulla destroyed the sites of both the Academy and the Lyceum. He is the earliest author to mention this: 'He laid his hands on the sacred groves, and he cut down the Academy, because of the suburbs it had the most trees, and the Lyceum too'.[52] Sulla cut down the trees of the Academy and the Lyceum, which had a religious significance, because he needed wood to build siege-engines.[53] Earlier sources describe the Academy in the decades after the sack without mentioning any damage. Strabo is silent on any Sullan destruction at the Lyceum or Academy, although he mentions both places as

---

48 Paus. 1.20.4: ἔστι δὲ πλησίον τοῦ τε ἱεροῦ τοῦ Διονύσου καὶ τοῦ θεάτρου κατασκεύασμα, ποιηθῆναι δὲ τῆς σκηνῆς αὐτὸ ἐς μίμησιν τῆς Ξέρξου λέγεται· ἐποιήθη δὲ καὶ δεύτερον, τὸ γὰρ ἀρχαῖον στρατηγὸς Ῥωμαίων ἐνέπρησε Σύλλας Ἀθήνας ἑλών. Translation adapted from Jones' Loeb edition.
49 E.g., Camp (2001) 185; Hoff (1997) 37, 41. Strabo mentions the Odeion but not the damage (9.1.17); it may already have been rebuilt by his lifetime. Ariobarzanes II of Cappodocia, who ruled from 65 to 52 B.C., paid for its reconstruction. See *IG* II² 3426 and Vitr. 5.9.1.
50 Cf. Arafat (1996) 101; Assenmaker (2013a) 400–401.
51 On Sulla as plunderer in Pausanias see also Miles (2008) 93–94. On Pausanias and Athens see Pretzler (2005); (2007) 142–153.
52 Plut. *Sull.* 12.3: ἐπεχείρησε τοῖς ἱεροῖς ἄλσεσι, καὶ τήν τ' Ἀκαδήμειαν ἔκειρε δενδροφορωτάτην προαστείων οὖσαν καὶ τὸ Λύκειον. Translation adapted from Perrin's Loeb edition.
53 The trees of the Academy were thought to be related to the sacred olive-tree on the Acropolis burned but not destroyed by the Persians: Hdt. 8.55; Paus. 1.27.2, 1.30.2. Appian also records that Sulla ordered the felling of trees in the Academy, but he does not mention the Lyceum (*Mith.* 30).

Athenian landmarks rich in history and myth (9.1.17). Similarly, in the opening of the last book of his *De finibus*, which is set in 79 B.C. and takes place in the Academy, Cicero omits any reference to the violence that would have taken place there just a few years previously; scholars have explained this as a pointed, intentional omission.[54] So perhaps the destruction in the Academy and the Lyceum was less severe than Plutarch has led some scholars to believe?[55] Strabo and Cicero (and, partially, Appian) did not necessarily suppress Sulla's actions in these areas, but they may have thought, possibly, that it was not on such a scale as to warrant discussion. If Plutarch exaggerated the Sullan violence at the Academy and Lyceum, one reason for this, as in the case of Pausanias, could be that it fitted well with his overall view of Sulla's actions at Athens and in Greece. Plutarch discusses Sulla's thefts from the sanctuaries at Delphi, Olympia, and Epidaurus at length. He describes in great detail which objects Sulla stole (and sometimes destroyed), their beauty, and their importance, and he contrasts Sulla's behaviour with that of other Roman generals who not only spared the sanctuaries but actually made dedications (*Sull.* 12.3–9).[56] When Sulla takes the Piraeus he destroys the Arsenal of Philo, which, Plutarch adds, was 'an amazing work' (θαυμαζόμενον ἔργον, *Sull.* 14.7). In Plutarch's narrative Sulla is emphatically presented as a destroyer of feats of Greek workmanship and of sites of Greek learning.[57]

On three occasions, finally, Plutarch refers to Sulla's attitude towards the history of Greece, but his comments seem contradictory. He speculates that Sulla was motivated to capture Athens, in part, because of its storied past (*Sull.* 13.1). Yet, when a peace embassy of the Athenians recalls the glories of the city's myths and history, Sulla rebuffs them saying that he 'was not sent to Athens by the Romans wanting to learn'.[58] Once the city has been taken Sulla, in turn, pardons the Athenians with reference to the Athenian past: 'By this time he was also sated with vengeance – he spoke some words in praise of the ancient Athenians, and said that he forgave a few for the sake of many, the living for the sake of the dead'.[59] Thein explains the contrast between the second and the third passage by arguing that Plutarch

---

[54] Eckert (2016a) 99–100 attributes this omission to the taboo status among Romans of Sulla's capture of Athens. Connolly (forthcoming) argues that Cicero wanted to recreate the Academy as an idealised, pacified place.
[55] See e.g. Hoff (1997); Mango (2010) 119, 122; Eckert (2016a) 96–97.
[56] Cf. Thein (2014) 180. The generals are T. Quinctius Flamininus, M'. Acilius Glabrio, and L. Aemilius Paullus: cf. Plut. *Aem.* 28.4; *Flam.* 12.6. On Sulla and the sanctuaries see also Diod. Sic. 38/39.7 and Paus. 9.7.5–6. See Ruggeri (2006) 320–322 for a detailed comparison of the Diodorus and Plutarch passages with regard to their sources.
[57] Plutarch may have been influenced by Sallust's account of Sullan looting in Asia Minor: Sall. *Cat.* 11; cf. Miles (2008) 157.
[58] Plut. *Sull.* 13.4: ἐγὼ γὰρ οὐ φιλομαθήσων εἰς Ἀθήνας ὑπὸ Ῥωμαίων ἐπέμφθην.
[59] Plut. *Sull.* 14.5: αὐτός τε μεστὸς ὢν ἤδη τῆς τιμωρίας, ἐγκώμιόν τι τῶν παλαιῶν Ἀθηναίων ὑπειπὼν ἔφη χαρίζεσθαι πολλοῖς μὲν ὀλίγους, ζῶντας δὲ τεθνηκόσιν.

contrasted his [Sulla's] severity towards Aristion during the siege with his clemency to the Athenians at its violent conclusion. Plutarch adopts this structure as the basis for his own narrative of how Sulla learns to become a philhellene: he is rudely dismissive of Athenian history in his words to the envoys of Aristion, but then as victor he praises the Athenians of the past and thus he presents his clemency as an act of philhellenism.[60]

I agree that Plutarch has Sulla present his pardon as an act of philhellenism, but the notion of a learning curve is complicated by Plutarch's earlier suggestion that Sulla was motivated by Athens' storied past from the start. In any case, the inclusion of the wry remark that Sulla was 'sated with vengeance' juxtaposed with Sulla's display of philhellenism shows, in my view, that in this passage Plutarch regards Sulla's remark as precisely that, a charade.

Roman philhellenism was a cultural strategy that first and foremost benefited Roman rule. Connolly takes Gruen's argument about Roman philhellenism one step further when she writes:

> [I]mperial Hellenism brought a particular payoff to the Romans. It functioned primarily not as a mode of Greek self-differentation but as an instrument of Imperial assimilation. Universal, globally appealing Hellenism mapped itself as the intellectual and ideological system for universal and globalizing (if not globally appealing) Roman empire.[61]

In my view Plutarch and his peers would, on some level, have been aware of this imbalance. Even if Greeks and particularly Athenians were sometimes able to play this Roman strategy to their own advantage,[62] I think the ironies and complexities of the conqueror's love and appropriation of Greek culture were not lost on them, especially not intellectuals like Plutarch and Pausanias. Donations and dedications to Athens or other Greek cities from Romans were forms of philhellenism that were valued and often rewarded. Romans purchasing art for export was also not an issue. But sending Greek treasures to Rome during wartime was considered looting by Plutarch, Pausanias, and other Greeks.

Conclusion

We started with an odd saying recorded in the Suda and attributed to Aelian: 'for what do a dolphin and an ox have in common, they say, and what Sulla and philosophers?' The first part was certainly a colloquialism, given that other instances and

---

60 Thein (2014) 181.
61 Connolly (2007) 31.
62 Well-known examples are the city selling Athenian citizenship to Romans, which was forbidden by Augustus (Cass. Dio 54.7.3), and allowing Romans to re-inscribe existing statues for themselves, see Dio Chrys. *Or.* 31; cf. Moser (2017).

variations of it are extant. As for the interjection 'they say', which signals that a proverbial expression is cited, it is placed in the middle of the sentence, so it can apply either to the first part alone, or to both the first and second parts. Did Aelian come up with the variation about Sulla and the philosophers himself, or was he repeating something that he had heard or read elsewhere? In the absence of other written attestations we cannot know the answer to this question, but even if Aelian improvised the second part himself, he clearly assumed that his audience would understand the reference and appreciate the joke.

I have argued that for most recipients of Aelian's witticism the 'Sulla and philosophers' part would have evoked the fact that Sulla appropriated the library of Apellicon and its supposed autographs of Aristotle and Theophrastus. The implication of the phrase is that Sulla had no interest in books of philosophy. In other words, 'what on earth does a man like Sulla want books of philosophy for?' To understand how such a joke works we must look to the broader context of the Greek memory of the capture of Athens in the Imperial period, notably the accounts of Plutarch and Pausanias which foreground (and in some cases possibly exaggerate) the thefts and the destruction of Greek cultural capital by Sulla or his men. That Sulla was also said to have violated the hallowed sites of philosophy, the Lyceum and Academy, is especially relevant.

Sulla and the philosophers have as little in common as dolphins and oxen. The persistence of such an idea, as well as the elliptical reference to Sulla's appropriation of Apellicon's books in Lucian's *The Ignorant Book Collector* show that within the broader context of Sulla's siege of Athens this event was remembered into the 3rd century A.D. In Greek discourse Sulla came to be associated with the destruction of Athens to such an extent that the possibility of him caring for the philosophers of Athens became the subject of ridicule, which, if indeed only the philosopher is *felix*, was another sign of his *infelicitas*. The crisis of the violent capture of Athens lived on through the centuries in memory, in language, and, ultimately, in a joke.[63]

---

63 This research has been undertaken as part of the 'After the Crisis' research project at Groningen University and the OIKOS Anchoring Innovation research agenda. I would like to thank the editors for their helpful comments and suggestions.

Alexandra Eckert
9 Reconsidering the Sulla Myth

The idea of the 'Sulla myth' traces its origins to a seminal article by Laffi entitled 'Il mito di Silla' published in 1967. The argument put forward by the Italian scholar in this study is that the characterisation of Sulla's personality and actions is uniformly negative in the ancient sources written after Caesar's civil war victory over Pompey. From this point, Greek and Roman historiography conveyed a highly unfavourable image of Sulla, defined by tyranny, cruelty, and the proscriptions. In Laffi's opinion, this negative view had not existed before Caesar's victory.[1] Even the exclusion from public office imposed by Sulla on the sons of the proscribed, a major violation of fundamental principles of Roman law, remained in force until 49 B.C. For Laffi this signalled that Sulla's reforms were not seriously challenged in the decades after his death, and the conclusion drawn from this is that a majority of the Roman elite held either a favourable or balanced view of the dictator.[2]

Laffi's ideas were adopted and developed seventeen years later in an article on the origins of 'le mythe de Sylla' by the French scholar Hinard. According to this study, contemporaries had a nuanced memory of Sulla, and this prevented the emergence of a 'Sulla myth' during the Late Republic. Only in the following generation did Sulla turn into a negative *exemplum* of cruelty.[3] Laffi saw the 'Sulla myth' as a product of Caesar's civil war victory, but Hinard took the position that it came into existence no earlier than the beginning of the principate. In his view, several 'historical accidents' contributed to the development of the 'Sulla myth': first, Caesar's victory in the civil war with Pompey; second, the proscriptions of the Second Triumvirate; and third,

---

[1] Laffi (1967) 274: 'L'esito della guerra civile con la vittoria di Cesare, l'anti-Silla, segnò il trionfo definitivo della tradizione ostile al dittatore ... Questa valutazione negativa di Silla influenzerà in maniera determinante tutta la tradizione letteraria dell'ultima età repubblicana e dell'età imperiale' ('The outcome of the Civil War with the victory of Caesar, Sulla's opponent, signified the final triumph of a tradition hostile towards the dictator ... This negative characterisation of Sulla significantly influenced the literary tradition of the late Republic and the Imperial period'). Translations are mine unless otherwise stated.
[2] Cf. Laffi (1967) 185–186. Gabba, a fellow Italian, adopted Laffi's terminology and argument. See Gabba (1972) 803: 'Certamente su questa tragica, inevitabile conseguenza della vittoria sillana insistettero la propaganda e la storiografia avverse a Silla, specialmente quella cesariana, e il mito della crudeltà di Silla si è trasformato in un dato sicuro' ('Certainly and tragically, the inevitable consequence of Sulla's victory was the rise of propaganda and historiography hostile to Sulla, specifically Caesar's propaganda; and the myth of Sulla's cruelty was transformed into an undisputed fact'). Badian (1970) accepted the reality of Sulla's violence and argued that the reforms were a failure, due to the disunity of his partisans in the years after his death. For the Sulla myth, see also the brief discussion in Zecchini (2018) 255.
[3] Hinard (1984) 83; 85. Dowling's position is similar, but she does not use the term 'Sulla myth'. See esp. Dowling (2000) 306. For the Sulla myth cf. also Urso (2016) 11.

Octavian's victory at the battle of Actium. Augustan propaganda attributed sole responsibility for the proscriptions of 43 to Mark Antony, and in the historiography of the Early Empire this image of Antony as a bloodthirsty tyrant was applied to Sulla, who had been the first to proscribe his fellow Romans. Hinard uses the term 'noircissement' to describe the gradual 'blackening' of Sulla's image. Twenty-four years later he modified his position. In his chapter 'L'énigme, l'exemplum et le mythe' published in 2008, he argued that Sulla's negative image reached its final form not under Augustus but in the time of Seneca the Younger.

The use of the term 'Sulla myth' by Laffi and Hinard provokes several questions. Is it true that ancient sources dating from the Late Republic are silent on the scale of Sulla's atrocities? Do depictions of Sulla as a cruel tyrant rest solely on him having been the first to introduce proscriptions? Could Sulla's image as a cruel tyrant have emerged without 'historical accidents' such as Caesar's civil war victory, the proscriptions of 43, or Octavian's emergence as Augustus? Is Sulla's portrayal as a bloodthirsty tyrant by authors of the principate defined by a suspicious level of hyperbole? In order to answer these questions this chapter will re-examine the Late Republican sources, in particular Cicero's speeches *Pro Sexto Roscio* (80 B.C.) and *De lege agraria* (63 B.C.), along with his philosophical treatises *De finibus* (45 B.C.) and *De officiis* (44 B.C.). This evidence offers clear testimony that it was possible, long before Caesar's dictatorship, to label Sulla a tyrant and to characterise the violence of his civil war victory as excessive in scale and marred by acts of transgressive cruelty. The readings offered by Hinard in response are not convincing: thus, for example, he argues that Cicero attributes *crudelitas* (cruelty) to Sulla only in the context of the public auction of assets confiscated from the proscribed, and that the word was used as a synonym for *avaritia* (avarice). In this view, the Latin word for cruelty refers to the Sullan vice of greed and not, or only to a negligible extent, to violence and bloodshed.[4]

Laffi and Hinard took the view that Sulla's image as a cruel tyrant was a 'myth' which did not exist in the decades after Sulla's death. This chapter challenges this idea of a 'blackening' of Sulla's reception in ancient writers. It argues that the enormous death toll of the punitive measures carried out by Sulla in 82/81 affected all strata of Roman society and encompassed much more than the proscriptions, which were directed at a substantial, but limited number of the senatorial and equestrian elite. Sulla's actions constituted a transgression of Roman values hitherto unknown in Roman history, and a majority of Romans perceived him in highly negative terms even during his lifetime. In the two decades after Sulla's death this consensus was reflected in a series of initiatives to mitigate or reverse aspects of Sulla's legacy.

---

4 Hinard (2008) 134–135

Cicero on Sulla's Cruelty

In 80, Sulla, as consul, was still the dominant force in Roman politics when Cicero delivered his defence of Sextus Roscius of Ameria on the charge of parricide.[5] It is clear that Cicero, in his first criminal trial, had to tread carefully, but there is one remarkable passage at the end of the speech in which he refers directly to the 'cruelty' of the civil war period.

Cicero's main target in the *Pro Sexto Roscio* is the Sullan freedman Chrysogonus, who is presented as the leading figure, along with two relatives of Cicero's client, in a conspiracy to kill the Elder Sextus Roscius and arrange for his proscription in order to secure legal tenure of his estates. The events are said to have taken place some months after the closure of the proscription lists on the 1st June 81, hence the proscription was illegal. As for the murder, the conspirators attempted to cover their tracks with a false accusation of parricide against the dead man's son, hoping that their connections with Sulla would suffice to secure a conviction. Cicero obtained an acquittal by exposing the true culprits, and by making sure to absolve Sulla from any responsibility for the death of the Elder Roscius: as dictator he was focused on affairs of state and could not possibly have known of his subordinate's criminal schemes.[6]

Cicero's strategy was to praise Sulla and focus his attack on Chrysogonus, hence Laffi concluded that Cicero's attitude to Sulla in the *Pro Sexto Roscio* was favourable.[7] In doing so, however, he ignored another line of argument that is of equal importance to the speech. In his final plea, Cicero describes the devastating impact of the proscriptions on Roman society as a whole and makes an appeal to the judges to banish cruelty from the *res publica*.

> There is no one among you who does not know that the Roman people, who were formerly considered to be most lenient towards their enemies, is today suffering from cruelty towards its own citizens. Ban this cruelty from the *res publica*, gentlemen; do not allow it to rage any longer in this Republic; for it not only involves this evil, that it has removed so many citizens by a most savage death, but it has also stifled all feeling of pity in the hearts of men generally most merciful, by familiarising them with all kinds of evil. For when, every hour, we witness or hear of an act of cruelty, even those of us who are by nature most merciful lose from our heart in this constant present of trouble all feeling of humanity.[8]

---

5 For the date of the speech cf. Dyck (2010), esp. 4.
6 Cic. *Rosc. Am.* 22 and 131.
7 Laffi (1967) 261–263.
8 Cic. *Rosc. Am.* 154: *vestrum nemo est quin intellegat populum Romanum qui quondam in hostis lenissimus existimabatur hoc tempore domestica crudelitate laborare. Hanc tollite ex civitate, iudices, hanc pati nolite diutius in hac re publica versari; quae non modo id habet in se mali quod tot civis atrocissime sustulit verum etiam hominibus lenissimis ademit misericordiam consuetudine incommodorum. Nam cum omnibus horis aliquid atrociter fieri videmus aut audimus, etiam qui natura mitissimi sumus adsiduitate molestiarum sensum omnem humanitatis ex animis amittimus.* Translation above: Loeb edition, J. H. Freese, adapted.

Anyone at the trial will have known who was ultimately responsible for the 'cruelty' at home suffered by the Roman people (*populum Romanum ... hoc tempore domestica crudelitate laborare*), or the 'most savage' deaths of so many citizens (*quod tot cives atrocissime sustulit*). Therefore, there was no need for Cicero to name Sulla, the author of the proscriptions, when he spoke of the threat to social cohesion and the humanity of Roman society resulting from the continuing atrocities that were witnessed or reported on an hourly basis (*cum omnibus horis aliquid atrociter fieri videmus aut audimus*). Cicero's message to the judges was that his client had to be acquitted in order to signal to Chrysogonus and other Sullan partisans that the arbitrary extension of the violence of the proscriptions had to end.

The implicit criticism of Sulla in the above passage shows that Laffi's reading of the speech as favourable to the dictator is not really satisfactory. One may also note how Cicero uses highly emotive language to describe Sullan violence, notably the words *atrox* and *crudelitas*. The passage offers a direct condemnation which cannot be explained by Hinard's theory that Cicero focused almost exclusively on greed and the confiscation of property not cruelty and physical acts of violence when he lamented the *crudelitas* of the proscriptions.[9]

Let us now turn to the philosophical work *De officiis*, written towards the end of Cicero's life, in 44 B.C. In one passage he laments that Rome's empire was no longer governed with justice and moderation after Sulla had shown such excessive cruelty to Roman citizens. The honourable, conservative cause championed by Sulla in the civil war was disgraced by his victory, and as an illustration Cicero recalls how Sulla dared to say he was selling his own booty (*praedam se suam vendere*) when he placed the spear of the auctioneer in the Forum to offer the property of Roman citizens for sale.[10] If we focus only on these lines and the auction context it might seem that Cicero does use the term *crudelitas*, as Hinard argued, to highlight the vice of greed, not cruelty.[11] However, Cicero continues his discussion by drawing the attention of his audience back to the present, and to the fact that auctions of confiscated properties had reappeared after Caesar's civil war victory: 'Never will seed and cause for civil wars be missing, as long as evil men (*homines perditi*) remember that blood-stained spear (*hastam illam cruentam*) and hope for its return'.[12]

---

9 Hinard (1984) 87–91; (2008) 135–136.
10 Cic. *Off.* 2.27: *Sensim hanc consuetudinem et disciplinam iam antea minuebamus, post vero Sullae victoriam penitus amisimus; desitum est enim videri quicquam in socios iniquum, cum exstitisset in cives tanta crudelitas. Ergo in illo secuta est honestam causam non honesta victoria. Est enim ausus dicere hasta posita, cum bona in foro venderet et bonorum virorum et locupletium et certe civium, praedam se suam vendere.*
11 Hinard (1984) 86; (2008) 134–135. Dowling (2000) 312 follows a similar line of argument, as does Zecchini (2002) 45 and 54.
12 Cic. *Off.* 2.29: *Nec vero umquam bellorum civilium semen et causa deerit, dum homines perditi hastam illam cruentam et meminerint et sperabunt ...*

The passage focuses on avarice and the cycle of civil war violence, but the spear is notably blood-stained, and Sulla's *crudelitas*, contrasted with Rome's clement treatment of its foreign subjects, clearly refers to the physical acts of violence that defined his civil war victory.

Cicero on Sulla's Tyranny

Sulla is linked with the vice of cruelty, and there are also texts in which Cicero labels him a tyrant. In 63, as consul, Cicero delivered three speeches against the agrarian law of the tribune Rullus, and in the second speech he urged an assembly of the people to reject the bill unless they wanted to see compensation paid to Sulla's partisans for estates acquired for much less than their true value in the Sullan auctions of estates confiscated from the proscribed in 82–81. There were also plans to establish the Sullan profiteers as legal owners of large plots of illegally-occupied land adjacent to the estates purchased in Sulla's auctions.[13] At one point Cicero reminds his audience of Sulla's arrogance at one of the auctions when he used the term booty (*praeda*) to refer to property confiscated from Roman citizens who had been proscribed on his orders without having been condemned by any court.[14]

In the third speech Cicero recalls the Valerian law, the enabling law of the Sullan dictatorship, which had been forced through an assembly of the Roman people at the end of 82, a period of terror within living memory for many in Cicero's audience.[15] In the *De lege agraria*, the Valerian law is described as most hateful and unjust, an allusion to the coercion with which it was passed into law. Cicero even calls Sulla a tyrant (*hic rei publicae tyrannum lege constituit*) in a summary of the exceptional powers the Valerian law granted to Sulla:

> Of all laws I think that this is the most unjust and least like a law, which Lucius Flaccus, the *interrex*, passed in regard to Sulla – that all his acts, whatever they were, should be ratified. For, why in all other states, when tyrants are set up, all laws are annulled and abolished, in this case Flaccus by his law established a tyrant in a Republic. It is a hateful law, as I have said, but there is some excuse for it; for it seems to be not the law of a man, but of the times.[16]

---

13 Cic. *Leg. agr.* 2.69–70.
14 Cic. *Leg. agr.* 2.56. For the wider implications of Sulla's statement, see Eckert (2016b) 139–140. For Sulla's veterans, cf. Keaveney in this volume.
15 App. *B Civ.* 1.98–99 illustrates how the Roman people ratified the Valerian law under compulsion.
16 Cic. *Leg. agr.* 3.5: *Omnium legum iniquissimam dissimillimamque legis esse arbitror eam quam L. Flaccus interrex de Sulla tulit, ut omnia quaecumque ille fecisset essent rata. Nam cum ceteris in civitatibus tyrannis institutis leges omnes exstinguantur atque tollantur, hic rei publicae tyrannum lege constituit. Est invidiosa lex, sicuti dixi, verum tamen habet excusationem; non enim videtur hominis lex esse, sed temporis.* Translation: Loeb edition, J. H. Freese, adapted.

Hinard argued that Cicero's use of the word 'tyrant' in this particular passage does not convey connotations of cruelty, violence, or bloodshed, but was meant to describe Sulla's exceptional power as dictator exclusively from an abstract legal perspective.[17] Yet a closer look at Cicero's third speech on the agrarian law calls this position into question. We may assume that a considerable part of Cicero's audience had first-hand knowledge of the Valerian law, the circumstances of its passage into law, and the fact that it ratified the killing and dispossession of citizens without trial. Indeed, Cicero had already recalled the negative associations of the Valerian law in the second agrarian speech when he revived memories of the proscription auctions and the illegal occupations of land by Sulla's partisans. In the third speech he introduces the Valerian law with the telling statement that it was the most unjust of all laws (*omnium legum iniquissimam*). This prepares the stage not for an abstract legal discussion of Sulla's powers, but for succinctly illustrating a key characteristic of Sulla's rule: arbitrariness and injustice. The Valerian law declared all of Sulla's acts to be ratified, even those which constituted major violations of Roman norms and values. In contrast with other polities where tyrants abolish all law, the Valerian law legalised the arbitrary injustice of Sulla's tyranny.[18] It is thus no surprise that Cicero concludes by stating the *lex Valeria* was a hateful law (*est invidiosa lex*).

In Cicero's philosophical treatise 'On Moral Ends' (*De finibus bonorum et malorum*), written in 45 B.C., three tyrannical vices are ascribed to Sulla. In the third book of this treatise, Cicero's interlocutor, Cato the Younger (95–46 B.C.), illustrates the key attributes of a man adhering to the Stoic ideals by describing counter-examples from Roman history.[19] According to Cato, Sulla was a master of three pestilential vices: licentiousness, avarice, and cruelty (*Sulla, qui trium pestiferorum vitiorum, luxuriae, avaritiae, crudelitatis, magister fuit*).[20] Sulla is here described as a 'master of cruelty', and in the *De lege agraria* he had been called a 'tyrant', and thus it might be argued that Cicero thought of Sulla as a 'cruel tyrant', but Hinard refrains from linking the two passages on the grounds that they come from works of different genres written almost 20 years apart in very different historical contexts. He also points out the difficulty of trying to determine if Cicero had rendered his own opinion on Sulla in the *De finibus* or Cato the Younger's.[21]

---

17 Hinard (1984) 84–85; cf. (2008) 133. Hinard disputed Lanciotti's position that the term 'tyrant' in Cic. *Leg. agr.* 3.5 encompasses cruelty. Cf. Lanciotti (1977) 130–131.
18 The Valerian law did not only ratify Sulla's acts retrospectively, but also proactively legalised all his future acts. Cf. Cic. *Verr.* 2.3.82: [...] *ut ipsius voluntas ei posset esse pro lege*; Schol. Gronov. in Cic. *Rosc. Am.* 125 (314 Stangl): *hic tulit legem: quicquid Sulla dixisset lex esset.*
19 For the Stoic ideas expressed in this passage see Annas/Woolf (2001) 89 n. 49.
20 Cic. *Fin.* 3.75.
21 Hinard (1984) 84–85, arguing against Lanciotti, who uses the passage in the *De finibus* to argue that key aspects of Sulla's image as a cruel tyrant already existed before the principate. See Lanciotti (1977) 140–142; (1978) 211.

Hinard raises important points, but from external evidence it is possible to make the case that both Cicero and Cato the Younger shared a negative view of Sulla's deeds. Cicero condemned the cruelty of the proscriptions in the *Pro Sexto Roscio*, and in the *De lege agraria* he spoke of Sulla's unjust and hateful empowerment as tyrant through the Valerian law. Cato was still a boy during Sulla's dictatorship, but in Plutarch's biography we are told that he was roused to thoughts of tyrannicide by the spectacle of the severed heads of the proscribed.[22] As for Cicero, it is known that he was aware of the importance of portraying the interlocutors in his dialogues as authentically as possible in order to match the expectations of his readers.[23] We may assume, then, that the *De finibus* offers a reliable portrait of Cato's position on Sulla. As a final point one may note that *avaritia* is very clearly distinguished from *crudelitas* in the above passage. Again this casts doubts on Hinard's assumption that Cicero referred primarily to Sulla's *avaritia* when speaking of his *crudelitas*.

Sulla and Extreme Violence

Hinard's position is that Late Republican authors did not associate Sulla with excessive violence or acts of cruelty such as torture and mutilation. Specifically, he notes that there are no descriptions or even mentions of the Villa Publica massacre, an atrocity in which several thousand prisoners of war were executed en masse, in spite of promises to spare those who surrendered, three days after the decisive civil war victory at the Colline Gate on the 1st November 82.[24] But if we assume that Sallust's letters to Caesar are authentic, then there is at least one testimony, from the transitional period between Republic and Empire, which tells us how the Roman populace was slaughtered in the Villa Publica 'like cattle' (*plebem Romanam in villa publica pecoris modo conscissam*).[25]

Cicero provides the earliest references to the enormous death toll of Sulla's civil war victory. In the *Pro Sexto Roscio*, he alluded to the display of the severed heads of the proscribed at a fountain in the Forum known as the Servilian Basin, highlighting the scale of the slaughter with a striking comparison with the Roman disaster at the battle of Lake Trasimene: 'We have witnessed many killed, not at Lake Trasimene,

---

22 Plut. *Cat. min.* 3.2–3.
23 Cic. *De or.* 2.9; Cic. *Att.* 13.16.1 (26th June 45 B.C.); Cic. *Fam.* 9.8.1 (11th or 12th July 45 B.C.). Cf. Eckert (2018a) 22–23 with notes 20 and 21.
24 Hinard (1984) 86; (2008) 134.
25 Sall. *Ad Caes. sen.* 1.4.1. The fictional date of the letter is 48 or 46 B.C. Eisenhut (1985) 462–467 argues in favour of Sallust's authorship. Ramsey (2015) 475–476 takes a more critical stance. Later testimonies for the Villa Publica massacre: Strabo 5.4.11; Livy, *Per.* 88; Val. Max. 9.2.1; Sen. *Clem.* 1.12.2; *Ben.* 5.16.3; Luc. 2.196–210; Plut. *Sull.* 30.2–3; Flor. 2.9.24; Cass. Dio fr. 109.5–8.

but at the Servilian basin' (*Multos caesos non ad Trasumennum lacum, sed ad Servilium vidimus*).²⁶ Cicero's testimony is remarkable as it presents Sulla as a new Hannibal and compares a Sullan atrocity with a battlefield defeat that resulted in the deaths of an estimated 15,000 Romans.²⁷ Cicero associates Sulla more explicitly with extreme loss of life in his third Catilinarian speech, delivered to the Roman people as consul in 63. In a catalogue of past civil war violence he describes the piles of dead Romans killed in the Forum during the civil strife between Cinna and Octavius in 87, then he moves on to the atrocities conducted by Marius and Cinna later in the same year. It is Sulla, however, who represents the climax in the escalation of violence: 'Sulla afterwards avenged the cruelty of this victory [sc. of Marius and Cinna]; it is not necessary to mention how large was the loss of citizens and how great a calamity befell the Republic' (*Ultus est huius victoriae crudelitatem postea Sulla: ne dici quidem opus est quanta deminutione civium et quanta calamitate rei publicae*).²⁸

These passages of Cicero's speeches, far from being rhetorical exaggerations, find confirmation in the figures given by Imperial sources to estimate the death toll of Sulla's civil war victory. A total of 4,700 Romans were proscribed, and, judging by the figures given by Strabo and Livy, somewhere between 3,000 and 8,000 prisoners were killed in the Villa Publica massacre.²⁹ There was also a massacre after the fall of Praeneste which claimed either 5,000 or 12,000 lives.³⁰ The violence of Sulla's victory extended beyond the proscriptions or the mass execution of prisoners, and it is said that as many as 9,000 people were killed in the city of Rome after Sulla gave his soldiers free rein to kill anyone they pleased: members of the opposite faction, personal enemies, or uninvolved persons alike.³¹ At a conservative estimate, Sulla was responsible for the violent deaths of between 20,000 and 30,000 Romans.³² At around 1,000 members of the Roman elite, at most, the death toll was significantly lower for the violence carried out by Marius and Cinna after the civil war of 87.³³

Republican sources do highlight the scale of Sullan violence, and there are also two Republican sources which discuss the death of the praetor M. Marius

---

26 Cic. *Rosc. Am.* 89. Cf. Dyck (2010) 154–157, on Cicero's allusion to the proscriptions. The reference to Lake Trasimene is discussed by Diehl (1988) 92; Stinger (1993) 36; Bücher (2006) 272; van der Blom (2010) 114; Eckert (2018b) 292.
27 Polyb. 3.85; Livy 22.7.
28 Cic. *Cat.* 3.24.
29 Proscriptions: Val. Max. 9.2.1. Villa Publica: Strabo 5.4.11; Livy, *Per.* 88.
30 Val. Max. 9.2.1; Plut. *Sull.* 32.1.
31 Oros. 5.21.
32 Cf. Dion. Hal. *Ant. Rom.* 5.77.5, for the figure of 40,000 citizens killed, some of them tortured, after they had surrendered to Sulla.
33 Mommsen arrived at a figure of 50 senators and 1000 Roman knights as the death toll of Marius and Cinna's killings in 87 B.C. Cf. Mommsen (2010) ⁹[1903/1904] 1.352 with n. 2. Cf. Eckert (2016a) 204 and 208 for more details.

Gratidianus – a victim of torture and mutilation, and the prime *exemplum* of Sullan cruelty for authors of the Imperial period. In his *In toga candida* of 64, Cicero attacked Catiline, a rival for the consulship, by accusing him of playing a leading role in the torture and public execution of Marius Gratidianus.[34] In the *Commentariolum Petitionis*, attributed to Cicero's brother, there is a graphic, almost lurid description of the cruelties inflicted on Gratidianus which matches anything found in the more extensive Imperial sources.

> Why should I speak of him [Catiline] as a candidate for the consulship, who caused M. Marius, a man most beloved by the Roman people, to be beaten with vine-rods in the sight of that Roman people from one end of the City to the other – forced him up to the tomb – rent his frame with every kind of torture, and while he was still alive and breathing, cut off his head with his sword in his right hand, while he held the hairs on the crown of his head with his left, and carried off his head in his own hand with streams of blood flowing through his fingers?[35]

The date and authorship of the *Commentariolum Petitionis* are disputed, but Balsdon offers a strong case for the authenticity of the text and its origin in the 60s.[36] The date of Cicero's *In toga candida* is secure, and from the fragments preserved in Asconius' commentary there can be no doubt that the execution of Gratidianus and the details of his torture and execution were the subject of public debate during Cicero's election campaign of 64.

Sulla's Legacy and the Sons of the Proscribed

Laffi has argued that the restoration of the full rights of the tribunes of the plebs and the readmission of equestrians as jurors in the Roman courts, two measures introduced in 70 B.C., did not represent a major overhaul of the reforms enacted by Sulla in 82–81.[37] In Laffi's opinion it is also highly significant that the prohibition on running for public office imposed by Sulla on the sons of the proscribed was not repealed for decades.[38] Although this ban was a major violation of fundamental

---

34 Asc. 84, 87, 89–90 (Clark).
35 Cicero, *Comment. pet.* 10: *Quid ego nunc dicam petere eum tecum consulatum qui hominem carissimum populo Romano, M. Marium, inspectante populo Romano vitibus per totam urbem ceciderit, ad bustum egerit, ibi omni cruciatu lacerarit, vivo stanti collum gladio sua dextera secuerit, cum sinistra capillum eius a vertice teneret, caput sua manu tulerit, cum inter digitos eius rivi sanguinis fluerent.* Translation above: Evelyn S. Shuckburgh.
36 Balsdon (1963).
37 Laffi (1967) 212–213. For the *lex Pompeia Licinia de tribunicia potestate* (restoration of tribunician rights) see Cic. *Verr.* 2.2.174, 2.3.97, 2.3.223; Cic. *Clu.* 130, 151. For the *lex Aurelia iudicaria* (re-admission of knights to the courts) see Vell. Pat. 2.32.3.
38 Laffi (1967) 185–187.

principles of Roman law, it remained in effect for more than 30 years until it was annulled by Caesar, a declared enemy of Sulla, in 49 B.C.[39] The conclusion drawn by Laffi from these two observations is that there was a generally positive attitude towards Sulla's reforms throughout the Late Republic, and that the negative image of Sulla the cruel tyrant was a myth that must have evolved after Caesar's civil war victory.

Laffi is right to argue that the two laws introduced in 70, on the tribunate and the law courts, should not be understood as a revolution against Sulla's reforms. That said, the restoration of the rights of the tribunes of the people and the removal of the courts from full senatorial control repealed two cornerstones of Sulla's legislation and readjusted the balance of power in the Roman political system.[40] One must assume, moreover, that the opposition to these two Sullan measures reflected a majority opinion in Roman society. Otherwise it is difficult to explain their repeal by the consuls Pompey and Crassus, two former Sullan partisans, only eight years after Sulla's death in 78. It is stated in fact that Pompey received a murmur of consent when he announced the law on the tribunes of the plebs in an assembly of the Roman people.[41] In his *De legibus*, written in the late 50s, Cicero argued that a proper balance of power was essential to the functioning of the *res publica*, and he praised Pompey and Crassus for restoring this balance with their law on the tribunes.[42] A similar imbalance, between senators and knights, was corrected by the reform of the law courts. Clearly, the reforms of 70 should be viewed as a milestone in a process of tackling Sulla's legacy.

Sulla's legacy included constitutional reforms as well as laws that legitimised the violence of his civil war victory. In particular, the Valerian law ratified all of Sulla's past acts.[43] The passage of this law can be dated to early December 82, thus it legitimised not only Sulla's actions in the civil war of 83–82, but also the extreme violence in the first weeks after his victory at the battle of the Colline Gate on the 1st November 82, notably the Villa Publica massacre and the manhunts resulting from the publication of the first proscription lists.[44] The legal basis for the proscriptions was given greater definition with the *lex Cornelia de proscriptione* passed at an early stage in Sulla's dictatorship. It awarded large bounties for the assassination of the proscribed and granted immunity to the perpetrators. In addition, wives

---

39 Plut. *Caes.* 37.1–2; Suet. *Iul.* 41; Cass. Dio 41.18.2; 43.50.1–2; 44.47.4. Cf. Rotondi (1963) 416 on the *lex Antonia de proscriptorum liberis*.
40 Hölkeskamp (2000) 217 argues that key parts of Sulla's reforms were repealed by Crassus and Pompey in 70 B.C.
41 Cic. *Verr.* 1.44.
42 Cic. *Leg.* 3.23–26
43 App. *B Civ.* 1.98–99; Cic. *Verr.* 2.3.82; *Leg. agr.* 3.5.
44 Cic. *Rosc. Am.* 125–126. For a detailed chronology of events after Sulla's victory on the 1st November 82, see Heftner (2006a) and Eckert (2016a) 144–146. Cf. also Eckert (2014).

of the proscribed lost their dowry, and sons of the proscribed were both disinherited and prohibited from standing for public office.[45] Sulla also enacted laws to inflict severe punishment on Italian municipalities which had sided with his civil war opponents, above all with the confiscation of land to be distributed to Sulla's veterans.[46]

The earliest reactions against Sulla's political and legislative acts can be traced to his own lifetime, for it was in 80 or 79 that Cicero successfully challenged Sulla's disenfranchisement of certain Italian municipalities in his defence speech for a woman from Arretium.[47] Lepidus, the consul of 78, planned to rescind the expropriations of land from the Italian municipalities and to restore the estates of the proscribed to their lawful owners.[48] Lepidus met firm resistance and died after legions sent by the Roman Senate put down the unrest he had kindled in Etruria.[49] In 77 and 76, some of Sulla's partisans were put on trial for extortion in the provinces: Dolabella, praetor of 81, was convicted, but there were acquittals for his relative Cn. Cornelius Dolabella, consul of 81, and C. Antonius Hybrida, one of Sulla's commanders in Greece.[50] In 75, the consul Cotta passed a law to repeal Sulla's prohibition on tribunes of the people running for higher public office.[51] Only three years later a law was passed to reclaim money which Sulla had remitted to buyers of the estates of the proscribed.[52] In 70, the tribunate was restored, senatorial control of juries was ended, and C. Verres, a prominent Sullan, was tried for extortion in Sicily: only exile saved him from conviction.[53] A census was conducted in 70, and as a consequence 64 senators were expelled from the Senate, among them well-known followers of Sulla such as Antonius Hybrida and Lentulus Sura.[54] In the same year the Senate also declared an amnesty for any of the proscribed who had survived Sulla's terror outside of Italy.[55]

In the 60s the reaction against Sulla's legacy gained momentum. An attempt to reclaim public money embezzled by Sulla during his dictatorship from his son

---

45 Livy, *Per.* 89; Vell. Pat. 2.28.4; Lucan 2.148–149; Plut. *Sull.* 31.
46 Cic. *Caecin.* 97–102; Cic. *Verr.* 2.3.8; Cic. *Dom.* 79; App. *B Civ.* 1.96, 1.100. For Sulla's confiscations and veteran settlements, cf. Keaveney (1982); Dahlheim (1993); Santangelo (2007) 147–157; Thein (2010); Santangelo (2016a).
47 Cic. *Caecin.* 96–97 and 101–102.
48 Sall. *Hist.* 1.55 (Maurenbrecher) = 1.48 (McGushin) = 1.49 (Ramsey); Gran. Lic. 36.35–36 (Criniti); Flor. 2.11.3, 2.11.5–8.
49 Flor. 2.11.5–8; App. *B Civ.* 1.107.
50 Cic. *Verr.* 2.1.41; Cicero, *Comment. pet.* 2; Cic. *Brut.* 317; Vell. Pat. 2.43.3; Val. Max. 8.9.3; Asc. 26, 74, 84 (Clark); Plut. *Caes.* 4.1–3. For the trials of Dolabella the consul and Antonius Hybrida, see Rosenblitt (2014) 425. For the Dolabellae cf. also Thein in this volume.
51 Sall. *Hist.* 2.49, 3.48 (Maurenbrecher) = 2.45, 3.34 (McGushin) = 2.44, 3.15 (Ramsey); Asc. 66–67 (Clark).
52 Cic. *Verr.* 2.3.81–82; Sall. *Hist.* 4.1 (Maurenbrecher), (McGushin), (Ramsey); Gell. *NA* 18.44.
53 Cic. *Verr.* 2.1.34–38 and 2.1.123–124.
54 Livy, *Per.* 98; Asc. 84 (Clark). Cf. Steel (2014a); (2014b).
55 Cass. Dio 44.47.4. Cf. Heftner (2013) 239–240.

Faustus was unsuccessful, but in 66 Sulla's relative P. Cornelius Sulla, consul elect for 65, was convicted of electoral bribery and expelled from the Roman Senate.[56] These initiatives against Sulla's family gained public attention, but far more spectacular were the murder trials initiated by Caesar and Cato the Younger against the Sullan bounty hunters. In 64, L. Luscius and L. Bellienus were put on trial for the killing of proscribed Roman citizens, and despite their plea that they had followed orders from the dictator Sulla, they were convicted and punished.[57] Contemporaries perceived this as a belated punishment of the dictator Sulla himself.[58] L. Bellienus was the uncle of Catiline, the most infamous of Sulla's assassins.[59] Cicero ran against Catiline for the consulship of 63 and during the election campaign he publicly attacked him for his Sullan-period crimes, proclaiming that if elected he would have Catiline put on trial.[60] As consul, Cicero successfully opposed the agrarian law of Rullus, which he felt served the interests of Sullan landowners, but Catiline was not put on trial for his Sullan crimes, and impoverished Sullan veterans who remembered the profits of Sulla's victory were among those who joined Catiline when he instigated a conspiracy to overthrow the Republic in 63.[61] The final anti-Sullan initiative of the decade came in 61: the praetor Octavius forced Sulla's partisans to return property that they had seized by threats and violence after Sulla's victory. In doing so, Octavius is said to have become a popular hero.[62]

The 70s and 60s saw the modification or repeal of key elements of the legal and political framework established by Sulla, and in many respects the legacy of his punitive actions was also mitigated. Cicero, Caesar, and Cato the Younger were the main actors, and it is therefore surprising that Cicero, as consul in 63, refused to support an initiative to rescind one of Sulla's most iniquitous acts, the exclusion of the sons of the proscribed from public office. In his lost speech *De proscriptorum liberis*, he admitted the injustice of the prohibition but argued against repeal on the grounds that it was not in the interests of the state.[63] Eight years later, in his speech *In Pisonem*, Cicero made the same case: he conceded that he had supported an unpopular position by opposing the rehabilitation of the sons of the proscribed, but

---

56 Faustus Sulla: Cic. *Clu.* 93; *Mur.* 42; Asc. 73 (Clark). Publius Sulla: Cic. *Sull.* 73–74 and 90–91; Sall. *Cat.* 18.2; Cic. *Fin.* 2.62; *Fam.* 15.19.3; Livy, *Per.* 101; Asc. 88 (Clark); Suet. *Caes.* 9.1; Cass. Dio 36.44.3.
57 Asc. 90–91(Clark); Suet. *Caes.* 11; Cass. Dio 37.10.1–3.
58 Plut. *Cat. min.* 17.5–7.
59 Asc. 91 (Clark).
60 On Catiline's crimes, cf. Cicero, *Comment. pet.* 10; Sall. *Hist.* 1.44, 1.55 (Maurenbrecher) = 1.36, 1.48 (McGushin) = 1.36, 1.49 (Ramsey); Livy, *Per.* 88; Val. Max. 9.2.1; Plut. *Sull.* 32.2. For Cicero's attack against Catiline in his speech *In toga candida*, cf. Asc. 82–83, 85–86, 93–94 (Clark).
61 Sall. *Cat.* 16.4 and 37.6.
62 Cic. *Q Fr.* 1.1.
63 Quint. *Inst.* 11.1.85 preserves this testimony of Cicero's speech *De proscriptorum liberis* in 63 B.C., which is lost otherwise. Cic. *Att.* 2.1.3 and Plin. *HN* 7.117 also attest to Cicero's speech.

he still maintained that the alternative would have been a risk to the stability of the Roman state.⁶⁴ Some of the *liberi proscriptorum* did in fact join Catiline's revolt.⁶⁵

Cicero's allusion in his *In Pisonem* to the unpopularity of the Sullan restrictions on the civic rights of the sons of the proscribed is instructive, for it suggests that Laffi was probably wrong to focus on the longevity of this one provision when he made his case for a mostly positive Late Republican view of Sulla's laws. He also placed too little emphasis on the repeal of Sulla's laws on the tribunes of the people and the composition of jury courts in 70, downplaying the importance of these reforms in an ongoing process of revision that started in Sulla's lifetime.

Conclusion

In 49, Caesar reinstated the sons of the proscribed to their full political rights in a move which recalled his leading role in the trials of the Sullan bounty hunters in the 60s and bolstered his famous declaration, in a letter written in the spring of 49, that he would be a champion of clemency who would not imitate Sulla's cruelty.⁶⁶ The memory of Sulla's cruelty, by now a well-established fact in the collective consciousness, would also inform the triumviral proscription edict. In a vain attempt to distance themselves from their model, the triumvirs promised to prevent unsanctioned violence by marauding soldiers as well as to proscribe significantly fewer of their enemies than Sulla almost forty years previously.⁶⁷ Ancient writers from Seneca the Younger and Pliny the Elder to Cassius Dio attest, however, that neither the text of the triumviral edict nor the attempt by Augustus as emperor to attribute sole responsibility for the proscriptions to Mark Antony proved successful. The fact that Augustus had been a member of the triumvirate which initiated proscriptions for the second time after Sulla remained problematic into the Imperial period.⁶⁸

Sulla was already negatively perceived during his dictatorship in 82–81 due to the extreme violence of his civil war victory. It was unprecedented in Roman history, and it had a significant impact on a broad spectrum of Roman society. Sulla was defined by his atrocities, and after his death he was remembered as the ultimate *exemplum* of cruelty. Already in 70, in his speech against Verres, Cicero made the highly emotional plea: 'May the immortal Gods grant that there may never be another [Sulla]!' (*di immortales faxint, ne sit alter!*).⁶⁹ The same year saw the repeal

---

64 Cic. *Pis.* 4.
65 Sall. *Cat.* 37.9.
66 Cic. *Att.* 9.7c.1 (5th March 49 B.C.). Cf. Cic. *Att.* 9.16.1–2 (26th March 49 B.C.).
67 App. *B Civ.* 4.8–10. The edict refers to Sulla not by his full name, but only by his surname 'Felix'.
68 Sen. *Clem.* 1.11.1–2; Plin. *HN* 7.147; Cass. Dio 47.14.1, 56.38.1.
69 Cic. *Verr.* 2.3.81.

of two of the most important Sullan reforms when the tribunes of the people regained the right to exercise their veto and propose laws, and the equestrian order was re-admitted to jury service.[70] During his dictatorship Sulla had reorganised the *res publica* by enacting laws but he had also utilised his powers to legitimise his atrocities, and so his peers and posterity found it difficult to distinguish Sulla the reformer from Sulla the cruel tyrant and thus they perceived much of his legislation as a necessary evil at best.[71]

Sullan violence tends to be viewed through the exclusive lens of the proscriptions and the Villa Publica massacre, but there was also a massacre at the fall of Praeneste, as well as a wave of killings in the city of Rome carried out by Sulla's army after the battle at the Colline Gate. The fullest testimonies come from authors of the Imperial period, but there are also Republican sources which attest to both the scale and brutality of the atrocities. Cicero speaks of witnessing or hearing of acts of violence on a daily, even hourly, basis in 80, when Sulla was consul, and in 64, in a bitter election campaign, he called to mind the gruesome spectacle of the torture and public execution of M. Marius Gratidianus. For eye-witnesses of traumatic events only a few words are required to evoke the painful experiences of the past. It is for this reason that Late Republican references to Sulla's atrocities are brief. Yet, these references do exist, and thus they pose a challenge to the idea that the image of Sulla the cruel tyrant was invented long after his death. The idea of the 'Sulla myth' is attractive, but it may well be a myth itself.[72]

---

[70] Tribunes: Cic. *Verr.* 1.44–45; *Leg.* 3.23–26. Equestrian juries: Cic. *Verr.* 1.18, 2.2.77; *Clu.* 151.
[71] Cic. *Verr.* 2.3.82.
[72] I would like to thank Alexander Thein and the UCD School of Classics for their hospitality during two Research Fellowships in 2017 and 2018/19. My particular gratitude goes to Alexander Thein for sharing his thoughts on the Sulla Myth with me.

Abbreviations

Abbreviations of ancient authors in this volume follow the *Oxford Classical Dictionary* (4th edition).

Agora XVIII	D. J. Geagan, *The Athenian Agora XVIII. Inscriptions: The Dedicatory Monuments*, Princeton 2011.
ANRW	H. Temporini & W. Haase (eds.), *Aufstieg und Niedergang der Römischen Welt*, Berlin/New York 1972–.
BÉ	*Bulletin Épigraphique*, published in *Revue des Études Grecques*.
BNJ	I. Worthington (ed.), *Brill's New Jacoby*, Leiden 2006–.
CID	*Corpus des Inscriptions de Delphes*, Paris 1977–2002.
CIL	*Corpus Inscriptionum Latinarum*, Berlin 1863–.
Clark	A. C. Clark, *Q. Asconii Pediani Orationum Ciceronis Quinque Narratio*, Oxford 1907.
Criniti	N. Criniti, *Grani Liciniani reliquiae*, Leipzig 1981.
DNP	H. Cancik & H. Schneider (eds.), *Der Neue Pauly. Enzyklopädie der Antike*, Stuttgart/Weimar 1996–.
FD	*Fouilles de Delphes*, Paris 1908–.
GL	H. Keil (ed.), *Grammatici Latini*, 8 vols., Berlin 1855–1923.
IDélos	F. Durrbach et al., *Inscriptions de Délos*, 8 vols., Paris 1926–1950.
IEleusis	K. Clinton, *Eleusis. The Inscriptions on Stone. Documents of the Sanctuary of the Two Goddesses and the Public Documents of the Deme*, 2 vols., Athens 2005–2008.
IG	*Inscriptiones Graecae*, Berlin 1873–.
IGRom	R. Cagnat et al., *Inscriptiones Graecae ad res Romanas pertinentes*, Paris 1906–1927.
ILLRP	A. Degrassi (ed.), *Inscriptiones Latinae Liberae Rei Publicae*, 2 vols., 2nd ed., Florence 1963–1965.
ILS	H. Dessau, *Inscriptiones Latinae Selectae*, 3 vols., Berlin 1892–1916.
IvO	W. Dittenberger & K. Purgold (eds.), *Inschriften von Olympia*, Berlin 1896.
IOropos	V. Petrakos, *Οι επιγραφές του Ωρωπού*, Athens 1997.
IThesp.	P. Roesch, *Les Inscriptions de Thespies*, Lyons 2007.
LSJ	H. G. Liddell & R. Scott, revised by H. S. Jones, *A Greek-English Lexicon* (9th ed.), Oxford 1925–1940.
Maurenbrecher	B. Maurenbrecher, *C. Sallustii Crispi Historiarum Reliquiae*, 2 vols., Leipzig 1891–1893.
McGushin	P. McGushin, *Sallust. The Histories*, 2 vols., Oxford 1992–1994.
MRR	T. R. S. Broughton, *The Magistrates of the Roman Republic*, 2 vols. and suppl., New York/Atlanta 1951/1952 and 1968.
OGIS	W. Dittenberger, *Orientis Graeci Inscriptiones Selectae*, 2 vols., Leipzig 1903–1905.
ORF[4]	H. Malcovati, *Oratorum Romanorum Fragmenta*, 2 vols., 4th ed., Turin 1976–1979.
Ramsey	J. T. Ramsey, *Sallust. Fragments of the Histories. Letters to Caesar*, Cambridge, MA 2015.
RDGE	R. K. Sherk, *Roman Documents from the Greek East*, Baltimore 1969.
RE	A. Pauly, G. Wissowa & W. Kroll, *Real-Encyclopädie der classischen Altertumswissenschaft*, Stuttgart 1893–1980.
RRC	M. H. Crawford, *Roman Republican Coinage*, 2 vols., Cambridge 1974.

SEG	*Supplementum epigraphicum Graecum*, Amsterdam 1923–.
Stangl	T. Stangl, *Ciceronis Orationum Scholiastae*, Vienna 1912.
*Syll.*³	W. Dittenberger, *Sylloge Inscriptionum* Graecarum, 4 vols., 3rd ed., Leipzig 1915–1924.
TLG	*Thesaurus Linguae Graecae*, Irvine, CA 1972–.

Bibliography

Adams (1973): J. N. Adams, 'The vocabulary of the speeches in Tacitus' historical works', *BICS* 20, 124–144.
Allély (2007): A. Allély, 'La déclaration d'*hostis* de 88 et les douze *hostes*', *Rev. Ét. Anc.* 109, 175–206.
Andersen/Woyke (2013): U. Andersen & W. Woyke (eds.), *Handwörterbuch des politischen Systems der Bundesrepublik Deutschland* (7th ed.), Heidelberg.
Annas (1993): J. Annas, *The Morality of Happiness*, Oxford.
Annas/Woolf (2001): J. Annas & R. Woolf, *Cicero. On Moral Ends*, Cambridge.
Antela-Bernárdez (2015): B. Antela-Bernárdez, 'Athenion of Athens Revisited', *Klio* 97, 59–80.
Appel (2013): H. Appel, 'Some Remarks on the *hostis declaratio* of 88 B.C.', in: D. Słapek and I. Łuć (eds.), *Lucius Cornelius Sulla: History and Tradition*, Lublin, 27–39.
Arafat (1996): K. W. Arafat, *Pausanias' Greece. Ancient artists and Roman rulers*, Cambridge.
Arena (2012): V. Arena, *Libertas and the Practice of Politics in the Late Roman Republic*, Cambridge.
Ash (1997): R. Ash, 'Warped Intertextualities: Naevius and Sallust at Tacitus *Histories* 2.12.2′, *Histos* 1, 42–50.
Ash (2010): R. Ash, '*Tarda Moles Civilis Belli*: The Weight of the Past in Tacitus' *Histories*', in: B. W. Breed, C. Damon & A. Rossi (eds.) *Citizens of Discord: Rome and Its Civil Wars*, Oxford, 119–131.
Ashton (2012): R. Ashton, 'The Hellenistic World: The Cities of Mainland Greece and Asia Minor', in: W. E. Metcalf (ed.), *The Oxford Handbook of Greek and Roman Coinage*, Oxford, 191–210.
Assenmaker (2013a): P. Assenmaker, 'Poids symbolique de la destruction et enjeux idéologique de ses récits: Réflexion sur les sacs d'Athènes et d'Ilion durant la premiére guerre mithridatique', in: J. Driessen (ed.), *Destruction: Archaeological, psychological and historical perspectives*, Louvain-la-Neuve, 391–414.
Assenmaker (2013b): P. Assenmaker, '*L. Sulla imperator* et *imperator iterum*: pour une réévaluation de la chronologie des émissions monétaires de Sulla (RRC 367–368 et 359)', *RN* 170, 248–277.
Assenmaker (2014): P. Assenmaker, *De la victoire au pouvoir. Développement et manifestations de l'idéologie impératoriale à l'époque de Marius et Sylla*, Brussels.
Assenmaker (2017): P. Assenmaker, 'La frappe monétaire syllanienne dans le Péloponnèse durant la guerre mithridatique: retour sur les monnaies "luculliennes"', in: E. Apostolou & C. Doyen (eds.), *Το νόμισμα στην Πελοπόννησο. Νομισματοκοπεία, εικονογραφία, κυκλοφορία, ιστορία. Από την Αρχαιότητα έως και τη Νεότερη Εποχή. Τόμος Α', Coins in the Peloponnese. Mints, Iconography, Circulation, History from Antiquity to Modern Times. Volume 1: Ancient Times* (BCH Supplément 57 – Ὀβολός 10), Athens, 411–424.
Astin (1958): A. E. Astin, *The Lex Annalis before Sulla*, Brussels.
Astin (1962): A. E. Astin, '"Professio" in the Abortive Election of 184 BC', *Historia* 11, 252–255.
Badian (1955): E. Badian, 'The Date of Pompey's First Triumph', *Hermes* 83, 107–118.
Badian (1958): E. Badian, *Foreign Clientelae (264–70 B.C.)*, Oxford.
Badian (1961): E. Badian, 'Servilius and Pompey's First Triumph', *Hermes* 89, 254–256.
Badian (1962): E. Badian, 'Waiting for Sulla', *JRS* 52, 47–61.
Badian (1965): E. Badian, 'The Dolabellae of the Republic', *PBSR* 33, 48–51.
Badian (1967): E. Badian, 'Cicero. Scripta Quae Manserunt Omnia. Fasc. 4. Brutus (review)', *JRS* 57, 223–230.
Badian (1970): E. Badian, 'Lucius Sulla: The Deadly Reformer' (Seventh Todd Memorial Lecture, University of Sydney), Sydney, 1–32.
Bahmer/Eckert (2015): F. A. Bahmer & A. Eckert, 'Phthiriasis – die geheimnisvolle Läusekrankheit der Antike: Fakt oder Fiktion?', *Der Hautartzt* 66, 143–148.

Balsdon (1951): J. P. V. D. Balsdon, 'Sulla Felix', *JRS* 41, 1–10.
Balsdon (1963): J. P. V. D. Balsdon, 'The Commentariolum Petitionis', *CQ* 13, 242–250.
Barnes (1997): J. Barnes, 'Roman Aristotle', in: J. Barnes & M. Griffin (eds.), *Philosophia Togata II. Plato and Aristotle at Rome*, Oxford, 1–69.
Bauslaugh (2000): R. A. Bauslaugh, *Silver Coinage with the Types of Aesillas the Quaestor*, New York, NY.
Beard et al. (1998): M. Beard, J. North & S. Price, *Religions of Rome* (2 vols.), Cambridge.
Beck (2005): H. Beck, *Karriere und Hierarchie. Die römische Aristokratie und die Anfänge des cursus honorum in der mittleren Republik*, Berlin.
Behr (1993): H. Behr, *Die Selbstdarstellung Sullas*, Frankfurt.
Bernhardt (1985): R. Bernhardt, *Polis und römische Herrschaft in der späten Republik (149–31 v. Chr.)*, Berlin.
Berry (2000): D. H. Berry, *Cicero: Defence Speeches*, Oxford.
Bicknell (1969): P. Bicknell, 'Marius, the Metelli, and the lex Maria tabellaria', *Latomus* 28, 327–348.
de Blois et al. (2005): L. de Blois, J. Bons, T. Kessels & D. M. Schenkeveld (eds.), *The Statesman in Plutarch's Works. Vol. II: The Statesman in Plutarch's Greek and Roman Lives*, Leiden.
van der Blom (2010): H. van der Blom, *Cicero's Role Models: The Political Strategy of a Newcomer*, Oxford.
van der Blom (2016): H. van der Blom, *Oratory and Political Career in the Late Roman Republic*, Cambridge.
van der Blom (2017): H. van der Blom, 'Sulla in the contio: an oratorical episode in pieces', in: J. Kwapisz, T. Derda & J. Hilder (eds.), *Fragments, Holes, and Wholes*, Journal of Juristic Papyrology Supplements 30, Warsaw, 181–195.
Blume et al. (1967) [1848]: F. Blume, K. Lachmann & A. Rudorff (eds.), *Die Schriften der römischen Feldmesser*, vol. 1, Hildesheim.
Boehringer (1991): C. Boehringer, 'Zur Geschichte der Achaischen Liga im 2. und im 1. Jh. v. Chr. im Lichte des Munzfundes von Poggio Picenze (Abruzzen)', in: A. D. Rizakis (ed.), *Achaia und Elis in der Antike*, Akten des 1. Internationalen Symposiums, Athen, 19.–21. Mai 1989, Athens, 163–170.
Boehringer (2008): C. Boehringer, 'Quelques remarques sur la circulation monetaire dans le Péloponnèse au IIe et au Ier siècle a.C.', in: C. Grandjean (ed.), *Le Péloponnèse d'Epaminondas à Hadrien*, Bordeaux, 83–89.
Bonner (1977): S. F. Bonner, *Education in Ancient Rome: From the Elder Cato to the Younger Pliny*, Berkeley, CA.
Bouchon (2007): R. Bouchon, 'Les "porteurs de toge" de Larissa', *Topoi* 15, 251–284.
Bouchon (2011): R. Bouchon, 'Réelles présences? Approche matérielle et symbolique des relations entre la Grèce balkanique et les officiels romains, de Mummius Achaicus à Antoine', in: N. Barrandon & F. Kirbihler (eds.), *Les gouverneurs et les provinciaux sous la République romaine*, Rennes, 53–74.
Bouchon/Helly (2015): R. Bouchon & B. Helly, 'The Thessalian League', in: H. Beck & P. Funke (eds.), *Federalism in Greek Antiquity*, Cambridge, 231–249.
Bowman/Cooley 2008: A. Bowman & A. Cooley (general editors), *The Customs Law of Asia*, eds. M. Cottier, M.H. Crawford, C.V. Crowther, J.-L. Ferrary, B. M. Levick, O. Salomies, & M. Wörrle and with papers by M. Corbier, S. Mitchell, O. van Nijf, D. Rathbone, & G.D. Rowe, Oxford.
Bremer (2005): J. M. Bremer, 'Plutarch and the Liberation of Greece', in: L. de Blois, J. Bons, T. Kessels, & D. M. Schenkeveld (eds.), *The Statesman in Plutarch's Works. Vol. II: The Statesman in Plutarch's Greek and Roman Lives*, Leiden, 257–268.
Brennan (1992): T. C. Brennan, 'Sulla's career in the 90s: some reconsiderations', *Chiron* 22, 103–158.

Brennan (2000): T. C. Brennan, *The Praetorship in the Roman Republic*, Oxford.
Brescia (1997): G. Brescia, *La 'scalata' del Ligure. Saggio di commento a Sallustio. Bellum Iugurthinum 92–94*, Bari.
Briscoe (1973): J. Briscoe, *A Commentary on Livy XXXI–XXXIII*, Oxford.
Brockliss et al. (2012): W. Brockliss et al. (eds.), *Reception and the Classics*, Oxford.
Broughton (1991): T. R. S. Broughton, 'Candidates defeated in Roman elections: some ancient Roman "also-rans"', *TAPhS*, 1–64.
Brunt (1986): P. A. Brunt, *Italian Manpower (225 B.C.–A.D.14)*, Oxford.
Bücher (2006): F. Bücher, *Verargumentierte Geschichte: Exempla Romana im politischen Diskurs der späten römischen Republik*, Stuttgart.
Büchner (1973): K. Büchner, 'Cottas Ansprache ans Volk', *C&M*, 246–261.
Büchner (1982): K. Büchner, *Sallust* (2nd ed.), Heidelberg.
Bugh (1990): G. R. Bugh, 'The Theseia in Late Hellenistic Athens', *ZPE* 83, 20–37.
Burnand (2000): C. J. Burnand, *Roman Representations of the Orator during the Last Century of the Republic*, PhD thesis, University of Oxford.
Cadario (2014): M. Cadario, 'Preparing for Triumph. Graecae Artes as Roman Booty in L. Mummius' Campaign (146 BC)', in: C. H. Lange & F. J. Vervaet (eds.), *The Roman Republican Triumph beyond the Spectacle*, Rome, 83–101.
Cagniart (1986): P. F. Cagniart, *The Life and Career of Lucius Cornelius Sulla through his Consulship in 88 BC. A Study in Character and Politics*, PhD thesis, University of Texas.
Cagniart (2007): P. F. Cagniart, 'The Late Republican Army (146–30 BC)', in: P. Erdkamp (ed.), *A Companion to the Roman Army*, Malden, 80–95.
Calabi (1950): I. Calabi, 'I commentarii di Silla come fonte storica', *Mem. dei Lincei* 8.3.5, 248–302.
Camp (1986): J. M. Camp, *The Athenian Agora*, London.
Camp (2001): J. M. Camp, *The Archaeology of Athens*, New Haven, CT.
Campanile (2007): D. Campanile, 'L'assemblea provinciale d' Asia in età repubblicana', in: G. Urso (ed.), *Tra oriente e occidente: Indigeni, Greci e Romani in Asia Minore*, Pisa, 129–140.
Campbell (1994): B. Campbell, *The Roman Army 31 B.C.–A.D. 337: A Sourcebook*, London.
Campbell (2000): B. Campbell, *The Writings of the Roman Land Surveyors*, London.
Carcopino (1931): J. Carcopino, *Sylla ou la monarchie manquée*, Paris.
Cargill Thompson Warren (1996): J. A. W. Cargill Thompson Warren, 'The Achaian League, Sparta, Lucullus: Some Late Hellenistic Coinages', in: D. Zapheripoulou (ed.), *ΧΑΡΑΚΤΗΡ, Αφιέρωμα στη Μάντω Οικονομίδου*, Athens, 297–308.
Cargill Thompson Warren (1997): J. A. W. Cargill Thompson Warren, 'After the Boehringer Revolution: the 'New Landscape' in the Coinage of the Peloponnese', *Topoi* 7, 109–114.
Cargill Thompson Warren (1999a): J. A. W. Cargill Thompson Warren, 'The Achaian League Silver Coinage Controversy Resolved: a Summary', *Num. Chron.* 159, 99–109.
Cargill Thompson Warren (1999b): J. A. W. Cargill Thompson Warren, 'More on the 'New Landscape' in the Late Hellenistic Coinage of the Peloponnese', in M. Amandry, S. Hurter & D. Berend (eds.), *Travaux de numismatique grecque offerts à Georges Le Rider*, London, 375–393.
Cargill Thompson Warren (2007): J. A. W. Cargill Thompson Warren, *The Bronze Coinage of the Achaian Koinon. The Currency of a Federal Ideal*, London.
Cartledge/Spawforth (2002) [1989]: P. Cartledge & A. J. S. Spawforth, *Hellenistic and Roman Sparta. A Tale of Two Cities* (2nd ed.), London.
Chaniotis (1995): A. Chaniotis, 'Sich selbst feiern? Städtische Feste des Hellenismus im Spannungsfeld von Religion und Politik', in: P. Zanker & M. Wörrle (eds.), *Stadtbild und Bürgerbild im Hellenismus*, Munich, 147–172.

Chausserie-Laprée (1980): J. P. Chausserie-Laprée, '"Retractatio" et Description Stylistique', in: Y. Burnand, C. Guittard, F. Hinard, J.-P. Néraudau, A. Novara & N.-M. Tupet (eds.), *Hommage à la mémoire de Pierre Wuilleumier*, Paris, 77–81.
Chlup (2013): J. T. Chlup, 'Sallust's Melian Dialogue: Sulla and Bocchus in the *Bellum Iugurthinum*', in: D. Côté & P. Fleury (eds.), *Discours politique et Histoire dans l'Antiquité*, Dialogues d'histoire ancienne Supplément 8, Besançon, 191–207.
Christ (2002): K. Christ, *Sulla. Eine römische Karriere*, Munich.
Chroust (1962): A. H. Chroust, 'The miraculous disappearance and recovery of the *Corpus Aristotelicum*', *C&M* 23, 50–67.
Cichorius (1922): C. Cichorius, *Römische Studien*, Leipzig.
Clarke (2002): K. Clarke, '*In arto et inglorius labor*: Tacitus' Anti-history', in: A. K. Bowman, H. M. Cotton, M. Goodman, & S. Price (eds.) *Representations of Empire: Rome and the Mediterranean World*, Oxford, 83–103.
Clinton (1989): K. Clinton, 'The Eleusinian Mysteries: Roman initiates and benefactors, second century B.C. to A.D. 267', *ANRW* II.18.2, 1499–1539.
Clinton (2003): K. Clinton, 'Maroneia and Rome: Two Decrees of Maroneia from Samothrace', *Chiron* 33, 379–417.
Connolly (2007): J. Connolly, 'Being Greek/Being Roman: Hellenism and Assimilation in the Roman Empire', *Millennium* 4, 93–119.
Connolly (forthcoming): J. Connolly, 'A new form of citizenship: imperial fantasies of "classical Athens"', in: N. Wiater & J. König (eds.), *Literature and Cultural Identity in the Late Hellenistic and Imperial Periods*, Cambridge.
Corish (1976): P. J. Corish, 'The Cromwellian Regime 1650–60', in: J. W. Moody, F. X. Martin & F. G. Byrne (eds.), *A New History of Ireland*, vol. 2, Oxford, 353–386.
Cornell (2013): T. J. Cornell (ed.), *The Fragments of the Roman Historians* (3 vols.), Oxford.
Cosmopoulos (2001): M. Cosmopoulos, *The Rural History of Ancient Greek City-States. The Oropos Survey Project*, Oxford.
Courrier (2014) C. Courrier, *La plèbe de Rome et sa culture (fin du IIe siècle av. J.-C. – fin du Ier siècle ap. J.-C.)*, Rome.
Cowan (2009): E. Cowan, 'Tacitus, Tiberius and Augustus', *Cl. Ant.* 28, 179–210.
Crawford (1985): M. H. Crawford, *Coinage and Money under the Roman Republic*, London.
Crawford (1994): J. W. Crawford, *Tullius Cicero. The Fragmentary Speeches*, Atlanta, GA.
Criniti (1970): N. Criniti, *L'epigrafe di Asculum di Gn. Pompeo Strabone*, Milan.
Cugusi (1974): P. Cugusi, *Ricerche sulla letteratura latina dell'età traianea*, Cagliari.
Dahlheim (1993): W. Dahlheim, 'Der Staatsstreich des Konsuls Sulla und die römische Italienpolitik der 80er Jahre', in: J. Bleicken (ed.), *Colloquium aus Anlass des 80. Geburtstages von Alfred Heuss*, Frankfurter Althistorische Studien 13, Kallmünz, 97–116.
Damon (2010a): C. Damon, 'Déjà vu or déjà lu? History as intertext', *PLLS* 14, 375–388.
Damon (2010b): C. Damon, 'The Historian's Presence, or, There and Back Again', in: C. S. Kraus, J. Marincola & C. Pelling (eds.), *Ancient Historiography and its Contexts: Studies in Honour of A. J. Woodman*, Oxford, 353–363.
Damon/Mackay (1995): C. Damon & C. S. Mackay, 'On the Prosecution of C. Antonius in 76 B.C.', *Historia* 44, 37–55.
Dart (2014): C. J. Dart, *The Social War, 91 to 88 BCE: A History of the Italian Insurgency against the Roman Republic*, Aldershot.
Daux (1935): G. Daux, 'À propos des monnaies luculliennes', *RN* 38, 1–9.
Daux (1964): G. Daux, 'Concours des *Titeia* dans un decret d'Argos', *BCH* 88, 569–579.

De Callataÿ (1998): F. De Callataÿ, 'The coins in the name of Sura', in: A. Burnett, U. Wartenberg & R. Witschonke (eds.), *Coins of Macedonia and Rome: Essays in honour of Charles Hersh*, London, 113–117.
De Callataÿ (2004): F. De Callataÿ, 'Le monnayage d'argent au type d'Athéna Parthénos émis au nom des Ainianes', in: L. Kypraiou (ed.), *Coins in the Thessalian region. Mints, circulation, iconography, history: ancient, Byzantine, modern*, Athens, 125–156.
De Callataÿ (2015): F. De Callataÿ, 'The Late Hellenistic didrachms of Leukas: Another case of Greek coinage of the Roman', in: P. G. van Alfen, G. Bransbourg & M. Amandry (eds.), *FIDES. Contributions to numismatics in honor of Richard B. Witschonke*, New York, NY, 239–270.
De Souza (1999): P. De Souza, *Piracy in the Graeco-Roman World*, Cambridge.
Dench (2005): E. Dench, *Romulus' Asylum. Roman Identities from the Age of Alexander to the Age of Hadrian*, Oxford.
Devillers (1993): O. Devillers, 'Le rôle des passages relatifs à Germanicus dans les *Annales* de Tacite', *Anc. Soc.* 24, 225–241.
Diehl (1988): H. Diehl, *Sulla und seine Zeit im Urteil Ciceros*, Hildesheim.
Dijkstra/Parker (2007): T. M. Dijkstra & V. Parker, 'Through Many Glasses Darkly. Sulla and the End of the Jugurthine War', *Wien. Stud.* 120, 137–160.
Dijkstra et al. (2017): T. M. Dijkstra, I. N. I. Kuin, M. M. Moser & D. Weidgenannt (eds.), *Strategies of Remembering in Greece Under* Rome *(100 BC – 100 AD)*, Publications of the Netherlands Institute at Athens VI, Leiden.
Dilke (1971): O. A. W. Dilke, *The Roman Land Surveyors*, Newton Abbot.
Dmitriev (2011): S. Dmitriev, *The Greek Slogan of Freedom and Early Roman Politics in Greece*, Oxford.
Dohnicht/Heil (2004): M. Dohnicht & M. Heil, 'Ein Legat Sullas in Messenien', *ZPE* 147, 235–242.
Domingo-Forasté (1994): D. Domingo-Forasté, *Claudius Aelianus: Epistulae et Fragmenta*, Stuttgart.
Dowling (2000): M. B. Dowling, 'The Clemency of Sulla', *Historia* 49, 303–340.
Drumann (1902): W. Drumann, *Geschichte Roms: Pompeius, Caesar, Cicero und ihre Zeitgenossen*, vol. 2, Leipzig.
Drumann (1906): W. Drumann, *Geschichte Roms: Pompeius, Caesar, Cicero und ihre Zeitgenossen*, vol. 3, Leipzig.
Drummond (2000): A. Drummond, 'Rullus and the Sullan *Possessores*', *Klio* 82, 126–153.
Ducroux (1978): S. Ducroux, 'Histoire d'un portrait, portraits d'historiens. Tacite lecteur de Salluste', *MÉFRA* 90, 293–315.
Dunant/Pouilloux (1958): C. Dunant & J. Pouilloux, *Recherches sur l'Histoire et les cultes de Thasos II. De 196 avant J.-C. jusqu'à la fin de l'Antiquité* (Études thasiennes V), Paris.
Düring (1957): I. Düring, *Aristotle in the Ancient Biographical Tradition*, Gothenburg.
Düring (1966): I. Düring, *Aristoteles. Darstellung und Interpretation seines Denkens*, Heidelberg.
Dyck (1998): A. R. Dyck, *A Commentary on Cicero De Officiis*, Ann Arbor, MI.
Dyck (2010): A. R. Dyck, *Cicero: Pro Sexto Roscio*, Cambridge.
Earl, D. C. (1961): D. C. Earl, *The Political Thought of Sallust*, Cambridge.
Eckert (2014): A. Eckert, 'Remembering Cultural Trauma. Sulla's Proscriptions, Roman Responses and Christian Perspectives', in: E.-M. Becker, J. Dochhorn & E. K. Holt (eds.), *Trauma and Traumatization in Individual and Collective Dimensions. Insights from Biblical Studies and Beyond*, SANT vol. 2, Göttingen, 262–274.
Eckert (2016a): A. Eckert, *Lucius Cornelius Sulla in der antiken Erinnerung. Jener Mörder, der sich Felix nannte*, Berlin/Boston.
Eckert (2016b): A. Eckert, '"There is nobody who does not hate Sulla": Emotion, Persuasion and Cultural Trauma', in: E. Sanders & M. Johncock (eds.), *Emotion and Persuasion in Classical Antiquity*, Stuttgart, 133–145.

Eckert (2018a): A. Eckert, 'Roman Orators between Greece and Rome. The Case of Cato the Elder, L. Crassus, and M. Antonius', in: C. Gray, A. Balbo, R. M. A. Marshall & C. Steel (eds.), *Reading Republican Oratory. Reconstructions, Contexts, Receptions*, Cambridge, 19–32.

Eckert (2018b): A. Eckert, 'Good Fortune and the Public Good: Disputing Sulla's claim to be Felix', in: C. Steel, H. van der Blom & C. Gray (eds.), *Institutions and Ideology in Republican Rome: Speech, Audience and Decision*, Cambridge, 267–282.

Eckert (forthcoming: a): A. Eckert, 'Death by Lice. Ancient Riddles and Modern Confusion', in: R. Arnott & R. Breitweiser (eds.), *Disease and the Ancient World*, Oxford.

Eckert (forthcoming: b): A. Eckert, 'Sulla's Dictatorship "rei publicae constituendae" and Roman Republican Cultural Memory', in: M. T. Dinter und C. Guerin (eds.), *Cultural Memory in Republican and Augustan Rome*, Cambridge.

Eckstein (1990): A. M. Eckstein, 'Polybius, the Achaeans, and the "Freedom of the Greeks"', *GRBS* 31, 1990, 45–71.

Edwards, R. (2012): R. Edwards, '*Devotio*, Disease, and *Remedia* in the Histories', in: V. E. Pagán (ed.), *A Companion to Tacitus*, Chichester, 237–259.

Eisenhut (1985): W. Eisenhut, 'Das Echtheitsproblem der Invektive und der Briefe', in: W. Eisenhut & J. Lindauer (eds.), *Sallusts Werke*, Munich, 462–467.

Engels (1999): J. Engels, *Augusteische Oikumenegeographie und Universalhistorie im Werk Strabons von Amaseia*, Stuttgart.

Epstein (1992): S. J. Epstein, 'More Speech and Allusion in Tacitus' Annales XIV', *Latomus* 51, 868–871.

Feig Vishnia (2008): R. Feig Vishnia, 'Written Ballot, Secret Ballot and the iudicia publica. A note on the leges tabellariae (Cicero, De legibus 3.33 39)', *Klio* 90, 334–346.

Felmy (1999): A. Felmy, *Die römische Republik im Geschichtsbild der Spätantike. Zum Umgang lateinischer Autoren des 4. und 5. Jh.s n. Chr. mit den exempla maiorum*, Berlin.

Ferrary (1988a): J.-L. Ferrary, *Philhellenisme et imperialisme: Aspects ideologiques de la conquete romaine du monde hellenistique*, Rome.

Ferrary (1988b): J.-L. Ferrary, '*Rogatio Servilia Agraria*', *Athenaeum* 66, 141–164.

Ferrary (2000): J.-L. Ferrary, 'Les gouverneurs des provinces romaines d'Asie Mineure (Asie et Cilicie), depuis l'organisation de la province d'Asie jusqu'à la première guerre de Mithridate (126–88 av. J.-C.)', *Chiron* 30, 161–193.

Ferrary (2001a): J.-L. Ferrary, 'À propos des pouvoirs d'Auguste', *Cahiers du Centre Gustave Glotz* 12, 101–154.

Ferrary (2001b): J.-L. Ferrary, 'Rome et la geographie de l'hellénisme: réflexions sur 'hellènes' et 'panhellènes' dans les inscriptions d'époque romaine', in: O. Salomies (ed.), *The Greek East in the Roman Context*, Papers and Monographs of the Finnish Institute at Athens 7, Helsinki, 19–35.

Ferriès/Delrieux (2011): M.-C. Ferriès & F. Delrieux, 'Quinctus Mucius Scaevola, un gouverneur modèle pour les Grecs de la province d'Asie?', in: N. Barrandon & F. Kirbilher (eds.), *Les gouverneurs et les provinciaux sous la République romaine*, Rennes 2011, 207–230.

Fletcher (1945): G. B. A. Fletcher, 'Some Certain or Possible Examples of Literary Reminiscence in Tacitus', *CR* 59, 45–50.

Fletcher (1964): G. B. A. Fletcher, *Annotations on Tacitus*, Brussels.

Flower (2010): H. I. Flower, *Roman Republics*, Princeton, NJ.

Fortenbaugh et al. (1992): W. W. Fortenbaugh, P. M. Huby, R. W. Sharples & D. Gutas (eds.), *Theophrastus of Eresus. Sources for his Life, Writings, Thought, and Influence* (2 vols.), Leiden.

Frei-Stolba (1967). R. Frei-Stolba, *Untersuchungen zu den Wahlen in der römischen Kaiserzeit*, Zürich.

Fündling (2010): J. Fündling, *Sulla*, Darmstadt.
Furneaux (1896): H. Furneaux, *The Annals of Tacitus. Vol.I: Books I–VI* (2nd ed.), Oxford.
Gabba (1967): E. Gabba, *Appiani Bellorum Civilium Liber Primus* (2nd ed.), Florence.
Gabba (1972): E. Gabba, 'Mario e Silla', *ANRW* I.1, 764–810.
Gabba (1976): E. Gabba, *Republican Rome: The Army and the Allies*, trans. P. J. Cuff, Oxford.
Gargola (1995): D. J. Gargola, *Lands, Laws, and Gods*, Chapel Hill, NC.
Gärtner (2011): T. Gärtner, 'Cotta bei Sallust und Perikles bei Thukydides – eine übersehene Parallele', *Historia* 60, 122–125.
Gautier (1980): P. Gautier, *Theophylacte d'Achrida. Discours, Traités, Poésies. Corpus Fontium Historiae Byzantinae*, Thessaloniki.
Geagan (1967): D. J. Geagan, *The Athenian Constitution after Sulla*, Princeton, NJ.
Geagan (1979): D. J. Geagan, 'Roman Athens. Some Aspects of Life and Culture', *ANRW* II. 7.1, 371–437.
Giardina (2012): A. Giardina, 'Silla sul Campidoglio', in E. Chevreau, D. Kremer & A. Laquerrière-Lacroix (eds.), *Carmina Iuris. Mélanges en l'honneur de Michel Humbert*, Paris, 333–344.
Gilbert (1973): C. D. Gilbert, 'Marius and Fortuna', *CQ* 23, 104–107.
Ginsburg (1981): J. Ginsburg, *Tradition and Theme in the* Annals *of Tacitus*, Salem, NH.
Ginsburg (1986): J. Ginsburg, 'Speech and Allusion in Tacitus, *Annals* 3.49–51 and 14.48–49', *AJPhil.* 107, 525–541.
Gisborne (2005): M. Gisborne, 'A curia of kings: Sulla and royal imagery', in: O. Hekster & R. Fowler (eds.), *Imaginary Kings Royal Images in the Ancient Near East, Greece and Rome*, Munich, 105–123.
Goodyear (1972): F. R. D. Goodyear, *The Annals of Tacitus: Books 1–6. Vol. I: Annals 1.1–54*, Cambridge.
Gossage (1975): A. G. Gossage, 'The Comparative Chronology of Inscriptions relating to Boiotian Festivals in the First Half of the First Century B.C.', *BSA* 70, 115–134.
Gottschalk (1972): H. B. Gottschalk, 'Notes on the Wills of the Peripatetic Scholarchs', *Hermes* 100, 314–342.
Grainger (2000): J. D. Grainger, *Aitolian prosopographical studies*, Leiden.
Grandjean (2003): C. Grandjean, *Les Messéniens de 370/369 au 1er siècle de notre ère*, Athens.
Graninger (2011): D. Graninger, *Cult and Koinon in Hellenistic Thessaly*, Leiden.
Griffin (1995): M. T. Griffin, 'Tacitus, Tiberius and the Principate', in: I. Malkin & Z. W. Rubinsohn (eds.), *Leaders and Masses in the Roman World*, Leiden, 33–57.
Griffin (1999): M. T. Griffin, 'Pliny and Tacitus', *SCI* 18, 139–158.
Grigoropoulos (2005): D. Grigoropoulos, *After Sulla: Study in the Settlement and Material Culture of the Piraeus Peninsula in the Roman and Late Roman Period*, PhD thesis, Durham University.
Gruen (1966a): E. S. Gruen, 'The Dolabellae and Sulla', *AJPhil.* 87, 385–399.
Gruen (1966b): E. S. Gruen, 'Political Prosecutions in the 90's BC', *Historia* 15, 32–64.
Gruen (1968): E. S. Gruen, *Roman Politics and the Criminal Courts 149–78 B.C.*, Cambridge, MA.
Gruen (1974): E. S. Gruen, *The Last Generation of the Roman Republic*, Berkeley, CA.
Gruen (1992): E. S. Gruen, *Culture and National Identity in Republican Rome*, Ithaca, NY.
Guilbert (1957): D. Guilbert, 'Salluste *oratio Lepidi consulis* et la IIe Olynthienne', *LEC* 25, 296–299.
Gurzadyan/Vardanyan (2004): V. G. Gurzadyan & R. Vardanyan, 'Halley's Comet of 87 BC on the Coins of Armenian King Tigranes?', *Astronomy & Geophysics* 45, 4.06.
Habicht (1997) [1995]: C. Habicht, *Athens from Alexander to Antony*, Cambridge, MA.
Habicht (2003): C. Habicht, 'Versäumter Götterdienst', *Journal of Ancient History* 4, 39–49.
Hague et al. (2016) [1982]: R. Hague, M. Harrop & T. McCormick, *Comparative Government and Politics: An Introduction* (revised edition), London.

Hall (1990): U. Hall, 'Greeks and Romans and the Secret Ballot', in: E. M. Craik (ed.), *Owls to Athens. Essays on Classical Subjects Presented to Sir Kenneth Dover*, Oxford, 191–199.
Hands (1959): A. R. Hands, 'Sallust and *dissimulatio*', *JRS* 49, 56–60.
Hantos (1988): T. Hantos, *Res publica constituta. Die Verfassung des Diktators Sulla*, Stuttgart.
Hardwick (2003): L. Hardwick, *Reception Studies*, Oxford.
Hardwick/Harrison (2013): L. Hardwick & S. Harrison (eds.), *Classics in the Modern World. A 'Democratic Turn'?*, Oxford.
Hardwick/Stray (2008): L. Hardwick & C. Stray (eds.), *A Companion to Classical Receptions*, Malden, MA.
Hardy (1913): E. G. Hardy, 'The Policy of the Rullan Proposal in 63 B.C.', *Journ. Phil.* 32, 228–260.
Harris (1971): W. V. Harris, *Rome in Etruria and Umbria*, Oxford.
Harter-Uibopuu (2003): K. Harter-Uibopuu, 'Kaiserkult und Kaiserverehrung in den Koina des griechischen Mutterlandes', in: H. Cancik & K. Hitzl (eds.), *Die Praxis der Herrscherverehrung in Rom und seinen Provinzen*, Tübingen, 209–231.
Harvey (1973): P. B. Harvey, 'Socer Valgus, Valgii and Quinctius Valgus', in: E. N. Borza & R. W. Carrubba (eds.), *Classics and the Classical Tradition: Essays presented to R.E. Dengler on the Occasion of his Eightieth Birthday*, University Park, PA, 79–94.
Harvey (1975): P. B. Harvey, 'Cic. *leg. agr.* 2.78 and the Sullan colony at Praeneste', *Athenaeum* 53, 33–56.
Harvey (1982): P. B. Harvey, 'Cicero, Consius and Capua: II. Cicero and M. Brutus' Colony', *Athenaeum* 60, 145–171.
Hatzimichali (2013): M. Hatzimichali, 'The texts of Plato and Aristotle in the first century BC', in: M. Schofield (ed.), *Aristotle, Plato and Pythagoreanism in the First Century BC: New Directions for Philosophy*, Cambridge, 1–27.
Heftner (2006a): H. Heftner, 'Der Beginn von Sullas Proskriptionen', *Tyche* 21, 33–52.
Heftner (2006b): H. Heftner, *Von den Gracchen bis Sulla. Die römische Republik am Scheideweg 133–78 v. Chr.*, Regensburg.
Heftner (2013): H. Heftner, 'Bemerkungen zu den Amnestie- und Restitutionsbestrebungen der nachsullanischen Ära', in: K. Harter-Uibopuu & F. Mitthof (eds.), *Vergeben und Vergessen? Amnestie in der Antike*, Vienna, 229–249.
Hellegouarc'h (1963): J. Hellegouarc'h, *Le vocabulaire latin des relations et des partis politiques sous la République*, Paris.
Henderson (1958): C. Henderson, 'The Career of the Younger M. Aemilius Scaurus', *CJ* 53, 194–206.
Heraeus (1905): W. Heraeus, 'Tacitus und Sallust', *Archiv für lateinische Lexikographie und Grammatik* 14, 273–276.
Hercher (1866): R. Hercher, *Claudii Aeliani: Varia historia, epistolae, fragmenta*, Leipzig.
Heubner (1983): H. Heubner, *P. Cornelius Tacitus, Tom. I: Annales*, Stuttgart.
Hill (1946): H. Hill, 'Roman Revenues from Greece after 146 B.C.', *CPhil.* 41, 35–42.
Hillard (1981): T. W. Hillard, 'The Seventies, the Senate and Popular Discontent. The Background to the "First Verrine" Part I', *Ancient History Resources for Teachers* 11, 12–21.
Hillman (1997): T. P. Hillman, 'Pompeius in Africa and Sulla's Order to demobilize (Plutarch, *Pompeius* 13, 1–4)', *Latomus* 56, 94–106.
Hinard (1984): F. Hinard, 'La naissance du mythe de Sylla', *Rev. Ét. Lat.* 62 (1984), 81–95.
Hinard (1985a): F. Hinard, *Sylla*, Paris.
Hinard (1985b): F. Hinard, *Les proscriptions de la Rome républicaine*, Rome.
Hinard (1988): F. Hinard, 'De la dictatures à la tyrannie. Réflections sur la dictature de Sylla', in: F. Hinard (ed.), *Dictatures*, Paris, 87–96.
Hinard (1999): F. Hinard, 'Dion Cassius et l'Abdication de Sylla', *Rev. Ét. Anc.* 101, 427–432.

Hinard (2007): F. Hinard, 'La dictature de Sylla: une magistrature inconstitutionelle?', in: C. Cascione & C. Masi Doria (eds.), *Fides humanitas Ius. Studi in onore di Luigi Labruna*, Naples, 1–13.
Hinard (2008): F. Hinard, *Syllana Varia. Aux sources de la première guerre civile romaine*, Paris.
Hinard (2011): F. Hinard, *Rome, la dernière République. Recueil d'articles de François Hinard*, ed. E. Bertrand, Paris.
Hinds (1998): S. Hinds, *Allusion and intertext: dynamics of appropriation in Roman Poetry*, Cambridge.
Hoff (1997): M. C. Hoff, *'Laceratae Athenae:* Sulla's Siege of Athens in 87/6 BC and its Aftermath', in: M. C. Hoff & S. I. Rotroff (eds.), *The Romanization of Athens*, Oxford, 33–51.
Hölkeskamp (2000): K.-J. Hölkeskamp, 'Lucius Cornelius Sulla – Revolutionär und restaurativer Reformer', in: K.-J. Hölkeskamp & E. Stein-Hölkeskamp (eds.), *Von Romulus zu Augustus. Große Gestalten der römischen Republik*, Munich, 199–218.
Hölkeskamp (2004): K.-J. Hölkeskamp, *Senatus populusque Romanus. Die politische Kultur der Republik – Dimensionen und Deutungen*, Stuttgart.
Holladay (1978): A. J. Holladay, 'The election of magistrates in the early Principate', *Latomus* 37, 874–893.
Hollard (2010): V. Hollard, *Le rituel du vote, les assemblées du peuple romain*, Paris.
Holleaux (1919): M. Holleaux, 'Décret de Chéronée relatif à la première guerre de Mithridates', *Rev. Ét. Grec.* 32, 320–337.
Holtmann (2000) [1991]: E. Holtmann (ed.), *Politik-Lexikon* (3rd ed.), Munich.
Hopkinson (2008): N. Hopkinson, *Lucian: A Selection*, Cambridge.
Howgego (1990): C. Howgego, 'Why Did Ancient States Strike Coins?', *Num. Chron.* 150, 1–25.
Hurlet (1993): F. Hurlet, *La dictature de Sylla. Monarchie ou magistrature républicaine? Essai d'histoire constitutionelle*, Brussels.
Janssen (1981): L. F. Janssen, 'Some Unexplored Aspects of *Devotio Deciana*', *Mnemos.* 34, 357–381.
Jauß (1970): H. R. Jauß, 'Proklamation einer Rezeptionsästhetik. Antrittsvorlesung Universität Konstanz 1967' (extended 1970), in: H. R. Jauß, *Literaturgeschichte als Provokation der Literaturwissenschaft*, Frankfurt, 144–206.
Jehne (1993): M. Jehne, 'Geheime Abstimmung und Bindungswesen in der römischen Republik', *Historische Zeitschrift* 257, 593–614.
Jehne (2010): M. Jehne, 'Der Diktator und die Republik', in: B. Linke, M. Meier & M. Strothmann (eds.), *Zwischen Monarchie und Republik*, Stuttgart, 187–211.
Johnson (2010): W. A. Johnson, *Readers and Reading Culture in the High Roman Empire: a Study of Elite Communities*, New York, NY.
Jones (1955): A. H. Jones, 'The elections under Augustus', *JRS* 45, 9–21.
Kallet-Marx (1995): R. M. Kallet-Marx, *Hegemony to Empire. The Development of the Roman Imperium in the East from 148 to 62 B.C.*, Berkeley, CA.
Kalliontzis (2016): Y. Kalliontzis, 'La date de la première célébration des Amphiareia-Romania d'Oropos', *Rev. Ét. Grec.* 129, 85–105.
Kaltsas et al. (2010): N. Kaltsas, S. Fachard, A. Psalti & M. Giannopoulou (eds.), Ερέτρια. Ματιές σε μια αρχαία πόλη, Athens.
Kay (2014): P. Kay, *Rome's Economic Revolution*, Oxford.
Keaveney (1981): A. Keaveney, 'Sulla, the Marsi and the Hirpini', *CPhil* 76, 292–296.
Keaveney (1982a): A. Keaveney, 'Young Pompey 106–79 BC', *Ant. Class.* 51, 111–139.
Keaveney (1982b): A. Keaveney, 'Sulla and Italy', *Critica Storica* 19, 499–544.
Keaveney (1983a): A. Keaveney, 'What happened in 88?', *Eirene* 20, 53–86.
Keaveney (1983b): A. Keaveney, 'Studies in the Dominatio Sullae', *Klio* 65, 185–208.

Keaveney (1984): A. Keaveney, 'Who were the Sullani?', *Klio* 66, 114–150.
Keaveney (2003): A. Keaveney, 'The Short Career of Q. Lucretius Afella', *Eranos* 101, 84–93.
Keaveney (2005a) [1982]: A. Keaveney, *Sulla. The Last Republican* (2nd ed.), London.
Keaveney (2005b): A. Keaveney, 'The terminal date of Sulla's dictatorship', *Athenaeum* 93, 423–439.
Keaveney (2006): A. Keaveney, 'The Exile of L. Cornelius Scipio Asiagenus', *Rh. Mus.* 149, 112–114.
Keaveney (2007): A. Keaveney, *The Army in the Roman Revolution*, Abingdon.
Keaveney (2009a): A. Keaveney, *Lucullus: A Life* (2nd ed.), Piscataway, NJ.
Keaveney (2009b): A. Keaveney, 'Crisis with Alternative. The Reformers of the Roman Republic', in A. Keaveney & L. Earnshaw-Brown (eds.), *The Italians on the Land*, Newcastle, 1–9.
Keaveney/Madden (1982): A. Keaveney & J. A. Madden, 'Phthiriasis and its Victims', *Symbolae Osloenses* 57, 87–99.
Keaveney/Strachan (1981): A. Keaveney & J. C. G. Strachan, 'L. Catiline Legatus: Sallust, *Histories* 1.46M', *CQ* 31, 363–366.
Keitel (1984): E. Keitel, 'Principate and Civil War in Tacitus', *AJPhil.* 105, 306–325.
Keitel (2010): E. Keitel, 'The Art of Losing: Tacitus and the Disaster Narrative', in: C. S. Kraus, J. Marincola & C. Pelling (eds.), *Ancient Historiography and its Contexts: Studies in Honour of A. J. Woodman*, Oxford, 331–352.
Kendall (2013): S. Kendall, *The Struggle for Roman Citizenship*, Piscataway, NJ.
Keppie (1983): L. Keppie, *Colonisation and Veteran Settlement in Italy 47–14 B.C.*, London.
Knoepfler (1991): D. Knoepfler, 'L. Mummius Achaïcus et les cités du golfe euboïque: à propos d'une nouvelle inscription d'Erétrie', *MH* 48, 252–280.
Knoepfler (1992): D. Knoepfler, 'Sept années de recherches sur l'épigraphie de la Béotie (1985–1991)', *Chiron* 22, 411–503.
Knoepfler (1997): D. Knoepfler, '*Cupido ille propter quem Thespiae visuntur*. Une mésaventure insoupçonnée de l'Eros de Praxitèle et l'institution du concours des Erôtideia', in: D. Knoepfler (ed.), *Nomen latinum. Mélanges de langue, de littérature et de civilisation latines offerts au professeur André Schneider à l'occasion de son départ à la retraite*, Neuchâtel, 17–39.
Knoepfler (2008): D. Knoepfler, 'Louis Robert en sa forge: ébauche d'un mémoire resté inédit sur l'histoire controversée de deux concours grecs, les Trophônia et les Basileia à Lébadée', *CRAI* 2008, 1421–1462.
Koestermann (1963): E. Koestermann, *Cornelius Tacitus: Annalen. Band I: Buch 1–3*, Heidelberg.
Kountouri (2001–2004): E. Kountouri, 'Αγρός Κ. Γκιζίμη (Τρόπαιο Σύλλα)', *Archaiologikon Deltion* 56–59, B2 Chron., 193–194.
Kountouri et al. (forthcoming): E. Kountouri, S. Zoumbaki & N. Petrochilos, 'The Tropaion of Sulla over Mithridates VI Eupator: A First Approach', in: V. Di Napoli, F. Camia, V. Evangelidis, D. Grigoropoulos, D. Rogers & S. Vlizos (eds.), *What's New in Roman Greece? Recent Work on the Greek Mainland and the Islands in the Roman Period*, Athens.
Krawczuk (2008): A. Krawczuk, 'La colonizzazione sillana (edizione italiana traduzione di Francecso Papagni con note di aggiornamento di Federico Santangelo)', *Simblos* 5, 7–99.
Krebs (2012): C. B. Krebs, '*Annum quiete et otio transiit*: Tacitus (*Agr.* 6.3) and Sallust on Liberty, Tyranny, and Human Dignity', in: V. E. Pagán (ed.), *A Companion to Tacitus*, Chichester, 333–344.
Kreiler (2007): B. Kreiler, 'Zur Verwaltung Kilikiens von 102 bis 78 v. Chr.', *Gephyra* 4, 117–126.
Kremydi (2004): S. Kremydi, 'Hoard Evidence from Thessaly in the Second and First Centuries BC: From a "Multi-Currency" to a "Double-Currency" System', in: L. Kypraiou (ed.), *Coins in the Thessalian region. Mints, circulation, iconography, history: ancient, Byzantine, modern*, Athens, 235–258.
Kuin (2017): I. N. I. Kuin, 'Anchoring Political Change in Post-Sullan Athens', in: T. M. Dijkstra, I. N. I. Kuin, M. M. Moser & D. Weidgenannt (eds.), *Strategies of Remembering in Greece Under*

Rome (100 BC – 100 AD), Publications of the Netherlands Institute at Athens VI, Leiden, 157–167.
Kuin (2018): I. N. I. Kuin, 'Sulla and the Invention of Roman Athens', *Mnemos.* 71, 616–639.
Kunkel/Wittmann (1995): W. Kunkel & R. Wittmann, *Staatsordnung und Staatspraxis der römischen Republik. Die Magistratur*, Munich.
Kuttner (2013): A. Kuttner, 'Representing Hellenistic Numidia, in Africa and at Rome', in: J. R. W. Prag & J. Crawley Quinn (eds.), *The Hellenistic West. Rethinking the Ancient Mediterranean*, Oxford, 216–272.
La Penna (1959): A. La Penna, 'L'interpretazione Sallustiana della congiura di Catilina', *Stud. Ital.* 31, 1–64, 127–168.
La Penna (1963): A. La Penna, 'Le Historiae di Sallustio e l'interpretazione della crisi repubblicana', *Athenaeum* 41, 201–274.
La Penna (1968): A. La Penna, *Sallustio e la 'rivoluzione' romana*, Milan.
La Penna (1978): A. La Penna, *Aspetti del pensiero storico latino*, Turin.
Laffi (1967): U. Laffi, 'Il mito di Silla', *Athenaeum* 45, 177–213, 255–277.
Laird (1999): A. Laird, *Powers of Expression, Expressions of Power: Speech Presentation and Latin Literature*, Oxford.
Lamberton (1997): R. Lamberton, 'Plutarch and the Romanization of Athens', in: M. C. Hoff & S. I. Rotroff (eds.), *The Romanization of Athens*, Oxford, 150–160.
Lanciotti (1977): S. Lanciotti, 'Silla e la tipologia del tiranno nella letteratura latina repubblicana I', *Quaderni di Storia* 6, 129–153.
Lanciotti (1978): S. Lanciotti, 'Silla e la tipologia del tiranno nella letteratura latina repubblicana II', *Quaderni di Storia* 8, 191–225.
Lange (2016): C. H. Lange, *Triumphs in the Age of Civil War: the Late Republic and the adaptability of triumphal tradition*, London.
Lange/Vervaet (2019): C. H. Lange & F. J. Vervaet, 'Sulla and the Origins of the Concept of *Bellum Civile*', in: C. H. Lange & F. J. Vervaet, *The Historiography of Late Republican Civil War*, Leiden, 17–28.
Lanzani (1936): C. Lanzani, *Lucio Cornelio Silla Dittatore*, Milano.
Le Rider (1968): G. Le Rider, 'Un groupe de monnaies crétoises à types athéniens', in: *Humanism actif. Mélanges d'art et de littérature offerts à Julien Cain*, vol. 1, Paris, 313–335.
Letzner (2000): W. Letzner, *Lucius Cornelius Sulla. Versuch einer Biographie*, Münster.
Levene (1992): D. Levene, 'Sallust's *Jugurtha*. An "Historical Fragment"', *JRS* 82, 53–70.
Levene (2009): D. Levene, 'Warfare in the *Annals*', in: A. J. Woodman (ed.), *The Cambridge Companion to Tacitus*, Cambridge, 225–238.
Levene (2010): D. Levene, 'Pompeius Trogus in Tacitus' *Annals*', in: C. S. Kraus, J. Marincola & C. Pelling (eds.), *Ancient Historiography and its Contexts: Studies in Honour of A. J. Woodman*, Oxford, 294–311.
Levick (1967): B. Levick, 'Imperial Control of the Elections under the Early Principate: Commendatio, Suffragatio, and "Nominatio"', *Historia* 16, 207–230.
Levick (1981): B. Levick, 'Professio', *Athenaeum* 59, 378–388.
Lewis (1991): R. G. Lewis, 'Sulla's Autobiography. Scope and Economy', *Athenaeum* 69, 509–519.
Linderski (1972): J. Linderski, 'The Aedileship of Favonius, Curio the Younger and Cicero's Election to the Augurate', *Harv. Stud.* 76, 181–200.
Lindsay (1997): H. Lindsay, 'Strabo on Apellicon's Library', *Rh. Mus.* 140, 290–298.
Linke (2005): B. Linke, *Die römische Republik von den Gracchen bis Sulla*, Darmstadt.
Lintott (1999) [1968]: A. Lintott, *Violence in Republican Rome* (2nd ed.), Oxford.
Low (2013): K. A. Low, *The Mirror of Tacitus? Selves and Others in the Tiberian Books of the* Annals, PhD thesis, University of Oxford.

Lundgreen (2009): C. Lundgreen, 'Geheim(nisvoll)e Abstimmung in Rom. Die leges tabellariae und ihre Konsequenzen für die Comitien und die res publica', *Historia* 58, 36–70.

Lundgreen (2011): C. Lundgreen, *Regelkonflikte in der römischen Republik: Geltung und Gewichtung von Normen in politischen Entscheidungsprozessen*, Stuttgart.

Ma (1999): J. Ma, *Antiochus III and the Cities of Western Asia Minor*, Oxford.

Ma (2002): J. Ma, '"Oversexed, Overpaid, Over Here": A Response to Angelos Chaniotis', in: A. Chaniotis & P. Ducrey (eds.), *Army and Power in the Ancient World*, Stuttgart, 115–122.

Ma (2013): J. Ma, *Statues and Cities. Honorific Portraits and Civic Identity in the Hellenistic World*, Oxford.

Mackay (2000a): C. Mackay, 'Sulla and the Monuments: Studies in his Public Persona', *Historia* 49, 168–177.

Mackay (2000b): C. Mackay, 'Damon of Chaeronea: The Loyalties of a Boeotian Town during the First Mithridatic War', *Klio* 82, 91–106.

Malitz (1972): J. Malitz, 'C. Aurelius Cotta cos. 75 und seine Rede in Sallusts Historien', *Hermes* 100, 359–386.

Malloch (2004): S. Malloch, 'The end of the Rhine mutiny in Tacitus, Suetonius and Dio', *CQ* 54, 198–210.

Malloch (2009): S. Malloch, '*Hamlet* without the prince? The Claudian *Annals*', in: A. J. Woodman (ed.), *The Cambridge Companion to Tacitus*, Cambridge, 116–126.

Mango (2010): E. Mango, 'Tanta vis admonitionis inest in locis. Zur Veränderung von Erinnerungsräumen im Athen des 1. Jahrhunderts v. Chr.', in: R. Krummeich & C. Witschel (eds.), *Die Akropolis von Athen im Hellenismus und in der römischen Kaiserzeit*, Wiesbaden, 117–155.

Marincola (2010): J. Marincola, 'The Rhetoric of History: Allusion, Intertextuality, and Exemplarity in Historiographical Speeches', in: D. Pausch (ed.), *Stimmen der Geschichte: Funktionen von Reden in der antiken Historiographie*, Berlin, 259–289.

Marino (1974): R. E. Marino, *Aspetti della politica interna di Silla*, Palermo.

Marshall (1969): A. J. Marshall, 'Romans under Chian Law', *GRBS* 10, 255–271.

Marshall (1997): B. A. Marshall, 'Libertas Populi: the Introduction of Secret Ballot at Rome and its Depiction on Coinage', *Antichthon* 31, 54–73.

Martin (1975): D. G. Martin, *Greek Leagues in the Later Second and First Centuries B.C.*, PhD thesis, Princeton University.

Martin (1953): R. H. Martin, 'Variatio and the Development of Tacitus' Style', *Eranos* 51, 89–96.

Martin (1969): R. H. Martin, 'Tacitus and his Predecessors', in: T. A. Dorey (ed.), *Tacitus*, London, 117–147.

Martin (1981): R. H. Martin, *Tacitus*, London.

Martin/Woodman, (1989): R. H. Martin & A. J. Woodman, *Annals. Book IV*, Cambridge.

Martindale (2006): C. Martindale, 'Thinking through Reception', in: C. Martindale & R. F. Thomas (eds.), *Classics and the Uses of Reception*, Malden, MA, 1–13.

Master (2014): J. Master, 'Allusive Concord: Tacitus *Histories* 2.37–38 and Sallust *Bellum Catilinae* 6', *Phoenix* 68, 126–136.

Maurenbrecher (1891): B. Maurenbrecher (ed.), *C. Sallusti Crispi Historiarum Reliquiae*, Leipzig.

Maxfield (1981): V. A. Maxfield, *The Military Decorations of the Roman Army*, Berkeley, CA.

Mayer (2008): M. Mayer, 'Sila y el uso político de la epigrafía', in: M. L. Caldelli, G. L. Gregori & S. Orlandi (eds.), *Epigrafia 2006, Atti della XIVe rencontre sur l'épigraphie in onore di Silvio Panciera con altri contributi di colleghi, allievi e collaboratori*, Rome, 121–135.

Mayor (2010): A. Mayor, *The Poison King: The Life and Legend of Mithradates, Rome's Deadliest Enemy*, Princeton, NJ.

McGing (1986): B. C. McGing, *The Foreign Policy of Mithridates VI Eupator, King of Pontus*, Leiden.

McGushin (1992): P. McGushin, *Sallust: The Histories*. Vol. 1, Oxford.
McGushin (1994): P. McGushin, *Sallust: The Histories*. Vol. 2, Oxford.
Meier (1997) [1966]: C. Meier, *Res Publica Amissa. Eine Studie zu Verfassung und Geschichte der späten römischen Republik*, Wiesbaden.
Meyer (2008): E. Meyer, 'New Inscription from Chaironeia and the Chronology of Slave-Dedication', *Tekmeria* 9, 53–89.
Meyer (1991/1992): H. Meyer, 'Rom, Pergamon und Antiochos III. Zu den Siegesreliefs von Sant'Omobono', *BCAR* 94, 17–32.
Miaczewska (2013): A. B. Miaczewska, 'Good General becoming Evil Tyrant. The Deconstruction of the Sullan Topos', in: D. Słapek & I. Łuć (eds.), *Lucius Cornelius Sulla. History and Tradition*, Lublin, 191–211.
Migeotte (1984): L. Migeotte, *L'emprunt public dans les cités grecques. Recueil des documents et analyse critique*, Québec.
Miles (2008): M. Miles, *Art as Plunder: The Ancient Origins of Debate about Cultural Property*, Cambridge.
Millar (1984): F. Millar, 'The Political Character of the Classical Roman Republic, 200–155 BC', *JRS* 74, 1–19.
Millar (1986): F. Millar, 'Politics, Persuasion, and the People before the Social War (150–90 BC)', *JRS* 76, 1–11.
Millar (1998): F. Millar, *The Crowd in Rome in the Late Republic*, Ann Arbor, MI.
Miller (1964): N. P. Miller, 'Dramatic Speech in Tacitus', *AJPhil*. 85, 279–96.
Moles (1998): J. Moles, 'Cry Freedom: Tacitus *Annals* 4.32–35', *Histos* 2, 95–184.
Mommsen (2010) ^{9}[1903/1904]: T. Mommsen, *Römische Geschichte*. Special edition with an introduction by S. Rebenich (2 vols.), Darmstadt.
Mommsen (1877): T. Mommsen, *Römisches Staatsrecht*, Leipzig.
Mommsen (1899): T. Mommsen, *Römisches Strafrecht*, Leipzig.
Morstein-Marx (2009): R. Morstein-Marx, '*Dignitas* and *res publica*: Caesar and Republican legitimacy', in: K.-J. Hölkeskamp (ed.), *Eine politische Kultur (in) der Krise?*, Munich, 115–140.
Morstein-Marx, R. (2011): R. Morstein-Marx, 'Consular appeals to the army in 88 and 87: the locus of legitimacy in late-republican Rome', in: H. Beck, A. Duplá, M. Jehne, & F. Pina Polo (eds.), *Consuls and Res Publica: Holding High Office in the Roman Republic*, Cambridge, 259–278.
Moser (2017): M. Moser, 'Public Honours for Roman Friends: The Past as a Political Resource on the Roman Acropolis', in: T. M. Dijkstra, I. N. I. Kuin, M. M. Moser & D. Weidgenannt (eds.), *Strategies of Remembering in Greece Under Rome (100 BC – 100 AD)*, Publications of the Netherlands Institute at Athens VI, Leiden, 169–181.
Mouritsen (2001): H. Mouritsen, *Plebs and Politics in the Late Roman Republic*, Cambridge.
Müller (1996): C. Müller, 'Les nomina romana à Thespies du IIe s. a.C. à l' édit de Caracalla', in: A. D. Rizakis (ed.), *Roman Onomastics in the Greek East. Social and Political Aspects*, Athens, 157–166.
Müller (2014a): C. Müller, 'A Koinon after 146? Reflections on the Political and Institutional Situation of Boeotia in the Late Hellenistic Period', in: N. Papazarkadas (ed.), *The Epigraphy and History of Boeotia. New Finds, New Prospects*, Leiden, 119–146.
Müller (2014b): C. Müller, 'Les Romains et la Grèce égéenne du Ier s. av. J.-C. au Ier s. apr. J.-C.: un monde en transition?', *Pallas* 96, 193–216.
Münzer (1901a): F. Münzer, 'Cn. Cornelius Dolabella (no. 134)', *RE* 4, 1297.
Münzer (1901b): F. Münzer, 'Cn. Cornelius Dolabella (no. 135)', *RE* 4, 1297–1298.
Münzer (1920): F. Münzer, *Römische Adelspartaien und Adelsfamilien*, Stuttgart.

Münzer (1927): F. Münzer, 'Q. Lucretius Ofella (no. 25)', *RE* 26, 1686–1687.
Münzer (1948): F. Münzer, 'M. Tullius Decula (no. 34)', *RE* 2.14, 1312.
Ñaco del Hoyo (2011): T. Ñaco del Hoyo, 'The Republican War Economy Strikes Back: a 'minimalist approach'', in: N. Barrandon & F. Kirbihler (eds.), *Les gouverneurs et les provinciaux sous la République romaine*, Rennes, 171–180.
Ñaco del Hoyo et al. (2009): T. Ñaco del Hoyo, I. Arrayás & S. Busquets, 'The Impact of Roman Intervention in Greece and Asia Minor upon Civilians (88–63 BC)', in: B. Antela-Bernárdez & T. Ñaco del Hoyo (eds.), *Transforming Historical Landscapes In The Ancient Empires*, Oxford, 33–51.
Ñaco del Hoyo et al. (2011): T. Ñaco del Hoyo, B. Antela-Bernárdez, I. Arrayás & S. Busquets-Artigas, 'The "Ultimate Frontier": War, Terror and the Greek *Poleis* between Mithridates and Rome', in: O. Hekster & T. Kaizer (eds.), *Frontiers in the Roman World*, Leiden, 291–304.
Nicolet (1959): C. Nicolet, 'Note sur Appien, B.C. I, 100, 467: Sylla et la réforme électorale', *MÉFRA* 71, 211–225.
Nicolet (1970): C. Nicolet, 'Cicéron, Platon et le vote secret', *Historia* 39–66.
North (1989): J. North, 'Religion in republican Rome', in F. W. Walbank, A. E. Astin, M. W. Frederiksen & R. M. Ogilvie (eds.), *The Cambridge Ancient History, Second Edition, Volume VII.2. The Rise of Rome to 220 B.C.*, Cambridge, 573–624.
North (1990): J. North, 'Politics and aristocracy in the Roman Republic', *CPhil.* 85, 277–287.
North (2011): J. North, 'Lex Domitia Revisited', in: J. H. Richardson & F. Santangelo (eds.), *Priests and State in the Roman World*, Stuttgart, 39–61.
Nünning (2008) [1998]: A. Nünning (ed.), *Metzler Lexikon Literatur- und Kulturtheorie*, Stuttgart.
O'Gorman (1995): E. O'Gorman, 'On Not Writing About Augustus: Tacitus' "Annals" Book I', *MD* 35, 91–114.
O'Gorman (2000): E. O'Gorman, *Irony and Misreading in the Annals of Tacitus*, Cambridge.
O'Gorman (2006): E. O'Gorman, 'Intertextuality, Time and Historical Understanding', in: A. L. Macfie (ed.), *The Philosophy of History*, London, 102–117.
O'Gorman (2009): E. O'Gorman, 'Intertextuality and historiography,' in: A. Feldherr (ed.), *The Cambridge Companion to the Roman Historians*, Cambridge, 231–242.
Oakley (2009): S. P. Oakley, 'Style and language', in: A. J. Woodman (ed.), *The Cambridge Companion to Tacitus*, Cambridge, 195–211.
Orlandos (1938): A. Orlandos, 'Ἀνασκαφαί Σικυῶνος', *Praktika tes en Athenais Archaiologikes Hetaireias* 1938, 120–123.
Osgood (2008): J. Osgood, 'Caesar and Nicomedes', *CQ* 58, 687–691.
Osgood (2010): J. Osgood, 'Caesar and the Pirates: or how to make (and break) an ancient life', *G&R* 57, 319–336.
Pagán (2000): V. E. Pagán, 'Distant Voices of Freedom in the *Annales* of Tacitus', *Studies in Latin Literature and Roman History* 10, 358–369.
Paladini (1957): V. Paladini, *Orationes et Epistulae de Historiarum Libris Excerptae*, Bari.
Papazarkadas (2011): N. Papazarkadas, *Sacred and Public Land in Ancient Athens*, Oxford.
Parker (2008): V. Parker, 'Between Thucydides and Tacitus. The Position of Sallust in the History of Ancient Historiography', *Antike und Abendland* 54, 77–104.
Pascucci (1975): G. Pascucci, 'I commentarii di Silla', in: S. Boldrini, C. Questa, S. Lanciotti & R. Raffaelli (eds.), *Atti del convegno gli storiografi latini tramandati in framenti*, Studi urbinati di storia, filosofia e letteratura 49, Urbino, 283–296.
Pasoli (1974): E. Pasoli, *Le Historiae e le Opere Minori di Sallustio*, Bologna.

Pasoli (1976): E. Pasoli, 'De orationibus atque epistulis de historiarum Sallusti libris excerptis', in: E. Coleiro (ed.), *Acta Omnium Gentium ac Nationum Conventus Latinis Litteris Linguaeque Fovendis*, Malta, 103–114.

Paterson (1985): J. Paterson, 'Politics in the Late Republic', in: T. P. Wiseman (ed.), *Roman Political Life 90 B.C.–A.D. 69*, Exeter, 21–43.

Paul (1984): G. M. Paul, *A Historical Commentary on Sallust's Bellum Jugurthinum*, Liverpool.

Payne (1984): M. J. Payne, *Aretas eneken: Honors to Romans and Italians in Greece from 260 to 27 BC*, PhD thesis, Michigan State University.

Pelling (2013): C. Pelling, 'Intertextuality, Plausibility, and Interpretation', *Histos* 7, 1–20.

Perl (1965): G. Perl, 'Die Rede Cottas in Sallusts Historien', *Philol.* 109, 75–82.

Perl (1967): G. Perl, 'Die Rede Cottas in Sallusts Historien (Fortsetzung)', *Philol.* 111, 137–141.

Perl (1975): G. Perl, 'Das Kompositionsprinzip der *Historiae* des Sallust (zu *Hist. fr.* 2, 42)', in: *Actes de la XIIe Conférence Internationale d'Études Classiques 'Eirene'*, Cluj-Napoca, 2–7 octobre 1972, Amsterdam, 317–337.

Perl (2005): G. Perl, 'Kontroverse Stellen in den "Historiae" Sallusts', *Hermes* 133, 178–195.

Picard (1989): O. Picard, 'Thasos dans le monde romain', in: S. Walker & A. Cameron (eds.), *The Greek Renaissance in the Roman Empire. Papers from the Tenth British Museum Classical Colloquium*, BICS Supplement 55, London, 174–179.

Picard (1979): O. Picard, *Chalkis et la confédération Euboéenne. Etude de numismatique et d'histoire (IVe-Ier siècle)*, Paris.

Piepenbrink (2013): K. Piepenbrink, 'Sulla', in: P. von Möllendorf, A. Simnonis & L. Simonis (eds.), *Historische Gestalten der Antike. Rezeption in Literatur, Kunst und Musik*, DNP Supplement VIII, Stuttgart, 961–970.

Pina Polo (1989): F. Pina Polo, *Las contiones civiles y militares en Roma*, Zaragoza.

Pina Polo (2011): F. Pina Polo, *The Consul at Rome: The Civil Functions of the Consuls in the Roman Republic*, Cambridge.

Pirenne-Delforge (2010): V. Pirenne-Delforge, 'Reading Pausanias: Cults of the Gods and Representation of the Divine', in: J. N. Bremmer & A. Erskine (eds.), *The Gods of Ancient Greece. Identities and Transformations*, Edinburgh, 375–387.

Pomptow (1921): H. Pomptow, 'Delphische Neufunde V', *Klio* 17, 153–203.

Prag (2010): J. Prag, 'Troops and Commanders: *auxilia externa* under the Roman Republic', in: D. Bonano, R. Marino & D. Motta (eds.), *Truppe e comandati nel mondo antico*, Palermo, 101–113.

Prag (2011): J. Prag, 'Provincial governors and auxiliary soldiers', in: N. Barrandon & F. Kirbilher (eds.), *Les gouverneurs et les provinciaux sous la République romaine*, Rennes, 15–28.

Pretzler (2005): M. Pretzler, 'Comparing Strabo with Pausanias: Greece in context vs. Greece in depth', in: D. Dueck, H. Lindsay & S. Pothecary (eds.), *Strabo's Cultural Geography. The Making of a Kolossourgia*, Cambridge, 144–160.

Pretzler (2007): M. Pretzler, *Pausanias: Travel Writing in Ancient Greece*, London.

Pretzler (2009): M. Pretzler, 'Form over substance? Deconstructing ecphrasis in Lucian's *Zeuxis* and *Eikones*', in: A. Bartley (ed.), *A Lucian for Our Times*, Newcastle, 157–171.

Raggi (2001): A. Raggi, 'Senatus consultum de Asclepiade Clazomenio sociisque', *ZPE* 135, 73–116.

Ramage (1991): E. S. Ramage, 'Sulla's Propaganda', *Klio* 73, 93–121.

Ramsey (2015): J. T. Ramsey, *Sallust. Fragments of the Histories. Letters to Caesar*, Cambridge, MA.

Rathmann (2010): M. Rathmann, 'Athen in hellenistischer Zeit. Fremdbestimmung und kulturelle Anziehungskraft', in: R. Krummeich & C. Witschel (eds.), *Die Akropolis von Athen im Hellenismus und in der römischen Kaiserzeit*, Wiesbaden, 55–94.

Raubitschek (1951): A. E. Raubitschek, 'Sylleia', in: P. R. Coleman-Norton, with F. C. Bourne & J. V. A. Fine (eds.), *Studies in Roman Economic and Social History in Honor of Allan Chester Johnson*, Princeton, NJ, 49–57.

Rawson (1974): E. Rawson, 'Religion and politics in the late second century BC at Rome', *Phoenix* 28, 193–212.

Rawson (1985): E. Rawson, *Intellectual Life in the Late Roman Republic*, London.

Reggiani (1994): R. Reggiani, 'Silla *peior atque intestabilior* e *scaevus Romulus* (nota a Sall. Hist. I, 55, 1 e 5 M.)', *Athenaeum* 82, 207–221.

Richardson (2019): E. Richardson (ed.), *Classics in Extremis. The edges of Classical Reception*, London/New York.

Reinach (1895): T. Reinach, *Mithradates Eupator. König von Pontos*, Leipzig.

Ridley (2000): R. T. Ridley, 'The Dictator's Mistake: Caesar's Escape from Sulla', *Historia* 49, 211–229.

Ridley (2010): R. T. Ridley, 'L. Cornelius Sulla as Untrained Master of Military Science', *Riv. Fil.* 138, 96–111.

Rigsby (1996): K. Rigsby, *Asylia. Territorial Inviolability in the Hellenistic World*, Berkeley, CA.

Riggsby (2007): A. M. Riggsby, 'Memoir and Autobiography in Republican Rome', in: J. Marincola (ed.), *A Companion to Greek and Roman Historiography*, Oxford, 266–274.

Rilinger (1976): R. Rilinger, *Der Einfluß des Wahlleiters bei den römischen Konsulwahlen von 366 bis 50 v. Chr.*, Munich.

Rizakis (2008): A. D. Rizakis, *Achaïe III. Les cités achéennes: épigraphie et histoire*, Athens.

Rizakis (2015): A. D. Rizakis, 'Expropriations et confiscations des terres dans le cadre de la colonisation romaine en Achaïe et en Macédoine', *MÉFRA* 127, 1–23.

Rögler (1962): G. Rögler, 'Die lex Villia annalis', *Klio* 40, 76–123.

Rohe (1994): K. Rohe, *Politik. Begriffe und Wirklichkeiten*, Stuttgart.

Rosenblitt (2011): J. A. Rosenblitt, 'The "*devotio*" of Sallust's Cotta', *AJPhil.* 132, 397–427.

Rosenblitt (2013): J. A. Rosenblitt, 'Sallust's *Historiae* and the voice of Sallust's Lepidus', *Arethusa* 46, 447–470.

Rosenblitt (2014): A. Rosenblitt, 'The Turning Tide: The Politics of the Year 79 B.C.E.', *TAPA* 144, 415–444.

Rosenblitt (2016): J. A. Rosenblitt, 'Hostile Politics: Sallust and the rhetoric of popular champions in the Late Republic', *AJPhil.* 137, 655–688.

Rosenblitt (2019): J. A. Rosenblitt, *Rome after Sulla*, London.

Rosillo-López (2010): C. Rosillo-López, *La corruption à la fin de la République romaine (IIe-Ier s. av. J.-C.): aspects politiques et financiers*, Stuttgart.

Roth (1999): J. Roth, *The logistics of the Roman army at war (264 B.C.–A.D. 235)*, Leiden.

Rotondi (1963): G. Rotondi, *Leges Publicae Populi Romani*, Hildesheim.

Rotroff (1997): S. I. Rotroff, 'From Greek to Roman in Athenian Ceramics', in: M. C. Hoff & S. I. Rotroff (eds.), *The Romanization of Athens*, Oxford, 97–116.

Rousset (forthcoming): D. Rousset, 'La confédération phocidienne aux époques hellénistique et impériale', in the proceedings of the international conference 'Ancient Phokis. New Approaches to its history, archaeology and topography' (30th March–1st April 2017).

Rowe (2002): G. Rowe, *Princes and Political Cultures: The New Tiberian Senatorial Decrees*, Ann Arbor, MI.

Ruggeri (2006): C. Ruggeri, 'Silla e la conquista di Atene nell' 86 a.C.', in: P. Amann, M. Pedrazzi & H. Taeuber (eds.), *Italo–Tusco–Romana: Festschrift für Luciana Aigner-Foresti zum 70. Geburtstag am 30. Juli 2006*, Vienna, 315–324.

Rüpke (2008): J. Rüpke, *Fasti Sacerdotum. A Prosopography of Pagan, Jewish, and Christian Religious Officials in the City of Rome, 300 BC to AD 499*, Oxford.

Rüpke (2012): J. Rüpke, *Religion in Republican Rome: rationalization and ritual change*. Philadelphia, PA.
Russell (1979): D. A. Russell, 'De Imitatione', in: D. West & A. J. Woodman (eds.), *Creative Imitation and Latin Literature*, Cambridge, 1–16.
Russo (2002): F. Russo, 'I commentarii Sullani come fonte della vita Plutarchea di Silla', *Studi Classici e Orientali* 48, 281–305.
Sailor (2008): D. Sailor, *Writing and Empire in Tacitus*, Cambridge.
Salerno (1999): F. Salerno, *'Tacita libertas': l'introduzione del voto segreto nella Roma repubblicana*, Naples.
Salmon (1970): E. T. Salmon, *Roman Colonization under the Republic*, Ithaca, NY.
Sandberg (2004): K. Sandberg, 'Consular legislation in pre-Sullan Rome', *Arctos* 38, 133–162.
Sandberg (2018): K. Sandberg, 'Sulla's Reform of the Legislative Process', in M. T. Schettino & G. Zecchini (eds.), *L'età di Silla. Atti del convegno. Istituto italiano per la storia antica, Roma 23–24 marzo 2017*, Rome, 167–190.
Santangelo (2006): F. Santangelo, 'Sulla and the Senate: a reconsideration', *Cahiers du Centre Gustave Glotz* 17, 7–22.
Santangelo (2007): F. Santangelo, *Sulla, the Elites and the Empire. A Study of Roman Policies in Italy and the Greek East*, Leiden.
Santangelo (2012): F. Santangelo, '*Sullanus* and *Sullani*', *Arctos* 46, 187–191.
Santangelo (2014): F. Santangelo, 'Roman Politics in the 70s B.C.: a Story of Realignments?', *JRS* 104, 1–27.
Santangelo (2016a): F. Santangelo, 'Performing Passions, Negotiating Survival: Italian Cities in the Late Republican Civil Wars', in: H. Börm, M. Mattheis & J. Wienand (eds.), *Civil War in Ancient Greece and Rome. Contexts of Disintegration and Reintegration*, Stuttgart, 127–148.
Santangelo (2016b): F. Santangelo, *Marius*, London.
Santangelo (2018): F. Santangelo, 'La marcia su Roma dell' 88 a.C.', in: M. T. Schettino & G. Zecchini (eds.), *L'età di Silla. Atti del convegno. Istituto italiano per la storia antica, Roma, 23–24 marzo 2017*, Rome, 191–204.
Sapere (2011): A. Sapere, 'La figura del cónsul Cota en el Libro II de las Historiae de Salustio', in: M. E. Steinberg (ed.), *Miscellanea Philologica: Lecturas de textos latinos clásicos en florilegios, ediciones, comentarios y traducciones de los siglos XII a XXI*, Buenos Aires, 193–207.
Scardigli (1971): B. Scardigli, 'Sertorio: problemi cronologici', *Athenaeum* 49, 229–270.
Scardigli (1979): B. Scardigli, *Die Römerbiographien Plutarchs. Ein Forschungsbericht*, Munich.
Schachter (1994): A. Schachter, *Cults of Boiotia 3. Potnia to Zeus*, BICS Supplement 3, London.
Schettino/Zecchini (2018): M. T. Schettino & G. Zecchini (eds.), *L'età di Silla. Atti del convegno. Istituto italiano per la storia antica Roma, 23–24 marzo 2017*, Rome.
Schietinger (2013): G.-P. Schietinger, 'Ein politischer Ziehsohn der Metelli? Biographische Anmerkungen zu Sulla', *Gymnasium* 120, 207–227.
Schmid (2000): S. G. Schmid, 'Sullan debris from Eretria (Greece?)', *Rei Cretariae Romanae Fautores* 36, 169–180.
Schneider (1977): H.-C. Schneider, *Das Problem der Veteranenversorgung in der späteren römischen Republik*, Bonn.
Scholz (2003): P. Scholz, 'Sulla's Commentarii – Eine literarische Rechtfertigung', in: U. Eigler, U. Gotter, N. Luraghi & U. Walter (eds.), *Formen römischer Geschichtsschreibung von den Anfängen bis Livius*, Darmstadt, 172–195.
Scholz (2011): P. Scholz, *Den Vätern folgen. Sozialisation und Erziehung der Republikanischen Senatsaristokratie*, Berlin.

Scholz/Walter (2013): P. Scholz & U. Walter (with C. Winkle), *Fragmente Römischer Memoiren*, Heidelberg.
Seager (1994): R. Seager, 'Sulla', in: J. A. Crook, A. Lintott & E. Rawson (eds.), *The Cambridge Ancient History, Second Edition, Volume IX: The Last Age of the Roman Republic, 146–43 B.C.*, Cambridge, 165–207.
Seager (2002) [1979]: R. Seager, *Pompey the Great: a political biography* (2nd ed.), Oxford.
Seemann (2019): L. Seemann, 'Die Tyrannenmörder auf dem Kapitol', *Historia* 88, 95–114.
Shackleton-Bailey (1999): D. R. Shackleton-Bailey, *Cicero: Letters to Atticus I*, Cambridge, MA.
Shannon (2011): K. Shannon, 'Livy's Cossus and Augustus, Tacitus' Germanicus and Tiberius: A Historiographical Allusion', *Histos* 5, 266–282.
Sherwin-White (1973) [1939]: A. N. Sherwin White, *The Roman Citizenship* (2nd ed.), Oxford.
Sherwin-White (1976): A. N. Sherwin White, 'Rome, Pamphylia and Cilicia, 133–70 B.C.', *JRS* 66, 1–14.
Sherwin-White (1984): A. N. Sherwin White, *Roman Foreign Policy in the East 168 B.C. to A.D. 1*, London.
Shotter (1967): D. C. A. Shotter, 'The Starting-Dates of Tacitus' Historical Works', *CQ* 17, 158–163.
Shotter (1991): D. C. A. Shotter, 'Tacitus' View of Emperors and the Principate', *ANRW* II.33.5, 3263–3331.
Siewert (2002): P. Siewert, 'Sulla und die 175. Olympiade (80 v. Chr.) bei Appian und in Olympia', *Aevum* 76, 77–79.
Smith (2009): C. J. Smith, 'Sulla's Memoirs', in: C. J. Smith & A. Powell (eds.), *The Lost Memoirs of Augustus and the Development of Roman Autobiography*, Swansea, 65–85.
Smith (2014): S. D. Smith, *Man and Animal in Severan Rome: The Literary Imagination of Claudius Aelianus*, Cambridge.
Sonnabend (2002): H. Sonnabend, *Geschichte der antiken Biographie. Von Sokrates bis zur Historia Augusta*, Stuttgart.
Spielberg (2017): L. Spielberg, 'Language, *Stasis* and the Role of the Historian in Thucydides, Sallust and Tacitus', *AJPhil.* 138, 331–373.
Steed (2008): K. L. S. Steed, *Memory and Leadership in the Late Roman Republic*, PhD thesis, University of Michigan.
Steel (2003): C. Steel, 'Cicero's *Brutus*: the end of oratory and the beginning of history?', *BICS* 46, 195–211.
Steel (2013): C. Steel, *The End of the Roman Republic 146 to 44 BC. Conquest and Crisis*, Edinburgh.
Steel (2014a): C. Steel, 'The Roman Senate and the Post-Sullan Res Publica', *Historia* 63, 323–339.
Steel (2014b): C. Steel, 'Rethinking Sulla. The Case of the Roman Senate', *CQ* 64, 657–668.
Steel (2016): C. Steel, 'Early-career prosecutors: forensic activity and senatorial careers in the late Republic', in P. du Plessis (ed.), *Cicero's Law: Rethinking Roman Law of the Late Republic*, Edinburgh, 205–227.
Steel (2018): C. Steel, 'Past and present in Sulla's dictatorship', in M. T. Schettino & G. Zecchini (eds.), *L'età di Silla. Atti del convegno. Istituto italiano per la storia antica, Roma 23–24 marzo 2017*, Rome, 225–238.
Stein-Hölkeskamp (2015): E. Stein-Hölkeskamp, 'Marius, Sulla, and the War over Monumental Memory and Public Space', in: K. Galinksy (ed.), *Memory in Ancient Rome and Early Christianity*, Oxford, 214–234.
Stephenson et al. (1985): F. R. Stephenson, K. K. Yau & H. Hunger, 'Records of Halley's Comet on Babylonian tablets', *Nature* 314, 587–592.
Stepper (2003): R. Stepper, *Augustus et sacerdos. Untersuchungen zum römischen Kaiser als Priester*, Wiesbaden.

Stinger (1993): P. Stinger, *The Use of Historical Example as a Rhetorical Device in Cicero's Orations*, Ann Arbor, MI.
Strasburger (1938): H. Strasburger, *Caesars Eintritt in die Geschichte*, Munich.
Strasser (2001): J.-Y. Strasser, 'Quelques termes rares du vocabulaire agonistique', *Rev. Phil.* 75, 273–305.
Sträterhoff (1997): B. Sträterhoff, 'Kolometrie und Prosarhythmus bei Sallust am Beispiel der Rede des Caius Aurelius Cotta', in: B. Czapla, T. Lehmann & S. Liell (eds.), *Vir bonus dicendi peritus: Festschrift für Alfons Weische zum 65. Geburtstag*, Wiesbaden, 399–406.
Strauch (1996): D. Strauch, *Römische Politik und griechische Tradition. Die Umgestaltung Nordwest-Griechenlands unter römischer Herrschaft*, Munich.
Straumann (2016): B. Straumann, *Crisis and Constitutionalism: Roman Political Thought from the Fall of the Republic to the Age of Revolution*, New York, NY.
Sumi (2002): G. S. Sumi, 'Spectacles and Sulla's Public Image', *Historia* 51, 414–432.
Sumner (1971): G. V. Sumner, 'The lex annalis under Caesar', *Phoenix* 25, 246–271.
Sumner (1973): G. V. Sumner, *The Orators in Cicero's Brutus: Prosopography and Chronology*, Toronto.
Syme (1939): R. Syme, *The Roman Revolution*, Oxford.
Syme (1958): R. Syme, *Tacitus*, Oxford.
Syme (1964): R. Syme, *Sallust*, Berkeley, CA.
Syme (2016): R. Syme, *Approaching the Roman Revolution. Papers on Republican History*, ed. F. Santangelo, Oxford.
Tatum (2011): J. Tatum, 'The Late Republic. Autobiography and Memoirs in the Age of the Civil Wars', in: G. Marasco (ed.), *Political Autobiographies and Memoirs in Antiquity. A Brill Companion*, Leiden, 161–187.
Taylor (1941): L. R. Taylor, 'Caesar's Early Career', *CPhil.* 36, 113–132.
Taylor (1942a): L. R. Taylor, 'Caesar's colleagues in the pontifical college', *AJPhil.* 63, 385–412.
Taylor (1942b): L. R. Taylor, 'Caesar and the Roman Nobility', *TAPA* 73, 1–24.
Taylor (1957): L. R. Taylor, 'The Rise of Julius Caesar' *G&R* 4, 10–18.
Taylor (1960): L. R. Taylor, *The Voting Districts of the Roman Republic. The Thirty-five Urban and Rural Tribes*, Rome.
Taylor (1966): L. R. Taylor, *Roman Voting Assemblies from the Hannibalic War to the Dictatorship of Caesar*, Ann Arbor, MI.
Terrenato (1998): N. Terrenato, '*Tam Firmum Municipium*: The Romanization of Volaterrae and its Cultural Implications', *JRS* 88, 94–114.
Thein (2002): A. Thein, *Sulla's Public Image and the Politics of Civic Renewal*, PhD thesis, University of Pennsylvania.
Thein (2006): A. Thein, 'Sulla the weak tyrant', in S. Lewis (ed.), *Ancient Tyranny*, Edinburgh, 238–249.
Thein (2009): A. Thein, '*Felicitas* and the Memoirs of Sulla and Augustus', in: C. J. Smith & A. Powell (eds.), *The Lost Memoirs of Augustus and the Development of Roman Autobiography*, Swansea, 87–110.
Thein (2010): A. Thein, 'Sulla's Veteran Settlement Policy', in: F. Daubner (ed.), *Militärsiedlungen und Territorialherrschaft in der Antike*, Berlin, 79–99.
Thein (2013): A. Thein, 'Rewards to Slaves in the Proscriptions of 82 B.C.', *Tyche* 28, 163–175.
Thein (2014): A. Thein, 'Reflecting on Sulla's Clemency', *Historia* 63, 166–186.
Thein (2015): A. Thein, 'Sulla and the Tarpeian Rock in 88 and 82 BC', *Anc. Soc.* 45, 171–186.
Thein (2016): A. Thein, 'Booty in the Sullan Civil War of 83–82 B.C.', *Historia* 64, 450–472.
Thein (2017): A. Thein, '*Percussores*: a study in Sullan violence', *Tyche* 32, 235–250.

Thein (2018): A. Thein, 'Proscriptions', in: R. S. Bagnall, K. Brodersen, C. B. Champion, A. Erskine & S. R. Huebner (eds.), *The Encyclopedia of Ancient History*, Malden, 1–2.
Themelis (1998): P. Themelis, 'Ἀνασκαφή Μεσσήνης', *Praktika tis en Athenais Arkhaiologikis Etaireias*, 89–126.
Thompson (1961): M. Thompson, *The New Style Silver Coinage of Athens*, New York, NY.
Thonemann (2015): P. Thonemann, *The Hellenistic World. Using Coins as Sources*, Cambridge.
Tosi (2010) [1991]: R. Tosi, *Dictionnaire des sentences latines et grecques*. Grenoble.
Troiani (1981): L. Troiani, 'Sulla "lex de suffragiis" in Cicerone, "de legibus" III, 10', *Athenaeum* 59, 180–184.
Tsangari (2007): D. Tsangari, *Corpus des monnaies d'or, d'argent et de bronze de la confédération étolienne*, Athens.
Twyman (1972): B. Twyman, 'The Metelli, Pompeius and Prosopography', *ANRW* 1.1, 816–874.
Ullmann (1927): R. Ullmann, *La Technique des Discours dans Salluste, Tite Live et Tacite*, Oslo.
Urso (2016): G. Urso, 'Cassius Dio's Sulla: *Exemplum* of Cruelty and Republican Dictator', in: J. M. Madsen & C. H. Lange (eds.), *Cassius Dio. Greek Intellectual and Roman Politician*, Leiden, 13–32.
Vaahtera (1990): J. Vaahtera, 'Pebbles, Points, or Ballots: The Emergence of the Individual Vote in Rome', *Arctos* 24, 161–177.
Valgiglio (1975): E. Valgiglio, 'L'autobiografia di Silla nelle biografie di Plutarco', in: S. Boldini, S. Lanciotti, C. Questa & R. Raffaelli (eds.), *Atti del convegno gli storiografi latini tramandati in framenti*, Studi urbinati di storia, filosofia e letteratura 49, Urbino, 245–281.
van den Berg (2012): C. S. van den Berg, 'Deliberative Oratory in the *Annals* and the *Dialogus*', in: V. E. Pagán (ed.) *A Companion to Tacitus*, Chichester, 189–211.
Verdejo-Manchado/Antela-Bernárdez (2015): J. Verdejo-Manchado & B. Antela-Bernárdez, 'Pro-Mithridatic and Pro-Roman Tendencies in Delos in the Early First Century BC: the case of Dikaios of Ionidai (ID 2039 and 2040)', *DHA* 41, 117–126.
Verdière (1957): R. Verdière, 'Notes de lecture', *Latomus* 16, 480–481.
Versnel (1976): H. S. Versnel, 'Two Types of Roman *Devotio*', *Mnemos*. 29, 365–410.
Versnel (1981): H. S. Versnel, 'Self-Sacrifice, Compensation and the Anonymous Gods', in: J. Rudhardt & O. Reverdin (eds.), *Le Sacrifice dans L'Antiquité*, Geneva, 135–185.
Vervaet (2004): F. Vervaet, 'The Lex Valeria and Sulla's Empowerment as Dictator', *Cahiers du Centre Gustave Glotz* 15, 37–84.
Vervaet (2018): F. Vervaet, 'The Date, Modalities and Legacy of Sulla's Abdication of his Dictatorship: A Study in Sullan Statecraft', *Historia Antigua* 36: 31–82.
Vowe (2007): G. Vowe, 'Politics, Policy, Polity', in: L. L. Kaid & C. Holtz-Bacha (eds.), *Encyclopedia of Political Communiction* (2 vols.), Thousand Oaks, CA.
Walde (2010): C. Walde, 'Vorbemerkungen', in: C. Walde (ed.) with B. Egger, *Die Rezeption der antiken Literatur*, DNP Supplement VII, Stuttgart, i–xiii.
Walter (2018): U. Walter, 'Die Dictatur Sullas – Ein Wendepunkt für die römische Historiographie', in: M. T. Schettino & G. Zecchini (eds.), *L'età di Silla. Atti del convegno. Istituto italiano per la storia antica, Roma 23–24 marzo 2017*, Rome, 239–251.
Ward (1977): A. M. Ward, *Marcus Crassus and the Late Roman Republic*, Columbia.
Watson (1969): G. R. Watson, *The Roman Soldier*, London.
Watt (1998): W. S. Watt, 'Tacitea', *Eikasmos* 9, 263–266.
Weigel (1992): R. D. Weigel, *Lepidus: the tarnished triumvir*, London.
Wells (1974): C. M. Wells, 'Emona and Cornuntum: Evidence for the start of Roman Occupation', in: E. Birley, B. Dobson & M. Jarrett (eds.), *Roman Frontier Studies 1969: Eighth International Congress of Limesforschung*, Cardiff, 185–190.
Westermeier (2016): J. Westermeier, *Hans Robert Jauß. Jugend, Krieg und Internierung*, Konstanz.

Wilkes (1963): J. J. Wilkes, 'A Note on the Mutiny of the Pannonian legions in A.D. 14', *CQ* 67, 268–271.
Williams (1997): M. F. Williams, 'Four Mutinies: Tacitus *Annals* 1.16–30; 1. 31–49 and Ammianus Marcellinus *Res Gestae* 20.4.9–20.5.7; 24.3.1–8.', *Phoenix* 51, 44–74.
Williamson/van Nijf (2016): C. Williamson and O. van Nijf, 'Connecting the Greeks: Festival Networks in the Hellenistic World', in: C. Mann, S. Remijssen, & S. Scharff (eds.), *Athletics in the Hellenistic World*, Stuttgart, 43–71
Winterling (2008): A. Winterling, '"Krise ohne Alternative" im Alten Rom', in: M. Bernett, W. Nippel & A. Winterling (eds.), *Christian Meier zur Diskussion*, Stuttgart, 219–240.
Wiseman (2009): T. P. Wiseman, 'Augustus, Sulla and the Supernatural', in: C. J. Smith & A. Powell (eds.), *The Lost Memoirs of Augustus and the Development of Roman Autobiography*, Swansea, 111–123.
Woodman (1977): A. J. Woodman (ed.), *Velleius Paterculus: The Tiberian Narrative (2.94–130)*, Cambridge.
Woodman (1979): A. J. Woodman, 'Self-imitation and the substance of history', in: D. West & A. J. Woodman (eds.), *Creative Imitation and Latin Literature*, Cambridge, 143–155.
Woodman (1988): A. J. Woodman, *Rhetoric in Classical Historiography*, London.
Woodman (1992a): A. J. Woodman, 'The Preface to Tacitus' Annals: more Sallust?', *CQ* 42, 567–568.
Woodman (1992b): A. J. Woodman, 'Nero's Alien Capital: Tacitus as paradoxographer (*Annals* 15.36–7)', in: A. J. Woodman & J. Powell (eds.), *Author and Audience in Latin Literature*, Cambridge, 173–188.
Woodman (1998): A. J. Woodman, *Tacitus Reviewed*, Oxford.
Woodman (2006): A. J. Woodman, 'Mutiny and Madness: Tacitus *Annals* 1.16–49', *Arethusa* 39, 303–329.
Woolf (1994): G. Woolf, 'Becoming Roman, Staying Greek: Culture, Identity, and the Civilizing Process in the Roman east', *PCPS* 40, 116–143.
Woolf (2006): G. Woolf, 'Playing games with Greeks: one Roman on Greekness', in S. Saïd & D. Konstan (eds.), *Greeks on Greekness: Viewing the Greek Past under the Roman Empire*, Cambridge, 162–178.
Worthington (1992): I. Worthington, 'Coinage and Sulla's Retirement', *Rh. Mus.* 135, 188–191.
Wray (2001): D. Wray, *Catullus and the Poetics of Roman Manhood*, Cambridge.
Wulff Alonso (2002): F. Wulff Alonso, *Roma e Italia de la Guerra Social a la retirada de Sila (90–79 a.C.)*, Brussels.
Wyetzner (2002): P. Wyetzner, 'Sulla's Law on Prices and the Roman Definition of Luxury', in: J.-J. Aubert & B. Sirks (eds.), *Speculum Iuris: Roman Law as a Reflection of Social and Eonomic Life in Antiquity*, Ann Arbor, MI, 15–33.
Yakobson (1995): A. Yakobson, 'Secret Ballot and its Effects in the Late Roman Republic', *Hermes* 123, 426–442.
Yakobson (1999): A. Yakobson, *Elections and Electioneering in Rome. A Study in the Political System of the Late Republic*, Stuttgart.
Yeoman et al. (1986): D. K. Yeoman, J. Rahe & R. S. Freitag, 'The History of the Comet Halley', *Journal of the Royal Astronomical Society of Canada* 80, 62–86.
Zachos (2013): G. Zachos, Ελάτεια. Ελληνιστική ρωμαϊκή περίοδος, Volos.
Zack (2013): A. Zack, 'Forschungen über die rechtlichen Grundlagen der römischen Außenbeziehungen während der Republik bis zum Beginn des Prinzipats. III. Teil: Der personenrechtliche Status der *amici, socii* und *amici et socii* und die *formula amicorum* und *formula sociorum*', *Göttinger Forum für Altertumswissenschaft* 16, 63–113.
Zecchini (1993): G. Zecchini, 'Momenti della fortuna tardoantica di Silla', in: G. Zecchini (ed.), *Ricerche di storiografia latina tardoantica*, Rome, 93–102.
Zecchini (2002): G. Zecchini, 'Sylla selon Salluste', *Cahiers du Centre Gustave Glotz* 13, 45–55.

Zecchini (2018): G. Zecchini, 'Per una nuova immagine di Silla', in: M. T. Schettino & G. Zecchini (eds.), *L'età di Silla. Atti del convegno. Istituto italiano per la storia antica, Roma, 23–24 marzo 2017*, Rome, 255–260.

Zoumbaki (2010): S. Zoumbaki, 'Elean relations with Rome and the Achaean Koinon and the role of Olympia', in: A. D. Rizakis & C. E. Lepenioti (eds.), *Roman Peloponnese III. Society, Economy and Culture under the Roman Empire: Between Continuity and Innovation*, Athens, 111–127.

Zoumbaki (2014): S. Zoumbaki, 'Römer und die griechischen Agone: Einstellung und Teilnahme', in: K. Harter-Uibopuu & T. Kruse (eds.), *Sport und Recht in der Antike*, Vienna, 195–216.

Zoumbaki (2015): S. Zoumbaki, 'The social and economic integration of Romans and Italiot Greeks in the Greek cities. Networks of mobility of "entrepreneurs", merchants and other professionals: the cases of Athens and the Ionian Islands', http://kyrtouplegmata.eie.gr/index.php/en/2015-03-08-11-36-11/1-4/ee2-2

Zoumbaki (2018): S. Zoumbaki, 'Sulla, the Army, the Officers and the Poleis of Greece: A Reassessment of Warlordism in the First Phase of the Mithridatic Wars', in: T. Ñaco del Hoyo & F. López Sánchez (eds.), *Wars, Warlords, and Interstate Relations in the Ancient Mediterranean*, Leiden, 351–379.

Zoumbaki (forthcoming): S. Zoumbaki, 'Communities of Romans and Italians abroad: Reflections on their elusive nature and organization', in: S. Skaltsa & C. Thomsen (eds.), *Corporate Groups and Communities: Convening in Private, Acting in Public*, Copenhagen.

Zychowicz (2013): A. Zychowicz, 'Lucius Cornelius Sulla and Athens (87–86 BC)', in: D. Słapek & I. Łuć (eds.), *Lucius Cornelius Sulla. History and Tradition*, Lublin, 79–90.

Index of Ancient Authors

Aelian 15, 143, 144, 145, 146, 148, 151, 153, 156, 157
Aëtius 146
Al-Farabi 150
Appian 2, 3, 4, 5, 6, 7, 8, 9, 10, 11, 22, 23, 24, 25, 26, 27, 28, 29, 33, 35, 36, 37, 40, 42, 47, 49, 50, 51, 56, 58, 60, 61, 64, 65, 66, 68, 69, 71, 72, 73, 74, 79, 81, 84, 85, 86, 92, 94, 96, 97, 101, 147, 151, 154, 163, 168, 169
Aristotle 147–151, 157
Arsenius 146
Asconius 36, 61, 75, 78, 79, 81, 89, 167, 169, 170
Athenaeus 147, 150, 151
Augustine 6, 7

Caesar 8
Cassius Dio 5, 6, 8, 12, 58, 65, 68, 69, 103, 156, 165, 168, 169, 170, 171
Charisius 116
Chrysocephalus 146
Cicero 3, 7, 8, 9, 12, 15, 19, 22, 23, 24, 26, 27, 29, 31, 36, 41, 49, 56, 57, 58, 59, 60, 61, 62, 65, 66, 67, 160, 161, 68, 72, 73, 74, 75, 78, 79, 80, 82, 85, 87, 88, 89, 90, 91, 92, 94, 95, 97, 98, 100, 102, 103, 127, 147, 150, 152, 155, 160, 161, 162, 163, 164, 165, 166, 167, 168, 169, 170, 171, 172

Dio Chrysostom 156
Diodorus Siculus 4, 15, 35, 36, 155
Dionysius of Halicarnassus 8, 12, 166

Florus 6, 7, 30, 96, 165, 169

Gellius 24, 74, 169
Granius Licinianus 26, 92, 96, 98, 169

Herodes Atticus 144
Herodotus 154
Hyginus 93, 98, 99, 100, 101

Juvenal 79

Livy 4, 5, 7, 8, 12, 40, 42, 43, 51, 58, 79, 91, 94, 95, 96, 98, 137, 138, 165, 166, 169, 170
Lucian of Samosata 5, 47, 146, 147, 148, 152, 153

Memnon of Heracleia 5

Nepos 152

Orosius 6, 7, 56, 73, 82, 166

Pausanias 4, 5, 11, 12, 15, 33, 36, 39, 40, 41, 47, 144, 145, 153, 154, 155, 156, 157
Philostratus 144
Plato 62, 145
Pliny (the Elder) 5, 7, 11, 47, 49, 82, 152, 170, 171
Plutarch 2, 3, 4, 5, 6, 7, 10, 14, 15, 19, 20, 21, 23, 25, 26, 29, 33, 35, 36, 37, 39, 42, 46, 48, 51, 56, 57, 58, 62, 63, 65, 66, 71, 72, 73, 74, 75, 77, 78, 79, 80, 81, 83, 84, 85, 92, 100, 107, 112, 123, 127, 143, 147, 149, 150, 151, 152, 153, 154, 155, 156, 165, 166, 168, 169, 170
Polybius 34, 40, 48, 51
Pompeius Trogus 126
Posidonius 143, 147, 150, 151

Quintilian 2, 68, 170

Sallust 7, 8, 12, 14, 15, 19, 21, 58, 61, 89, 96, 98, 100, 101, 107, 108, 110, 111, 112, 113, 114, 115, 117, 118, 119, 120, 121, 122, 124, 125, 126, 127, 128, 129, 130, 131, 132, 133, 134, 135, 136, 137, 138, 139, 141, 142, 152, 155, 165, 169, 170, 171
Seneca (the Younger) 2, 6, 11, 29, 160, 165, 171
Serenus 11
Siculus Flaccus 98, 100
Sisenna 109, 112
Strabo 6, 9, 15, 33, 35, 40, 47, 98, 148, 149, 150, 151, 153, 154, 155, 165, 166

Suetonius 58, 68, 69, 73, 75, 76, 98, 168, 170

Tacitus 8, 15, 75, 102, 125, 126, 127, 128, 131, 132, 133, 134, 135, 136, 137, 138, 141
Theophylact of Ohrid 145
Thucydides 116, 127, 130, 147

Valerius Maximus 4, 6, 7, 11, 12, 25, 63, 75, 84, 91, 98, 152, 165, 166, 169, 170
Velleius 4, 5, 7, 8, 12, 58, 65, 68, 76, 102, 107, 167, 169
Vitruvius 154

Index of Ancient Persons and Deities

Achaeans 38
Adherbal 110, 113, 114
Aemilius Lepidus, M. (cos. 78) 2, 63, 72, 75, 76, 77, 81, 82, 83, 86, 87, 96, 97, 98, 135, 169
– Sallust's Speech of Lepidus 14, 15, 89, 92, 96, 100, 101, 102, 103, 125, 129, 131, 132, 133, 139, 141, 142
Aemilius Lepidus, Q. (cos. 21) 69
Aemilius Paullus, L. (cos. 182, 168) 33, 42, 43, 149, 155
Aemilius Scaurus, M. (cos. 115) 59, 81, 82, 83, 85, 110
Aemilius Scaurus, M. (Sulla's stepson) 72, 78, 83, 85, 87, 88
Aesillas 37
Aetolians 37
Afella. *See* Ofella
Agrippa Postumus 138
Amatokos 35
Anaxidamos 35, 51
Ancharius, Q. 38
Andronicus of Rhodes 149
Antiochus III (king of Syria) 121
Antonius Hybrida, C. (cos. 63) 75, 76, 79, 169
Antonius, M. (cos. 99) 79, 80
Antony (Mark) (triumvir) 58, 68, 160, 171
Apellicon 15, 147, 148, 149, 150, 151, 153, 157
Aphrodite 41, 44
Apollo 39, 78, 126
Appuleia (wife of Lepidus, cos. 78) 82
Archelaus 25, 39, 143
Ariobarzanes II (king of Cappodocia) 154
Aristion 143, 147, 154, 155, 156
Arminius (Germanic leader) 128
Aspar 120
Athena 78, 145, 154
Athenion 143, 147
Atius Labienus, T. (tr. pl. 63) 58
Atticus (T. Pomponius Atticus) 24, 49, 61, 62, 147, 149, 152
Augis 34
Augustus (emperor) 2, 14, 15, 49, 68, 69, 93, 101, 102, 103, 127, 128, 138, 142, 150, 160, 171
Aurelius Cotta, C. (cos. 75) 22, 75, 76, 140
– Sallust's Speech of Cotta 15, 126, 134, 135, 141, 142
Aurelius, Q. 100

Bellienus, L. 170
Blaesus 134
Bocchus (king of Mauretania) 19, 21, 110, 113, 115, 116, 117, 118, 119, 120, 121, 122, 123
Braetius Sura, Q. 38

Caecilia Metella (Sulla's wife) 51, 78, 81, 87
Caesar (L. Iulius Caesar (cos. 90)) 20
Caesar (C. Iulius Caesar (dictator))
– early career 72, 73, 75, 76, 77, 83, 84, 86, 98
– later career (in the 60s) 58, 68, 100, 135, 170
– civil war and dictatorship 2, 3, 15, 31, 68, 69, 93, 102, 103, 159, 160, 162, 165, 168, 171
Caligula (emperor) 69
Calpurnius Bestia, L. (cos. 111) 114
Calpurnius Bibulus, L. 147
Calpurnius Piso, C. (cos. 67) 63
Carbo (Cn. Papirius Carbo (cos. 85, 84, 82)) 7, 27, 63
Castor 65
Catiline 2, 15, 98, 125, 129, 167, 170, 171
Cato the Elder 21
Cato the Younger 84, 130, 131, 164, 165, 170
Catulus the Elder (cos. 102) 19
Catulus the Younger (cos. 78) 63, 73
Chrysogonus 161, 162
Cicero 3, 12, 15, 24, 29, 31, 60, 61, 62, 78–79, 90, 91, 92, 103, 149–150, 155, 161–168, 170, 172
Cinna (L. Cornelius Cinna (cos. 87–84)) 3, 5, 12, 24, 27, 56, 61, 67, 73, 76, 82, 166
Claudius Pulcher, Ap. (cos. 79) 75
Cleopatra VII (queen of Egypt) 150
Cloatii (brothers) 49
Clodius (tr. pl. 58) 22, 31
Clutorius Priscus 135
Cornelia (Cinna's daughter) 73, 76
Cornelius, C. (tr. pl. 67) 78
Cornelius, Cn. 81, 82

Cornelius Lentulus, Cn. (cos. 97) 82
Cornelius Lentulus, L. 80
Cornelius Lentulus Sura, P. (cos. 71) 73, 84, 87, 169
Cornelius Sulla, P. (pr. 186) 109
Cornelius Sulla, P. (elected cos. 65) 169
Coruncanius, Ti. (cos. 280) 58
Crassus (M. Licinius Crassus (cos. 70, 55)) 100, 168

Dabar 120, 122
Damasippus, L. (pr. 82) 27
Dionysus 153, 154
Dolabella (Cn. Cornelius Dolabella (cos. 81)) 14, 64, 71, 72, 74, 75, 76 , 77, 78, 84, 86, 169
Dolabella (Cn. Cornelius Dolabella (pr. 81)) 14, 65, 72, 78, 79, 80, 81, 82, 83, 84, 85, 86, 87, 88, 169
Domitius Ahenobarbus, Cn. (tr. pl. 104, cos. 96) 58, 59
Drusus Caesar 138

Fabius Maximus, Q. 33
Faustus (Sulla's son) 124, 150, 170
Flamininus (cos. 198) 51
Flavius Fimbria, C. 26
Fufidius, L. 30
Fulvius Nobilior, M. (cos. 189) 33

Gabinius, A. (cos. 58) 85
Gellius, L. (pr. 94) 80
Germanicus 102, 138
Glabrio (M'. Acilius Glabrio (cos. 191)) 155
Gracchus, Gaius (tr. pl. 123–122) 116
Gracchus, Tiberius (tr. pl. 133) 94
Granius of Puteoli 73, 84
Gratidianus. *See* M. Marius Gratidianus

Hannibal 1, 132, 166
Herennius, C. (tr. pl. 80) 65
Hermodoros 41
Homoloichos 35, 51
Hortensius, Q. (cos. 69) 75

Iunius Brutus, M. (tr. pl. 83) 93, 94

Jugurtha 1, 14, 19, 21, 107, 110, 113, 114, 115, 116, 117, 118, 119, 120, 121, 122, 123

Labienus (T. Atius Labienus (tr. pl. 63)) 58
Laelius, C. (cos. 140) 59
Lentulus Sura. *See* P. Cornelius Lentulus Sura 169
Lepidus. *See* Aemilius Lepidus, M. (cos. 78)
Licinius Crassus, C. (tr. pl. 145) 59
Licinius Murena, L. 51, 79, 85, 87
Livius Drusus, M. (tr. pl. 91) 94
Lucullus (L. Licinius Lucullus (cos. 74)) 36, 37, 38, 38, 51, 66, 149
Luscius, L. 170
Lysander 14, 29, 71, 77, 78, 79

Macer (C. Licinius Macer (tr. pl. 73, pr. 68))
– Sallust's Speech of Macer 15, 129, 130, 131, 132, 133, 136, 140, 141, 142
Malleolus, C. 78
Manlius, A. 21, 114
Manlius Agrippa, Cn. 51
Manlius Torquatus, L. 74
Marcius Censorinus, C. 21
Marius Gratidianus, M. (pr. 85) 15, 56, 166, 167
Marius the Elder 1, 19, 21, 22, 24, 31, 56, 59, 61, 107, 108, 109, 110, 111, 112, 113, 114, 115, 116, 117, 118, 123, 124, 166
Marius the Younger (cos. 82) 3, 65, 74
Masinissa (king of Numidia) 120
Memmius, C. (tr. pl. 111) 129
Metellus, C. 30, 84
Metellus Creticus Q. (cos. 69) 141
Metellus Numidicus, Q. (cos. 190) 107, 109, 112, 114, 118
Metellus Pius, Q. (cos. 80) 5, 30, 65, 100
Micipsa 114
Minucius Thermus, M. (pr. 80) 75
Mithridates VI Eupator (king of Pontus) 33
Mucius Scaevola, Q. (cos. 117, known as 'augur') 25
Mucius Scaevola, Q. (cos. 95, known as 'pontifex') 42, 51
Mummius, L. (cos. 146) 33
Munatius Plancus, L. 51
Myron 154

Naevius, Sex. 78
Nasicae (branch of the *gens Cornelia*) 19
Neleus 148, 149, 150

Index of Ancient Persons and Deities — 201

Nicomedes IV Philopator (king of Bithynia) 76, 143
Nonius Sufenas, Sex. 55
Norbanus, C. (cos. 83) 56, 96

Octavian (future Augustus) 69, 94, 159, 160
Octavius, C. (pr. 61) 170
Octavius, Cn. (cos. 87) 166
Ofella (Q. Lucretius Ofella, or Afella 9, 27, 28, 65, 66, 67, 71, 73, 83, 84, 85, 95
Oppianicus 100
Oppius, Q. 80

Palicanus (M. Lollius Palicanus (pr. 69)) 63
Papius Mutilus, C. 96
Percennius 15, 128, 129, 130, 131, 132, 133, 134, 136
Pericles 154
Philip II (king of Macedon) 132
Pompeius Rufus, Q. (cos. 88) 22, 61
Pompeius Strabo, Cn. (cos. 89) 81, 82
Pompey 3, 15, 55, 71, 73, 79, 81, 83, 84, 85, 87, 95, 96, 159
Postumius Albinus, A. 114
Ptolemy II Philadelphus (king of Egypt) 150
Pyrrhus (king of Epirus) 132

Quinctius, P. 78

Romulus 139, 140
Roscius (Sextus Roscius of Ameria, father and son) 98, 100, 161
Rullus. *See* P. Servilius Rullus

Saturninus (tr. pl. 103, 100) 67, 82, 93
Scipio Aemilianus (cos. 147) 66
Scipio Asiagenes, L. (cos. 83) 27, 56, 68
Scipiones
– (branch of the *gens Cornelia*) 19
Scribonius Curio, C. (cos. 76) 51
Segestes (Germanic leader) 128
Sertorius, Q. (pr. 83) 9, 56, 65
Servilius Caepio, Q. 59, 81, 85
Servilius Glaucia, C. 67
Servilius Rullus, P. (tr. pl. 63) 60, 89
Servilius Vatia Isauricus, P. (cos. 79) 56, 75, 78, 79, 80

Servius Tullius (king of Rome) 67
Sulla
– early life 19, 109
– war with Jugurtha 1, 19, 21, 107, 108, 109, 113, 114, 115, 116, 117, 118, 119, 120, 121, 122, 123, 124
– war with Teutons and Cimbri 1, 19
– praetorship 20, 21
–governor of Cilicia 20, 80
– Social War 1, 20
– consulship and first march on Rome 1, 3, 22, 23, 24, 25, 56, 63
–war with Mithridates 1, 3, 4, 5, 25, 26, 33, 35, 36, 37, 39, 40, 41, 42, 43, 44, 45, 46, 47, 48, 49, 50, 51, 52, 53, 79, 143, 144, 145, 147, 148, 152, 153, 154, 155, 156
–civil war and violence
    1, 5, 6, 7, 26, 27, 28, 29, 56, 74, 76, 77, 82, 99, 100, 111, 140, 160, 161, 162, 163, 165, 166, 167, 168, 169, 171
–dictatorship and reforms 1, 2, 7, 8, 9, 10, 29, 30, 31, 55, 57, 58, 59, 60, 61, 62, 64, 65, 66, 67, 68, 71, 72, 73, 74, 75, 83, 84, 85, 87, 89, 90, 92, 93, 94, 95, 96, 127, 131, 163, 164, 165, 171
– retirement 2, 77
Sulpicius, P. (tr. pl. 88) 22, 23, 30

Terentius Varro Lucullus, M. (cos. 73) 75
Tiberius (emperor) 14, 69, 102, 128, 136
Timotheus 145
Titius, Q. 50
Trophonius 50
Tullius Decula, M. (cos. 81) 64, 65, 74, 77
Tyrannio 148, 149, 150, 151

Valerius Flaccus, L. (cos. 100) 7, 64, 163
Valerius Messalla Corvinus, M. (cos. 31) 147
Valgus C. Quinctius Valgus 90, 91, 100
Verres, C. 78, 79, 83, 87, 88, 171
Vibulenus 133, 134, 135
Volcacius, C. 78
Volux 118, 119, 120

Xerxes 153

Zeus 39, 152

Index of Ancient Places

Academy. *See* Athens
Achaea 53
Acraephia 47, 51
Acropolis. *See* Athens
Aegean 5, 79
Aegium 38, 51
Aesernia 96
Aetolia 35
Africa 1, 22, 71, 73, 84, 85, 93, 108, 111
Alalcomenae 12, 145, 147, 154
Alexandria 150
Ambracia 33
Anthedon 5
Argos 51
Arretium 67, 72, 97, 98, 99, 169
Asia (Minor) 1, 5, 26, 42, 51, 80, 121, 143
Athens 1, 4, 5, 25, 33, 34, 35, 49, 51, 78
– Academy 15, 154, 155, 157
– Acropolis 11, 143, 153, 154
– Erechtheion 5
– Lyceum 15, 154, 155, 157
– Odeion 154
– Stoa of Zeus Eleutherios 154
– Theatre of Dionysus 153
– Xerxes' tent 154

Bithynia 76, 143
Black Sea 145
Boeotia 1, 36, 42, 46, 143, 145
Bononia 94, 101
Bruttium 100

Campania 1, 20, 27
Cape Malea 47
Capsa 107
Carystus 42
Casinum 100
Chaeronea 1, 35, 41, 50
Chalcis 40, 51
Chios 5, 41
Cilicia 1, 20, 65, 72, 75, 76, 78, 79, 80, 81, 82, 84, 85
Cirta 113
Colline Gate. *See* Rome
Corinth 33, 34, 40

Corinthian Gulf 34
Cormus 5
Cos 5
Crimea 143
Cumae 9, 149

Dardanus 1, 4, 5, 26, 143
Daulis 33
Delos 34, 40, 49, 50, 78, 147
Delphi 4, 36, 37, 39, 48, 155
Dyme 33

Elatea 41
Eleusis 143
Emona 91, 102, 103
Ephesus 26, 42
Epidaurus 4, 36, 39, 155
Epirus 33
Erechtheion. *See* Athens
Eretria 33
Esquiline Gate. *See* Rome
Euboea 39, 42

Faesulae 92, 98
Forum Holitorium. *See* Rome
Forum. *See* Rome

Greece 1, 3, 5, 13, 25, 26, 33, 34, 35, 36, 37, 38, 39, 40, 42, 43, 46, 48, 49, 50, 51, 52, 56, 143, 152, 153, 154, 155, 169
Gytheion 36, 49

Halae 5
Hellespont 4
Hypata 51

Ilium 5
Imbros 40
Ister, River 145
Italy 1, 2, 3, 5, 7, 9, 22, 24, 26, 27, 47, 56, 71, 79, 84, 96, 108, 111, 123, 144, 147, 148, 169

Kalamai 49
Kotyrta 49

Larinum 100
Larissa 51
Larymna 5
Latium 78, 89, 108
Lesbos 40
Liternum 91
Lyceum. *See* Athens
Lycia 5

Macedonia 35, 40, 42, 43, 72, 75, 77
Magnesia 5
Mahdia 47
Maroneia 41
Mauretania 110
Messene 51
Messenia 34
Minturnae 3
Moluccha 107, 111, 121
Mytilene 96

Naples 6, 152, 153
Nola 22
Numantia 113
Numidia 19, 85, 121, 124

Odeion. *See* Athens
Olympia 4, 36, 39, 155
Orchomenus 1, 4, 5, 13, 25, 44, 46, 154
Oropus 41, 42, 47, 51

Pannonia 102, 103, 128, 133, 138
Parthia 20
Peloponnese 34, 35, 36, 37
Peparethos 40
Pergamum 148
Perusia 94
Philippi 94
Phocis 42
Piraeus 1, 4, 33, 143
– Arsenal of Philo 155
Pisidia 103
Pontus 1, 33, 143
Praeneste 6, 7, 65, 84, 166, 172

Rhine 136
Rhodes 76, 149

Rome
– Colline Gate 1, 5, 6, 7, 12, 27, 29, 56, 63, 74, 76, 77, 99, 140, 165, 168, 172
– Esquiline Gate 3
– Forum Holitorium 82
– Forum 1, 2, 6, 9, 27, 65, 73, 84, 141, 162, 165, 166
– Servilian Basin 165
– Temple of Bellona 6, 29
– Temple of Castor 65
– Villa Publica 6, 7, 165, 172

Sabine Hills 76
Sacriportus 6, 74, 76, 77
Salapia 90
Samnium 20
Samothrace 79
Sciathos 40
Scyros 40
Servilian Basin. *See* Rome
Sicily 71, 84, 169
Sicyon 46, 49
Sipontum 90, 91
Spain 9
Sparta 33, 36, 37
Stoa of Zeus Eleutherios. *See* Athens
Stratoniceia 5, 30

Tabae 5
Teanum 27
Temple of Bellona. *See* Rome
Temple of Castor. *See* Rome
Teos 47
Thasos 38, 40
Theatre of Dionysus. *See* Athens
Thebes 4, 39, 46, 154
Thespiae 5, 47, 50, 51
Thessaly 34, 35, 36
Trasimene, Lake 165
Tuder 100

Villa Publica. *See* Rome
Volaterrae 9, 67, 72, 97, 98, 99

Xerxes' tent. *See* Athens

General Index

aedileship 19, 66
Aenianes 37, 38
ager publicus 90
agrarian law 163, 164, 170
Agrimensores 89, 93, 100
ambitus. *See also* electoral bribery 61
Amphiaraeia Rhomaia 47, 51
anarchy 6, 7
army, Roman 1, 3, 4, 23, 36, 39, 113
Asculum inscription, consilium of Pompeius Strabo 81
Asian Vespers 4
Athamanes 38
Athens, sack of 15, 143–157
atrocities 6, 162, 166, 171, 172
auctoritas 62, 69, 93
avaritia (greed) 160, 165

battle casualties 4, 6
Battle of Actium 160
Battle of Arausio 59
Battle of Chaeronea 1, 35, 51
Battle of Colline Gate 1, 6, 77, 168, 172
Battle of Lake Trasimene 165
Battle of Orchomenus 1, 4, 25, 26
Battle of Philippi 94
Battle of Sacriportus 78
booty 4, 6, 7, 10, 29, 40, 79, 100, 127, 162, 163

centuriate assembly 25
Chaeroneans 35
Cimbri 1, 123
Cinnans 100
citizenship 56, 60, 67, 89, 97, 102, 144
civil war 1, 2, 3, 5, 7, 8, 10, 11, 12, 14, 15, 24, 26, 27, 56, 63, 72, 74, 75, 76, 77, 81, 82, 83, 84, 86, 89, 111, 124, 127, 140, 141, 159, 160, 161, 162, 163, 165, 166, 168, 169, 171
civil war violence 163, 166
clemency 2, 156, 171
coin hoards 34
coinage 13, 34, 37, 39
colonisation. *See* veteran settlement
comitia 58, 64, 67, 69

confiscation 40, 169
– of property 162
– of territory 39
constitution/constitutional reform 2, 12, 70, 94, 96, 168
consulship 2, 8, 9, 15, 20, 24, 28, 56, 58, 59, 63, 64, 65, 66, 67, 69, 72, 73, 81, 84, 87, 89, 95, 108, 123, 167, 170
contio (public meeting) 21, 23, 25, 27, 28, 30, 32, 56, 62, 63, 140
Cornelii (10,000 ex-slaves) 9
corruption 10, 13, 57, 58, 61, 62, 67, 73, 79, 86
courts 8, 13, 20, 31, 57, 72, 75, 76, 81, 83, 86, 101, 148, 163, 167, 168, 171
crisis 3, 20, 22, 157
crudelitas (cruelty) 160, 162, 163, 165
cursus honorum 8, 57, 58, 67, 87

debt 4, 5, 15, 73, 112, 150
demagogue 25, 133, 137
devotio 134, 141, 142
dictator 7, 9, 10, 13, 19, 27, 30, 55–70, 73, 85, 87, 92, 93, 95, 97, 159, 161, 162, 164, 170
dictatorship 1, 4, 7–9, 10, 11, 12, 13, 15, 26–31, 32, 55, 56, 57, 64, 71, 72, 73, 77, 79, 81, 85, 86, 87, 94, 97, 127, 160, 163, 165, 168, 169, 171, 172
– abdication 2, 65

economy 34, 39, 43, 112, 129
elections 8, 13, 14, 55, 56, 57, 58, 60, 61, 62, 63, 64, 65, 66, 67, 68, 69, 70, 86
electoral bribery *(ambitus)* 61, 170
Eleusinian mysteries 149, 152
Eleutheria 51
embezzlement *(peculatus)* 169
Ἐρωτίδεια Ῥωμαῖα 47, 51
ephebeia 50
epinikia-games 46, 47
equestrians 2, 8, 160, 167, 172
euergetism 48–49, 52
executions 7, 166, 167, 172
extortion *(repetundae)* 72, 75, 78, 85, 169

famine 5, 6
felicitas 2, 11, 111, 145

Felix, title of 2, 11, 29, 111, 145, 157
festivals 43–48, 50, 51
fetiales 119
fides 120, 121

grain dole 8
Greek poleis 39, 46, 48, 52
Greek sanctuaries 4, 36, 39, 47, 48, 154, 155

hostis (public enemy) 4, 25, 40, 43, 50, 52, 127, 140
hostis-declaration 3, 40

imperium 23, 26, 27, 69, 72, 80, 84
indemnities (after Mithridatic War) 40, 42
invidia 89, 90, 91, 92, 103
Italians 2, 6, 8, 9, 49, 56, 62, 76, 93, 159, 169

Jugurthine War 93, 107

knights 8, 9, 69, 118, 168 *See also* equestrians
koinon 34, 35, 37, 38, 39

land. *See* confiscation
leadership 59, 108, 112, 114
lectio Senatus 8
legatus 51, 78
leges Corneliae 94
legislation. *See* Sulla, reforms
lex Antonia de proscriptorum liberis 68
lex Aurelia iudicaria 167
lex Calpurnia 57
lex Cassia tabellaria 61
lex Cornelia Baebia de ambitu 57
lex Cornelia de ambitu 57
lex Cornelia de magistratibus 66
lex Cornelia de proscriptione 8, 168
lex Cornelia sumptuaria 57
lex Domitia de sacerdotiis 58
lex Gabinia 61
lex Labiena 58, 60
lex Licinia 59
lex Maria tabellaria 62
lex Ogulnia 58
lex Papiria tabellaria 61
lex Pompeia Licinia de tribunicia potestate 167
lex Valeria 64, 67, 94, 164
lex Villia annalis 58
libertas 23, 131, 132

Library of Apellicon 148, 157
lice 11, 65, 146
Ligurians 107, 114
Lucullan coins 37, 48
ludi Victoriae 140
luxuria 110

magister equitum 64
magistrates 25, 28, 30, 32, 37, 38, 39, 42, 43, 49, 51, 56, 60, 61, 64, 66, 68, 69, 122, 130
march on Rome 1, 3, 55, 81
mass killing 7, 166
Mauretanians 110
military recruitment 37, 52
Mithridatic War 13, 25, 33, 34, 36, 38, 40, 41, 42, 43, 46, 47, 48, 52, 143, 147, 148
monuments 13, 38, 44, 46, 50, 51, 123, 124
Moors 115, 116, 117, 118, 119, 123
Muceia 51
mutinies 15, 127, 128, 132, 133, 135, 137, 138
Mysians 145

new citizens 23, 31
Numidians 113, 114, 115, 120

Odryssae 35
Olympic Games 47
oracles 41
oratory 13, 19, 20, 21, 23, 24, 26, 27, 30, 31, 32, 129, 133, 148

Paelignians 108
paideia 152–156
Panhellenic sanctuaries 4, 36
patronage 9, 10, 62, 81, 88, 98
peace 26, 33, 43, 48, 56, 116, 122, 123, 129, 143, 155
Peace of Dardanus 1, 4, 5
peculatus (embezzlement) 169
people. *See also populus*
Perusine War 94
philhellenism 152, 153, 156
philosophy 139, 147, 150, 151, 157
Phocians 4, 38
phthiriasis 11
piracy 79, 80
policy 2, 8, 9, 10, 14, 31, 47, 79, 81, 89, 136
politics 1, 8, 9, 10, 12, 13, 14, 15, 20, 22, 35, 48, 50, 55, 63, 73, 74, 76, 81,

86, 87, 88, 110, 126, 127, 128, 139, 140, 141, 142, 153, 161
politics, definition 10
pomerium 3, 27
pontifex maximus 58, 59, 60
pontiffs 13, 58–60, 67, 76
populus 19, 29
possessores 90, 91, 99
praeda 127, 140, 163, *See also* booty
praetorship 1, 20, 31, 58, 66, 67, 78, 81, 82, 109, 141
priestly colleges 8, 59
proscriptions 2, 7, 8, 11, 12, 27, 28, 29, 94, 99, 159, 160, 161, 162, 165, 166, 168, 171, 172
provinces 1, 8, 39, 43, 53, 72, 75, 79, 80, 81, 87, 101, 137, 169
publicani 41, 42

quaestorship 19

reception 11, 13, 14, 15, 27, 125, 160
res publica 7, 15, 19, 22, 23, 25, 27, 29, 30, 31, 32, 68, 121, 128, 140, 142, 161, 168, 172
rioting 1, 22, 141

secret ballot 13, 61, 62, 67
Senate 3, 6, 8, 13, 14, 21, 22, 25, 26, 27, 29, 30, 32, 41, 56, 61, 62, 63, 66, 67, 70, 73, 84, 85, 110, 117, 118, 122, 169, 170
senatus consultum ultimum 67
siege warfare 127, 136
slaves 3, 48, 60, 116, 128, 129, 130, 140
Social War 1, 20, 22, 24, 56, 81
sons of the proscribed 7, 159, 167, 169, 170, 171
sortitio (lot) 63
Soteria 47, 51
speeches 13, 15, 21, 25, 26, 27, 29, 30, 32, 78, 89, 120, 128, 132, 134, 139, 140, 141, 142, 160, 163, 166
statues 51, 79, 153
strategy, military 115
Sulla
– memoirs 2, 4, 21, 24, 25

– military experience 20, 108, 111
– military reputation 1
– myth 15, 159–172
– reforms 2, 12, 13, 43, 55, 59, 67, 68, 159, 168, 172
– Sallust's portrait of 109, 110, 111, 112, 113
– *as exemplum* 2, 12, 15, 159, 167, 171
Sullani (Sullan faction) 9, 10, 14, 86
Sylleia 38, 51
'Sullan constitution' of Athens 43, 86

taxation 40, 41, 42, 43, 79
Teutons 1, 123
Thessalians 35, 37
Titeia 51
trials 3, 6, 72, 75, 77, 78, 79, 83, 86, 88, 161, 162, 164, 169, 170, 171
tribes (voting) 8, 56, 59, 60
tribunate 21, 31, 56, 60, 102, 132, 168, 169
tribunes of the plebs 8, 30, 61, 68, 69, 167, 168
tribute 40, 41, 42, 43, 48
triumph 4, 29, 56, 73, 75, 84, 85, 140
trophies 43–48
Tyche 45
tyranny 10, 15, 27, 64, 67, 139, 159, 163–165

Vestals 76
veteran settlement 8, 9, 14, 72, 89
veterans 14, 73, 89, 90, 91, 92, 93, 97, 99, 100, 103, 130, 131, 169, 170
Villa Publica massacre 6, 165, 166, 168, 172
violence 1, 3, 6, 7, 9, 11, 12, 15, 23, 67, 140, 148, 149, 151, 153, 155, 160, 162, 163, 164, 165, 166, 168, 170, 171, 172
voting 25, 28, 55, 57, 58, 60, 61, 62, 65
votive offerings 15, 36

warfare 13, 33, 111, 127, 136

Zeuxis 152, 153

www.ingramcontent.com/pod-product-compliance
Lightning Source LLC
Chambersburg PA
CBHW080411230426
43662CB00016B/2370